CHRISTIANS
IN CONTEMPORARY RUSSIA

CHRISTIANS IN CONTEMPORARY RUSSIA

NIKITA STRUVE

translated by
Lancelot Sheppard
and A. Manson

from the
second revised and
augmented edition

CHARLES SCRIBNER'S SONS
New York

FOREWORD

The aim of this book is to provide an entirely
objective account of Christian life in Soviet Russia.
I have tried to gather as much concrete information
as possible not only about the position in which
Christians have been placed by the first Socialist
State, but about the spiritual characteristics of the
Russian people as these are becoming evident today.
With some rare exceptions, my sources of information are all of Soviet origin – the *Review of the
Patriarchate of Moscow, Science and Religion* (the
propaganda journal of the anti-religious movement), anti-religious pamphlets and articles, contemporary Soviet literature. In addition, after
making certain of their authenticity, I have used
private letters from Soviet citizens and reports from
Western tourists. This work owes much to the
valuable help I have received from a number of
people. I hope that they will accept this expression
of my profound gratitude.   *N.S.*

This translation has been made from the second
revised and augmented French edition of my book;
during its preparation I further revised the text in
order to bring the English edition up to date.

15th March 1966

CORRIGENDA

The author has used the French form for Russian names throughout the text and index. In many instances the most acceptable
English form of the names would vary slightly. The partial list
below illustrates how the gallicized spelling differs from anglicized
on certain names.

French Form	*English Form*
Asseev	Aseev
Beschapochniki	Besshaposhniki
Bojzhi	Bozhy
Bojzhi Deti	Bozhy Deti
Chavrov	Shavrov
Chelepin	Shelepin
Chernychevsky	Chernyshevsky
Cheromukin	Cheryomukhin
Chichkine	Shishkin
Doroche	Dorosh
Isidore	Isidor
Isadore	Isidor
Karlovtsky	Karlovtsy
Kruschev	Khrushchev
Kruititsy, Pitirim	Krutitsy, Pitirim, Metropolitan of
Kunovsy	Kunovsky
Mikhailovich, Tsar Alexis	Alexis Mikhaylovich, Tsar
Ogorodmikov	Ogorodnikov
Preobajensky	Preobrazhensky
Stravropol	Stavropol

CONTENTS

Contents

CHAPTER I

RUSSIA AND CHRISTIANITY

All Russians are Christians. They always have been and always will be.
Anonymous letter to the weekly *Krokodil*, 20th June 1962

AS A UNIFIED COUNTRY AND NATION, Russia owes its existence
to Christianity. Every nation has chosen or been given a name that
is meant to express its essential quality: La Doulce, la Belle France,
Germany das Volk der Denker und Dichter, Old or Merry England. The Russian people chose the name Holy Russia. This title,
though in considerable disrepute today because it is mistaken for
a value judgement, expresses an essential aspect of Russia's vocation. Orthodox Christianity and the USSR present an inseparable
duality to anyone who would understand the Russian soul. Today,
Russia is turning her back on her original vocation: not content
with disregarding it, she is seeking to destroy its every trace and
even all memory of it. To what degree, then, can atheist USSR
be considered the legitimate heir and successor of Christian Russia?
The question is inevitable, but should not be over-simplified. It is
certainly no accident that Communism which, before it was
polluted by the most massive dose of lying known to history, was
a demand for justice, should have taken root in a country that
wished itself Christian. On the other hand, the survival, after
forty-five years of implacable persecution of some tens of millions
of active and fervent Christians, shows that the last word has not
yet been said as to the ultimate orientation of Modern Russia. The
first *Soviet* writer to receive the Nobel prize for literature was a
Christian: is this not both a symbol and a sign?

9

The birth of the Russian State coincided with the introduction of Christianity. The Eastern Slavs, organized and led by the Varegians or Normans who had come down from Scandinavia, made contact with Byzantine Christianity through the Bulgarian Slavs in the eighth century, long before the political unification of the Russian State. When the Norman ruling class became Christian, they were better able to adopt Slavonic culture and to identify themselves with the native population. The first mass-conversion took place about 860 after the blockade of Byzantium by the Russian fleet had failed. This was a characteristic feature of the period: Byzantium succeeded in repelling the repeated assaults of the Slavonic hordes only by converting them to Christianity. Conversely, the adoption of the new faith enabled these peoples to consolidate their national personality. Indeed it seems unquestionable that it was due to Christianity that the Slavs, and especially those of the east, achieved and secured their nationhood. At a later date, the Baltic Slavs were to disappear as a nation and to be completely absorbed by the Germans, because they obstinately resisted conversion, and remained loyal to paganism at the cost of their corporate existence.[1]

During the ninth and tenth centuries, 'two Russias' (one Christian, the other pagan) were already in existence; both are acknowledged in the legal documents of the period. The example of Olga, the widow of Igor, converted in 955 and received as a Christian princess in Constantinople, was not followed by the nation as a whole, but is evidence of the slow yet sure advance of the Christian faith which was making its way into the upper classes and through them became widespread. In 988 Prince Vladimir, after trying to re-establish paganism and shedding the blood of the first Russian martyrs, was himself converted through a combination of personal conviction and political calculation. In compensation, he obtained the hand of the Princess Anne, sister of the Byzantine Emperor. He commanded the people to receive baptism; the ancient gods were overthrown and the idols flung into the rivers; no resistance

[1] Notes will be found on page 421 *et seq.*

Russia and Christianity

was encountered except at Novgorod in the north, where force had to be used. Thus at the dawn of the second millennium of modern history, in the course of a few years, Christianity became the national religion of the Russians. To a historian, the remarkable fact about what is commonly called 'the baptism of Russia' is the extraordinary speed with which this general conversion was accomplished. The Russians absorbed Christianity as 'a sponge absorbs water', thus showing an *anima naturaliter christiana*, or at least an undeniable predisposition to Christianity.

The success of Christianity in Kievan Russia was amazing. In less than a century, the country from Kiev to Novgorod was covered with churches and influential monasteries. A national Christian literature came into being; in his sermon-like treatise on 'Law and Grace', written in vivid and remarkable Russian, the Metropolitan Hilarion develops the theme of Russia's entry into the concert of the Christian nations, her accession to the new *oikoumene* constituted by Europe. Similarly, in the racy *Chronicle* of the monk Nestor (1057–1117) one can feel Russia becoming aware of her universal vocation. During the eleventh and twelfth centuries, Kievan Russia was one of the most prosperous and enlightened countries in Europe. The Russian Middle-Ages – if we can speak of a medieval period in Russia – were altogether brilliant. Vladimir the Great was still illiterate; his son Yaroslav won the title of the Wise for his efforts to promote a Christian civilization, and his grandson Vladimir Monomachos (reigned 1113–25) was both a model ruler and a first-class writer. Cathedrals dedicated to St Sophia, the Holy Wisdom, were built at Kiev and Novgorod. Kievan Russia aimed at being not only the heir, but the equal of Byzantium.

The Gospel humanized the new and recently barbaric State, influenced its ethics and deeply affected the masses of the people; the Russian word for 'peasant' (*Krestianin*) is a variant of the word *Khristianin*, Christian. And when, less than two hundred and fifty years after the baptism of Russia, the Mongol invasion submerged the country and cut it off from the West (1237–1448) it was as Christians that the mass of the people opposed the pagan invader.

But well before this historic catastrophe a specifically Russian Orthodox Christianity had developed, distinct from that of Greece, Bulgaria or Serbia, with which, however, it remained in full communion.

The first saints revered by the people and canonized by the Church were the Princes Boris and Gleb, treacherously murdered by their brother: martyrs not for the faith, but for justice, they were dear to the heart of the people on account of their humility and their unresisting acceptance of death as a way of sharing in the sufferings of Christ. St Theodosius, the founder of the Laura (monastery) of the Caves in Kiev, and of Russian monasticism (1051), rejected the extreme forms of asceticism, replaced them by continual work and prayer and sought to develop the virtues of humility, poverty and practical charity. Humility and renunciation, illuminated by the joy of the Resurrection and the promise of a transfiguration of the whole world, are the virtues most cherished by the Russian people ever since those distant centuries.[2]

Successive Mongol invasions laid waste the country and sapped the moral and spiritual energies of the people for more than a century (1240–1340). Novgorod, which alone was spared, thanks to the marshes surrounding it, suffered repeated assaults from Western Christians, the Knights of the Sword (1240), and the Teutonic Knights (1242). Alexander Nevsky, who repulsed these new crusaders and secured the neutrality of the Tartar Khans, was canonized as the saviour of his country. Papal Rome, through its policy of domination, lost its last chance in Russia and irremediably compromised the unity of Christendom. The Schism between Rome and Constantinople, formal since 1054, became a reality, a feature of the national consciousness.[3]

Under the Mongol yoke, Russia lost its political centre, its sense of vocation and moral vigour. But the Church gradually re-created the personality of the country. Three great characters, three saints symbolize that spiritual, national and political resurrection. The monk Alexis, raised to the metropolitan dignity (1353–78), gave the full support of his authority to the unification of the Russian lands round Moscow, where one of his predecessors, the Metropolitan Peter, had earlier taken up residence (*c.* 1320). St Alexis made frequent and dangerous journeys to the Golden Horde in order that Russia might escape further disasters, checked the encroachment of Catholic Lithuania, which was growing in rivalry with Moscow, and persuaded the disunited princes to submit to the Muscovite Grand Duke. St Stephen, Bishop of Perm (1379–96), carried the light of faith to the tribes of the north. Following the example of the Byzantine missionaries, he proclaimed the Gospel in the language of the country for which he composed an alphabet. Through his work Russia regained the sense of her mission and her role in history. Finally, the Abbot of the Monastery of the Trinity, Sergius of Radonej (1314–92), through his example, his spiritual teaching and by the creation of numerous monasteries where characters were formed and souls made firm, inspired the Russian people with confidence in their moral resources. He gave his blessing to Prince Dimitri Donskoi when he attacked the Mongols and the victory of Kulikovo (1380), although it was not decisive, marked the beginning of the end of Tartar domination.

Through his Christian virtues of poverty, humility, sober mysticism and practical charity, as well as by his political work for the unification of the country, St Sergius seems like an incarnation of the popular consciousness; the Monastery of the Trinity became a national sanctuary, where, from the fourteenth to the twentieth century, hundreds of millions of believers came seeking comfort in misfortune, renewal of their strength, or help.[4]

The fifteenth century, forearmed and fertilized by St Sergius, his colleagues and disciples, was one of the richest in the history of Russian spirituality. It was the period in which the icon – profiting from the Byzantine renaissance – rose to its apogee as an art of universal meaning in the work of Andrew Rublev (d. 1460) and of the master Denis. In these icons the Russian faith finds complete expression, not as a discovery of intellectual truths, but as a vision of the divine beauty, a theology no less than a theophany. Rublev's vision embraces both Christ in glory and Jesus of Nazareth, the Incarnation and the Resurrection.[5] The Russian faith is not only contemplative: monastic hermitages spread far into the forests of the north and the monk, a forester and a workman, was closely followed by the peasant. In this way, the Church collaborated in the peaceful colonization of the vast unpopulated spaces.

In the fifteenth century occurred an historical event with important consequences for the political, religious and spiritual future of Russia: in 1439, the Patriarch and the Emperor of Constantinople and all the members of the Orthodox hierarchy (with the exception of Mark of Ephesus) who were present at the Council of Florence, signed an act of union with Rome. This union was not accepted by the Orthodox peoples; hostility to it was particularly strong in Russia, where the Metropolitan of Kiev, the Greek Isidore, one of the signatories of the union, was driven from the country. The Russians decided on their own account to enthrone a new Metropolitan: the Russian Church became autocephalous (1448). The fall of Byzantium, a few years after it had abdicated its autonomy, deeply impressed the Russian imagination. Was not Moscow thenceforth the centre of Orthodoxy, the last refuge of the unaltered faith, the one independent Orthodox country? 'Two Romes have fallen, the third is Moscow', and national pride, but also a feeling that the end of the world was at hand, added that: 'there will not be a fourth'. This ambitious doctrine stimulated the national consciousness of the country and hastened the formation of a theocratic empire. The marriage between the Grand Duke Ivan III and the Byzantine Princess Zoë (Sophia) Paleologus, was seen as a symbol: Moscow was the direct heir of the Byzantine Empire.[6]

Ivan IV drew the logical conclusion, and was the first to assume the title of Tsar and receive the unction of the Church: Holy Russia made way for the sacred Empire.

This transformation of the State was accompanied by a conflict within the Church. Two different ideals of the monastic life, two kinds of holiness equally legitimate, instead of being complementary, now turned against each other. Nilus of Sora (1433–1508) and his disciples, who inherited the spiritual tradition of Kievan Russia, stood for the eremitic form of monasticism, for absolute poverty, intellectual freedom and toleration. Joseph of Volokolamsk (1439–1515) and the monks trained in the austerity of his monastery wanted an organized monasticism, disciplined, wealthy, and socially and politically active. They supported the State in its centralizing and theocratic aims, and the State in return supported them, in their struggle against the opponents of ecclesiastical possessions. The tendency that Joseph represented won the day, and the disciples of Nilus were condemned and scattered.[7]

The success of Joseph's policy, founded as it was on the temporal power, on discipline and ritual observance, seemed hardly favourable to the development of spiritual life. It brought the Church into confrontation with the State which began to fear the wealth and power of the monasteries; and fostered a religion of formal worship, whose ultimate aberrations, a century later, provoked the schism of the Old Believers.

The sanguinary despotism of Ivan the Terrible during the second half of his reign revealed the frailty of the alliance between Church and State. The Metropolitan Philip of Moscow (1566–8) refused to condone the Tsar's crimes and himself fell a victim to repression. Russian princes and tsars no longer aroused the veneration of the faithful. A new form of sanctity made its appearance and became widespread: the *iurodivye* or the 'Fools for Christ's sake' who voluntarily renounced the light of reason, and assumed as a prophetic ministry the denunciation of the crimes of those in power.[8]

During the period of the *Time of Troubles* (1605–13) which followed Ivan's dictatorship, the Church alone stood firm for national independence. The Trinity-Saint-Sergius Monastery, besieged from September 1608 until 1610, kept the bulk of the Polish forces at bay and gave the country breathing space to organize its defence. When the siege was raised, the monastery put all its material resources at the disposal of the people. The Patriarch Hermogenes paid with his life for his loyalty to the Muscovite throne (1612). It was his summons that had stirred the cities of the north and east to rise and drive out the occupying power.

In 1596, the Metropolitan of Kiev, and almost all the bishops in Poland and Lithuania, yielding to government pressure, signed an act of unity with Rome at Brest-Litovsk, but the majority of the laity, organized in fraternities, remained faithful to the Orthodox Church. These two events, the Polish attempt to dominate Moscow, and the union imposed by force upon the dioceses situated outside Russia, gave the Russians of the seventeenth century an implacable hatred of Catholics. More than ever, 'Latin' became a synonym for an enemy of the religion and the nation.

As she emerged from the *Time of Troubles*, the Church felt an urgent need for renewal, and the more enlightened members of the clergy put forward proposals for moral reform and the spread of education. The Patriarch Nikon (1652–88) decided to correct the liturgical books and ritual practices according to Greek norms. But had not Byzantium disowned Orthodoxy? Was she not under the yoke of the infidel? Could she still claim that her faith was pure? Nikon, however, authoritarian and even despotic, proceeded with the reforms in spite of the protests of his former friends. From revolt to secession was but a step; the zealots who opposed him declared that the third Rome had fallen in its turn, and since there must be no fourth, the only thing left was to withdraw from history into the woods, or else go to the stake. This was the *Raskol*, or schism of the Old Believers, which afterwards (1693) gave birth to a number of sects. The loss of vital energy which it cost both the Church and the country had grave and lasting consequences for the spiritual destiny of Russia.[9]

Nikon, whose tactlessness made him incapable of preventing the schism, was also responsible for a further disaster to the Church. In his desire to assert the supremacy of spiritual over temporal power, he lost all sense of proportion. Tsar Alexis Mikhailovich, who was his spiritual son and his best friend, obtained his deposition and condemnation by a Council at which the Eastern Patriarchs (of Alexandria and Antioch) were present (1666–7). The Church now became an easy prey for the State. When the Patriarch Adrian died (1700), Peter the Great (1682–1725) opposed the election of a successor and provisionally entrusted the government of the Church to a Synod. Twenty years later, when he at last found the puppet he was looking for to do it (Theophan Procopovich), he abolished the Patriarchate and reorganized the Synod on the lines of the other departments of State. Religion became simply one public function among the rest subject to the State and controlled by it (1721). The Church became Westernized, receptive to Roman and Protestant influences. Peter the Great looked to the Ukrainian clergy, educated in the schools of the West, to help him in the task of remodelling the face of Russia. His successors carried on his secularizing policy. Monastic property was confiscated and the monasteries were allowed only a minimum of novices. The Government attacked the clergy, brutally reduced the supernumerary priests to lay status, and offered material advantages to those who would unfrock themselves voluntarily. The priest ceased to be a servant of God and became the lowest functionary in the State. The ancient religious culture was sacrificed to the elaboration of secular techniques and of civilization. It was in the eighteenth century that the great intellectual schism began: the people and the Orthodox Church, on the one hand; the ruling class, addicted to Voltaire and Positivism, on the other. For the Church, the eighteenth century was the period of humiliation.

But the people kept their faith intact. Gradually, truly miraculously, what followed was an astonishing monastic and spiritual renaissance. The 'Jesus prayer' (Lord Jesus Christ, Son of God, have mercy upon me a sinner) and the *Philokalia*, a synthesis of patristic spirituality translated into Slavonic by Paissy Velichkovsky (1793), nourished and universalized this spontaneous movement arising from the hearts of the people.[10] In the first half of the nineteenth century St Seraphim of Sarov (1759–1833) showed, by his radiant life and by his teaching upon the acquisition of the Holy Spirit, the vitality and originality of Russian Christianity.[11] Communities of monks surged up everywhere; hermits again took up their abode in the impenetrable Russian forests. Ecclesiastical seminaries increased in number, gave up Latin which, paradoxically, had become the language of instruction, replaced the scholastic manuals with works more in the Orthodox tradition. The great preacher and theologian Philaret Drozdov, Metropolitan of Moscow (1783–1867) initiated a return to biblical and patristic sources. Also during this period, the Church regained her sense of missionary calling. Macarius Glukharev (1792–1847), imbued at first with the Pietistic ideas of his time, ended by accepting the pure teaching of the Gospel and the Hesychast tradition; he chose for his mission field the almost inaccessible region of Altai in Siberia, where he and his new-formed communities were worthy of the earliest apostolic times. With Innocent Venyaminov (1797–1879), the Orthodox faith crossed the boundaries of Asia and entered America.[12]

The renaissance of the Church was accompanied by another miracle: the flowering of Orthodox culture. According to a well-known epigram, the challenge thrown down by Peter the Great was taken up by Russia, a hundred years later, in Pushkin (1799–1837). In the early nineteenth century the Bible dethroned Voltaire. In his *Gabriliada* (1821) Pushkin, who had taken lessons in 'pure atheism', grossly parodied, in perfect verse, the mysteries of our Lady. But after reflection, and through his artistic intuition and his contact with the people, he discovered the ancient Russia, its history, its religion and its soul. *Boris Godunov* (1825) is a Christian tragedy. And Pushkin's heroes, above all his heroines, Tatiana in *Evgeny Onegin* (1830) and Masha in *The Captain's*

Daughter (1836), belong to Christian Russia. Their virtues are those of renunciation in love of duty, humility and integrity.

A constellation of thinkers and writers, the Slavophils, rediscovered the Church by reflecting upon the destiny of the Russian people: Khomyakov (1804–60), an intuitive of genius in every sphere of human activity and a remarkable lay theologian; Ivan Kireyevsky (1809–56), converted by his wife from the idealism of Shelling to the Orthodox faith, and translator of the Fathers of the Church. Gogol (1809–52) studied Greek and Nicholas Cabasilas to give his readers an explanation of the Divine Liturgy, and sacrificed his work as a novelist and his life to the demands of holiness. Dostoevsky (1821–81), who learnt 'the terrible power' of humility and the meaning of suffering in a convict settlement in Siberia, proclaimed a faith that was all the stronger for having been tested in the fire of doubt. At a later date, Tolstoy (1828–1901) abandoned his art to preach Christ as a moral and social reformer.

The Monastery of Optino at Kozelsk was the spiritual centre towards which both the people and the intellectuals converged. Kireyevsky settled in the neighbourhood so that he could translate the Fathers of the Church, under the direction of Father Ambrose. Gogol, finding it difficult to continue *Dead Souls*, for he wanted it to be a *Divine Comedy*, came there to seek advice. Dostoevsky and Vladimir Solovyev were frequent visitors. C. Leontyev (1831–91), who had come to believe in the decline not only of the West but of all human civilization, lived there for more than fifteen years. Even Tolstoy, although excommunicated by the Church, felt the attraction of Optino. Before he went away to die, he spent hours wandering around the monastery, but could not make up his mind to go in.

The alliance between secular culture and the institutional Church was by no means complete. The Archimandrate Theodore Bukharev (1824–71), who took up the defence of Gogol and secular art, was obliged to resign from the priesthood. The monks of Optino rejected the description of monasticism given by

Dostoevsky in *The Brothers Karamazov* as too humanistic. The fact was that the Church was excessively subordinated to the State, too bureaucratic – every official was, at least in principle, obliged to receive Holy Communion at least once a year – and too timid. All the lower clergy were married, and their office was hereditary; they formed a closed caste (in 1860, Professor A. Gorsky caused a scandal by becoming a priest unmarried). In the countryside, priests were very poor, often illiterate and drunkards. There were too few bishops (it was the close-fisted Ministry of Finance that settled what new dioceses should be established) and they were out of touch with the people. The episcopate was thus at once too authoritarian and too servile. Positivism and Socialism found no difficulty in spreading among the cultivated class – the intelligentsia – which grew in numbers every year. The ecclesiastical seminaries, still too wedded to scholasticism and outworn educational methods, became seed-beds of atheists. The Church taught an ideal of social justice to which the reality, supported by this same Church, failed to correspond, if it did not contradict it – despite the revolutionary reforms of Alexander II. Those who thirsted for justice, those who were impatient, turned to revolutionary agitation. The Positivist literary critic N. Dobrolyubov (1836–81) and Chernychevsky (1828–89) the one consistent materialist produced by Russia in the nineteenth century, were both sons of priests. In spite of Dostoevsky, the years 1860–70 saw the triumph of Positivism and revolutionary atheism. There was now a threefold division: the ruling class, the newly fledged intellectuals, and the people.

During the last quarter of the nineteenth century, the writings of Vladimir Solovyev (1853–1900) rehabilitated Christian dogma by rationalizing it. His mystical experience and apocalyptic vision gave rise to the Symbolist movement (A. Blok, 1880–1921; A. Bely, 1880–1934; V. Ivanov, 1866–1949) which was a religious as well as a literary phenomenon. The twentieth century began with a religious revival akin to the almost contemporary one in France under the influence of Bergson. A group of eminent

Marxists, Berdyaev (1874–1948), Bulgakov (1871–1944), Frank (1877–1951), Struve (1870–1944), etc., were converted first to idealism and then to the Orthodox faith and initiated a new philosophy of religion. The 'Conferences on Religious Philosophy' held in Petersburg (November 1901–April 1903 ; 1907–17) and in Moscow and Kiev, brought into personal contact members of the clergy and representatives of the intelligentsia in an attempt to reconcile the Church and the world.

The Church herself was in a flourishing condition. Every kind of theology, from dogmatics to Byzantine, Islamic and Amharic studies prospered brilliantly. The chaplains of the Russian embassies abroad, open-minded and informed theologians, were among the real forerunners of the Ecumenical Movement. Foreign missions reported magnificent successes in Japan, China and Korea. Only one obstacle still prevented the Church from bearing her full witness to the world: her subservience to the State, which, despite the 1905 Revolution, remained hardly less stifling than before.[13]

CHAPTER II

THE CHURCH AND THE REVOLUTION

Come, comrade, have no fear, take your gun, and we'll fire a shot into Holy Russia; into the Russia of the forests, the land of huts; the land with the fat behind. Away with the cross! Away with the cross!

A. Blok, *The Twelve*, II, 1918

STRANGE THOUGH IT MAY SEEM, the Church was better prepared than the State to face the Revolution. Ever since 1905 had opened the path to freedom, all ranks in the Church had begun an examination of conscience, and a huge programme of reforms was under way. The diocesan bishops recorded their criticisms and their demands in five large volumes, published with the full official sanction of the Holy Synod. A preconciliar commission, composed of bishops, priests and expert laymen, set to work energetically and added a further six volumes (1906–7), a striking witness to the fact that the council was being prepared in depth. In 1912, a new preconciliar consultative committee was appointed with the same end in view, and published five more volumes (1912–16). Preparations were all the more thorough, because the imperial authorities, who feared the Church's emancipation, delayed summoning the council. Commission followed commission, but no council appeared. The war, and the decisive influence of Rasputin on the Government, increased the Church's subjection to the State. The few bishops who ventured to protest were removed from their sees and confined to monasteries. More than ever before, the Church longed to recover her freedom from State control.

The Church and the Revolution

The preparation for the Council

This explains why the fall of the imperial power 'established by the grace of God', and its replacement by the provisional Government, created by the will of the people (2nd March 1917), were accepted by the Holy Synod with submission and humility. On the proposal of the new Chief Procurator, V. Lvov (for the moment, the former links between Church and State were retained), the Holy Synod sent a proclamation to every parish asking for loyalty to the new régime and ordering prayers to be said for it during church services. V. Lvov began by purging the Church of the most reactionary elements, those known to be attached to the old order or to have been friendly or compliant towards Rasputin. A dozen bishops were sent into retirement, among them the aged Metropolitans of Moscow and Petrograd. But this measure was not enough, and in order to hasten the summoning of a general council of the Church, Lvov, making use of the privileges of the former imperial procurators, entirely reorganized the composition of the Holy Synod. Of its original members, he retained only Mgr Sergius of Vladimir (the future custodian of the Patriarchal throne, and afterwards Patriarch) and Mgr Platon as president. The State was undoing what it had established two hundred years before.

The new Synod appointed a new preconciliar commission and actively set to work on preparations for the Council, a matter of increasing urgency because the Church was in ferment from top to bottom: parishioners were agitating against their priests, priests against their bishops, and all were clamouring for reform. In order to canalize this revolutionary fervour, the temporary Synod published a series of provisional decrees which introduced the elective and representative principle into the life of the Church, and granted a broad administrative autonomy to the parish and the diocese. General elections followed; most of the diocesan bishops were re-elected and confirmed in their office. Certain

23

notoriously reactionary prelates, however, such as Antony Khrapovitsky (1863–1936) the leader of the conservative wing, and Seraphim Chichagov, were deposed, but nevertheless invited to the Council by co-option. In the two capitals, which had been deprived of their Metropolitans, the election results were rather unexpected. In Petrograd, the majority vote was for Mgr Benjamin Kazansky, a young auxiliary bishop, a man of kindly and humble character, very popular among the workers (as we shall see, he was martyred in 1922). In Moscow, Mgr Tikhon of Vilnius (1863–1925), the future Patriarch, was elected; he had been obliged to leave his see when the Germans advanced, and in these few years his simplicity and humility had won him the sympathy of the people.

At the beginning of July 1917, A. Kartachev, President of the Society of Religious Philosophy, replaced V. Lvov as Chief Procurator. But almost at once he gave up this title because it smacked too much of the old régime, took that of Minister of Worship and declared the Holy Synod to be completely autonomous. Meanwhile the preconciliar commission had decided – in opposition to a minority of conservative bishops – that the council should be composed not only of bishops, but also of priests and laymen. Each of the sixty-five dioceses was to send to the council its bishop and five delegates, two of them priests and three laymen, elected according to a threefold system, chiefly designed to ensure that the clergy and laity should be equally represented. There were four hundred diocesan representatives, and to these were added the members of the Holy Synod, those of the preconciliar commission, delegates from the monasteries, from the military chaplaincies, from the academies of science, the universities, the Duma and the Council of State. Total membership thus amounted to 564; paradoxically, laymen were in the majority (314 laymen; 250 ecclesiastics). As a safeguard against any situation which might threaten to impair the authority of the bishops, the Council adopted the parliamentary system of two chambers: it was divided into the General Assemblies in which the votes of the bishops and laymen had equal weight and the Episcopal Meetings which scrutinized all the decisions taken by the General Assemblies. If a decision was rejected by a majority of three-quarters of the bishops, it was sent back to the General Assembly. On a second rejection by the bishops, it would not obtain force of law. Thus the authority of the bishops was established as final, and the Council was protected against taking hasty decisions.

The sessions of the Council and the restoration of the Patriarchate

The Council began with great ceremony and in a mood of considerable optimism, in spite of the disturbing news from the front. Considered as a whole, the Council was composed of moderate men; the first symptoms of the approaching revolution had produced a pronounced shift to the right. The conservatives, headed by the impressive personality of Mgr Antony Khrapovitsky, an eminent theologian and a spiritual leader with a large following, seemed to be in the majority. The centre, less numerous but also less clerical, was perhaps more influential; it was led by a great Russian philosopher, Prince Eugene Trubetskoi and by Sergius Bulgakov who was to become one of the greatest theologians of our time. Finally, the left, an odd collection, for it allied anti-episcopal priests to professors from theological academies with advanced political views, was in a minority. But these divergent tendencies did not impair the fundamental unity of the Council.

In its session of 18th August, the governing body of the Council was appointed. These initial elections were of special importance, because to some extent they foreshadowed the election of the Patriarch. To the surprise of all, it was the new Metropolitan of Moscow, the lowly Tikhon, who secured by far the greatest number of votes; 406 out of 432. His chief competitors, Mgr Arsenius Stadnitsky of Novgorod and Mgr Antony Khrapovitsky, were appointed as coadjutors.

Urged on all sides to lend support to political movements
(General Kornilov's revolt, for example) the Council contrived
to resist such temptations and had the wisdom to exercise its
authority only in exhorting the people to order and the authorities
to clemency.[1] On the other hand it was unsuccessful in deciding
whether the time had come to restore the Patriarchate. The right
wing was in favour of doing so, but the left, whose main fear was
the despotic authoritarianism of the episcopate, wanted a Synod
that would be elected and periodically renewed. The discussions
dragged on until the dramatic seizure of power by the Bolsheviks
on 25th October 1917, suspended the debate. On 28th October,
the very day when the Bolsheviks crushed the resistance of the
officer-cadets entrenched in the Kremlin, the Council voted
unanimously for the re-establishment of the Patriarchate at the
same time clearly stating that the supreme power in the Church
must reside in the 'local council, summoned periodically and on
fixed dates'. Thus, by the pressure of events, the monarchical
and conciliar principles in the government and administration of
the Church were reconciled. On 31st October the process of
electing the Patriarch began; three candidates were to be selected,
and the final choice decided by drawing lots. The results were
practically similar to those of the election of the governing body;
Antony of Kiev, Arsenius of Novgorod and Tikhon of Moscow
were again elected, but this time Antony came first and Tikhon
took his place as third. It was clear that the Council had moved
further to the right.

On 5th November, after the liturgy had been celebrated in
the Cathedral of the Holy Saviour, an aged monk, who lived
as a recluse, was given the task of drawing the lots. The first
voting paper bore the name of Mgr Tikhon. So the drawing
of lots confirmed the initial elections to the governing body.
The members of the Council and the faithful did not fail to
be impressed by this identity between the voice of the people and
the voice of God. Tikhon's election was hailed with unanimous
joy.[2]

The Church and the Revolution

The Council in conflict with the new power

Even before the new Patriarch was solemnly enthroned on 21st November, in the Cathedral of the Assumption, the Council, stirred by the extension of the Revolution and the civil war, had on 11th November issued a message calling on the whole Russian Orthodox Church to 'offer penitential prayers for the great sin of those of her sons who, through ignorance, have become victims of illusion and fallen into fratricide and the sacrilegious destruction of the sacred patrimony of the nation . . .' and urging those who had gone astray 'to give up the foolish and impious dream of the false teachers who are calling upon you to bring about universal brotherhood by means of universal conflict'.[3] This was a scarcely veiled condemnation of Marxism and class-warfare, and also the beginning of a struggle between Church and State which, in spite of appearances, has never ended.

In December the first decrees were issued limiting the Church's freedom and the means at her disposal. On 4th December all agricultural production, including that of the Church, came under State control; on 11th December, all the ecclesiastical schools, primary, secondary and high, were nationalized and, in consequence, closed. Shortly afterwards, the proposed decree on the separation between Church and State was published; its terms were such that all personal belongings and real estate became the property of the State.[4] Relying on this proposal alone, the local authorities, presumably encouraged by directives from above, began a series of acts of violence and pillage, and an attempt was made to seize the monasteries by armed force. During one of the struggles for the possession of the Laura Alexander Nevsky, the aged arch-priest Peter Skipetrov was killed by a bullet; almost everywhere the blood of the first martyrs began to flow. Orthodox believers sprang to the defence of their sanctuaries and organized huge processions which the police, in some cases, dispersed by rifle and machine-gun fire. Summary executions multiplied. The Patriarch Tikhon, though he had no liking for extreme measures, brought the full weight of his authority into the conflict and on 19th January 1918, hurled his anathema against 'the open and clandestine enemies of the truth of Christ', who 'persecute that truth and are trying to ruin Christ's work. Echoes reach us every day of horrible and cruel massacres whose victims are innocent people, and even those lying on a bed of sickness whose only fault was that they had honestly done their duty to their country and worn themselves out in the service of God and the people . . .

'. . . . The power that has promised to establish order in Russia is everywhere exhibiting shameful lawlessness and unbridled violence towards everyone, and particularly towards the Holy Orthodox Church.

'Foolish men, return to your senses and cease your massacres . . . by the authority committed to us by God, we forbid you to approach the mysteries of Christ, we anathematize you, you at least who still bear Christian names and, though it be only by your birth, belong to the Orthodox Church.'

Lastly, the Patriarch called upon 'the faithful children of the Church to rise up and defend the Church and to suffer, if necesary, for the cause of Christ'.[5]

In Petrograd, where the memory of the attack on the Laura was still vivid, 'the Patriarch's message was enthusiastically greeted in a procession in which a number of parishes took part and the people sang the "Christ is risen" and other Easter canticles'.[6]

The anathema was never withdrawn, but it can be validly argued that the Communists were not explicitly mentioned in it and that it was aimed only at those who, at the beginning of the Revolution, were guilty of murderous deeds.

On 20th January the decree on the separation of Church and State was given official sanction. The Church was not merely separated from the State; she was stripped of all her property and of all her legal rights; in short, outlawed.[7] The Council made no mistake about the real meaning of this decree, barely concealed by its proclamation of complete freedom of conscience. This decree, according to the decisions adopted by the Council in its session of 27th January, 'gives legal sanction to open persecution of the Orthodox Church and also of all religious bodies whether Christian or not . . . under the pretext of separating the Church from the State, the Soviet of People's Commissars is endeavouring to make the very existence of Churches, ecclesiastical institutions and clergy, impossible. Under the pretext of confiscating ecclesiastical property, the decrees aim at destroying the very possibility of worship and public services . . . The most sacred objects intended to be used in worship . . . have been put at the disposal of the civil power which can either return or not return them to their use . . . Since the confiscation of the printing presses, even the publication by the Church of the holy Gospels and, generally, of all the sacred and liturgical books, with the complete purity and integrity of text that they require, becomes impossible . . . Even the teaching of religion in schools, not only public but private, is unauthorized . . . The Church is deprived of the possibility of training her own pastors . . .[8]

Unfortunately, the Council's apprehensions were not only justified, but far exceeded by what the reality was to be. The Church, bound hand and foot, was delivered up to the good will of an anti-Christian State. The decree of 23rd January was soon to be used, and is used to this day, as legal cover for the physical annihilation of the Church.

Publication of this decree was accompanied by an ominous pointer to the future: two days afterwards, the aged Metropolitan of Kiev, Mgr Vladimir, was savagely assassinated a few hundred yards from the Laura of the Caves where he was living. His sacrifice inaugurated the long martyrology of the Russian episcopate.[9]

The Council did not confine itself to condemning the decree; it tried with precise instructions to combat its effects. In a circular letter of 21st February 1918, the Patriarch and the Holy Synod urged the people of the parishes, monastic communities, and teaching staffs of ecclesiastical schools, to form themselves into benevolent or other societies that enjoyed legal rights, in order to defend the sacred vessels and the property of the Church from profanation and to fight against the closure of monasteries and schools. In exceptional cases these societies were even authorized to declare themselves the owners of Church property, to avoid its falling into the hands of the non-Orthodox.[10]

In March 1918, the Patriarch Tikhon made a strong protest against the signature of a separate peace treaty with Germany. The Church considered this to be a betrayal of the promise given to the Russian people and the allies.[11]

The legislative work of the Council

Although its attention was thus repeatedly diverted by historical happenings to Russia, the Council managed, before its dissolution in September 1918, to create a remarkable body of legislation, and to endow the Church with new canonical forms.

At the base of the reformed organization of the Church, we note the conciliar principle. Supreme authority in the Church was to be exercised by the Council, summoned periodically, at least every three years. The Council appointed two supreme organisms to administer the Church in the periods between the Councils, under the presidency of the Patriarch: the Holy Synod, composed solely of bishops and entrusted with questions of doctrine, liturgy, religious education and discipline; and the High Commission of the Church, composed of three bishops, five priests, one monk, and six laymen, to deal with problems of administration. These arrangements which settled the forms of the ultimate authority of the Church quickly encountered the opposition of the Soviet Government and could not be carried into effect.

The diocese was given a status analogous to that of the Church as a whole. The bishop governs the diocese with the help of a diocesan council of priests and laymen, elected by a diocesan assembly, summoned periodically (every three years) and itself elected by the parochial assemblies.

The law passed on 8th April 1918, dealing with the *Regulation of Parishes*, was of even greater importance, for it established the autonomy of the parish, the security of tenure of priests, and the responsibility of the intimately associated laymen, under the presidency of the rector, for the administration of the parish. It was due to this almost providential arrangement that the laity found themselves in the forefront of the Church's defenders during the persecutions.

Thus the Church was reorganized from top to bottom according to the conciliar principle, dear to Orthodox theology. The Council's legislative activity deserves serious study and a discriminating appraisal. In any case, we can say it was largely due to these solid canonical foundations that the Church was able to stand up to the manifold attacks of her enemies.[12]

The response of faith

The Church's reaction was not only expressed in countermeasures: in compliance with the Patriarch's request, she responded with a great outburst of faith, manifested in all classes of the people. In June 1918, Sergius Bulgakov gave up his post as professor of political economy in the university of Moscow to become a priest.[13] At the same period the poet Sergius Soloviev (1885–1941), nephew of the renowned philosopher, the publicist V. Sventsitsky, and the essayist S. Durylin became priests.[14]

The people gave the Patriarch an enthusiastic welcome: his visit to Petrograd in May 1918, was a veritable triumph. Standing up in his carriage all the way from the station to the Laura, he blessed the crowds who knelt as he passed by. The Ascension Day procession gathered outside the Cathedral of Kazan – a sea of humanity, which did not disperse until four o'clock in the afternoon.[15]

This popular support enabled the Patriarch, in October 1918, on the first anniversary of the Revolution, to address a strong letter to the Soviet of People's Commissars; after a recital of the crimes of the new Government, the Patriarch pleaded that the first anniversary of its existence should be marked by the cessation of bloodshed, violence and the persecution of the faith, and by the liberation of those who had been imprisoned.[16]

The firm line taken by the head of the Church and by the faithful, led the authorities to a provisional mitigation of their anti-religious policy. A lengthy circular from the Commissar for Justice, dated December 1918, lists the various kinds of oppression that had accompanied the application of the decree of 23rd January: 'the arbitrary closing of churches, the confiscation for the purposes of the Revolution of objects used in worship, such as the casings of the icons, the cross, the pall, vestments; the arrest of ministers and the searches carried on in church during public worship; the assignment of priests to labour at road building, the prohibition of preaching', etc. This eloquent summary gives some idea of the violence of the first wave of persecution. These oppressive measures were condemned and the local Soviets instructed not to wound the feelings of the faithful.[17]

But the respite, if respite there were, did not last long. The same Commissar for Justice decided shortly afterwards (the circular is dated 1st March 1919) to launch an attack on what the people held most sacred, namely the holy relics. More than fifty tombs were opened, catalogued and expertly valued. There was no stopping half-way in so profitable an enterprise. A further circular, in August 1920, gave the order 'to proceed to the complete liquidation of the cult of corpses and mummies', by transferring them to the State museums and by bringing legal action against anyone responsible for false statements.[18]

It seems that the faithful accepted with resignation this fresh onslaught on their religious feelings and freedom of worship. Did they realize that this was only the beginning of their trials?

How the civil war affected the issues

The civil war, which lasted four years with varying fortunes for the two sides, offered a constant temptation to the Church.

The Church and the Revolution

In some regions, the clergy, persecuted by the Bolsheviks, welcomed the soldiers of the white army as liberators; on the return of the reds those who had compromised themselves had either to abandon their flocks, or else perish as victims of a savage repression. The worst consequences were, however, avoided, thanks to the wisdom of the Patriarch Tikhon who refused to take sides even tacitly in the conflict. To the bishops who found themselves in territories controlled by the whites, he granted every facility to administer their dioceses autonomously (decree of 20th November 1920) but remained deaf to all appeals for support from the whites. Prince Gregory Trubetskoi, before leaving Moscow for south Russia, had an interview with the Patriarch, and asked him to send his blessing, under seal of secrecy, to one of the white leaders. The Patriarch, however, felt he could not do this, without compromising the Church. On 25th September 1919, he made his position plain by ordering the clergy to stand aloof from politics of any kind.[19]

CHAPTER III

THE GREAT TRIALS

O Life, wherefore art thou dead? What has brought thee to the grave?
Service for Holy Saturday

IN THE SUMMER OF 1921, after the revolt when the sailors of Kronstadt were slaughtered (in May) Lenin, faced with the fearful famine raging in the regions of the Volga, altered his course and proclaimed the 'new economic policy'. A general liberalization of the régime and of intellectual life ensued. Only towards political opposition and the Church was the former severity maintained.

The famine and the seizure of sacred objects

The famine provided the pretext for provoking, dividing and decimating the Church. The Soviet Government had gladly sought help for the starving from the capitalist countries, but obstinately refused it from the Russian Church. Already in August, Patriarch Tikhon had written to the heads of the various Christian Churches (the Orthodox Patriarchs, the Pope, the Archbishop of Canterbury, the head of the Episcopalian Church of America) and asked them to come to the assistance of his people threatened by death. During the same period a national ecclesiastical committee was set up to succour the starving and collections were taken in every church. But the Government would not recognize this committee and compelled it to disband. The money that had been collected was handed to the Committee of State. On 19th

February 1922, the Patriarch asked the parochial councils to surrender the articles of value in the churches for the benefit of the starving, with the exception of those used for the sacraments. The Government authorized the publication of this request in the papers and its transmission to the people, but later changed its mind and, on 28th February, issued a decree ordering the confiscation of all objects of value, *including* those used for the sacraments.[1]

In a fresh pastoral letter, dated 28th February, the Patriarch renewed his appeal to the generosity of the faithful, but forbade them to hand over, even voluntarily, articles consecrated for liturgical use.[2] This was precisely what the Government needed in order to discredit the Patriarch and provoke a schism. The people were far more fiercely opposed than the bishops to the seizure of articles of value and wanted to contribute their money-value instead.[3] They had not forgotten the looting of the churches in 1919. When the seizures began, there were violent brawls between the people and the soldiers of the Red Army. A total of 1,414 incidents involving bloodshed occurred[4] – to quote only one example, at Schuiia, near Moscow, machine-gunners opened fire on the crowd, killing four people and wounding ten.[5] After these incidents which led to a number of arrests, forty-five priests and laymen were brought to trial; twelve of them, nine priests and three laymen, were condemned to death.[6] The Patriarch was first summoned as a witness at this trial, and then put under house arrest and forbidden to carry out the duties of his office (10th May 1922).[7]

The origin of the schism

A few days later a group of secular priests from Petrograd, led by Alexander Vvedensky, came to see the Patriarch and asked him to entrust them with the Patriarchal chancellery 'in order that there might be no interruption in the conduct of the Church's affairs'. The Patriarch had just passed on his authority to the aged

Metropolitan, Agathange Preobzajensky, who was then in Yaroslavl: he granted Vvedensky's request, but made it clear that he did so only until Mgr Agathange arrived in Moscow. This was all Vvedensky needed: relying on the help of bishop Antoninus Granovsky, an unstable intellectual, and bishop Leonides Sicobeev, a coarse and unscrupulous man, who was later to be disowned and silenced by his own followers, Vvedensky brought about a revolution in the constitution of the Church. He suppressed the Patriarchate and set up a provisional ecclesiastical administration which was to carry on until the meeting of the next Council. The so-called Living Church had come into being. The Soviet Government which had made the schism possible by arresting the Patriarch, now went on to offer it moral and material support, and especially the co-operation of the police. The new leaders of the Church succeeded in convincing some of the bishops (Mgr Sergius Stragorodsky, for example) that their reform had the approval of the Patriarch. But, more often, persuasion was backed with force. When Mgr Agathange was requested to recognize the new administration, he flatly refused; he was immediately arrested and, notwithstanding his great age, was exiled to the far north. In spite of its professed principles, the Government interfered brutally in the affairs of the Church.[8]

The trial of the Metropolitan Benjamin

Even more criminal was the collusion between the Living Church and the Soviet power in Petrograd: the Metropolitan Benjamin not only refused to recognize the new administration but also excommunicated Vvedensky who belonged to his diocese. When the Soviet newspapers heard of this they expressed their indignation in violent language. The Metropolitan was accused of opposing the State seizure of valuables and arrested. The bad faith of the authorities was obvious. For, in fact, Mgr Benjamin had adopted a most liberal attitude on the subject and on two occasions had succeeded in reaching an agreement with the State representatives on the procedure for handing over these valuables. On 10th April 1922, *Pravda* had published an appeal from the Metropolitan in which, anxious to quieten public feeling, he asked the faithful to give what they had with a good will. As a result, the seizure of valuables in the diocese had taken place without any serious incidents. Nevertheless, the Metropolitan was arrested and tried with eighty-six other people. The trial was one of the last in which some of the forms of 'bourgeois' justice were respected. Mgr Benjamin was brilliantly defended by a Jewish lawyer, Gurovitch, who was allowed to speak with complete freedom and had no difficulty in proving that the charge was inane and the tribunal prejudiced. The Metropolitan won the admiration of all those present by his calmness, his dignified bearing and his humility. Later, Gurovitch remarked: 'there went a saint.' On 5th July sentence of death was passed on the ten principal accused. For six of them (including N. Chukov, rector of the Cathedral of Kazan, who, twenty-five years later, was to become the Metropolitan of Leningrad) the sentence was commuted to ten years imprisonment. On the night of 12th–13th August 1922, Mgr Benjamin, the Archimandrite Sergius Schein, formerly a deputy in the Duma, and who, during the trial, had displayed an eagerness for martyrdom worthy of the early Christians, G. Novitsky, a young professor of criminal law, and I. Kovsharov, a former legal consultant, were shot not far from Petrograd. No official communiqué was issued to confirm that the sentence had been carried out. For a long time the people refused to believe that their bishop was dead.

The responsibility for the blood of the Metropolitan Benjamin and his three companions must ultimately be laid at the door of the instigators of the Living Church, whose leaders, A. Vvedensky and Krasnitsky, had been summoned as hostile witnesses at the trial.[9]

Throughout Russia similar trials were taking place: anyone who opposed the new Church was removed. Towards the end of 1923, sixty-six bishops (among them Mgr Alexis, the future

Patriarch) were in prison or exiled.[10] The treatment of ordinary clergy was even more brutal; during 1922, 2,691 secular priests, 1,962 monks and 3,447 nuns were liquidated. The total number of victims was 8,100.[11]

The brief triumph of the Living Church

When the 'new administration' had made certain of the control of the parishes and dioceses, it convoked a General Council on 29th April 1923. This Council revealed what the real tendencies of the movement were: social and political collaboration with the Soviet Government, increased power for priests at the expense of episcopal authority and lay responsibility, rejection of the monastic life, and a liberalistic interpretation of dogma. On 3rd May, the Council of the Living Church decided to abolish the Patriarchate as 'incompatible with the conciliar principle'; accordingly it reduced the Patriarch Tikhon to the position of a layman, and gave unconditional support to the Soviet Government as 'the only one in the world that achieves on earth, by governmental means, the ideals of the Kingdom of Heaven'. The grievances of the secular clergy were made startlingly prominent. The Council ratified the institution of married bishops, which had formed part of the programme of the Living Church from its beginning, and authorized widowed priests to remarry. The left wing minority, defeated in the Council of 1917–18, was taking its revenge. Personal ambitions and the desire for security also played their part.[12]

Although from the outset the schismatic movement had been split into three distinct groups: the *Living Church*, led by Krasnitsky; the *Union of the communities of the earliest apostolic times*, with Vvedensky as its head and the *Renaissance of the Church*, the party of Mgr Antoninus – the Coalition Council was a success. The parishes in Moscow that remained faithful to Patriarch Tikhon could have been counted on the fingers.

Suddenly, in June 1923, a spectacular change of front occurred, under pressure from foreign governments,[13] and in return for a formal profession of guilt the Patriarch, whose trial had been announced on several occasions, was released. To save the Church from disintegration he agreed to draw up a curious statement:

As I was brought up under a monarchist régime and, until my arrest, was under the influence of people opposed to the Soviet, I was hostile to the present régime; sometimes this hostility ceased to be merely passive and found expression in such actions as the following: the statement made when the peace of Brest was signed in 1918; the anathema pronounced against the régime in that same year; the protest against the decree on the seizure of the treasures of the Church, issued in 1922. All my anti-Soviet actions, apart from a few inaccuracies, are exposed in the Supreme Tribunal's 'act of accusation'. I recognize that the Tribunal's decision sentencing me for anti-Soviet activity, according to the norm of the criminal code, mentioned in the 'act of accusation', was well founded. I deplore these offences against the established régime, and I beg the Supreme Tribunal to commute my punishment; that is, to free me from imprisonment.

I further declare to the Supreme Tribunal that henceforth I cease to be an enemy of the Soviet régime. Once for all, and resolutely, I separate myself from both the foreign counter-revolution and the counter-revolution of the monarchists of the white army in the interior.[14]

Whether this statement was made freely or under compulsion, it marks a decisive and irrevocable turning point in the relationship between the Church of the Patriarchate and the Communist régime. From this time onward, the Church gave up her prophetic function with respect to the régime, and completely submitted to the *de facto* authority. In two consecutive statements, published in *Isvestia* on 28th June and 1st July, the Patriarch clarified his thought: he declared that all the decisions of the Council of the Living Church were null and void, and he explained at length that he was not guilty of the accusation of being a counter-revolutionary which the Council had brought against him. He recalled the facts that, since the beginning of 1919, he had tried to free the Church from its attachment to the Tsarist régime; that in September of that year he had made it plain in a public statement that the Church would take no part in politics of any kind, and that he personally would accept the decisions of the Government in so far as these did not conflict with his faith and devotion.[15]

The Patriarch's statement procured his own freedom and stemmed the advance of the Living Church: many parishes returned to the obedience of the Church of the Patriarchate; Mgr Sergius Stragorodsky did public penance, dressed as an ordinary monk, and received the white *klobuk*, the insignia of his office, from the hands of the Patriarch. The Government continued nevertheless to support the Living Church and gave no legal recognition to the Patriarch's administration. Tikhon was closely watched and constantly subjected to pressures of various kinds. On 9th December 1923, his *keleïnik* (a kind of private secretary who looked after the material needs of a bishop or a monastic superior) was assassinated. His own health declined and in January 1925 he was obliged to enter a hospital. Three months later, on 7th April, he died; his last words were: 'The night will be very long and very dark.' Many people believed that he had been poisoned by the Soviet police, but this plausible hypothesis could never be proved. Three hundred thousand people attended his funeral, and from the day after his death he was revered in the hearts of the faithful as a martyr and a saint.[16]

The interregnum

A week later *Izvestia* published a statement, said to have been signed by the Patriarch on the day he died, committing the Church even more completely to the path of submission to the State.[17] But the authenticity of this document – of which the heading itself was inaccurate: it described Tikhon as 'Patriarch of Moscow and of the whole Russian Church', a title quite unknown to ecclesiastical parlance – was immediately disputed and the succeeding Patriarchs have never referred to it.[18]

Tikhon did, however, leave an authentic will which was ratified by fifty-nine bishops present at his funeral. In it he designated three *locum tenentes* who alone would have power to elect his successor, and who would inherit his authority until the summoning of a General Council. These were the Metropolitans Cyril, Agathange and Peter. The first two were in exile, so it was the third, Mgr Peter Poliansky, the Metropolitan of Krutitsy, who took office.[19] On 28th July, he issued a pastoral letter in which he stated that he would be faithful to his predecessor's policy and remain loyal to the civil authorities.[20]

The dissident Church, still supported by the Government, encountered considerable opposition from the people. It summoned a new Council which devoted its attention to a complete reorganization of its constitution. It gave up the name of the Living Church; replaced the Supreme Council by a Synod on traditional lines; severed its connection with the groups led by Mgr Antoninus and Rev Krasnitsy, and adopted a series of sensible liturgical reforms: the introduction of the Russian language, the establishment of an order of deaconesses, the extension of corporate prayer, etc.[21]

This was its splendid hour. Including the autocephalous 'renewed' Churches of the Ukraine and White Russia, it numbered 192 bishops, 16,540 priests and 12,593 parishes, published its own review and possessed a theological Institute in Petrograd, a school for higher studies in Kiev, and ran courses of pastoral theology in a number of cities.[22] Its influence was felt even in countries to which Russians had emigrated. The Ecumenical Patriarch gave it his recognition: Protestants attended its congresses[23] in the belief that this was the dawn of a Reformation in Russia; even Catholics expressed their sympathy, with the secret hope that they could direct it Romewards.[24] All it lacked was the support of the faithful and the sanction of the hierarchy of the Patriarchate. Mgr Peter met every approach of the 'Renewed Church' and every pressure from the Government's representative, with a point blank refusal. As a result he was arrested on 10 December 1925 and exiled to Siberia. He had arranged for Mgr Sergius Stragorodsky to take his place as the provisional occupant of the Patriarchal throne.[25] Mgr Sergius was unquestionably one of the most remarkable personalities in the Russian episcopate. He was an excellent theologian; his book on the doctrine of salvation has proved of lasting value. He had been, successively, a missionary in Japan; a priest in the Russian Embassy in Athens; Rector of the Ecclesiastical Academy in St Petersburg; an eminently tactful president of the meetings of the society of religious philosophy; Bishop of Finland, where, long before the council of 1917, he had introduced the custom of diocesan assemblies consisting of both priests and laymen; a member of the provisional Synod entrusted with the preparatory work for the Council, etc. In short he had taken part in all the major initiatives of the first part of this century. He was highly esteemed by all the clergy and the people.

Forbidden to live in Moscow, he governed the Church from Nijny-Novgorod; he tried to obtain official recognition of the Church, on the basis of the decree on the separation between the Church and State. [26] This was also the desire of the bishops who had been exiled to the Solovki Islands; they circulated a manifesto throughout Russia disclaiming all direct influence in temporal affairs, but asking that the Church's internal freedom should be respected by strict and loyal observance of the decree of 1918. This manifesto, written by Professor I. V. Popov (who finally disappeared in 1937) and Mgr Hilarion Troitsky (died in prison in 1929) was closely argued at a high intellectual level.[27] But it also showed a certain naïvety of outlook; these confessors of the faith wanted to believe that they were co-operating with an honest partner. In fact, however, the State had no intention of implementing the 1918 decree but desired to bring the Church into subjection the better to destroy it.

The only answer Mgr Sergius received to his request for legalization was his arrest on 26th December 1926.[28] After various vicissitudes, since Mgr Joseph, Mgr Cornelius and Mgr Thaddeus, the designated successors to Mgr Sergius, were all in exile, the government of the Church fell to Mgr Samoilovich. He was living in Uglich, and he too was prevented from coming to Moscow. He voluntarily limited his authority, appointed no successor, and told the bishops to govern their dioceses autonomously.[29]

Eight years of persecution had imprinted upon the Church a new character which, in its main features, has endured until now. After a preliminary phase of confusion, caused by the upheaval of the Church, during which there was some movement towards Catholicism and the Protestant sects, the Church recovered itself and responded to the attacks upon it by an intensification of faith.

There was a great renovation of worship. The offices were now celebrated at full monastic length and with a quite new magnificence. The people spent long hours in prayer. A real 'eucharistic movement' developed, regular communion at each celebration of the liturgy was no longer the custom of a few devotees and became a regular practice for all. In addition, private devotion was intensified and believers transformed their dwellings into oratories. The closing down and destruction of churches was accompanied by supernatural signs: particularly in Southern Russia, the cupolas and icons suddenly shone with a new light that was observed by many witnesses. What the Church lost in quantity she gained in quality. It was Christian thought rather than Christian life that lost the most in these new circumstances: Christians still studied and wrote but without hope of publication.[30]

The declaration of 1927 and the schism of the right

On 9th March 1927, Mgr Sergius was released from prison; he was permitted to resume his duties and to establish a provisional

Synod that received official Government recognition. This partial success did not extend to the administration of the dioceses, and it was paid for dearly. On 24th July, Mgr Sergius issued what amounted to a declaration of obedience to the Soviet Government.[31] This was sure to provoke a new schism in the Church. When, in the name of the Church as a whole, he declared that 'we wish to be Orthodox, and at the same time to recognize the Soviet Union as our civil fatherland, whose joys and successes are our joys and successes, and whose failures are our failures . . .' he was making the Church an active ally of the Soviet Government. By putting all the blame on the clergy for the deterioration of relations between Church and State, and by expressing his 'thanks to the Soviet Government for the concern it shows for all the needs of religion', he deeply wounded the feelings of all those who were suffering for the faith and for Christ; he was leading the Church into the path of half-truths, if not of actual untruth. And when he asked those who had emigrated to foreign countries to proclaim their loyalty to the Soviet Government, he was being politic to the point of absurdity.

Most of the clergy and laity understood this as a necessary sin, if the Church was to survive; they followed the Metropolitan Sergius with death in their hearts. The bishops deported to the Solovki Islands disapproved of the declaration in principle, but adjured everyone not to destroy the Church's unity. The chief supporters of the Patriarch Tikhon, Mgr Nicander Fenomenov, Mgr Hilarion Troitsky and Mgr Arsenius Stadnitsky came out on Mgr Sergius's side.[32]

But a number of bishops, while never ceasing to proclaim their loyalty to the established power, did not hesitate to dissociate themselves from Mgr Sergius's declaration. They held that he had overstepped his legal rights as *locum tenens* for the guardian of the Patriarchal throne, by setting up a Synod chosen by himself, and by imposing upon everybody his own policy of active collaboration with the persecutors. Before the Church had even overcome the schism on the left it was faced with one on the right. This is usually called the Josephite schism, from the Metropolitan of Leningrad, Mgr Joseph Petrovykh who was its recognized leader. The schism was limited – to mention only its principal centres – to the dioceses of Yaroslavl (five bishops, including Mgr Seraphim Samoilovich and Mgr Agathange), Leningrad, Serpukhov (Mgr Maximus Jijilenko), Voronej (Mgr Alexis Biuf), Kazan (Mgr Cyril Smirnov), Gluknov (Mgr Damascene), Usting (Mgr Ieropheus) and Ufa. It made its way even into the concentration camps, and although it did not involve the people as a whole, members of the episcopate and the clergy of the highest integrity were implicated. Among these were the first two successors of Mgr Tikhon, Mgrs Cyril and Agathange, the theologian P. Florensky, the publicist V. Sventsitsky, etc.

The opponents had various complaints. Some, such as Mgr Cyril, insisted that the new Synod was contrary to the canon law; others, for example Mgr Joseph, objected to the illegal transference of bishops (he had been prevented from coming to Leningrad, and was appointed to Odessa by Mgr Sergius, but refused to obey); while others argued that the martyrs had been implicitly betrayed and that the declaration contained a subtle untruth (Mgr Seraphim, Mgr Damascene, etc.)[33]

The bishops of the opposition proclaimed that their dioceses were autocephalous until the summoning of the General Council which alone, in their view, would be competent to pass judgement on their actions. They justified their attitude canonically by their fidelity to the *locum tenens*, the Metropolitan Peter Poliansky. What the latter really thought was never known, for he was exiled in the far north and allowed no correspondence with the outside world. It appears that he had not repudiated Mgr Sergius,[34] yet the Soviet authorities, pleased with their success in again dividing the Church, were very careful not to set him free. Far from it; they increased his isolation to keep up the uncertainty.

In the attitude of the dissidents of the right there was an element of pride, but also a great deal of courage. They chose to suffer rather than betray the truth.[35]

The first attempt to liquidate the Church

Mgr Sergius reckoned that the concessions which he made would bring important advantages to the Church: a Council might be summoned, schools of theology opened, a review published, some of the martyrs released from prison. The administrator of the Patriarchate, the young Metropolitan Sergius Voskresensky, defined the policy of the 'deputy to the *locum tenens*' in the following words:

To restrict as far as possible the destruction of the Church by the Bolsheviks has always been the Patriarchate's chief concern. Its aim has been to preserve the dogmatic purity and canonical rectitude of the Orthodox Church, overcome the schisms, safeguard the legitimate succession in the transmission of authority; to ensure for the Russian Church its rightful position among the other Orthodox Churches, and thus enable it to move towards a better future, when, after Bolshevism has fallen, the Church may once more be re-born. But to work towards the accomplishment of these tasks the Patriarchate had first to make sure of its own existence, which was in grave danger.

The Soviet Government and the Church confronted one another as two hostile forces, each compelled, for different reasons, to accept a mutual compromise. But when the Bolsheviks came to terms with the Church by making concessions, they deceived the Church, for they afterwards made those 'concessions' illusory. Even the legalization of the Patriarchate did not produce the results that had been hoped for. Juridical recognition was limited to it alone, and not to the Church as a whole. It was a paradoxical situation: the Patriarchate became the legal organ of an illegal organism. The Bolsheviks were tolerating the existence of the Patriarchate in their own interests. For the sake of the Church we resigned ourselves to our humiliating situation. The Patriarchate remained as the only legal organ in the Church; it

46

alone had the power to introduce a modicum of order into the Church's life and to limit the Bolsheviks' destruction of the Church.[36]

But even this last possibility soon proved illusory. In 1929, with the launching of its first Five-Year-Plan and the collectivization of agriculture, the Soviet Government began a pitiless offensive against the Church. Her legalization was followed, almost without an interval, by liquidation.

On 8th April, a law was promulgated which was of fundamental importance to religion; it reaffirmed the existing legislation, but with increased State control over parochial life; local authorities were given the right to remove members of the parish executive organizations without explanation. Besides this, their activity was still further restricted by the prohibition of every kind of charitable work and all cultural and social manifestations.[37] Then, on 22nd May, article 13 of the Constitution was amended; instead of 'freedom for religious and non-religious activities', the phrase 'freedom for religious belief and for anti-religious propaganda' was substituted. In other words, freedom for religious propaganda – the limits of which are not easily defined – became a criminal offence against the State, as a semi-official commentary soon made clear:

Henceforward all propaganda or agitation promoted by the representatives of religion and the Church cannot and must not be regarded as legally allowable. On the contrary, these exceed the bounds of confessional freedom granted by law and fall under the criminal and civil code. Such activities should be condemned in accordance with the articles 58 (10) and 59 (7) of the criminal code. The revised article means that the activity of religious bodies must henceforth be confined to worship. No other activity outside the satisfaction of religious needs is allowed. Even religious propaganda is no longer authorized.[38]

The week of uninterrupted work, laid down by the decree of 27th August, eliminated the observance of Sunday or any other day as a common rest day. Ministers of religion and their families were ranked with kulaks and deprived of their civil rights (*lishentsy*). This meant that they could no longer claim food coupons – vital in that time of scarcity – or medical assistance or medicines. In addition, they were burdened with exceptionally heavy taxes and their children were now prevented from attending secondary and high schools. As a result many priestly homes were broken; wives repudiated their husbands rather than see their children die of hunger or from lack of vital medicines. The Synod even had to issue instructions against the nominal divorces of priests who legally (though not in reality) separated themselves from their wives to enable their families to escape from the rigours of their situation.[39]

Priests in rags began to line up in front of the churches, begging for alms. Direct measures were added to these legal restrictions. A vast number of churches were closed;[40] arbitrary taxes beyond the income of the parishes were imposed; people were expelled from the community, arrested, deported, executed, at the whim of the local authorities, without any reason or explanation. In 1930 the number of exiled bishops rose to 150; in some places where there had been five priests, only one remained.[41] Collectivization often began by the closing of the village church and the deportation of the priest as a kulak. During this period a priest could be seen mounting the pulpit in his underclothes – all that he had left.[42] The background to this picture was the massive extermination of those peasants (numbering several millions) who resisted collectivization, and the famine.

A memorandum of demands presented by Mgr Sergius on 19th February 1930, clearly shows how despotically the Church was treated. It may be useful to quote this in its entirety, the more so since the years 1929–30 offer a striking parallel to the new wave of persecutions in 1959–62:

1. The property tax bears so heavily upon the churches, especially in the countryside, that the communities are

unable to make use of them. The tax on churches should be lowered (it should not be calculated as though they were buildings used for profit) and also the rate of assessment.

2. The collection of a composer's royalties for the benefit of the playwrights' union must be kept within the limits laid down by the law, that is, they must only be collected when music performed in a church is either national property or belongs to a particular individual, and not simply because it was sung in church and especially during public worship. Ministers who are engaged in divine worship cannot be considered as artists giving a musical performance. And therefore churches cannot be compelled to pay five per cent of all the revenues of the clergy, that is, of all the sums collected for religious services in the church or outside it.

3. Collection of insurance premiums for the cantors (it was suppressed in 1929) must be stopped. The money is demanded for the years when it was not paid (sometimes since 1922). When the interest is added this sometimes amounts to considerable sums (more than 4,000 roubles).

4. The churches must be released from taxes on various agricultural products (bread, grain, wood, etc.) as well as special agricultural taxes; for tractors, industrialization, State loans, etc. Since the churches possess no landed property, these taxes fall on the members of the religious communities and constitute a new kind of tax on their faith which the faithful must pay over and above those to which they are liable, like all the other citizens.

5. The instructions of the NKF (the Peoples' Commissariat for Finance) on 5th January 1930 (No. 195), according to which the penalties and confiscations for non-payment of taxes by the Church cannot involve the personal property of the parochial councils, must also be applied to the tax on real estate, royalties, etc.

6. It should be explained that the members of parochial councils, sacristans, vergers and all those who have some

particular function must not be treated as kulaks and compelled in consequence to pay particularly heavy taxes.

7. It should be explained to the local justices, who receive
complaints from the Orthodox communities and clergy, that
they must not refuse them legal protection in cases where
their rights have been infringed by local administrative
authorities, or any other organization.

8. It must be accepted as a general rule that when it is proposed to close a church, the decisive factor should not be
what unbelievers want, but the presence of believers who
are likely to use the church in question. When a church is, in
fact, given up by a community it can only be placed at the
disposition of another Orthodox community. If a church is
closed, for whatever reason, the members of the Orthodox
community retain the right to ask a priest to celebrate any
service for their families in their own homes.

9. Explanations are needed about the coming into force of
the decree of the SNK (the Soviet of the People's Commissars) of 8th April 1929, that deals with religious bodies,
and also about the instructions of 1st October 1929, and the
other regulations on the same subject, for sometimes the
local authorities do not accept the requests for legalization
made by the religious communities (congregations) and go
so far as to forbid the taking of any steps towards such
legalization. (The law had definitely fixed 1st May 1930,
as the final date on which religious bodies desiring to continue in existence could be registered.)

10. *Desiderata of the clergy.* Ministers of religion, having no
paid staff, should be registered as members of a liberal
profession and not as non-workers and still less as kulaks.

11. The amount of taxation must not be decided in an
arbitrary manner, nor exceed the means of the person
concerned. For example, Bishop Sinesius Zarubin was
taxed 10,300 roubles and in addition was required to pay
more than 7,000 roubles in advance on the following year.

The clergy should be taxed as members of a liberal profession.

12. The local authorities in the countryside should be given instructions as to the exact limits and amounts of the local taxes and dues which ministers of religion are to pay as non-kulaks.

13. Since ministers of religion are not engaged in farming, cattle breeding, hunting, etc., they should not be made to pay the tax on agricultural products such as bread, grain, wool, butter, game, etc. The payment of this tax is sometimes demanded within twenty-four hours.

14. When it happens that the goods of a minister of religion are seized for non-payment of taxes, he should be allowed to keep a minimum of furniture, clothing and footwear.

15. When forced labour is imposed upon a minister of religion, the amount of it should be fixed within reasonable limits. In the village of Liuk, in the Vot district, for example, the priest was compelled to fell, saw up, and remove some 1,500 feet of timber. The individual's age and health should be taken into consideration.

16. Ministers of religion must not be deprived of the means of living within their parish boundaries and near to the church, even in the case of villages that have been transformed into collective farms. Furthermore, those who let them rooms should not be taxed more heavily on this account.

17. The children of the clergy must be allowed to attend the primary and secondary schools, and those who were registered in the autumn of 1929 as university students must not be excluded by reason of their parentage. Those who have already been excluded must be authorized to return to the university and to complete their studies.

18. Professional or amateur singers, members of RABIS (the artists' union) or of other unions, who take part in church choirs to add to their income, should not, on that account, be excluded from RABIS or other unions.

19. In the summer of 1929 the opening in Leningrad of an institute of higher theological studies for the Orthodox Patriarchal Church was discussed. It is highly desirable that the requisite authorization be granted, if only in order to put our Church on an equal footing with the 'Renewed Church' which has an Academy.

20. The Patriarchate has long felt the need for a periodical publication, if only a monthly bulletin, in which the decrees, the pastoral letters of the central authorities of the Church, etc., which concern the Church as a whole, may be published.

21. Confronted by a press campaign for a revision of the Constitution of the USSR with the aim of prohibiting all religious propaganda and restricting Church activity, we ask for protection and for the maintenance of the rights granted to the Orthodox Church by the laws at present in force in the USSR.[43]

This list is already eloquent enough; to it must be added the countless legal trials of priests and layfolk referred to in the Soviet press of this period and also an outbreak of vandalism unprecedented in modern times. Between 1929 and 1934, hundreds, if not thousands of churches were destroyed, including many monuments of historical value. It is to be hoped that an inventory of this vandalism, unfortunately still continuing, will some day be undertaken. Let us mention, for example: the destruction in Moscow of the Cathedrals of the Holy Saviour and of our Lady of Kazan, the Monasteries of the Miracles in the Kremlin, of St Simeon (fourteenth century), the Chapels of the Virgin of Iberia, of the Virgin of Unexpected Joy – nearly fifty religious buildings in all were razed to the ground in the capital.[44] In Kiev, we may only mention the destruction, in spite of protests from the Academy, of the Monastery of St Michael (eleventh century), the Church of the Three Holy Doctors at the court of Yaroslav (twelfth century) and the Cathedral of the Assumption of the Virgin at Podol (twelfth century).[45]

Icons and religious books were burnt by the thousand, by whole cartloads.[46] Bell ringing was forbidden; the bells were pulled down and melted and their metal used for industrial purposes. 'The air was filled with the sound of bells, bells falling, bells crashing to the ground with a thud.'[47]

On 14th March 1930, the Party's Central Committee decided to slow down the speed of collectivization and of the anti-religious campaign; a famous resolution, the *Delirium of Success*, denounced the 'illegal deviations undergone by the Party line in the fight against religious prejudices, and especially the closure of churches without the consent of the overwhelming majority of the village'.[48] All the same, no attempt was made to repair the previous wrongs, and the Church continued to suffer violent persecution until the end of the year 1932.

The material destruction of the Church was accompanied by anti-religious propaganda on a vast scale.

The anti-religious movement

The anti-religious movement did not await the Five-Year-Plan before taking shape. In February 1922, the first anti-religious publishing house, 'The Atheist', was established.[49] In November of the same year a study group was set up in Moscow to discuss the means of opposing religion. During Christmastide the first carnival, organized to ridicule the nativity of Christ, paraded the streets of the capital. Previously the attacks on religion had been sporadic; they now became the most important branch of communist propaganda and activity.[50] In 1923, anti-religious newspapers made their first appearance: *Atheist*, published every five days in different editions to appeal to various types of reader; *Bezbojnik u Stanka* (The godless at the work-bench), a crudely illustrated monthly magazine. At Easter, the carnivals were extended to all the large towns: the 'gods', from the God of Israel to Buddha were burnt in effigy.[51] Anti-religious pamphlets were published, fifty, seventy and even a hundred thousand copies at a time, enormous numbers for that period. Children were recruited for this campaign; at school uplifted hands voted for the 'death' of God, or, more concretely, for the elimination of every kind of religious practice.[52]

On 7th February 1925, a Jew, Emilien Yaroslavsky (his real name was Gubelmann) founded the League of Militant Atheists which became the vanguard of the fight against religion. Two new publications were issued: the *Bezbojnik*, a fighting journal, and the *Anti-religioznik*, a fortnightly review of science and methodology aimed at a more limited and educated public. In 1929 the League published its own Five-Year-Plan, whose objectives were no less exaggerated than those of the economic plan. Naturally, these were not attained, but the results achieved were impressive: instead of seventeen million members which the League counted on having by 1932, there were only five-and-a-half million; the *Atheist* had only 471,000 subscribers instead of a million and a half; the *Bezbojnik* had 199,500 instead of 250,000; the *Anti-religioznik* 31,900 instead of 60,000. However, books and pamphlets poured out in fantastic numbers; 820,000 copies of the Anti-religious Manual alone had been sold by 1st January 1932. Yaroslavsky was triumphant, and declared that the real number of the godless had risen to almost thirty millions.[53]

These successes moved the League to promote a second Five-Year-Plan, even more ambitious than the former, since its aim was the total eradication of every aspect of religion by 1937. The details were worked out with naïve precision. In 1932–3 all external signs of religion were to be destroyed; during 1933–4 all religious pictures in books or people's homes were to disappear; during 1934–5 the whole country and particularly its youth, were to be subjected to intensive atheistic propaganda; during 1935–6, any places of worship still standing would be destroyed; and finally, during 1936–7, religion would be routed out from its most secret hiding-places.[54]

The Great Trials

A brief respite

But the League had taken little account of realities, or of the possible fluctuations in government policy. The years 1932–3 marked the culminating point of the campaign against religion, and after 1934 government pressure was relaxed. During the years of collectivization the bow had been stretched too tightly and it was at breaking point. Once the main objectives had been attained, it was essential to give the exhausted country time to breathe. The years preceding the promulgation of Stalin's Constitution show points of similarity with the thaw of 1954–7. In 1934 many bishops and priests who had given up all hope for the future were set free, and resumed their duties. Many schismatics returned to the Patriarchal Church. Liberalization was extended to all the different sections: during 1935–6 there existed at Ufa, with full legal sanction, a 'Josephite' diocese that did not accept the authority of the Metropolitan Sergius, and whose bishop did not scruple to keep up a correspondence abroad.[55]

The *Messenger of the Patriarchate* during these years (it resumed publication at the end of 1931 and continued until 1935) bears witness to a definite strengthening of the Church's organization and even the timid revival of a kind of interior life. Practically all the Episcopal Sees had fallen vacant during the persecutions, but were now occupied by new bishops. Since there was no theological college, the Patriarchal administration bestowed the degree of master of theology on the priest N. Konoplev, for his thesis on the saints of the Vologda regions. Lay people wrote to the Metropolitan Sergius to ask for permission to receive Holy Communion daily, even during Lent. (In the Orthodox Church, the eucharistic liturgy is celebrated only on Saturdays and Sundays during the long Lent preceding Easter. In order that the faithful may not have to wait too long for the sacraments, a 'liturgy of the pre-sanctified' is celebrated on Wednesdays and Fridays. The remaining days are aliturgical.)

At the Congress of the Godless in 1935, E. Yaroslavsky noted that clerical activity was on the increase, that the number of atheists was diminishing, and that interest in the propaganda against religion was slackening. In that same year the blasphemous carnivals were prohibited, and the sale of Easter cakes in State stores was authorized. On 29th December, a decree abolished discrimination between the children of workers and those of priests for entrance into the schools and eligibility for the various degrees and offices. Stalin's Constitution of 1936 ratified the amendment of 1929 which granted only 'freedom of religious worship' as against 'freedom of propaganda against religion'. The census of 1937 included the question 'Are you a believer?' which was in direct contradiction with the constitutional principles of the régime. The result of this religious referendum was never published, but from a well-informed source it appears that answers in the affirmative amounted to 70 per cent: in any case, it is certain that the majority of the people professed belief in God.[56]

In December 1936, news reached Moscow of the death in exile of Mgr Peter of Krutitsy. His death deprived the Josephite schism of any possible justification and left Mgr Sergius as the sole legitimate guardian of the Patriarchal throne. But already there were premonitory signs of the drastic purges of 1937–40, which were to obliterate the hard-won gains of this brief period of thaw.

The third attack on the Church

The Church was the favourite victim in those years of universal terror during which, in the words of N. Kruschev at the twenty-second Party Congress, 'no one was safe from arbitrary arrest or from the repression.'[57] For the Church, it was like a cyclone that swept everything before it. Churches were closed by the thousand; bishops and priests went back to prison, but this time hundreds of them were summarily executed.[58] To quote only one example, in Orel, the bishop and several priests were 'pitilessly punished' for a whole series of religious delinquencies: struggle against 'Renewed Church', attempts to attract young people to church, the practice of general confession which was condemned as an anti-Soviet 'meeting', the installation of a confessional at home, the transference of priests who had been dismissed from the towns to religious work in the country, inciting people to demand the re-opening of the churches, baptizing children who had reached school-age, etc.[59]

The Metropolitan Sergius was attacked through his relatives: his sister, a nun, and his *keleïnik*, perished in the purges.[60]

In the period immediately preceding the war the Church presented a picture of total desolation. In the whole of Russia not a hundred churches remained open for worship. Rostov-on-the-Don, a large industrial city with a population of 600,000, provides an example that illustrates many others. Its Archbishop, Seraphim Silichev, had been exiled to the far north in 1930, where he soon died. Shortly afterwards, his Vicar, Mgr Nicholas Ammasisky, was sent to the steppes of Astrakhan to graze a flock of sheep. In 1938 he was again arrested and this time shot, but miraculously recovered from his wounds. Meanwhile, the authorities continued to close the churches. In Rostov itself, even the former Cathedral of St Nicholas was transformed into a zoo; the new Cathedral of St Alexander Nevsky was razed to the ground; the huge Church of All Saints turned into a workshop, and the Greek Church became an anti-religious museum. Only one chapel in the Armenian cemetery remained for the use of the faithful, but there were no services there, because there were no priests. Throughout the whole province, one single church, served by a very old priest, was still functioning in a village close to Taganrog.[61] Outwardly, all that remained was a church in ruins.

During 1939–40 the annexation of the Baltic countries, of the western half of Poland, and of Bessarabia, brought a breath of fresh air to a dying organism. Several millions of Orthodox Christians, active members of Churches that were very much alive, became citizens of an atheist State which had succeeded in destroying all visible forms of religion. Mgr Sergius deputed the few bishops who had escaped death to work in these regions, and to effect a reunion of these Churches under the religious authority of Moscow. At the same time, the Soviet civil authorities took their preliminary administrative measures against these newly-incorporated Churches, a fact which did not make the task of the Patriarchate any easier. The patch of new cloth fitted badly on to the old garment.[62]

CHAPTER IV

RESURRECTION

Christ is risen from the dead, Through death he has overcome death

Trope for Easter

AT THIS POINT an event of supreme importance occurred which was to alter the whole situation for the Church: namely, the *war*. On 21st June 1941, according to the State calendar, and on the Sunday dedicated to the feast of all Russian saints, according to the ecclesiastical calendar, the German troops crossed the Russian frontier. The Metropolitan Sergius heard the news as he was coming back from the cathedral where he had been celebrating the liturgy.[1] After a few moments of thought and a short prayer he came to the historic decision which was to secure the Church's survival. *On that same day*, without waiting for the situation to develop or for any declaration of the Government's policy, the head of the Church drew up and sent out to the people a pastoral letter condemning the aggressor and invoking God's blessing upon all Orthodox Christians so that they might spring to the defence of their threatened country.

Our Orthodox Church has always shared the destiny of her people. She has suffered with them in their trials and has been consoled by their successes. And today, no less surely, she will not forsake her people. She gives her heavenly blessing to this sacrifice now to be made by the whole nation. . . . May God grant us victory.[2]

In this letter, the head of the Church did not mention the Government or even the Army. Anxious to respect the separation between Church and State with scrupulous care, and to avoid arousing the susceptibilities of anyone, he went straight to the inner meaning of the conflict; it was not the régime, but the nation, the very existence of Russia, that was at stake. By urging the faithful to join in the struggle, the Metropolitan Sergius took his place in the line of Russia's illustrious spiritual leaders, Alexander Nevsky, Sergius of Radonej, the Patriarch Hermogenes, etc. Through his summons he forestalled the head of the State, restored the Russian Church that had been humiliated and mocked, to her original vocation, and endowed her once more with a leading position in the life of the nation. Crushed by her enemy and left for dead, the Church, contrary to all expectations, rose up and sounded the battle cry. Four days after the outbreak of war, in the Cathedral of the Epiphany, Sergius held a solemn Te Deum for Russia's victory. On this occasion he gave a brief but resolute discourse in which he branded those who would default, and again called for the mobilization of all the nation's spiritual, moral and physical forces. This old man of seventy-four had no hesitation in expressing himself within the walls of the Church in the words of a naval command:

All hands on deck . . . Our country is in danger and is calling all of us . . . to defend our native land, its independence . . . shame on anyone who remains deaf to this appeal and allows others to sacrifice themselves for the common good while he himself waits to see which will be the most profitable side on which to serve. It would be especially shameful, and indeed sinful, if among these so-called sons who are really traitors to their country, any members of the Orthodox Church were to be found. . . . Those who imagine that the enemy will not attack our sanctuaries or our beliefs, are greatly mistaken. What we know of life in Germany makes us take a very different view. . . .

Let the storm come. We know that it will bring not only misfortune, but alleviation also; it will cleanse the air and blow away noxious vapours.

May the oncoming storm of battle purify the spiritual climate and sweep away the poisonous mists: indifference to the country's welfare, two-faced activity, the pursuit of personal gain, etc. We already see certain signs of this disinfection.[3]

The reference to those who were hesitating was aimed not only at members of the Church. Indeed, the clarity, courage and rapid decision of the Metropolitan contrasted vividly with the 'wait and see' attitude of a great part of the population and of those in government circles. Stalin himself, believing the attack to be merely an act of provocation, evaded a final decision for ten days, before issuing his first appeal to the people; and in this he addressed them in the classic terms of Christian preaching: 'Comrades, citizens, *brothers and sisters*, my friends.'[4] The hope that the storm would cleanse the atmosphere, fouled by the recent purges, was shared by numerous Soviet citizens. Fifteen years later, a Soviet poetess, Julia Neumann, recalling the extraordinary atmosphere of 1941, used words that echo the message of the head of the Church: 'O my contemporaries, be frank about it. Pure as a flame was that year when, for the first time in those days of camouflage, we tore off our masks.'[5]

The unusually large congregation that crowded inside and outside the church – some witnesses say there were twelve thousand present – was rightly seen by the Metropolitan Sergius as the first fruits and the pledge of the national awakening.

A special prayer, authentically liturgical, and sober and moderate, was introduced into public worship;[6] and a special petition for victory over the enemy was added to the litanies in common use.

At the outset, this definite attitude brought little change in the relations between Church and State. But from September onwards, the anti-religious periodicals were suppressed and the League of Atheists was dissolved. There could be no question of carrying on the internal conflict while the country was in danger. In October, when the German drive towards Moscow began,

Sergius, though ill, was abruptly ordered by the authorities to leave the capital. After an exhausting journey which lasted five days and might well have proved fatal, the aged prelate arrived at Ulianovsk (Simbirsk) where no preparations had been made to receive him; in fact, he had to spend the first weeks in the railway coach that had brought him. The position of the Church in Simbirsk, as everywhere else, was lamentable. A single parish church had remained open, or had just been reopened, but there was no priest to serve it. One of the Metropolitan's first tasks was to send the priests who were with him into the parishes of the region to form the necessary 'groups of twenty' (presumably the terrorized laity did not dare to form such groups themselves) and reopen the churches in order to create a little life in the neighbourhood of what was to be Russia's religious capital during the war.[7] It was from this place, in fact, that the head of the Church regained contact with the few eastern bishops who were still free; from here he sent out his numerous patriotic proclamations and his appeals for the collection of gifts to be devoted to the defence of the country; and then, as a gesture that was at once more symbolical and more tangible, for the formation of an armoured division, christened with the name of the Russian prince Dimitri Donskoi. It was here also that he held the first episcopal consecrations since 1937.

The religious and patriotic activity of the head of the Church was seconded at the outposts of Leningrad and Moscow, by his two oldest collaborators, the Metropolitans Alexis and Nicholas.

To Leningrad, under blockade and starving, the Metropolitan Alexis became the living symbol of the Church's presence amid its trials. He shared the privations of the people (a photograph of 1943 shows him terribly emaciated) and gave constant encouragement to his flock, urging them not only to accept suffering, but also to fight on until final victory. He celebrated the liturgy continually, and organized processions. By 15th January 1943, the Orthodox laity of Leningrad had contributed more than three million roubles to the 'Fund for the defence of the country'.[8]

The attitude of the Metropolitan Nicholas, on the other hand, at first seems to have been ambiguous. When he was driven from Lutsk by the German advance he was in no hurry to establish contact with Moscow, and remained in the area of the front 'moving from place to place'. On 15th July, Sergius, having had no news of him, and perhaps fearing that his career might end in schism, promoted him to the dignity of Metropolitan of Kiev and Galicia, and Exarch of the whole Ukraine. This promotion could be nothing but honorary, for the Ukraine was in process of being occupied by the Germans, but it flattered Nicholas's self-esteem and compelled him to return to Moscow. He was soon in charge of the business of the Patriarchate. As the spokesman for the Church he took his stand on the statements issued by Sergius, and went beyond them in the virulence of his patriotism.[9]

In 1942, a curious book, *The Truth about Religion in the USSR*, was published with his authority. It was symptomatic of the ambiguity of the alliance between the Church and her former adversary. This voluminous book – 457 pages, published in a luxury edition of 50,000 copies, with a bright blue binding and many illustrations – was the first visible sign of a radical change of policy towards the Church. A year previously the Church had still been socially outcast, and now the Government authorized, even patronized, the publication of a collection of testimonies and documents to the glory of this same Church. But the real aim of the book was different. As Sergius remarks in the Introduction,[10] it was intended, first, as an answer to 'the so-called Fascist crusade for the liberation of the Orthodox Church'; secondly, it was a reply to the more general question: 'Does our Church regard herself as persecuted by the Bolsheviks?' Mindful of his honour, the head of the Church could not explicitly deny the reality of the persecutions, and his answer was diplomatic. 'What our enemies call persecutions, our Orthodox people consider to be simply a return to the days of the apostles.'[11]

The unhappy task of repudiating and calumniating the martyrs was left to an anonymous article, issued from the editorial office:

It must be stated categorically, that the Constitution which guarantees complete freedom of worship in no way restricts the religious life of believers or of the Church in general. After the October revolution many ecclesiastics were put on trial. Why was judgement passed on them? For one reason only; because under cover of their cassock and protected by the name of the Church, they were working against the Soviet régime. These trials were political, and had nothing whatever to do with strictly ecclesiastical life of religious organizations or with the purely pastoral work of priests. The Orthodox Church herself has resolutely and publicly condemned these renegades who had betrayed her frank policy of scrupulous loyalty to the Soviet authority. . . . No, the Church can make no complaints against that authority.[12]

This obvious contradiction of the truth, repeated later in the official propaganda, was supported by the evidence of three priests and in an interview granted by Andrew, Archbishop of Saratov, to the correspondent of the Associated Press, on 24th December 1941. Thus even in wartime and in spite of the complete loyalty of the religious authorities, the Government insisted that the Church should publicly repudiate her martyrs and deny her sufferings.

The remaining sections of the book described the patriotic enthusiasm of the Orthodox people and clergy, and the atrocities of the Germans, depicted as the prime enemies of the Church. The evidence produced of Nazi extortions from the clergy appears pale indeed in contrast with the persecutions which the Church had recently undergone, but one feels that the exploitation of this theme concealed a twofold intention. If Fascism was condemned as a pagan doctrine opposed to Christianity was this not an indirect hit at Communism also? In depicting the Germans as destroyers and profaners of the sanctuaries, may not the authors have had the idea of forestalling a similar attitude on the part of the Soviet authorities when they succeeded in regaining the occupied territories? In his pastoral letter of 2nd April 1941, which forms the conclusion of the book, Sergius stated emphatically:

In Fascist Germany it is said that Christianity has failed and that there is no room for it in the future development of the world. Germany, therefore, whose aim is to control the world, must forget Christ, and pursue a course of its own. . . . The alternatives are these: either there must be a free and peaceful co-existence of nations, with their belief in Christ, their thirst for truth, for all the enlightenment that the world contains, or else Hitler with his Fascism and his darkness. . . . Not the swastika, but the cross is called to reign over our Christian civilization and over our lives as Christian people.[13]

Is not a twofold condemnation hidden in those words, a condemnation of Fascism, of course, but also of Communism, which also holds that Christianity 'no longer serves any useful purpose in this world'?

Normal relations between the Church and State came to be established only in September 1943, when the outcome of the war had ceased to be problematic and was merely a question of time. As we have seen, preparations had been made for this by mutual concessions. At Easter 1942, in spite of the danger of air attack, the curfew was lifted in Moscow, so that the people might attend the midnight service. The Metropolitans Alexis and Nicholas were invited to take part in the work of the commissions of inquiry into the atrocities committed by the German armies. Their appeals for the intensification of the resistance movement were dropped from military aircraft over territories still under occupation. On the twenty-fifth anniversary of the 'socialist republic' (November 1942) the Metropolitans Sergius and Nicholas sent telegrams of congratulation to Stalin, and these were published in the press.

In the name of the clergy and laity of the Orthodox Russian Church, loyal sons of our country, in a cordial and prayerful spirit, in your person I salute the head, chosen by God, of all our military and cultural forces, who is leading us to victory over the barbarian invaders, to the peaceful prosperity of our country and to the radiant future of its peoples. May God crown with success and glory your mighty deeds of valour in the defence of the country.[14]

In a telegram to Stalin in January 1943, the head of the Church informed him of the amount of the first collection of funds for an armoured division; the Metropolitan Alexis followed his example. These telegrams, written in a deferential and emphatic style, were honoured with brief and cool replies. This was the first peaceful dialogue between Church and State since the Revolution.

On 4th September 1943, the historic interview took place between the highest dignitaries of the Church and Marshal Stalin. The day following, *Izvestia* announced that the Government had authorized the summoning of a Council for the election of a Patriarch. Three days afterwards, an unpretentious gathering of bishops, nineteen in all, met for this purpose. The Metropolitan Sergius gave an account of the Church's patriotic activity. The meeting then proceeded to the election. On the proposal of the Metropolitan Alexis, this was done by acclamation. It was a confirmation rather than an election, for Sergius had been the *de facto* head of the Church for seventeen years. The final act of this diminutive Council was to excommunicate 'all those who had betrayed their faith and their country' – an ambiguous excommunication, because it combined two crimes of a completely different nature and it seems to have had no practical application whatever.[15]

From a legal point of view the Council had certain defects. It could be objected, for instance, that only a very small part of the Church was represented at it, and especially that those who had suffered persecution were absent from it; that the rules laid down by the Council of 1917 for the election of a Patriarch, were not observed, etc. Nevertheless, its validity was universally accepted, not only by the eastern Patriarchs, but even by the Bulgarian Church, which was within the German sphere of influence. Only the Synod of Karlovtsy, which had opted for collaboration with Hitler, persisted in its refusal to recognize the new Patriarch.

On 12th September the Patriarch Sergius was solemnly enthroned. At the end of the same month, after an interval of eight years, the first number of the Church's official bulletin, the *Review of the Moscow Patriarchate*, made its appearance.

The restoration of the Patriarchate had profound repercussions both at home and abroad. For the allies it was an indication that the Soviet Government had definitely committed itself to the path of compromise with the Church, and this augured hopefully for the future. At home, the Orthodox Church had regained a head who was recognized by the State and which led to the gradual decline or disappearance of the various schisms. Though the schisms of the Right, less important numerically, lingered on in the concentration camps and in clandestine forms elsewhere, the great schism of the Left, the Renewed Church, lost every reason for its existence, and the vast majority of its members did penance for their fault. The Orders conferred during the schism were declared invalid and the clergy were received in the Orthodox Church according to the rank that each had held before the schism. However, where there was no canonical impediment, they were soon reordained and confirmed in their ministries. Only a few isolated persons such as Alexander Vvedensky, the head of the Living Church, refused to submit, and remained more than ever the 'shepherd without a flock'.[16]

Sergius had time only to initiate the great work of the reorganization of the Church. On the morning of 15th May 1944, less than nine months after his election to the Patriarchate, he died suddenly from a cerebral haemorrhage. Death overtook him while he was still fully active; on the two previous days he had officiated at and presided over episcopal consecrations.[17] He died at peace; his policy that had caused so much bitterness and disillusion was at last beginning to bear fruit.

The resumption of religious life, tolerated but not encouraged in the territories remaining under Soviet control, had the value of a symbol rather than of a mass movement. It had a very different effect in the territories occupied by the Axis armies. Religious liberty was one of the rare if not the only liberty granted by the occupying authorities. They were not interested in the religious question, adopted no definite policy but left things as they were, and, when it was their business, gave any authorization required for the conduct of the religious life.

Here, as we know from all the evidence, the religious revival was general, massive and spontaneous. The people in both towns and villages, in the north and the south, took into their own hands the reopening of the churches, their provisional restoration and decoration. The articles used in worship, the Church plate, the icons which had been carefully hidden by the people were dug up. Choirs were organized spontaneously and sang the services while waiting for the arrival of a priest of their own or one who could supply their needs temporarily. The people thronged to the sacraments; baptisms by the hundred, burials and marriages by the dozen, such was the rhythm of parochial life under the occupation.

Some regions owed the restoration of religious life to their own efforts alone. But others benefited from the help of neighbouring Orthodox Churches: the regions of Novgorod and Pskov were served by a mission organized from the Baltic States; the Ukraine owed its remarkable religious revival to the presence in the formerly Polish Volhynia, of a strong ecclesiastical organization; the region of Odessa came under the protection of the Rumanian Church.

The mission of Pskov was a forbidden subject in the Soviet Union.[18] Even the *Review of the Patriarchate* has never mentioned it. Yet this was one of the most glorious and dramatic pages in the Church's history during the war.

It was the work of the Exarch of the Metropolitan of Moscow in the Baltic States, the young Metropolitan, Sergius Voskresensky. Born in 1899, the son of a Moscow priest, Dimitri Voskresen-sky was unable to complete his studies at the seminary on account of the Revolution. He entered the Monastery of St Daniel in Moscow, in which Bishop Theodore (the last Rector of the ecclesiastical Academy of Moscow – he was shot in 1935 or thereabouts) had established a régime of exceptional asceticism. He left it in 1924 in order to become Secretary of the Chancellery of the Patriarchate. In 1929, when thirty years old, he was con-secrated bishop and became the chief adviser to the head of the Church and, in fact, his second in command.

Clear evidence about his activity during this period is lacking. Some people accused him of collusion with the Soviet police with whom his duties brought him into frequent contact. He was a strange person, remarkable in many ways but full of contradic-tions. He was exceptionally intelligent, extremely tactful, speaking French and English, interested in theological problems, but self-taught and authoritarian to a degree. He had his weaknesses: this former monk of one of the most austere monasteries in Russia was an excellent player of bridge, by preference, with a liking for vodka, and poked fun at religiosity   of a monk who pros-trated himself till his forehead touched the ground, he remarked: 'If he is so very pious, he can't be very intelligent.' He dreamed of a modernization of the Russian Church which, in his view, was threatened by too much piety and a monastic passivity. Though suspected by some, in the Baltic States he proved an exceptional leader. So long as the Soviet occupation lasted, he took no important decision, and won general sympathy through his tact and discretion. When the German troops arrived the Soviet authorities told him to withdraw, he did not comply but hid himself in the crypt of the Cathedral of Riga in order to be arrested by the Gestapo. He came out after four days, without having disowned his allegiance to the Metropolitan of Moscow.

In less than two months the Germans had occupied the Pro-vinces of Pskov, Novgorod, and Leningrad. Throughout these regions the material and moral situation was deplorable; the misery was unrelieved. Hardly a remnant of the Church remained: in the Pskov and Novgorod regions not a single parish; in the immediate approaches to Leningrad only five. There was not one bishop, scarcely a hundred priests, and these, dispirited and exhausted by their trials, were in no hurry to come out of hiding. Besides, many of them no longer had strength enough to run a parish.

The Exarch acted promptly. He considered that these new provinces over which, in theory, he had no jurisdiction, were *de facto* under his authority. He had at his disposal a number of secular priests who were comparatively well educated; some had completed their studies at the St Sergius Institute in Paris. He ordered fourteen of these young men to set out for Pskov to organize the mission. These involuntary missionaries expected to find only a spiritual desert in the USSR, and to be greeted with mistrust and hostility. On their arrival at Pskov on 18th August (the vigil of the Transfiguration), they were very surprised to see the former anti-religious museum stripped of its blasphemous posters and inscriptions, and to find themselves taking part in vigil services attended and chanted by thousands far into the night. The astonishment was mutual; on the following day, when the people saw this group of well-dressed, healthy-looking young priests, they could hardly believe their eyes; they crossed themselves, wept and asked them for their blessing. . . . No hostility, in intellectual circles there was some indifference and above all great ignorance, but among the people an unquenchable thirst for faith, for communion with God. Such was the impression made upon all these missionaries.

With what speed the churches were restored, cleansed by the tears of the people as soon as the first prayers were uttered! With what emotion they chanted the services! This spontaneous enthusiasm of the Russian people for its Orthodox Church and its holy places had to be seen to be believed. Outside observers may question it, but we who were the witnesses of that nostalgia for God's justice, declare that the mass of the Russian people are still believers, and are even perhaps the most believing people upon earth.

According to another priest: 'On the feast of the Intercession the entire Soviet population of Ostrov sang the Magnificat with one voice. The people came up to the Gospel book to kiss it and receive the blessing. Suddenly the singing ceased and gave place to weeping and lamentation. What made the people weep? Was it joy at being able again to celebrate the feast? Was it the memory of their martyred priests and of their relatives in exile? Was it the disasters of the war? There were many reasons for their weeping: I can remember only one thing; that, sharing their sorrow, I wept with them.'[19]

Deprived of the means of grace for years, the people literally thronged to the sacraments: five hundred to a thousand received Holy Communion at every Eucharist celebrated, the individual sacraments had become collective.

Under the Exarch's energetic influence, the mission rapidly developed. Its centre was established at Pskov, where five churches were reopened; the Kremlin there contained a candle factory, a workshop for icons, a printing press and a library. In August 1942 there appeared (well before the *Review of the Patriarchate*) the first number of the mission's monthly magazine, *The Orthodox Christian*, a modest leaflet of four to eight pages, which provided official news of the mission, celebrated the glory of the new martyrs (at the very moment when Moscow was disowning them), discussed the relations between faith and science, but never dabbled in politics. In 1943 the mission already included eighty-five priests serving more than 220 parishes. Particular attention was paid to the young who had been affected by Marxism. Priests were authorized to teach the catechism in the primary schools; special courses on religion were organized for adolescents, and requests for admission exceeded the limits of space and staff available. In Pskov study circles met five times a week. Neither were social activities neglected by the mission, so far as the occupying power allowed them. In 1943 each parish adopted a prison camp and entrusted the young with the task of collecting food, and clothing, etc., for it.

All this religious, educational and social activity was able to proceed without the Exarch having to repudiate his canonical allegiance to Moscow. It is significant that when the Metropolitan Sergius had to pronounce upon the case of his Exarch he avoided any condemnation, confining himself to a mild request for explanations and a change of policy. In every parish of the Mission it was Alexis, the Metropolitan of Leningrad whose name was invoked. (In 1943, when pamphlets calling for armed resistance and signed by Alexis were dropped by the military over occupied territory, such mention of his name became impossible.) In addition, when he was asked by the Germans to give his opinion on the election of the Patriarch Sergius, the Exarch did not hesitate; he not only accepted the validity of that election, but also persuaded the Germans to accept it, and to incorporate it in their propaganda. In order to ensure the existence of his Mission, the Exarch played a dangerously double game. Though he declared that he was radically anti-Bolshevik, and may even have hoped that the régime would collapse by being defeated in the war, he made no secret of his contempt for the Germans: 'As we have been successful in deceiving the NKVD, the deception of these sausage-eating amateurs will scarcely present much difficulty.' The Mission found itself caught between two fires. As the fighting grew nearer and nearer, the resistance movement grew more and more aggressive and political in character (some priests of the Mission fell by the partisans' bullets) and the Germans more anxious and suspicious. The Exarch's personal position became untenable. Early in 1944, in one of his last public statements, he reaffirmed his loyalty to the Patriarch of Moscow, but expressed his doubts about the sincerity of the new orientation of the Soviets' religious policy. 'Stalin is not Saul and will never become Paul.' A few weeks later the tragedy occured. On 28th April 1944, on hearing that his friend Smirnov, a famous tenor, had died, he left Vilnius for Riga where the burial was to take place. The following day his body, with those of other travellers, was found on the roadside riddled by bullets. What happened was never explained. The Germans imputed the crime to Communist partisans, but the inquiry was quickly suppressed. Persistent rumours said that the Metropolitan Sergius was struck down by killers of the Gestapo, which feared his independent spirit and his influence.

The Mission of Pskov not only provides an illustration of the religious revival among the Russian people; it also shows what the activity and life of the Church might have been, had she been given her freedom; an activity not only liturgical, but educational and social. It also shows us the extent to which the attitudes taken up by the dignitaries of the Church depended on circumstances. Had he remained in Moscow, the Exarch Sergius would certainly have been one of the contributors to the book *The Truth about religion in the USSR* in which the reality of the persecutions is denied. When he was out of the reach of Soviet control he enthusiastically proclaimed the glory of the new martyrs. And yet his conduct gives no grounds for supposing that he was governed by political or personal aims. His one concern seems to have been to discover the best means of making Christ known and of serving his Church.

In the Ukraine and White Russia,[20] the religious revival was as spontaneous and intense as in the northern provinces. But here the reconstruction of the Church was made easier by the existence, in what had been Polish Volhynia, of a traditional Orthodox Church with several million members, which had been made active and alert by being obliged to resist the pressure of the Catholic Church. Its clergy were militant and it had several monasteries renowned for their austerity and spiritual influence (for example the Laura of Pochaev).

The episcopate of Volhynia, subject to Moscow since 1940, assembled on 18th August 1941, in the Laura of Pochaev and decided to extend its activity to Soviet Volhynia and beyond.

At the same time it was careful to reaffirm its canonical obedience to Moscow, and not to transgress the canonical rules against bishops exceeding the limits of their jurisdiction.

Unlike the Orthodox region of Volhynia which was incorporated in Poland, the former Soviet Ukraine was, from an ecclesiastical point of view, a desert. And so Volhynia was the natural basis from which to proceed to the restoration of the Church's life in the Ukraine territories that had been liberated from Bolshevism. To fulfil this task in unity and in order, it was necessary that Volhynia, which had been split into two dioceses (one Polish, the other Soviet), should be reunited under the authority of one diocesan bishop. This bishop should have jurisdiction over the whole of Volhynia, as it existed in 1917, and with the help of his auxiliary bishops, he should use every means at his disposal to reconstruct the Church in East and South-East Ukraine. Thus was formed the autonomous Church of the Ukraine, with Archbishop Alexis Gromadsky, an eminent prelate extremely popular with the Ukrainians, as its president. Unfortunately, at the same time, those Ukrainians who were in favour of absolute separation from Russia, decided that this was an opportune moment for restoring the autocephalous Ukrainian Church which had enjoyed a transitory existence after the Revolution. This uncanonical Church – a Church cannot make itself autocephalous but must be given that status by the mother Church upon which it depends – was headed by Polycarp Sikorsky, Bishop of Loutsk. It became still more uncanonical by incorporating a sectarian group – the Lipkovtsy, whose orders were not recognized as valid by any Orthodox Church. Thus two parallel hierarchies each comprising fifteen bishops, were established in the Ukraine and competed with each other. The people, overjoyed at regaining the Church, were at first indifferent to the schism, the only visible difference being the use of Ukrainian in the liturgy by the autocephalists. But later, and in certain places, the battle between the two Churches was bitter. The church of the town of Spasskaia, for example, changed hands three times.

The autocephalists were supported by the nationalist partisans, the benderovtsy,[21] who seized churches by force of arms and did not shrink from assassinating bishops and priests.[22] In order to prevent the schism from damaging the reconstruction of the Church, the Metropolitan Alexis Gromadsky began talks with the autocephalous hierarchy and, on his own authority, even agreed in principle that the two jurisdictions should be combined.[23] But his auxiliary bishops refused to ratify this agreement and asked their Metropolitan either to resign or to withdraw it. He chose to withdraw it. This decision cost him his life: on 7th May 1943, he was shot by the Ukrainian separatist partisans.

This dramatic antagonism between two rival jurisdictions had little effect upon the reconstruction of the Church. The autocephalist Bishop of Kiev, Nicanor Abramovitch – of Jewish origin and brother of an eminent professor of literature in the University of Leningrad – declared: 'We were receiving up to a hundred delegates a day, each of whom came to beg for a priest for his parish. In the first months of 1942 we were successful in putting 298 communities on their feet, and these were served by 455 priests, 136 of them newly ordained.' In 1942 the autonomous Church in this same diocese of Kiev included 410 parishes and 434 priests in active work. For this diocese we can also give precise statistics which provide an estimate of the extent of the Church's reconstruction:

	1914	1940	1942	
Churches	1,710	2	318	
Monasteries	23	*none*	8	
Priests	1,437	3	434	(600 in 1943 ; 300 of
Deacons	277	1	21	them newly
Cantors	1,411	2	86	ordained)
Monks	5,193	*none*	387	

If, therefore, we combine the real potential of both jurisdictions in 1943, we find that there were about 1,000 priests in active work, that is more than two-thirds of the pre-revolutionary potential.

The results were not so spectacular everywhere, and varied according to the regions, but everywhere huge crowds could be observed taking part in public worship. In Dniepropetrovsk, for example, on the feast of the Epiphany, sixty thousand people went in procession to the Dnieper for the blessing of the waters. At Easter, the congregation in the cathedral was so great that the doors, which are shut during the procession before matins, could not be reopened. There were so many communicants that on more than one occasion the eucharistic elements proved to be insufficient.

One notable feature of the religious awakening in the Ukraine was the restoration of monastic life. In the diocese of Kiev alone, eight monasteries (five in Kiev itself) were reopened. Religious communities, particularly of nuns, were formed in most of the large towns, Odessa, Poltava, Dniepropetrovsk, etc. Altogether there were over a thousand nuns. The organization of religious instruction was a more difficult matter – there were many vocations and many were ordained, but the intellectual level of the candidates was extremely low. In western Volhynia, the seminary of Cholm, suppressed by the Soviet authorities in 1939, started to function again, and continued for two years. Plans for a seminary in Kiev could not be carried out for lack of time. At Poltava, on the other hand, each of the two jurisdictions managed to arrange a course of theological studies, and the course given by the 'autonomous' Church attained a high scientific standard. In the sphere of secondary education little or nothing was done; the Germans having prohibited the teaching of catechism in the schools.

All this exuberant and somewhat unco-ordinated activity stopped with the arrival of the Soviet army. The autocephalous episcopate emigrated *en masse*. Those of the autonomous Church who were courageous enough to stay were exiled to Siberia.

With every obstacle removed, the religious revival under the German occupation was an event of capital importance for Russia during the war. After twenty-four years of persecution, the people grasped the first opportunity to give free rein to religious feelings which were all the stronger from having been so long repressed. To an even greater extent than the loyalty of the Patriarch Sergius, it was this revival that moved Stalin to alter his policy towards the Church. It would have been against the interest of the Communist Government to let this religious sentiment develop on its own. By restoring a recognized, lawful head to the Church, under the protection of the State, it was contributing to a realignment of the country's religious forces in a closely controlled and politically neutral organization.

The re-establishment of religious practice in the occupied territories had, moreover, a profound effect upon the religious structure of post-war Russia. For although the Soviet authorities continued to oppress the bishops and Church dignitaries, they did not dare to destroy the whole ecclesiastical organization. This brought about the marked disproportion in the USSR between the number of churches open for worship in the western and southern provinces, which had benefited from the few years of religious liberty, and those of the eastern and northern provinces which remained under Soviet control. In Odessa, for example, with a population of 600,000, twenty churches remained open for worship until 1960, whereas in Sverdlovsk, a town of equal importance, there were only two; Kherson, on the Black Sea coast, could offer its 100,000 inhabitants the choice of seven churches in different parts of the town, whereas Murmansk had only one. . . .

While the people of the occupied territories were enjoying religious liberty, there was a similar religious revival among the Soviet soldiers facing danger and death. In that stern testing time of deadly conflict, faith was the most spontaneous and the most necessary quality: an absolute faith in the orders given by superiors, in the future, in survival, and beyond that, however dim and unreflective, faith in a Supreme Being. Thus it was due to the war and its manifold results that the Church recovered her life and regained her position within a social system that excluded her.

CHAPTER V

THE ORGANIZATION OF THE CHURCH

We were all living in God's hands, very close to him, at his side. Standing on the mausoleum, he was stronger, fiercer, wiser than that other whose name was Yahweh; he dismembered him, tortured him, burnt him to ashes; and then pulled him out of the abyss and settled him in a corner where he could just eat and sleep.

Boris Slutsky, 1955

IN HIS WILL of 12th October 1941, drawn up in the train which was taking him, a very sick man, to Simbirsk, Mgr Sergius provisionally delegated the leadership of the Church to the Metropolitan of Leningrad, Alexis.[1] The transference of authority, even provisionally, is explicitly forbidden by canon law, but the circumstances of the time excused it. In 1941, as later in 1944 although to a lesser extent, the Church still had no properly settled organization. The Council of 1943 had been too restricted to be able to tackle canonical problems. Moreover, when Mgr Sergius appointed the Metropolitan Alexis, he was not in fact infringing the canons then in force among most of the Orthodox Churches, according to which authority during the interregnum is normally exercised by the bishop senior in order of consecration. In this case it was Alexis. In addition, his eminent personal qualities marked him out as Sergius' successor. Born in 1877, in a noble family closely connected with the court, Sergius Vladimirovich Simansky was a man of great erudition in both theological and secular subjects (before beginning theology he had completed his studies in the faculty of law). In 1915 he was consecrated bishop, and after the Revolution he became auxiliary to Benjamin, the Metropolitan of Petrograd. In the conflict with the Living Church he displayed great determination, and was rewarded by being exiled to Semipalatinsk in the Kazakhstan – an event omitted, of course, from all his official biographies.[2] In 1927 he resolutely took his stand by the side of the Patriarch Sergius, became a member of his provisional Synod and titular Bishop of Leningrad. Spared during the great purges, he was often accused of sacrificing his principles for the sake of his personal career.[3] But later on, during the blockade of Leningrad, his heroic conduct won universal acclaim. He was wholly committed to the two great principles of his predecessor's policy; unwavering fidelity to the Church's canons and complete loyalty to the State.

At the Patriarch's funeral, Mgr Alexis addressed the dead man in these words: 'Beseech the Almighty that we and all your disciples may be endowed with unshakable tenacity in keeping to the one path which you laid down for us and to the teaching you bequeathed to us, and which we hold sacred.'[4]

The first public act of the new guardian of the patriarchal throne was to write what amounted to a letter of allegiance to Stalin. In it he gave the news of the Patriarch's death and recalled the feelings of 'sincere love' which the latter had always encouraged towards the head of the State, and declared that his own policy would conform to his predecessor's in every detail. 'By working in complete unison with the Council for the affairs of the Orthodox Church, I myself and the Synod instituted by the late Patriarch will be safeguarded against all error and mistaken action. I beg you, most honoured and dear Joseph Vissarionovich, to accept these assurances with the same confidence as that which they express, and to believe that all the active members of the Church who have now been committed to my guidance, are motivated by feelings of the deepest love.'[5] The terms of this letter are those of absolute submission; the Patriarch Sergius' policy was not simply to be continued but extended to its uttermost implications. Servility was to succeed loyalty. This servility was moreover demanded from every citizen. Paraphrasing the psalmist, it may be said without exaggeration that this was the watchword of that period: 'Let everything that hath breath praise Stalin.'

After this profound cajolery, Mgr Alexis felt sure of the dictator's neutrality, and he could set himself to the great work of reorganization which the Church expected from him; the recovery of control in the territories that had been liberated from occupation, the organization of the dioceses, the reconstitution of the episcopate, the creation of a network of seminaries, and, above all, the development of a constitution for the Church and the election of a new Patriarch.

To effect all this, it was necessary to make preparations for the meeting of a Council. The arrangements made by the Council of 1917, inapplicable and unapplied, could be canonically changed only by another Council elected according to the same principles, that is, with not only bishops taking part, but with the clergy and laity also. Mgr Alexis wanted to avoid being accused of exceeding his powers as *locum tenens* and also to see that no novelty that might endanger Church and State relations was suddenly introduced. He therefore summoned a preliminary meeting of bishops (21st–23rd November 1944). The work of these bishops was to give their opinion on the plan for the settlement of the Church's administration and to appoint the candidate who should succeed the Patriarch Sergius. Naturally there was no discordant note; everything was unanimously, and it may be presumed sincerely, approved.

The atmosphere was highly optimistic. The members of the Synod were received on 24th November by the President of the Council entrusted with the affairs of the Orthodox Church, G. Karpov, who greeted them with reassuring words:

What is at present happening in the life of the Church in its relationship to the State is not an unexpected accident, not a merely provisional arrangement, not a diplomatic move, as some ill-willed people try to insinuate or as is sometimes said by those who are ill-informed. No: these measures are a direct result of tendencies which had begun to appear even before the war and matured during it. These measures taken by the Soviet Government harmonize perfectly with the Constitution of the USSR and are an expression of approval of the attitude adopted by the Church towards the State during the last ten years before the war and especially during the war.[6]

The Council of 1945

The Soviet Government gave material assistance to the Council, which opened on 31st January 1945, and lasted only three days. Its membership was not very great; only 170 delegates in all. Each diocese was represented by its bishop, a priest and a layman. These latter were not elected, but nominated by the Synod. The delegates of the Russian Church were joined by thirty-four representatives from related Orthodox Churches. This broad international participation was useful, both for the purposes of the Church – the Patriarchate was publicly seen and recognized by the Orthodox Church as a whole – and for those of the Soviet Government which thus provided visible proof of its respect for the Church.

The sessions of the Council were solemn, but brief. The first day was devoted to official matters. G. Karpov was allowed to speak first: he greeted the foreign guests with respect; he stressed the historical contribution of the Russian Church to the defence of the country, and he praised the freedom of conscience granted by the socialist October Revolution 'which not only delivered our people from slavery and gave them liberty, but also released the Russian Orthodox Church from the shackles that chained her down and frustrated her inner development'. The guests replied, and Mgr Alexis gave an account of the Church's patriotic activity. Then the Regulations for the Church's administration were unanimously adopted, without the slightest criticism, or even the smallest amendment.

The second and final session of the Council (2nd February) was entirely devoted to the election of the new Patriarch. Again, nothing unexpected happened. Voting was by individuals in open ballot. One after another, the bishops stood up, with the representatives of their dioceses, and gave the name of the elected candidate. There was complete unanimity. After the election, Mgr Philip Stavitsky, the senior bishop present, in a courageous speech, reminded the newly elect of the duties incumbent upon a Patriarch: he must 'follow the path laid down by the Metropolitans of Moscow, Philip, Hermogenes, Alexis and Jonas, and be the guardian of the truth of Christ with the arms of justice in both hands'.

On the following day, 4th February, the Patriarch was solemnly enthroned. Out of the many speeches on this occasion, we may select that of G. Karpov. In it he made these noteworthy remarks: 'The Russian Orthodox Church, with its Patriarch and his Holy Synod, is pursuing a course which is honest, unmistakable and straightforward; it is the course pursued by the late Patriarch Sergius and his clergy. Both the Government and the people realize this and it moves them to sympathize profoundly with everything done by the Russian Orthodox Church.' The Patriarch Alexis then thanked the Government, and the head of the Church and the representative of the State exchanged the three-fold embrace.[7]

From a purely ecclesiastical point of view, the Council of 1945 could only be disappointing: it was absolutely passive and asked for nothing more than the ratification of orders issued by superiors. But for a true judgement of the historical significance of this Council, we should remember the condition to which the Church had been reduced only a few years previously.

Now, however, after twenty-five years of persecutions and chaotic existence, she had rules for her administration, approved by the whole episcopal body, which provided her with a legal status. With all their defects, these regulations can be considered as an important victory over the forces of disorganization and destruction.[8]

The settlement of 1945 and the organization of the Church

The settlement achieved in 1945 was really a compromise between the regulations decreed by the Council of 1917 which ensured complete autonomy for the Church, with a truly catholic and conciliar constitution, on the one hand, and the rigid restrictions imposed by Soviet laws, on the other. The Council 'summoned periodically and composed of bishops and laymen' continued to be the supreme power in the Church in matters of doctrinal teaching, administration, and as an ecclesiastical court. But this clause gives the impression of being a statement of principle rather than a real factor in the Church's life. For in fact no single rule fixes any definite times for conciliar meetings or settles their composition. Bishops, of course, are *de jure* members, but we do not know how the clergy and laity are to be chosen. Are they to be present *ex officio*, or to be elected? When, however, 'important ecclesiastical problems' have to be solved, the Patriarch should preferably summon a council of bishops alone (1, 7). The Council is to be summoned only 'when it becomes necessary to hear views of the clergy and laity and when the position at home makes its meeting possible'. In any case, it is obvious that the Soviet Government could not permit the Church to function in a democratic way, when it denied that right to its own citizens. During the seventeen years that have elapsed since the adoption of the regulations, the Council has never in fact been summoned, and it is now clear that this will occur only on the death of the Patriarch Alexis, when his successor has to be elected.

Yet an imperative need for the views of the clergy and the laity became evident in 1961 when the Holy Synod was compelled to revise several articles of the regulations. Canonically, only a new council had the power to do this. But, in all probability, the external circumstances which would have enabled a Council to be summoned, 'did not present themselves', and in 1961 the Patriarch Alexis had to be content with summoning a gathering of bishops alone, the first since 1945.

The Church's organization is definitely centralized. At the head we find the Patriarch, who, in conjunction with the Holy Synod, governs the Church. The diocesan bishops are at the head of the dioceses entrusted to them, but they are nominated by a decree of the Patriarch and they can also – this is not categorically stated, but pre-supposed – be moved or deposed merely by decree. The unity of the 'ecclesia' is therefore considered to be that of the Russian Church as a whole, and not, as a sound theology would suggest, that of each diocese on its own. If a bishop can be moved or deposed at will, his authority is thereby lessened. This centralized, not to say 'papalized', organization, is a concession to circumstances to enable the Soviet Government to remove and get rid of any bishop whom it finds undesirable.

However, the diocesan bishops do share in the administration of the Church by means of the Holy Synod. This latter, with the Patriarch as president, is composed, in accordance with the regulations of 1945, of three permanent members – the incumbents of the Metropolitan sees of Leningrad, Kiev and Krutitsy (Moscow) – and of three temporary members, selected in order of seniority from each of the regions (south, centre and east) into which the dioceses are divided, to attend for one session of six months. In 1961 the president of the office for external affairs and the bishop responsible for the business of the Patriarchate, were made permanent members of the Synod.[9] The result is that the ordinary diocesan bishops are in a minority; this constitutes a fresh attack on the conciliar principle and on the Church's freedom. In fact, the Church is now governed by a permanent Synod.

The Patriarch and the Holy Synod govern the Church as a whole, but the diocesan bishop, according to local circumstances, is either the sole administrator of his diocese, or else he acts in co-operation with a diocesan council composed of three to five members of his clergy. Thus on the diocesan level the laity are excluded from the administration of the Church. This measure, in contradiction to the decree of the Council of 1917 which gave the laity a share in every stage of the administration, is perhaps a concession to prudence, a cleric being *a priori* 'safer' than a layman. The regulations provide for the establishment, subject, of course, to authorization by the competent officials, of courses in theology, and of factories for the manufacture of candles and other furniture of worship. But there is no mention at all of the need or possibility for bishops to convoke diocesan assemblies on the lines of the local Council that would include both clergy and laity, as the Council of 1917 decreed. Diocesan gatherings of this kind were, however, convened by a few bishops after the outbreak of war, but these manifestations of religious democracy do not seem to have met with encouragement from the local authorities.[10]

Most of the dioceses are of vast extent and are divided into deaneries: the 'deans' see to the proper running of the parishes in their deaneries. Every half-year they send a report to their local bishop, and each bishop sends a yearly report to the Patriarch. The arrangements made for the organization of the parishes are more in accordance with the spirit of the Council of 1917.

By Soviet law, the care and supervision of ecclesiastical property (both furniture and buildings) are entrusted to an executive commission of three, a churchwarden, his assistant, and a treasurer, elected by the parish as a whole in open ballot. The regulations of 1945 made the parish priest the *ex officio* president of this executive committee. Thus the priest is not restricted to his purely spiritual duties, he also administers, in partnership with laymen, the material possessions of the parish. Or, more accurately, spiritual and material activities are not divided, but form a single whole. In this way the unity of the parish is safeguarded, and its priest, by virtue of his office, holds the first place in it. This parochial organization is that which was laid down by the Council of 1917. The decisions of that Council meant that the prestige and authority of the clergy were increased, but they were explicitly contradicted by the Decree of 1929. That Decree envisaged no such activity for priests, they were to limit themselves to their work as ministers at public worship. For more than fifteen years, however, the Soviet Government tolerated this discrepancy between the regulations decreed by the Church and the legislation of the State, until it decided to combat the Church's influence. Then, in 1961, the Government ordered the Patriarch to alter the parochial organization and bring it into conformity with the wording of the Decree of 1929. The head of the Church could only obey, and simply by a decree of the Holy Synod, dated 18th April 1961, the settlement of 1945 was amended. This uncanonical procedure met with some opposition from the hierarchy. Three bishops were sufficiently courageous to say that the regulations for the Church decreed by a general Council could be altered only by a Council of equal status. An Assembly of bishops was thereupon convoked (July 1961) which ratified the decision of the Holy Synod without qualification 'until such time as a general Council is summoned'.[11]

The consequence was that the parish lost its unity: its priest became no more than an official strictly confined to its spiritual guidance; the laity alone became responsible for the management of parochial property, without any reference to the priest; state control tightened, the Decree of 1929 gave local authorities the right to remove any member of the executive Committee whom they found unacceptable (§ 14).

Financial resources of the Church

As we have seen, the Church owns no property; places of worship and articles used in worship are simply loaned to her by the good will of the State. Paradoxically, not only the upkeep, but the repair and restoration of churches in use (including those classified as historical monuments) are charged not to the owner, but to the tenant. Restorations are undertaken at the expense of the parishes, sometimes assisted by diocesan or Patriarchal funds. The Church receives no material aid from the State, at least not officially. This does not exclude the fact that the Soviet Government has financed the Church in some of her external activities. For her internal affairs the Church has to depend entirely upon her own resources which come from offerings made at public worship, donations, the sale of candles and of the bread that has been blessed.

Collections are taken at every service. The people's offerings are of a generosity that is perhaps unique in the world. The four huge collecting plates sent round during the services are brimful not merely with coins but with bank-notes. In a study of the business of the bank of Moscow, an author notes that its small change is provided mainly by the transport services and the churches.

The sale of candles provides, according to some authorities, almost half the income of the parishes. The Patriarchate of Moscow has organized the production of candles on a vast scale, so that 'every church is now provided with them at the most moderate cost'.[12] Some dioceses have their own candle factories: Ivanovo, Voronej, Astrakhan, Central Asia, Kazan, etc.

The parishes make a handsome profit on their sales. The great number of believers and their generosity widen the margin of profit, for often ten times more candles are bought than there are sockets available for them. Unused candles are later resold, in some cases several times in succession. The apostate priest, N. Spassky, dean of the region included in the province of Stalingrad (Volgagrad), declared that in the ten parishes in his deanery, candles bought by the diocesan administration for 195,843 roubles were resold for 1,109,783 roubles. The blessed bread also provides an appreciable income. According to the same Spassky, in 1958, the ten churches he is discussing sold this bread, bought for 13,192 roubles, for 160,859.[13]

The income from the parishes is divided into three unequal parts: the first is set apart for the parish; the second, which amounts to 20 per cent, for the diocese; the third, for the Patriarchate.

To this parochial income, the personal income of the clergy must be added; this is derived from the administration of certain sacraments, the dues for which vary according to the diocese. There is evidence to suggest that the tariff for baptism is 25 roubles, burials 100, and marriages about 170. In some dioceses the clergy live on these personal emoluments; in others they are expected to hand them over to the parish which allocates a fixed salary to them. This amounts on an average to 3,000–4,000 roubles and is higher than that of a skilled engineer. But since 1959 taxation has become so heavy that the temptations of wealth have again been replaced by the trials of poverty, if not of destitution.

The departments of the Patriarchate

The Patriarchal administration which receives about a third of the parochial revenues is the one section of the Church able to spend large sums of money. It includes and maintains the following departments:

1. *The administration of the affairs of the Patriarchate* which carries out the decisions of the Patriarch and the Synod and maintains contact with the dioceses.

2. *The Office of external relations*, responsible for maintaining the relationship between the mother Church and the numerous Exarchates, deaneries, parishes and missions abroad. In most cases the Patriarchate grants substantial financial assistance to all the external institutions which owe obedience to it. This office also has the duty to maintain contact through correspondence and an exchange of delegations with the other orthodox or heterodox Churches. In some cases (the Patriarchates of Antioch and Alexandria, the Russian monasteries on Mount Athos, etc.) contact includes considerable financial assistance. The reception of delegations is a heavy expense and the Patriarchate repays the Intourist agency for the huge costs incurred on account of them.

3. *The Committee in charge of theological instruction.* The Patri-

archate provides for the needs of the theological schools and co-ordinates their activity.

4. *The Committee for pensions* is the only benevolent organization that the authorities tolerate, because it operates within the very narrow limits of the clergy. Pensions are granted to clerics who, on account of age or sickness, become unable to carry on their duties in the pastoral ministry, and also to widows of the clergy and individuals who have been regularly employed by the Church.

5. *The Office for publications.* The Patriarchate has no printing press of its own. Its publications are printed by the various State presses. Contrary to what was hoped, and, it seems, to some assurances given by Stalin himself, there has been little progress in publishing. The Church only publishes a single review, the *Review of the Moscow Patriarchate.* It is issued monthly, although appearing very late, and it averages 70–80 pages. The number of copies published has never been declared. Until 1950 the review made known the terms of subscription to it, but from 1953 the indication of its cost disappeared from its cover. In practice, from this date, the review ceased to be sold in public, even upon Church premises, and may be compared to a house organ. An impressive number of copies, out of all proportion to requirements, is regularly sent abroad. A mysterious review in Ukrainian is published in Lvov; it appears to have been authorized as a means of confirming the uniates who had been converted to Orthodoxy in their new faith.[14]

Since 1942, the sum total of the Patriarchate's publications has amounted to some fifteen works devoted to contemporary problems, not to say political propaganda (the position of the Church, international meetings, speeches for the promotion of peace, etc.), a dozen liturgical books, the Bible (25,000 copies), the Gospels, the sermons of the Metropolitan Nicholas, and three numbers of a periodical review of theology. The authorities always allege a paper shortage when they do not want to meet the Church's needs.[15]

The monasteries

I have been unable to determine how far the monasteries in the USSR have the security of a legal existence. The law of 1929, the only law with authority in religious matters, does not envisage the existence of monastic communities, and it was, in fact, in 1929 that the last of the then existing communities was closed.

The Church even recently reckoned the number of monasteries at about sixty-seven, but these were either in territories annexed to the USSR in 1945, or had been opened during the war under the German occupation. The Trinity of St Sergius at Zagorsk, is the only one whose reopening was authorized by the Soviet authorities. No list of monasteries has ever been published, and nothing, or practically nothing is known of their inner life. Officially, the monasteries are governed by regulations approved by the Patriarch, but these have never been made public.

'By virtue of the law at present in force,' notes the work on the Church's position, 'the State admits that monasteries have the right to own a certain amount of land, cattle, and of material necessary for the organization and functioning of their workshops.' The Monastery of St Flora is famous for its embroidery. That of the Protection of the Holy Virgin in the same city has workshops for tailoring, mattress-making, book-binding, icon-painting. The nuns of the convent of the Virgin's Nativity in Bielorussia excel in the making of ecclesiastical vestments, shrouds, etc.[16] Since 1959 the State has forbidden all economic activity to monasteries with the result that many of them have been closed.

Church and State

Since 1944 the Church has adopted an attitude of complete loyalty towards the State, which she cannot go back upon; in fact, it can only be amplified.

At first, the Church could live by her patriotic ardour, her encouragement of collections for financial aid to war-widows, orphans and the seriously wounded. For example, on the twenty-ninth anniversary of the Revolution, the diocese of Saratov contributed 570,000 roubles to the State Bank for the victims of the war.[17] But once wartime and post-war services were accomplished, it was necessary to resort to more political forms of assistance to the State. This assistance was rendered most effectively in the external policy of the Moscow Patriarchate which we shall examine in detail in the next chapter. The Church has also assisted the State by giving her moral support to the external and internal policy of the Soviet Government. In February 1946, Father Michael Zernov, now Bishop Cyprian, asked the laity to give their votes to the Communist and non-party bloc because in no country 'does the Church enjoy such favourable conditions for her existence as in the USSR.'[18] The Church, like the Russian nation as a whole, sacrificed herself to the cult of personality. On the thirtieth anniversary of the Revolution, the Patriarch Alexis asked his flock to intensify their prayers for the Russian nation, for the authorities 'presided over by the most wise Leader whom Divine providence has chosen and established, to lead our country to prosperity and glory'.[19] On Stalin's seventieth birthday, the *Review of the Patriarchate* published a photograph of the Leader and the text of a long letter of congratulation signed by all the members of the episcopate which concluded with these words:

At every moment of our civil and religious life we experience the positive results of your wise guidance. We cannot hide our feelings and, in the name of the whole Church, we express, dear Joseph Vissarionovitch, on this your seventieth birthday, our deepest gratitude, and, together with our warm congratulations on this day of such significance for us who love you, we offer our prayers for the preservation of your strength and the happiness of our great country, and we bless the heroism (*podvig*) with which you are serving it; it is a heroism which is an inspiration for ourselves.[20]

It would be impossible for the expression of servility to go further.

It is true, of course, that this was the period when millions of schoolchildren were singing with the sincerity natural to their young hearts:

> *Stalin is our smile*
> *Stalin is our harvest.* . . .

And their spirit was in harmony with that of the 'great' writers, composers, painters, artists, etc.

The Patriarchate entered wholeheartedly into the Peace Movement in both the international (cf. the next chapter) and the national spheres. This movement had the backing of the Government. Since 1949 the *Review of the Patriarchate* has published in every number one or more articles on the maintenance of peace. In May 1952, at the instigation of the Patriarchate, the monastery of the Trinity-St-Sergius, received representatives from all the denominations and religious bodies officially recognized in the USSR, the speech of each delegate was not only an appeal for peace, but concluded with the invariable *gloria* to Stalin.[21]

Lastly, in all international disputes, the Patriarchate supported the Soviet Government by declarations published in the State press. In 1952 the Synod condemned, in terms of unusual violence, the imperialist aggression in Korea, and the alleged use of bacterial weapons: 'Let us hope that the Lord will cover with shame the bloodthirsty Baal of modern times who is trying to draw the whole world into his net. Let us hope that the terrible hand of Providence will re-establish the truth that has been mocked.'[22]

In 1956, in a calmer tone, the Russian Orthodox Church, 'observed with grief the misfortune of war that has fallen upon Egypt, raised her voice against those who hate peace, and condemned the perfidious deeds of the aggressors'.[23] The uprising in Hungary was referred to by the Patriarch in his New Year Message in deliberately vague if not ambiguous terms: 'In Hungary an attempt was made by forces hostile to the people to disturb the peaceful course of existence, and this threatened to create enormous international complications.'[24] The Metropolitan

Nicholas was more explicit: 'The powers of darkness,' he declared, 'are not asleep. They provoked bloodshed in Hungary. Now they are again trying to send agents, spies and assassins into countries which do not meet with their approval'.[25] The psychological shock produced by the Soviet intervention in Hungary was so considerable that several bishops were asked to contradict the reports of the excesses committed during the repression. Mgr Palladius, Archbishop of Lvov, wrote in the local press: 'In the name of the clergy and laity of the western regions of the Ukraine, I testify that we who live in the immediate neighbourhood of the Hungarian frontier, linked with Lvov by the only railway out of Lvov, have no knowledge of Hungarian citizens being deported into the Soviet Union.' Mgr Barlaam, Bishop of Mukachevo, another province adjoining the Hungarian border, declared in words that are equivocal to the point of absurdity: 'Every day I receive very many clergy and layfolk, but not one of them has seen or heard [sic] deported prisoners. The reason is obvious: there were none.'[26] On 28th April 1962 the Patriarch Alexis sent a personal letter to President Kennedy deploring the resumption of nuclear tests in the atmosphere.[27] In November 1962, he sent a message to all heads of government, asking them to do everything in their power to avert a new world war, and protesting against the American blockade of Cuba.[28]

State and Church

In 1943, the State, resigning itself to the Church's existence, granted her the possibility of subsistence, but without any official commitment towards her. The concordat between Church and State rested entirely on verbal assurances.

But throughout the twenty years which this concordat lasted, the State's attitude to the Church was not uniform. *Grosso modo*, four successive periods can be distinguished in the State's policy. The first, from 1943–7, is that of the concordat as a reality: the State did not oppose the Church's resurrection and even to some extent assisted it. From 1948 until Stalin's death, the State tried to enslave the Church, put obstacles in the way of her progress, but did not resort to direct persecution. After the tyrant's fall, the Church enjoyed a period of relative freedom, which began in 1954, reached its peak in 1957, and ended abruptly in 1958. In 1959 the Government began to put into operation a concerted plan for the final liquidation of the Church. The concordat of 1943 is, in fact, broken, although outwardly it is always observed.

The outward signs of the Church's recognition by the State are unchanged: the Government encourages the external relations of the Patriarchate; it bestows honours upon the principal ecclesiastical dignitaries (the Patriarch Alexis has been decorated three times with the order of the Red Flag – in 1948 when the Moscow conference was held; in 1952 on his seventy-fifth birthday; and in 1962 when he was eighty-five[29] – it publishes the Patriarch's and the Synod's declarations of policy in the press; it invites representatives of the Church to important official receptions (at least since Stalin's death), and it authorizes a representative of the Patriarch to use the medium of the radio once a year to broadcast a message to the Christians of the whole world.

Officially, all relations between the Church and State take place through the intermediary of the Committee for the affairs of the Russian Orthodox Church. This committee has representatives in every province and republic of the USSR.

CHAPTER VI

THE EXTERNAL RELATIONS OF
THE MOSCOW PATRIARCHATE

THE EXTERNAL RELATIONS of the Moscow Patriarchate deserve a study in depth. This is the domain in which the dependence of the Church upon the State is most palpable; and in which it is not always easy to distinguish between motives that are genuinely religious and spiritual and political objectives pursued on the Government's account.

The importance of the Patriarchate's influence over the other Orthodox Churches is largely explicable by the preponderant position occupied by the Russian Church during recent centuries, and by the prestige of Imperial Russia. In Bulgaria, for example, the name of Tsar Alexander II, the liberator of the Bulgarians, is still solemnly commemorated at every Eucharist. The Serbs are not likely to forget the unshakeable alliance of the Russians in 1914. In the Middle East, Russia has always been regarded as untainted by any colonialist ideology, and as the disinterested protector of the Holy Places against the claims of Islam and Catholicism. The Greek, alone among the Orthodox Churches, does not share this spontaneous and instinctive sympathy for everything Russian. And it is the Greeks alone – and those Patriarchates in which the Greek element is predominant – who have shown a vigorous and effective resistance to the 'imperialistic designs' of Moscow.

Once the Russian Church had regained her freedom of action she sought to recover her former position of leadership within the Orthodox world. To make Moscow the centre of Orthodoxy

95

once again – this was to be the aim of the Patriarch Alexis' external policy, at least until Stalin's death. It was a policy that suited Stalin's diplomatic purposes admirably; the Church was to be made use of in order to establish the Russian influence in the Balkan countries and in the Middle East, and to neutralize the propaganda of the Russian emigrants in the nations of the West. It is difficult to decide how far the Patriarch allows himself to be guided by his religious conscience, and where the carrying out of the governmental commands begins. An intimate dependence upon the State inevitably creates an equivocal situation: the Patriarch Alexis may consider that by serving the State he is only sacrificing the Church's integrity to the stability of her existence.

The Council of 1945

This Council gave the Russian Patriarchate its first opportunity to invite the heads of the Orthodox Churches to visit Moscow. The Patriarchs of Antioch and Alexandria came in person. The other Churches were represented by distinguished prelates. Only the Greek Church, which had suffered from the Communist insurrection of 1945, was absent. The Soviet Government displayed great concern for the guests of the Russian Church, provided them with warm clothing, buses for their journeys to and fro, and lodged them in the best hotels. In his inaugural address, the Patriarch Alexis took pains to emphasize that 'on account of its composition, this Council is in reality an Ecumenical Council, for it may be said that the entire Orthodox Church ... is represented at it. However,' he added, 'we humbly restrict our authority, and we shall confine ourselves to discussing and regulating the affairs of our own Church alone.' The foreign guests took no part in either the discussions or the voting. They were, however, singled out for a special welcome by the Government's representative, and were given the opportunity to speak, both in the Council and in the various receptions held in their honour.

The Patriarch of Antioch, Alexander III, expressed 'the gratitude of the whole Orthodox Church to the Government of the USSR which is doing its utmost to promote the increase and development of the material and spiritual strength of the Russian people and is manifesting great generosity towards the Holy Synod and the Russian Church'. Christopher, the Patriarch of Alexandria, went further in his praise of the Soviet Government and of Marshal Stalin, 'one of the great men of our time who has confidence in the Church and sympathizes with her'. His self-confessed aim in these words was to obtain material assistance from the Russian Church or Government: 'the Eastern Patriarchs presume to hope that after these events (the end of the war), the care and attention of Russia will be extended to them in a purely Christian spirit'.[1]

The obsequious attitude of these two Patriarchs was in contrast with that of the other guests, especially with that of the representatives of the Serbian Church and of the Ecumenical Patriarch. The delegate of this latter, Mgr Germanus, confined himself to congratulating the newly elect and encouraging him to be resolute. He made no reference to the relations between the Church and State. All the Orthodox delegates did, however, sign an 'appeal to the Christians of the whole world' which contained, in addition to an exhortation to combat Fascism, a remark aimed at the Vatican, as personifying 'those who presume to call themselves Christians . . . and recommend forgiveness for child-murderers and traitors'.[1]

From the Council of 1945 to the Inter-Orthodox Conference of 1948

Soon after his enthronement, Patriarch Alexis was received by Marshal Stalin, and as a result of this interview made a journey to the Middle East in an aeroplane specially chartered by the Soviet Government. During his pilgrimage to the various Holy Places and on his way through Egypt, he was welcomed by enthusiastic crowds, whose cheers were intended for the head of the Church as much as for the Russian people, Stalin and the Soviet army. This journey, the first ever made to the Middle East by a Russian Patriarch, had considerable repercussions, and helped to consolidate the prestige of both the Church and the Soviet Government. In the same year Russian delegations visited Bulgaria and Yugoslavia, and a Rumanian delegation arrived in Moscow to re-establish the relationship which had been compromised by the war. In May 1946, Patriarch Alexis made a personal visit to Bulgaria, on the thousandth anniversary of the death of the great Bulgarian saint, John of Ryla. In 1947 he returned the visit of Nicodemus, Patriarch of Rumania, which the latter had paid to him the previous year. It would be tedious to enumerate all the visits and interchanges of delegations which took place during those years, with the aim of strengthening the links between the Patriarchate of Moscow and the other Orthodox Churches.

The Churches of the emigration, not attached to Moscow,[2] were a considerable embarrassment to the Patriarch's activity, for their very existence, as well as what they said, proved that the Church in Russia was not entirely free. The Patriarch's delegates spared no effort in order to conciliate them, but after some initial successes, the attempt ended in failure.

In the countries occupied by the Soviet armies, the Moscow Patriarchate naturally met with no resistance. The four prelates of the Russo–Chinese Metropolitan area in Manchuria, which owed its origin to the Synod of Karlovtsy, asked the Patriarch Alexis, on 26th June 1945, to accept them as members of his obedience. The same request was made by Seraphim, Metropolitan of Bulgaria, by Bishop Sergius of Prague, and by the Russian parishes of Yugoslavia.

In the free countries, however, matters did not go so smoothly. In China, for example, although the Archbishop of Peking followed the example of the Manchurian prelates, Shanghai remained loyal to the émigré Synod. In September 1945, the Metropolitan Nicholas visited France and there succeeded in reconciling the Exarchate of the Ecumenical Patriarch with the

Russians of Western Europe whose primate was the Metropolitan Eulogius (1864–1946), and also a small group of parishes under the Metropolitan Seraphim, a member of the émigré Synod. But when Bishop Eulogius died (August 1946) his coadjutor, Bishop Wladimir, with the support of most of his clergy, alleged that this reconciliation lacked the consent of the Ecumenical Patriarch, and rejected the obedience of Moscow. His action was subsequently approved by the Ecumenical Patriarch who officially appointed him his Exarch and informed the Patriarch Alexis that he meant to protect this diocese from any kind of political pressure.[3]

The delegates of Moscow were hardly more successful in America. The pan-American Council which met at Cleveland on 26th November 1946, decided by a large majority to re-establish relations with Moscow 'on condition that it retained complete autonomy, including the right to elect the head of the Church'.[4] This solution Moscow found hard to accept. After a second journey of the Metropolitan Gregory to the United States, as fruitless as the first, the Patriarch Alexis placed the American metropolitan area under an interdict, of which, however, no notice was taken.[5]

Finally, the émigré Synod of Karlovtsy, which had moved first to Munich and then (1949) to the United States, refused to join in discussions with the Moscow Patriarchate.

In Czechoslovakia the Orthodox were divided into three jurisdictions: the Russian parishes were under that of Paris; some of the Czech parishes were under the Serbian Patriarch, and the others under the Ecumenical Patriarch. The Moscow Patriarchate tried to unify these divisions and appointed Mgr Eleutherius, a safe man, Archbishop of Prague and Exarch of the Patriarch of Moscow, head of the single Church thus formed.[6] The Soviet Government was an interested spectator of this action on the part of the Russian Church, and G. Karpov, President of the Council for the affairs of the Orthodox Church, on this occasion made his only official visit abroad. But the Russian Church, by acting in Czechoslovakia in this unilateral way, had overstepped its rights at the expense of the Serbian and Ecumenical Patriarchs, and the dispute with the Serbian Church was further exacerbated, in August 1946, by the incorporation of the Hungarian Orthodox parishes which up to then had been administered by the Serbian Patriarchate. The latter considered Moscow's action to be illegal.[7] Some months afterwards, however, the Serbian Church, in accordance with the principle that the unity of each Church is based upon the unity of its territory, voluntarily surrendered to the Russian Church the jurisdiction over the diocese of Mukachevo in sub-Carpathian Russia, a former province of Czechoslovakia which had been incorporated in the USSR (April 1947).[8]

The Russian Church quarrelled with the Ecumenical See over the Russian Exarchate of Western Europe, and also by trying to extend her influence over Finland, Poland and Albania.

The Orthodox Church of Finland, which, before the Revolution, had been merely a diocese of the Russian Church, in 1923 took advantage of the country's independence and placed herself under the jurisdiction of the Ecumenical Patriarch who granted her autonomy. In September 1945, Mgr Gregory visited Finland with the aim of securing the return of the Finnish Church. The head of that Church, Mgr Germain, turned to the authority of the Ecumenical Patriarch for protection, and he, in spite of many urgent appeals from the Patriarch Alexis, declined to surrender the liberty of the Finnish Church;[9] thereupon the Moscow Patriarch broke off communion with it.

After the Revolution, the Orthodox Church of Poland had followed the Finnish example, but since her numbers were far greater – four millions at this period – she was allowed by the Ecumenical See to become autocephalous, that is, completely independent. In 1945, her most populated dioceses were incorporated in the USSR, but for a time she was left undisturbed by the Moscow Patriarchate. At the beginning of 1948, however, the latter abruptly denounced the autocephalous status recently granted to the Polish Church by Constantinople, and severed communion with Mgr Denis, the Metropolitan of Warsaw, who had previously been betrayed by his diocesan bishops. Moscow then granted its own kind of autocephalous status to the Polish Church[10] and soon appointed a safe man at her head.[11]

Finally, the influence of the Moscow Patriarchate extended as far as Albania whose Church, before the establishment of the Communist régime, had maintained a close relationship with Constantinople. The policy of the Albanian Government was, at first, to isolate the head of the Albanian Church, Archbishop Christopher, by arresting his two diocesan bishops. Then the Moscow Patriarchate intervened and gave its support to the consecration of a former communist partisan, the Archimandrite Paissy Voditza, who was more or less illiterate. After a brief but stormy interlude, he replaced Mgr Christopher.[12]

This policy of expansion and hegemony, only too obviously supported by the Soviet Government, was bound to provoke mistrust and opposition from the Ecumenical Patriarch and from some other Orthodox Churches. For example, when, in the spring of 1947, Patriarch Alexis announced his decision to summon a genuine pan-Orthodox Council in Moscow during November, with the special purpose of discussing the attitude to be adopted to the Vatican, to the Ecumenical Movement and to Anglican ordinations, the replies from Constantinople, Alexandria and the Churches of Greece and Cyprus were frankly negative. The Ecumenical Patriarch maintained that the initiative for summoning a Council could only come from him.[13] The Patriarch of Alexandria added that the choice of Moscow, the seat of a revolutionary régime, was not a very happy one.[14] The Patriarch of Moscow was obliged to adjourn the Council, but he did not withdraw his claims.

In the spring of 1948 he again invited the heads of the Orthodox Churches, but this time it was to take part, first, in the jubilee celebrations in honour of the achievement of autocephalous status by the Russian Church, and then in the pan-Orthodox conference which was to follow them. This ambiguous invitation produced some wavering among the Eastern Patriarchs. In the end, the

Patriarch of Jerusalem and Archbishop Macarius of Cyprus declined the invitation; the Ecumenical Patriarch and the Greek Church agreed to send delegations to the jubilee celebrations alone, and once more, the Patriarch of Antioch was alone in not refusing anything; he decided to attend both events. The Patriarch of Alexandria, after changing his mind several times, decided that he would be represented by Antioch.[15]

In spite of these numerous abstentions, the Conference was held from the 9th–17th July, after pompous jubilee celebrations marked by the solemn translation of the relics of St Alexis, Metropolitan of Moscow, from the Kremlin to the Patriarchal Cathedral. The programme originally put forward by Moscow was carried through. In the work of the commissions, serious divergences made their appearance between the delegates of the Serbian, Bulgarian and Rumanian Churches, who were trying to approach the issues objectively, and some of the Russian delegates. These latter were, in their turn, overborne from the left by the Albanians, who adopted partisan views and a violent controversial tone. In the plenary sessions, in spite of certain proposed amendments and some reservations, extreme views invariably prevailed. The Vatican was condemned without qualification, and in terms of exceptional violence, for its dogmatic deviations, and also for its political misdeeds. A brief extract will illustrate the point:

The popes have always been on the side of the powerful of 'this world', and against the weak and the exploited. So today, Vatican activity is directed against the interests of the workers. The Vatican is the centre of international intrigues against the interests of the peoples, especially the Slav people, and is the centre of international Fascism. The essence of Christian morality is our Saviour's call to charity, whereas the Vatican has been one of the instigators of two imperialist wars and is at present taking an active part in promoting another war and, in general, in the political attack against world democracy. . . . Men everywhere must be made to see the abyss into which the papacy is leading them.

The External Relations of the Moscow Patriarchate

The Ecumenical Movement which had sent an official invitation to the Patriarch to take part in the Assembly at Amsterdam in September 1948, received hardly better treatment. The final resolution declared that 'the attempt being made by the Ecumenical Movement to organize political and social life and to create an Ecumenical Church as an international power, is, in fact, a yielding to the temptation which Christ withstood in the wilderness' and it accused Protestantism of trying to obtain a 'factitious form of union' which would 'reduce Christian doctrine to a belief which even demons would find acceptable'. The proposal of a French Orthodox delegate that this message should be taken to Amsterdam 'as an expression of courtesy towards fellow Christians', was rejected and its mere publication considered sufficient.

Although the Albanians tried to identify Anglicanism with English imperialism, the question of the validity of Anglican Orders, because much of it was both highly technical and *a priori* non-political, was discussed with more objectivity. Nevertheless, the solution finally adopted, of Russian inspiration, was severely critical of Anglicanism.[16]

The Conference concluded by drawing up and adopting an appeal to Christians throughout the world. In the preparatory commission, the two projects drawn up were purely religious and theoretical. But, in the full assembly, both were set aside and replaced by a completely different document, of a political and crudely polemical nature. There is some evidence to suggest that this document originated outside the formal ecclesiastical conference.[17]

In appearance, the Conference was a great success for the Moscow Patriarchate. The friendly relations with the Patriarchate of Antioch and the Serbian and Bulgarian Churches were cemented by granting them places of worship (*metochies*) in Moscow, where they would thus be permanently represented. But in reality the Conference sanctioned Moscow's influence within the Communist block, and in only one instance outside it – that of the

Patriarchate of Antioch.[18] The result of the openly political and anti-Western character of the resolutions and of the final appeal, was to divide the Orthodox Church into two antagonistic groups and to isolate the Russian Church from the rest of the Christian world.

From the 1948 Conference to the death of Stalin (1953)

This isolation of the Russian Church increased with Tito's breach with Stalin. Patriarch Alexis and his collaborators made haste to return the decorations received from the Yugoslav Government in 1945.[19] Contact between the two Patriarchates ended and the Serbian Church in Moscow was suppressed. Even so, the Moscow Patriarchate, while consolidating its gains in Poland and Czecho-slovakia, did not give up its claim to hegemony, and, in the period following 1948, it tried to assume the leadership of the Christian world by involving it in the campaign for peace.

On 3rd March 1950, Patriarch Alexis sent an 'Appeal' to the heads of all the Orthodox Churches, written in carefully qualified terms, which 'called to mind the duty to establish peace on earth which should be sacred to the pastors of Christ's flock'. Only the Bulgarian, Rumanian and Albanian Churches, and the Patriarch of Antioch, gave a positive response to this appeal.[20]

In August of the same year, Patriarch Alexis paid a visit to the Catholicos of Georgia at Tbilissi; the Armenian Catholicos was also present. Together, the three ecclesiastical leaders signed a *Message to the Christians of the whole world*. This was accompanied by explanatory letters and was sent to all those concerned.[21] The Archbishop of Canterbury answered it by a condemnation of the political and partisan attributes of the 'peace movement'.[22] During the same period (July 1950) the Metropolitan Nicholas and other ecclesiastics took part in an inter-Christian conference for peace at Luhacovici in Czechoslovakia.[23] In July 1952, the annual celebrations of St Sergius of Radonej provided the oppor-tunity for a meeting in Moscow between Alexander III, the

Patriarch of Antioch; Justinian, the Primate of Bulgaria, and the Catholicos of Georgia. These all signed a fresh appeal to Christians throughout the world, asking them to strive for a pact of peace between the great nations. This appeal, like its predecessors, had no effect outside the Communist world.[24]

In Czechoslovakia, the enforced conversion of the uniates to Orthodoxy increased the numbers of the Czech Orthodox Church, and thus Moscow was enabled to grant this Church autocephalous status, although it retained a bishop of Soviet nationality at its head. A Soviet bishop, Mgr Macarius of Lvov, was also appointed as the Primate of the Polish Church. As its last move, Moscow encouraged the Holy Synod of Bulgaria to re-establish a Bulgarian Patriarchate, without any reference to the Ecumenical See. All these initiatives, taken without the agreement of the Orthodox Churches as a whole, completed the breach between Moscow and Constantinople.

On two later occasions, 12th February and 25th September 1952, the Ecumenical Patriarch again put forward the idea of summoning an Orthodox pro-synod. But on the very day of Stalin's death, 7th March 1953, Patriarch Alexis replied to him in a long and somewhat bitter letter in which he listed all the points of disagreement between the two Churches: non-recognition by Constantinople of the autocephalous status of the Polish and Czechoslovakian Churches; non-recognition of the legitimacy of the election of the Archbishop in Tirana; the unlawful retention of the Russian Exarchate in Western Europe and the 'so-called' Church of Finland; communion with the Russian schismatic Churches of America, etc.[25]

Humanly speaking, reconciliation seemed impossible.

After Stalin's death: the first signs of a thaw

But, one among the many consequences of Stalin's death was an alteration in the relations between the various Orthodox Churches. In the eight years that followed the tyrant's death and the abandonment of the 'personality cult', the external policy of the Moscow Patriarchate developed in a direction diametrically opposite to that which it had followed in the eight previous years. The Russian Church steadily surrendered its centralizing ambitions, took the initiative in settling its dispute with the Ecumenical See, put an end to its vituperations against the Vatican, displayed a deep interest in the Ecumenical Movement. This new direction, corresponding with the new style of Mr Kruschev's diplomacy, was crowned in 1961 by a twofold success: the participation of the Russian Church in the pan-Orthodox conference of Rhodes and her admission to the World Council of Churches.

This new policy emerged only gradually, step by step with the liberalization of the régime. In August 1953, the *Review of the Moscow Patriarchate*, still with the pro-synod in mind, violently attacked the Ecumenical See which was accused of 'neo-papism', and of harming the Orthodox Church by its 'claims to special rights and privileges'.[26] During the same period, the Metropolitan Nicholas made another attempt to separate the Church of Finland from Constantinople. It again proved futile.[27]

In the early months of 1954, the *Review of the Moscow Patriarchate* published successively several articles on the Ecumenical Movement, which had previously been ignored. The movement was severely criticized, but it was agreed that 'fundamentally it displayed a genuine desire to achieve unity among Christians'.[28]

In 1956, the Moscow Patriarchate, in reply to a letter from the Central Committee of the World Council of Churches, still saw no grounds for collaboration except in the Peace Movement, and postponed till later the study of the documents of the Evanston conference (1954 World Council of Churches).[29] An initial meeting was planned to take place in January 1957 but, owing to the Hungarian rising and the Suez crisis, it was deferred at Moscow's request.[30] In 1956 relations with the Serbian Church were also renewed; the Patriarch of Yugoslavia came personally to Moscow where he was received by N. Bulganin, then president of the Council.[31] A similar approach was made to Constantinople.

With the Metropolitan of Beirut as intermediary, the Patriarch Alexis sent a message and a present to the Ecumenical Patriarch, who returned thanks warmly and without delay.[32]

It was in 1957, however, that the most spectacular step was taken, one which showed a profound change in the external policy of the Russian Church. At a meeting on 20th April the Patriarch and the Holy Synod decided to wipe out all the 'canonical disputes and the misunderstandings' which had arisen between the Russian and Finnish Churches, and to recognize the *status quo*, that is, the autonomy of the Finnish Church within the jurisdiction of the Ecumenical See; and to re-establish the communion between the two Churches which had been interrupted in 1923. This was not only an abandonment of the cause maintained with intransigent vigour[33] for more than ten years; it was also an explicit recognition of the legitimacy of the Ecumenical Patriarch's jurisdiction outside the geographical boundaries of his Church.[34]

Evidence of the thaw appeared in another direction. On the 14th March 1957, the Synod sent an appeal to the 'Churches of the emigration' urging them to be re-united with the mother Church now that 'the causes which had provoked the separation had ceased to exist'. The appeal ended with an invitation to the tens of thousands of Soviet citizens who had left their country during the Second World War, to return to the USSR without delay, for the Presidium of the Supreme Soviet, by a decree of 17th September 1955, granted a complete amnesty 'to all citizens who had collaborated with the German occupying forces, including those who are now still abroad'.[35]

Some months previously, resurgent nationalism in the countries that were satellites or allies of the USSR compelled Moscow to recall the head of the autocephalous Church of Czechoslovakia, Mgr Eleutherius, whom the Czechs found undesirable, and also the Exarch of China, Mgr Victor, as well as all the Russian collaborators in the Chinese mission.[36] A Russian, Mgr John Kukhtine, was again elected (not nominated) as head of the Czechoslovic Church. And he was an émigré. The Church of

China, although numerically insignificant, was granted autonomy, and this was made a practical reality by the consecration of a second Chinese bishop in Moscow.[37]

So, willingly or unwillingly, the Moscow Patriarchate renounced its former policy of direct domination. To give a public manifestation of this change, Patriarch Alexis invited all the heads of the autocephalous Orthodox Churches to Moscow, to take part in the celebrations of the fortieth anniversary of the restoration of the Patriarchate in Russia (May 1958). This was no longer a question of a pan-Orthodox conference, still less of a council. It was simply something that had happened within the Russian Church, to which the other Orthodox Churches were invited to bear witness. And this time the replies were positive: Jerusalem and Cyprus, owing to their special political situations, were the only ones to abstain.

The meeting of 1958

After the customary greetings and speeches, Metropolitan Nicholas read a paper entitled *Orthodoxy and the modern world*, in which he outlined the new policy of his Church in external affairs. He refrained from any discussion of problems that concerned the Orthodox Churches as a whole, 'because the Ecumenical Patriarch was soon to take action in these matters'. This was an official admission by the Russian Church that the privilege of summoning a Council belonged to the Ecumenical See. Later in his speech he declared that the Russian Church would now increase her contacts with the Ecumenical Movement. This change of policy was explained in terms that were somewhat confused; it was said to be due to 'new historical circumstances and to an evolution of the Ecumenical Movement towards a greater political objectivity and a more thorough appreciation of tradition'. Mgr Nicholas dwelt on the prohibition of atomic weapons and on the importance of the Peace Movement, but he went no further into the political situation. He was careful to distinguish between international peace and the peace of Christ, and said, with emphasis, that in the struggle for peace there was no necessity to 'enlist under a foreign flag or to join any organization of fighters for peace; it was enough to say that the whole Orthodox Church was sharing in the world's anguish'. All along the line, therefore, it was clear that the Moscow Patriarchate had abandoned its previous position. It would not be an exaggeration to say that the meeting of 1958 annulled that of 1948 and made reparation for it.[38]

The road to Rhodes

After the meeting of 1958, the pan-Orthodox conference became a possibility. In December 1960 Patriarch Alexis, with an impressive entourage, made a second pilgrimage to Jerusalem and visited the Churches of the Middle East. A comparison between this journey and that made by the Patriarch in 1945 – as a prelude to the conference that was to have been held in Moscow in 1947 – is unavoidable. This time the journey was a prelude to the coming Orthodox pro-synod. Alexis did not, as in 1945, visit the Patriarchates of the Arab countries alone; he also visited the Church of Greece and the Ecumenical Patriarch.

The official accounts of the journey do not supply us with much information.[39] In his own official statements, Patriarch Alexis made much of the struggle for peace. His private discussions invariably took place in the presence of interpreters, even when such aid was not required (Alexis speaks English and French perfectly and Archbishop Nicodemus can make himself understood in Greek and Arabic). In the Arab countries, he was cordially welcomed, but the enthusiasm of 1945 was wholly absent. In so far as we have confidential information about the discussions between the two Patriarchs, it would seem that at Constantinople the head of the Russian Church submitted to the Ecumenical Patriarch the conditions that would be necessary if he was to take part in a future pro-synod: the recognition of the Bulgarian Patriarchate, created with the support of the Russian Church; the autocephalous status of the Czech and Polish Churches; the acceptance of the legal position of the Archbishop of Tirana; and the transfer of the Russian Churches of the emigration which had been until then under the protection of the Ecumenical See.

The Ecumenical Patriarch was anxious, on the eve of the Vatican Council, to remove the last obstacles blocking the way to the Orthodox Council, and he gave way on the first three points. In any case, this was only to give *de jure* recognition to what the whole Orthodox world had already admitted *de facto*. The establishment of a Bulgarian Patriarchate was in itself lawful. The death of Mgr Denis, the head of the Polish Church while it depended upon Constantinople, and then of his Soviet successor, Mgr Macarius, had paved the way for the recognition of the autocephalous status of that Church. In Czechoslovakia the influence of Constantinople had always been negligible.

But on the question of the Russian emigration the Ecumenical Patriarch would not give way and merely promised to settle the problem later, in the best interests of all concerned. He also refused to recognize the legality of the position of Mgr Paissy – if indeed it is true that Patriarch Alexis warmly pleaded the cause of a friend of Enver Hodja. However that may be, the Albanian Church was not, in fact, invited to Rhodes. The conference that met to prepare for the pro-synod – the product of mutual concessions, which, we do well to remember, had been begun by Moscow – held its first sessions in Rhodes on 21st September 1961. The Russian delegation, led by Archbishop Nicodemus, his co-adjutor Mgr Alexis Ridiger (both of them then only thirty-two years old!) and Mgr Basil Krivocheine, a member of the emigrant Church attached to Moscow, behaved with discretion, and seemed anxious not to embitter issues that were in dispute. Thus the Russian delegation, which had begun with the proposal that presidency should be granted by rotation to the various Orthodox Churches, ended by accepting the sole presidency of the Ecumenical See – upon whose territory the conference was being held. But it insisted that in the future pro-synod the words 'mission' and 'struggle with atheism' should be omitted, and seemed unashamed of this proof that its dependence on the Soviet Government extended into the realm of ideas. It is essential to realize that the Rhodes conference had a limited aim; its purpose was to prepare the programme for the pro-synod, to draw up a catalogue of questions. The discussions rarely went down to fundamentals. Thus delimited, this collaboration between Churches behind the iron curtain and those in the free countries proceeded without any shocks, and to a satisfactory result.[40]

The road to New Delhi

In August 1958 there at last took place the first official encounter between the representatives of the Russian Church (Mgr Nicholas, Metropolitan of Krutitsy, Michael Chub, then Bishop of Smolensk, and A. Buevsky, the Secretary of External Affairs) and those of the central committee of the World Council of Churches (Visser't Hooft, Mgr James, then Metropolitan of Melita, and Mgr Fry). The discussions dealt with five points: The Russian Church and the Ecumenical Movement; the problem of Christian unity in its work for the defence and stabilization of peace; the attitude of the Russian Church towards political and social life (questions introduced at the request of the Russian Church); the World Council of Churches and the unity of the Church; the common concern of the Churches to ensure religious freedom (a question introduced by the World Council). Mgr Nicholas admitted that his Church as yet knew little about the World Council of Churches; he said that there were serious reservations to be made with regard to the political activity of that body and the inadequacy of its dogmatic foundations. He mentioned 'various' reasons which prevented some Churches from forming a relationship with the Ecumenical Movement, but he concluded with a reasonably broad proposal for collaboration that included the sending of observers to the sessions of the Central Committee, the exchange of periodicals and books, the organization of theological discussions, the publication of statements agreed upon in common, etc.[41]

This plan, which Mgr Nicholas wished first to submit to the Churches who had signed the Conference of 1948, was soon put into effect; in June 1959 two representatives of the Patriarchate, Father Vital Borovi and the interpreter (?) V. Alexeev were sent to Geneva for a month's study on the spot of the organization and working of the various departments of the World Council of Churches. In the following month the same two were sent as observers to the session of the Central Committee of the Council held in Rhodes between 19th and 29th August.[42] On this occasion Mgr Nicholas sent a message to those taking part in the session; its extreme warmth was in marked contrast with the reservations made a year previously at Utrecht:

We Orthodox Christians regard the Ecumenical Movement with deep sympathy, for we believe that our brethren in the West are sincerely trying to overcome the ruinous divergencies of belief. . . . We cannot fail to sympathize with the various means taken by the Council to solve the numerous social problems of our time. . . . Our common moral purpose is the struggle to end the testing of nuclear weapons and to secure their absolute prohibition. . . . At the same time, I feel bound to express the hope that the social concerns of the Council will not relegate to the background the Ecumenical Movement's main purpose – the achievement of that unity of belief which has been shattered by a variety of deviations. We Christians must rise above the political contradictions of our time, and show divided mankind an example of unity and peace, of brotherhood and love, by giving up any easy contentment with our own position and any unfriendly attitudes to one another. . . . I express my satisfaction that the representatives of the Russian Church have for the first time been able to follow the work of the Ecumenical bodies and thus to contribute to our mutual understanding.

The reading of this message produced an 'extraordinary impression'; it was greeted with genuine, unanimous and prolonged applause, culminating in an outburst of enthusiasm. Everyone praised 'the friendly tone, the moderation and dignity' of this statement which passed a sponge over all the grievances previously evoked, and showed the Russian Church about to co-operate wholeheartedly with the Ecumenical Movement.[43]

Mgr Nicholas was not allowed to see the success of the work he had undertaken. Renewed persecutions did not alter the policy of the Moscow Patriarchate, but they involved an important change in personnel. Mgr Nicholas was first removed and then, most probably, assassinated. Mgr Michel who had accompanied him to Utrecht was also removed from all international activity.

It was on 30th March 1960, that the formal acceptance by the Russian Church of membership of the World Council of Churches was sent to Geneva. The meeting of the Russian episcopate in July 1961 did no more than ratify what had been done. The Moscow Patriarchate sent an impressive delegation to the General Assembly at New Delhi (December 1961): five young bishops, several priests and a number of laymen of more than doubtful competence and position. The bishops, always accompanied by these strange persons, could exchange views with each other only during services in church. The general supervision was all in the hands of I. Varlamov, whose name, in the official list, is the only one followed by no qualification at all.

Practically unanimously the Russian Church was admitted as a member: out of 150 votes, 142 were in favour; 3 were against, and 4 abstained, 1 vote was not cast. The representative of the reformed Hungarian Church of America, Zoltan Beky, expressed the apprehensions of some members who either resigned themselves to vote in favour of the motion, or else abstained:

> Our Church feels itself to be at one in Christian charity with
> the great Russian Orthodox Church. Thousands of martyrs
> in the recent persecutions bear witness to the glorious Christian belief and the fidelity of the clergy and laity of that great
> Church. If the official delegates who present themselves as

nominees of that Church do correctly represent it, then we agree to its admission. But if the official representatives of the Russian Orthodox Church wish to use this platform for political ends, contrary to the spirit of the Russian Church, and if they mean to make themselves spokesmen of their Government's point of view (based on the principles of atheistic materialism and of the undemocratic system of party dictatorship) then, in that case, our Church wants to see its opposition noted in the report of the proceedings. In the meanwhile, we will abstain.

Only the future will show whether the apprehensions expressed by Zoltan Beky are justified or not. At New Delhi, the attitude of the Russian delegation was on the whole discreet. The luxurious reception given by the Soviet ambassador to his delegation, the number and the watchfulness of the agents appointed to supervise the bishops, showed that the Soviet Government was far from being unconcerned with the activity of the Russian Church at the World Council.[44] Mgr John Wendland, then the Exarch of central Europe, produced an unpleasant surprise in the commission for refugees, when he emphatically insisted that it was a matter of urgency for the refugees to be repatriated. At the meeting of the Executive Committee in Paris (August 1962), he took the opportunity to put forward his Government's views on the problem of Berlin. The entry of the Russian Orthodox Church into the World Council brought with it that of the satellite countries (Bulgaria and Rumania) and, a little later, five other Churches of the USSR: the Orthodox Church of Georgia, the Armenian Church, the Lutheran Churches of Lithuania and Esthonia, and the Baptist Alliance. The Soviet group entered the Ecumenical arena in full strength.[45]

The road to Vatican II

After Stalin's death the attacks against the Vatican by representatives of the Moscow Patriarchate decreased in intensity, and by

1956 had practically ceased. On the death of Pius XII, the Patriarchate, after a week's silence, offered its condolences to the Roman Church, praising the late Pope's appeals for Peace, and expressed the hope that his successor 'will intensify the efforts of Christians of the Roman Church towards the establishment of peace among the nations and the prosperity of all mankind.'[46] The *Review of the Patriarchate* saw no need to adopt any special position when the Second Vatican Council was summoned, and indeed did not even inform its readers of the fact until a notice appeared in *Tempo* (May 1959) with the announcement that discussions were taking place between Mgr Della Riane and representatives of the Russian Church. The Patriarch immediately published a formal denial and declared that in his view the proposed Council was entirely a domestic concern of the Roman Church.[47] It was not until May 1961 that the *Review* again referred to the Roman Council, and, in an unsigned article (hence issuing from the editorial board) entitled *Non possumus* explained the theological reasons why the Russian Church would not send a delegate or even an observer to the Roman Council.[48] Meanwhile, the political attacks against the Vatican were renewed. In November 1960, in the same review, the editor in chief, P. A. Shishkine, accused the Vatican of failing to put the principles of Christian love into practice, and of pursuing a policy of aggression. He pointedly remarked: 'We have adopted an attitude of reserve towards Pope John XXIII, in spite of the pacific nature of his pronouncements.'[49] At the world congress for peace at Prague, Mgr Nicodemus presented a lengthy paper full of accusations of a kind that had been out of fashion since the Stalin era: 'the aspiration to dominate is driving papal Rome, as it has always done, to be the activating power of different aggressive political associations. . . . It is no accident that the gulf dividing progressive mankind from the Vatican grows deeper day by day.'[50] But three months later there was a change in tone. For in the meanwhile N. Kruschev had commented favourably on the message of Pope John XXIII on 10th September 1961. In an interview given to the correspondents of *Pravda* and *Izvestia*, he said that 'an appeal of this kind was a good omen'.[51] Then, as a reinforcement of his changed outlook, he sent birthday greetings to the Pope on 23rd November, through the apostolic nuncio at the Quirinal. This was public permission to the Russian Church to reconsider her attitude.

As the Council drew near, Rome had to face the practical problem of the invitations to be issued to the Orthodox Churches. In order not to be presented with refusals as in 1870, the Vatican decided to approach these Churches first of all through the Ecumenical Patriarch, and to issue invitations only when sure of their acceptance. This useless precaution enabled the Moscow Patriarchate to play a subtle and remunerative diplomatic game. Patriarch Alexis, in the course of his various journeys (to the Middle East and Yugoslavia) and Mgr Nicodemus (to the four corners of the earth) let it be known that the Russian Church, while sending no observer to the Council, still refrained from shutting the door to possible future discussions. Mgr Nicodemus was constantly telling people that, so far, his Church had not been invited. At New Delhi he observed that on a number of occasions he had been asked whether observers would be ultimately sent to the Council and that this had been embarrassing for him. 'We are almost ashamed at being unable to answer. But how can we reply, when we have not yet been invited?'[52]

For his part, the Ecumenical Patriarch, unwilling to create a rift in the Orthodox world, was awaiting an answer from Moscow before sending his final decision to Rome. It was known that he personally was much in favour of sending observers. In August 1962, in Paris, Mgr Nicodemus met Mgr Willebrands, the secretary of the Secretariat for Christian Unity, and intimated that Moscow's answer might be affirmative, if he would make a personal visit to Moscow, as he had done to the Eastern Patriarchates. The Vatican gave its approval, and he stayed in Moscow from 27th September to 2nd October 1962. After the insults and affronts which the Vatican had received from the Soviet Government and the Russian Church, this was an indisputable diplomatic victory for Moscow. Mgr Willebrands was given no definite answer, on the grounds that the final decision must be taken by the Synod, and several days must elapse before it could meet. The Synod, in fact, only disclosed its decision to send two observer delegates on the day the Council opened, and at the same time the Tass agency, in its foreign news service, praised the work for peace undertaken by John XXIII.[53]

On the night before, the Ecumenical Patriarch, having given up hope, had telegraphed to Rome and Moscow that he would refrain from sending observers to the Council, as he had no wish to be a lonely knight-errant. Paradoxically, therefore, the Moscow Patriarchate, which until then had been the most hostile to Rome, was the only Orthodox Church to be represented at the first session of the Vatican Council. By the second session matters had righted themselves, but the position of prestige remained with Moscow. Diplomacy, in the new flexible style, has shown itself to be more effective than in the aggressive style of Stalin.

A revival of the peace movement

In June 1958, a specifically Christian movement for peace was launched in Prague, which from the outset received the whole-hearted support of the Russian Church. The Prague conferences became annual, and in July 1961 were transformed into a pan-Christian congress for the maintenance of peace; Moscow sent a delegation that was even more impressive than that which was about to be sent to New Delhi; it was led by the Metropolitan of Krutitsy Pitirim, and included five bishops, six priests (four of whom were professors), a protodeacon, seven laymen – among them I. V. Varlamov who seems to have been present on every journey – and five members of a youth organization.[54] The Congress established two permanent bodies: a working committee of sixteen members, with J. Hromadka as president, and Archbishop Nicodemus as vice-president; and a consultative committee of a hundred and ten members representing the four continents.[55]

The Prague movement is visibly tending to become a replica of the World Council of Churches: a meeting between the representatives of the two organizations took place in Geneva on 27th March 1962.[56] But in spite of its Christian character and its wish not to seem to be wholly committed, the Prague movement remains definitely confined to the East. It has had little success among the Orthodox Churches outside the sphere of Soviet influence. Only the Patriarchate of Antioch has given its support.

The development of external relations

The external relations of the Moscow Patriarchate are not conducted only through the activities of such central organizations as those of Rhodes, Geneva, the Vatican and Prague. Bilateral relationships (the exchange of delegations, conferences) are constantly on the increase, not only with the Churches of the West (America, England, Norway, etc.) but also with the Churches of Africa and Asia.

For some years now, the Soviet Government and the Moscow Patriarchate have had friendly dealings with Ethiopia and its ancient Monophysite Church. In January 1959, the Archimandrite Nicodemus Rotov, accompanied by the Orientalist M. Dobrynin, visited Addis-Ababa.[57] In July of the same year, the emperor Haile Selassie, during an official visit to the Soviet Union, was warmly received by Patriarch Alexis who gave him the decoration of the Order of St Vladimir.[58] A month later, an official delegation from the Ethiopian Church, led by Theophilus, the Metropolitan of Harrar, spent three weeks in Russia. A bishop of the Ethiopian Church took part in the Congress at Prague. In 1962 the representative of the Moscow Patriarchate in Alexandria undertook a long journey through Africa.[59]

In November 1961, Mar Klemis Abragam, the Malabar Metropolitan of the Monophysite Church of India, paid a visit to

Patriarch Alexis in Moscow; and when the New Delhi conference was held, several members of the Russian delegation paid a visit to the Church of Malabar.[60] Paradoxically, it is at a moment when the internal activity of the Moscow Patriarchate is practically paralysed by persecution, that its external relationships have become more extensive and animated than ever before.

CHAPTER VII

THEOLOGICAL SCHOOLS AND STUDIES

In a seminary everything should be directed towards training the students in the spiritual life.

Patriarch Alexis, 1949

BEFORE THE REVOLUTION, the training of the Russian clergy was ensured by fifty-eight seminaries, with 20,000 students, and by about 200 ecclesiastical schools, or minor seminaries. The children of the clergy were obliged to enter the seminaries, whatever their personal vocation. This was the weak point of these establishments, which, often frequented by unwilling students, became seed-beds of atheism.

Above the seminaries were four brilliant ecclesiastical academies that gave theological teaching of exceptional value and were devoted to scientific research. Each was concerned with a special branch of ecclesiastical learning. The Moscow Academy had undertaken and almost completed a full translation of the Greek Fathers. That of Kiev, nearer to the West, was translating the Latin Fathers. At Petersburg, the historical disciplines flourished under Bolotov (d. 1900) and his disciples; Byzantine studies under Sokolov and Andreev; liturgy under Dimitrievsky; dogmatics under Glubokovsky. Kazan was the school for future missionaries; there, the study of Arabic, of Islam and Buddhism had pride of place. Each academy had its monthly theological review. The standard of teaching was so high that at a later period the academies were criticized for having given a predominant position to reason and for pursuing learning for its own sake.[1]

The students, carefully selected from among the best of the seminarists, or already equipped with a sound secondary or university education, formed a homogeneous audience. They saw their future in teaching, research, the episcopate, or, more rarely, in the pastoral ministry. Many foreign students, Greeks, Slavs, Rumanians, Arabs, etc., became members of the academies.[2]

On 6th September 1918, as a result of the decree on the separation of the Church from the State, and of schools from the Church, all ecclesiastical establishments were obliged to close their doors. In theory, the Government's commission on education leaves room for the Church to arrange theological courses for the training of her ministers, on condition that all general subjects are excluded and that the minimum age of the students is kept at eighteen. Father Nicholas Chukov made desperate efforts to exploit this possibility and to restore theological teaching in Petrograd. In 1919 he succeeded not only in establishing lectures on pastoral theology, but also a remarkable institute of theology, which included among its members some of the most notable professors of the former academy (Glubokovsky, Brilliantov, Karabinov, Sokolov, etc.) and of the university (the distinguished Orientalist Turaiev, a member of the Academy of Sciences; the philosophers L. Karsavin and N. Lossky, expelled from the USSR in 1921; the historians M. Priselkov and S. Besobrasov – the latter Bishop Cassian, rector of the St Sergius Institute in Paris, etc.). In 1920, a hundred students, thirty-two of whom had already completed their advanced studies, entered for their first year's course. But the very success of the enterprise led to its downfall. The Institute only lasted three years, and held only one distribution of degrees, at which twenty-three students received diplomas. Its organizer and rector was condemned to death at the trial of Mgr Benjamin, but afterwards pardoned. Only the pastoral lectures continued to be given; in 1925 these became a course in advanced theology. This too, was ephemeral; the course came to an end in 1928. A final attempt was made in 1929 by the indefatigable Nicholas Chukov, who had been released from prison, but he was obliged to desist, because 'neither a building nor a library' could be obtained.[3] In the other towns theological teaching could not be resumed.

For more than a quarter of a century, if we omit the theological lectures in Leningrad, which were of little practical significance, the Russian Church had to give up all intellectual life and was deprived of the power to give its ministers a theological training. The restoration of a system of schools of theology was an indispensable condition for the Church's survival, and accordingly it was among the first issues put to the Soviet Government in August 1943, when the normalization of the relations between Church and State was under discussion. Stalin agreed in principle.[4] The same Nicholas Chukov, who had become Archbishop (later Metropolitan) Gregory, put forward in October 1943, a very modest proposal for the organization of an institute of theology in Moscow and for ordinary pastoral lectures in Leningrad.[5]

On 16th June 1944, the Metropolitan Alexis, then *locum tenens* of the Patriarchate, officially inaugurated the re-establishment of theological studies in Moscow, and defined the spirit of the new school as being 'strictly ecclesiastical, without the least concession to the spirit of the age'.

The first year was especially difficult. The Metropolitan Gregory had planned a course of studies lasting three years; he thought the maturity of the students would compensate for its brevity. But it was the reverse that happened. Twenty-five years of secularist, materialist teaching had borne its fruit. The students arrived with a sincere belief in God, with the desire of serving the Church, but their lack of preparation was catastrophic. They were supposed to attend lectures on dogma or on Russian religious thought, when most of them did not know the catechism. The gulf between the standards demanded by the masters and the intellectual and moral level of the students was so wide that it became necessary to simplify the syllabus, and, instead of professorial lectures, substitute a course of questions and answers. There also had to be a ruthless exclusion of those who did not present sufficient guarantees, or were disinclined to submit to the austere discipline of the school. These initial troubles led to a profound reorganization of the institute which served as a model for the other seminaries.

In 1945 it was planned to found seminaries in at least seven of the most important dioceses after Moscow: in Leningrad, Kiev, Odessa, Lutsk (Volhynia), Minsk (White Russia), Saratov (in the Volga basin), and Stavropol (Kuban), and to restore three of the former academies, in Moscow, Leningrad and Kiev. This minimum programme became in fact a maximum, and contrary to all expectations took more than three years of striving for its accomplishment. The Kiev Academy never became more than a plan, and from 1947 onwards the Government opposed any further extension of the network of ecclesiastical schools.

The organization of the seminaries

In order to be admitted to the first year's lectures, postulants must be at least eighteen, and have completed their studies at a secondary school of seven forms (roughly corresponding to our A level Certificate)[6] or have received corresponding private tuition. They must bring with them a reference from their parish priest or diocesan bishop, and a baptismal certificate issued by a priest or by three witnesses.[7] Candidates are subjected to an exclusively oral examination, with the aim of discovering whether the future seminarists know by heart and in a stable and intelligent manner, the essential prayers of the Orthodox faith; morning and evening and some liturgical prayers; the Creed; the Ten Commandments; the Beatitudes; Psalms 50 and 90. No charge is made for studies, apart from board and lodging; seminarists are given an allowance of twenty new roubles, which is increased or diminished according to the results obtained by the students.[8] Unlike other Soviet students, seminarists are not dispensed from military service. But since the clergy are exempt from it, seminarists try to get ordained before they conclude their studies.[9]

These studies last for four years. The first two years are considered as introductory, and form the elementary stage. The students learn the foundations of the Christian faith and the indispensable ecclesiastical disciplines: sacred history, catechism, liturgical rubrics, Slavonic. These two years originally sufficed to receive the priesthood and an appointment to a rural parish. Later, when the standard was raised, the first two years merely equipped students with the right to minor orders and offices (cantor, deacon). The third and fourth years constitute the central period. It is then that the theological disciplines begin to be studied: the Old and New Testaments; dogmatic, fundamental, moral, pastoral and comparative theology; the history of the early Church and of the Russian Church; homiletics; the refutation of the *raskol* and the various sects; liturgy; and the study of Greek and Slavonic. The Metropolitan Gregory tried to introduce the study of Russian religious thought, but this subject soon disappeared from the syllabus.[10]

We have little information about the life of the seminaries, especially about those in the provinces. Their beginnings appear to have been humble and arduous; the buildings were small, and the livelihood poor (in 1947 the seminary of Odessa was unheated and food there was insufficient);[11] numbers were few (eleven students entered for their first year studies in 1947 at the Seminary of Kiev);[12] the general surroundings were often ill-suited to their work, etc. The *Review of the Patriarchate* stopped giving definite reports on the seminaries from 1948 onwards. This silence, enforced by the censorship, meant that they were developing well. In 1956, the Seminary of Stavropol, one of the smallest (55 students in 1955) was enlarged with new buildings 'on account of the regular and continuous increase of requests for admission'.[13]

In 1960, when persecution was resumed, the Government requisitioned the buildings that had housed the seminaries of Kiev, Stavropol and Saratov. That of Odessa, also threatened with

expulsion, prudently withdrew to the suburbs. The Seminary of
Minsk, established in the Monastery of Jirovitsy (from the time
of its first Degree Day up to 1951 it had granted twenty-six
diplomas for completed studies)[14] and that of Lutsk (whose
students, to judge by the photographs published by the Moscow
Patriarchate,[15] were especially numerous) had to close their
doors in 1964. In 1961, the *Review of the Patriarchate* was at
last authorized to disclose the total number of degrees granted:
179 in 1960, 66 of whom were admitted to the Academies for
the continuation of their studies, and 113 were appointed to
parishes. But this abnormally low figure is not an accurate record
of the output of the seminaries during the ten years of their
normal existence.[16]

The organization of the academies

The theological schools of Moscow and Leningrad are better
known to us. Many tourists have been able to visit them and
have gathered some details which complete the information supplied by the *Review of the Patriarchate*.

Although the studies in the academies are more advanced than
in the seminaries, their chief purpose is still that of training priests
and not theologians.

'Theology must be neither a scholastic exercise of the (speculative) reason, nor a theoretical conspectus of Christianity, but pre-
eminently and primarily a guiding principle for life . . . The
knowledge of the Orthodox truths is important and useful only
if these truths become realities that are loved and are applied
to life . . . The new theological school disowns any duality of
purpose, and must be centred solely on the training of priests
who are convinced of the truth of the Church and enlightened
by it.'[17]

These words of one of the original promoters of the Moscow
Institute of Theology are a perfect illustration of the practical,
existential direction given to the new academies. The discipline

imposed in the academies is quasi-monastic, even stricter than in the seminaries: the day is divided between 'prayer – the great work of communion with God – and sustained work considered as life turned into prayer'.[18] Students are required not only to attend the Vigils and Eucharists of feast-days, but also to take an active part in the chant, the lessons, and in the sermons at morning and evening prayers. During meals there is silence; as in the monasteries, one of the students on duty reads from the lives of the saints. Lectures begin at 9 a.m. – six are given every day – and continue until 3 p.m. After the meal there is free time until 6 p.m. From then until 9 p.m. there is free time for study, or, for those students on duty, there is a part to be taken in the evening services. The day ends with a meal and communal night-prayers.[19]

Five new subjects appear in the syllabuses of the Academies: patrology, canon law, Byzantine studies and the history of the Slav Churches, archaeology and Christian art, and Hebrew. The academic syllabus originally included a complete scheme of philosophical subjects: logic, psychology, history of philosophy, metaphysics, history of Russian religious thought.[20] In 1953–4, however, logic alone was mentioned,[21] and in 1958 no philosophical subject whatever was taught in the academies.[22] Apparently in the eyes of the Soviet authorities, philosophical problems could only be safely dealt with by State instruction.

The syllabuses of the academies, unlike those of the seminaries, are not of a general nature; the teaching aims at investigating a single aspect of the subject, as the former academies had done. During his first three years a student must produce three dissertations and deliver at least one sermon. Specialization begins only with the fourth year which is set apart for the writing of the thesis for the degree. The most deserving graduates are kept on in the academy as Fellows of the Foundation.[23]

The professors are elected by the Council of the Academy which includes all the professors, except those engaged in teaching (*prepodovateli*), and are confirmed in their position by the Patriarch. The latter alone has the power to appoint the rector.

Theological Schools and Studies

The Seminary and the Academy of Moscow

The institute and the courses in pastoral theology were transformed into a seminary and an academy in 1946. During 1948–9 the students were transferred from Moscow to the Trinity-St-Sergius Monastery which had housed the academy before the Revolution. As a centre of prayer and a place of pilgrimage, this monastery enabled the Moscow Seminary and Academy to be a school where religious devotion and belief were really practised. The library, which had to be reconstructed from nothing, now includes 150,000 volumes. In 1951 a notable museum of Christian archaeology was created. The number of students has constantly increased: from 161 in 1946 it became 184 in 1950; in 1960, in spite of the measures taken to slow down recruitment, it rose to 212. The students are young: the immense majority are between the ages of eighteen and twenty-five.[24] A tourist who took part in the reopening, records that nowhere else in the USSR had he seen faces of such serenity, faces that were grave but shining. The theses for degrees presented by students between 1940 and 1960 covered a great variety of subjects. Here are the subjects of some fifty theses, classified according to the principal disciplines:

The Old and New Testaments: The Old Testament, an inspired book; the messianic prophecies of the book of Genesis; the immortality of the soul according to the Old Testament; the priestly ministry in the Old Testament; the Apostle Paul's testimony on his apostolate (refutation of liberal interpretations); St Paul's eschatology in 1 Corinthians (patristic texts and commentaries): the inherent liability of the human race to sin, according to St Paul; the bondage of the Law and the freedom of the Gospel according to St Paul, etc.

Dogma: The dogma of redemption in Russian theology during the last fifty years; the dogma of redemption as expressed in St Athanasius, St Basil and St Gregory Nazianzen; the doctrine of salvation according to the Orthodox liturgical documents; the

doctrine of the sacraments in the Fathers of the Church during
the first and second centuries; the doctrine of grace in the teaching
of Theophanus the Recluse.

Moral theology: The conflict with the passions according to the
Fathers of the Church; the doctrine of the Fathers on the spirit,
the body and the soul; the significance of the heart in the moral
perfecting of man according to the Scriptures; the ascesis of
repentance; an analysis of the progressive development of sin and
its various forms; the way to moral perfection according to
Isaac the Syrian.

Patrology: The dogmatic and ethical teaching of St Irenaeus of
Lyons; the doctrine of the Church in the Christian literature of
the first two centuries; the Holy Trinity in the teaching of St
Gregory Nazianzen.

Liturgy: The Trebnik of Peter Mohila; St John Chrysostom,
theologian of the liturgy; the sacramental system in the Russian
Orthodox Church from the seventeenth century to the present
time, etc.

History of the early Church: The apostolic writings as historical
documents; the significance of martyrdom in the Church of the
first three centuries; the ancient world and Christianity in the
writings of the Apologists of the first three centuries; Constantine
the Great and his position in the history of the Church.

History of the Russian Church: The Orthodox Church in Latvia
up to the middle of the nineteenth century; Orthodoxy among
the Chuvaches up to the middle of the nineteenth century;
Bishop Sophronius of Vracha; the Union of Brest; the con-
fraternities in the Ukraine and Bielgorod, bulwarks of Orthodoxy; history of the conflict between the Orthodox Church and
the Catholic Uniate movement of the twentieth century and the
liquidation of the Uniate Churches in 1949; the history of the
Monastery of the Holy Spirit at Vilnius; the Uniate movement
and Orthodoxy in White Russia from the Council of Zamoisky
to 1839; the life and work of Paissy Velichkovsky; the relations
between the Russian and Bulgarian Churches up to the period of

the Bulgarian schism; the Patriarchate of Antioch and its relationship with the Russian Church after the fall of Constantinople; the Russian Palestinian Society and its scientific and cultural work in the East.

Pastoral theology: The duties of a pastor according to St Tikhon of Zadonsk; Bishop Theophan of Vychen as pastor of souls; St John Chrysostom, pastor of souls; the pastoral teaching of the apostolic writings.

Fundamental theology: The Christian doctrine of the destiny of mankind; the basis of Christian belief in miracles; the theological basis of the doctrine of the creation of the world; the preparation of the world for the reception of the Gospel message.

Christian art: The theological ideas in the work of Rublev; the Church of Dubrovitsy.

Canon Law: The Orthodox teaching on autocephalous Churches; the juridical relations between the Russian Church and Byzantium up to the fall of Constantinople.

Homiletics: Preaching and its significance in the pastoral ministry; Philaret of Moscow as a preacher; Father Rodion Putiatin, preacher.

The Rector of the Academy who has supplied this information[25] is gratified to find that most of the students have been attracted by patrology and Russian religious thought: 'Only a thorough, and not merely episodic study of the works of the Fathers of the Church and of Russian religious thought . . . will enable a number of theological issues to be fully developed, deeply understood and clarified, and a new theological outlook to be created, derived from pure and unblemished patristic origins'. This conclusion, even though stated in the future tense, seems a trifle optimistic. The list of subjects for a degree shows an inevitable but excessive traditionalism; the complete absence of any confrontation with the modern world or with the theology of the non-Orthodox Churches is all too apparent. The theological studies give the impression of being developed in a hot-house. It is difficult to judge the quality of the theses, of which only brief extracts have been published in the *Review of the Patriarchate*. But the Orthodox theologian, Vladimir Lossky, during a stay in Moscow, was able to inspect some of them. He said that they were 'conscientious', but he was impressed by the difficulty that these students found in expressing their ideas in suitably philosophical language and by their complete ignorance of theological works written in the West since 1917.[26]

We have little information about the professorial body whose members are frequently changing. The first professors were confirmed in their function and status by a certifying commission formed for this purpose. Actually not one of the thirteen professors of the restored academy had previously taught the higher stages of theology. Their qualifications were modest; only five held the degree of doctor of theology; five merely had a diploma in theology; three had graduated in secular studies.[27] In the beginning there was a new Rector almost every year. But since 1950 until his death in 1965 this post was held without interruption by the Archpriest Constantine Rujitsky, an excellent administrator, a man of outstanding spiritual life, but with a mere diploma in theology (in 1960 he was given a doctorial degree for a manual of moral theology to be used during the fourth year at the seminary).[28] The scientific activity of the professorial body seems to be rather limited. The first Rector of the Academy, Father Chepurin, gave his colleagues the modest task of producing manuals for the students.[29] In 1947 a former professor of the Petersburg Academy, Father B. Veriujsky, defended a thesis for the doctorate on *The Bulgarian Church during the schism* before a jury, which, paradoxically, included no doctor of theology. That same year the professor of Old Testament studies, V. Vertogradov, defended a doctorial thesis on *The Orthodox Church in Galicia*.[30] In 1948, the teacher of patrology, Benjamin Milov (d. 1955) offered for the doctorate a thesis on *Divine love according to the Bible and the teaching of the Orthodox Church*.[31] N. Doktussov (d.1959), who was originally the professor of logic and psychology and then of the New Testament, chose *The Armenian Church* as the subject for his thesis.[32] It is obvious from these few examples that specialization among the professors is not very advanced.

During recent years, however, there has been a marked rejuvenation of the staff as the result of new appointments. The new Rector Filaret Denissenko, appointed in 1965, is a bishop of thirty-six; the speech at the beginning of the academic year in 1960 was read by a young director of Studies, Father A. Ostapov.[33] But the scientific standard of the professorial body, which still includes no doctor in its ranks, remains low.

The Seminary and Academy of Leningrad

The Ecclesiastical Schools of Leningrad came into existence a year later than those of Moscow, and their beginnings were more modest; in 1946, twenty-eight and thirty students were admitted respectively to the first and third year of the seminary, and sixteen to the first year of the academy, making a total of only seventy-four students.[34] But thanks to the experience and energy of the Metropolitan Gregory Chukov, these schools developed more rapidly and, in their scientific work, definitely outdistanced Moscow.

Gregory attached great importance to the reconstruction of the library. He secured the return of the former library of the Petersburg Academy (80,000 volumes) from the Government; and personally acquired a number of private libraries.[35] The library at present contains 200,000 volumes.

A special feature of the Leningrad schools was the creation of a department for correspondence courses. These were meant originally for priests in the dioceses of Leningrad and Novgorod, but they have been extended to the Church as a whole. Layfolk, however, may not take part in them, because the State would regard this as amounting to religious propaganda, which as we have seen, is forbidden by the Constitution. Suggestions for methods of study and books are sent to priests by correspondence. Three times a year they are summoned to Leningrad for a ten-day session, during which they can profit from special lectures and consultations, and can take their examinations. The department is concerned with the last two years of the seminary course and the four years of the academy course. In principle, each 'year' covers eighteen months. So that, in fact, nine years are necessary to complete the seminary and the academy courses. This is the optimum period, which may permissibly be shortened. Father G. Pogorsky and the Archimandrite John Wendland (both subsequently consecrated bishops) completed their academy studies in less than four years, that is, even more quickly than the students at the academy. In 1955, when the department had only been in existence for seven years, a hundred priests had completed the correspondence seminary course, and over ten that of the academy.[36] In 1955, the academy conferred eighteen degrees on the completion of studies. The theses presented by the students have covered the following subjects: six dealt with biblical theology (the symbolism of the vine in the Scriptures; the pastoral ministry in the major prophets; a critical examination of Old Testament studies that have appeared in Russian periodicals (two diplomas); the Messiah according to the Gospel of Matthew; the origin of Luke's Gospel); five were devoted to the history of the Russian Church (Macarius of Optino; Venelin and his function in the Bulgarian National Renaissance; Podogin and his position in the Renaissance of the Slav world; the function of the clergy in the reunion between the Ukraine and Russia; Christianity among the Latvians in the twelfth and thirteenth centuries); three were on patristic subjects (Cyprian of Carthage; the theological ideas of Simeon the New Theologian; the letters of Basil the Great as an historical source for his life and work); two on moral theology (prayer in Russian periodical literature; the ethical and spiritual characteristics of the Russian Episcopate from the eleventh to the fourteenth centuries); one on homiletics (the special features of Russian preaching at the end of the nineteenth and beginning of the twentieth centuries); and lastly, a thesis incorporating both dogmatic and moral theology (the significance for man's moral and religious life of the dogma of the union between God and man).[37]

The striking thing about this list is the absence of theses on philosophical or dogmatic subjects; the political and even patriotic trend of those on the history of the Church; and the historical nature of the majority of them. In addition, no thesis seems to have been concerned with the dialogue with the outside world, with the heterodox Churches or the doctrines of atheism.

In Leningrad, as in Moscow, the tendency of theological studies seems to be traditionalist and conservative. On the other hand, the teaching body of the academy had and continues to have, higher qualifications than that of Moscow. During its first years, three former professors of the Petersburg Academy, Father V. Chetyrkine, author of a monumental thesis on the Apocalypse, published in 1916, A. Sagarda (d. 1950), a specialist in the study of Clement of Rome, and Father Veriujsky, author of several works on the history of the Church, ensured continuity with the tradition of the ancient schools.[38] Some previous émigrés, Father Bogoiavlensky (Bishop Isadore, first rector of the Academy, who died in 1949); his protégé and disciple, A. Ossipov, who ten years after his master's death was to deny Christ publicly; Father Chichkine of Prague; Father A. Sergueenko, a graduate of the St Sergius Institute in Paris; Father A. Borovoi, a graduate of the Faculty of Theology in Warsaw, later the man who did most to bring the Russian Church into the Ecumenical Movement, all these men returned to Russia bringing with them more up-to-date knowledge and more open and liberal tendencies. In 1952 two young graduates of the Academy were appointed to the teaching staff.[39] At present, the professorial body includes two doctors (N. Uspensky, professor of liturgy, and A. Ivanov, a New Testament specialist, but one who in 1960 defended a thesis for his doctorate on *The Byzantine Church*); seven professors of theology; and several former students of the academy as lecturers . . .[40]

Although Leningrad Academy is more progressive than that of Moscow, it has suffered some resounding defections. In 1952, a former graduate of the Academy, appointed to lecture in the Seminary of Saratov, left the Church and proclaimed himself an atheist.[41] In March 1958 one of his friends and colleagues, who had been a priest for three years in a Leningrad church, renounced his orders and began to attack the Church and religion with great violence.[42] Lastly, in September 1959, after taking part in the examinations for the autumn session, the Professor of the Old Testament, A. Ossipov (a former priest, suspended for remarrying) suddenly and without any warning denied Christ and professed the most elementary ideas of anti-religious propaganda.[43]

The primary, most imperative and urgent, task of the theological academies continues to be the training of pastors, of the cadres of the Church. The acquisition of knowledge is secondary. In 1960, thirty-seven students (and in addition to these, six foreign students: Lebanese, Rumanian, Polish and Czech) successfully completed their higher studies in theology: thirty-six of them were given parochial appointments.[44] But it should also be stressed that the segregation forced upon the Church and her theological schools is hardly favourable to the development of learning. Those who first collaborated in the academy were returning to theology after an interruption of thirty years. Between 1945 and 1955, the isolation of Soviet Russia was so complete that no foreign books got past the frontiers, not even to libraries. And if by chance a book did reach its destination, no professor, or research worker, would dare take account of it in his work.

It is only six years since Russian theologians began to enter into relations with the West. In September 1955, they took part for the first time in a great international conference, the second Patristic Congress in Oxford. The Leningrad Academy sent its Vice-Rector, L. Pariisky, Professor of Liturgy, and Professor K.

Sbovovsky, as delegates to it. Their papers were eagerly awaited and were listened to with attention. But they proved to be very disappointing and could bear no comparison with the standard of Western patrology.[45] In 1956 there was an important theological exchange of views between Anglicans and Orthodox in which Michael Ramsay, then Archbishop of York (now Primate of England) and two young Russian bishops, graduates of the new schools, took part. The Orthodox contributions were expressed in the most dogmatic terms and were entirely lacking in any structural arguments.[46] Courtesy visits, with discussions, take place periodically between Russian theologians and the evangelical Churches in the Rhineland and Westphalia.[47] The entry of the Russian Church into the World Council of Churches could not fail to be a stimulus to theological studies.

Contacts with the West have been resumed – though fresh obstacles are to be feared and the absence of the Russian delegate from the second International Conference of New Testament Studies in London was a sign of things to come.[48] – yet the separation from secular intellectual life is more complete than ever. The elimination of the philosophical disciplines is evidence of this. For it is hard to see how such disciplines as dogmatic and fundamental theology and patristics can develop without the study of philosophy. Moreover, is it possible for any form of scientific knowledge to exist and grow when it cannot be expressed? The academies may not publish any theological work, and this perhaps explains why so few theses have been defended. The *Review of the Moscow Patriarchate* only publishes short articles, and these are mostly historical and apologetic. As long ago as 1945, the Patriarchate asked for the authorization to publish a theological review: it was granted only fourteen years later. The first number of *Theological Studies*, published conjointly by the two academies, with equal representation on the editorial board, appeared in 1959–60.[49] This journal of 180 pages, which bears no indication of its price or of the number of copies printed, and is therefore not on sale commercially, contains five articles, all written by professors of the Leningrad Academy, which goes to confirm the scientific superiority of the Leningrad Academy over that of Moscow. Professor Uspensky's study of Orthodox Vespers is conscientious but contains little that is new (pp. 7–52). Professor A. Ivanov's article on the manuscript tradition of the New Testament would make an excellent inaugural lecture for a course on the New Testament, but is entirely lacking in originality (pp. 58–83). Father V. Borovoi attempts to identify the compiler of the *Collectio Avelanna*; this is an admirable historical study distinguished by the value of its documentation and by its concern to produce an original solution (pp. 85–109).

An outline of the Old Catholic movement by Fr A. Sergueenko, who has since given up his work at the Academy, does not exceed the limits of a conscientious but secondhand study (pp. 141–73). Lastly, the historical dogmatic study by the hieromonk Paul Cheromukin, which deals with a still little known area of Byzantine theology in the twelfth century (the Council of Constantinople of 1157 and Nicholas, Bishop of Methone) appears to be substantial. Unlike the other contributors to the journal – Uspensky and Ivanov received their education before the Revolution, Borovoi and Sergueenko abroad – Father Cheromukhin is a young graduate of the Leningrad Academy and the only one of his year (1955–6) to qualify as a lecturer.[50]

Theological Studies was to be a biennial and later an annual review.[51] But in fact three years passed before the second number appeared; the Minister of Culture had refused to allocate the paper necessary for its production.[52] These two numbers show once again that theological studies are developing in a one-sided manner – liturgical and historical subjects, or subjects treated historically, are predominant – and that their standard is still far below that of the West.

But too much should not be expected from a Church under the conditions imposed in the USSR. The mere fact that Schools of Theology are able to exist is of considerable importance. The seminaries and academies not only ensure the supply of ministers to the Church and keep at least some theological learning in existence; they are also the only schools in the USSR that provide instruction that is non-Marxist. The Soviet authorities have realized the ideological danger which they represent, and are now trying by all available means to limit their increasing influence over some of the élite of Soviet youth.[53]

CHAPTER VIII

THE CLERGY

A holy people makes a virtuous clergy.

1. *The higher clergy*

A SERIOUS STUDY of the episcopate is of interest from many points of view. First of all, this is the one domain about which we are relatively well informed: every episcopal consecration, every change of diocese, every bishop who is asked to resign, and (with very few exceptions) every bishop's death, receives a notice in the *Review of the Moscow Patriarchate*. A detailed and precise description of the episcopal body can therefore be given. Secondly, although the bishops are not the whole of the Church, they do, in a sense, sum it up. It is true that for a number of reasons, and in every Church, it is not always the best or the most capable members who become bishops, but that is just what makes the episcopate a pretty accurate reflection of the state of the Church, of her strong and her weak points. Lastly, in the absence of precise information about the lower clergy, what we shall say about the episcopate can be applied – *mutatis mutandis* – to the clergy as a whole. For the problems of recruitment, and the difficulties encountered in the work of the ministry are common to them all.

THE RE-CONSTITUTION OF THE EPISCOPATE. We have seen that during the persecutions, the vast majority of the episcopate proved worthy of their calling and their function: that of bearing witness to Christ. The bishops were the persecutors' favourite target and, with four or five exceptions, they faced martyrdom with courage. The only way of compensating for the wholesale arrests of bishops was to increase the number of episcopal consecrations. Paradoxically, the Russian episcopate was never so numerous as during the persecutions. According to a reliable estimate, in 1927 the number of bishops loyal to the Patriarchal throne rose to 260.[1] But by 1939, only six or seven were still functioning.[2] Most of them had died either by violence during the purges, or from exhaustion in forced labour; some were continuing to suffer in the concentration camps.[3]

The episcopate had thus to be recreated practically from nothing. It was a long and arduous task; constantly held up by changes in government policy, it has not been complete or final. The following stages mark its numerical progress. In 1942, the condemnation of the autocephalous Ukrainian Bishop, Polycarp Sikorsky, was signed by eleven bishops.[4] In September 1943, the number of bishops assembled in Council for the election of the Patriarch was still only nineteen. But in the second Council, in 1945, the episcopate, owing to new consecrations, numbered forty-six. After the Council this number continued to increase, until 1949, when it reached the record figure of seventy-four (for seventy-three dioceses and several vicariates). From 1950 onwards, until the very last days before Stalin's death (1st March 1953) episcopal consecrations were prohibited, and this naturally led to an appreciable diminution in available strength. Strange disappearances in addition to normal deaths made the loss greater, and the number of bishops was reduced to sixty-two. After Stalin's death, episcopal consecrations again became more frequent: ten in 1953–4; eleven in 1955–6. And numbers were further increased by the return of bishops who had been pardoned. However, the ceiling of 1949 was not reached again. At present the position is more unstable than ever; dismissals, arrests and episcopal consecrations alternate with exceptional irregularity.

But in 1952, as later in 1962, the crisis of the episcopate was due more to external obstacles than to internal difficulties. Immediately after the war matters had been different: no limit was then set to the consecration of bishops – on an average, there were ten every year. But, contrary to what might have been expected, the restoration of more normal relations between Church and State did not involve a large scale return of the bishops who had been condemned or exiled: a total of only thirteen bishops (six in 1942, two in 1944, five in 1945) was added to the group that had survived the persecutions.[5] The Church did, however, benefit from two sources of increase from outside: that of the penitent bishops from the Living Church (seven in all); and that of the émigré bishops (there were seven of these also) who asked that they might be allowed to return.[6]

The new consecrations, more numerous than these intermittent additions from without, appreciably altered the traditional characteristics of the Russian episcopate. In the Orthodox Church, a bishop must be free from all family ties. Before the Revolution, it was customary for bishops to be chosen almost exclusively from monks with an advanced degree in theology. But when all the monasteries and the faculties of theology had been suppressed (1919–44), this practice was an anachronism: candidates with these two qualifications were no longer available. The only thing the Church could now do was to consecrate widowed secular priests as bishops. It is a noteworthy fact that out of twenty-six bishops consecrated between December 1941 and January 1945, twenty-three were former parish priests, all, with one exception, with a theological degree. In view of the requisite qualifications (widowhood, theological studies) it is not surprising that the average age of these bishops was high – about sixty (the oldest being seventy-nine). The same trend continued, although not so markedly, in subsequent years. Out of forty-nine bishops consecrated between January 1945 and 1950, thirty-five came from the secular clergy and fourteen were regulars. The average age remained high (sixty) and the theological standard low, but it should be added that from 1947 to Stalin's death, the *Review of the Moscow Patri-*

archate refrained from supplying biographical information about the new bishops.

A transitional episcopate was thus produced, which enabled the Church to overcome the most acute phase of the recruiting crisis. One advantage of the call to former parish priests was that it helped to break down the well-known psychological barrier between the higher and lower clergy. It gave the dioceses experienced and unassuming bishops, who, to their cost, had known the difficulties of a priest's life during the years of persecution.

After Stalin's death, the Church began to have new opportunities for recruiting. The taboo that had weighed so heavily upon the years of the war and the occupation was at last lifted; the Church was enabled to draw more freely on the recruits returning from emigration or living in the regions annexed after the war. For example, four of the six bishops consecrated in 1956 had lived outside the USSR until 1944. In 1959, a graduate of the Institute of Orthodox Theology in Paris was given the crozier. But the most distinctive feature of the post-Stalin period is the appearance of young bishops who have lived all their life, at least all their adult life, under the communist régime, and have received their theological formation in the new schools created since the war. From 1956–63, twenty-one bishops, aged from thirty-one to fifty, introduced young blood into the episcopate and imparted a new style to it. From 1956 onwards, the average age of priests consecrated as bishops has continued to decrease. In 1956 and 1960 it was fifty; in 1962 it was only forty-one. In this sphere, the Russian Church holds a world record; four of her bishops were less than thirty-two when consecrated.[7]

NOMINATION, TRANSLATION AND RETIREMENT OF BISHOPS. The Council of 1917 had restored the practice of electing bishops by the whole diocesan community. But under the conditions imposed upon the Church by the Soviet authorities, the abandonment of the elective principle was inevitable. From 1927 until the present day, candidates for the episcopate have been chosen by the head of the Church and the Holy Synod. Neither the laity, the clergy nor the episcopal college as a whole has a vote in the election. In addition, every episcopal consecration and nomination must be given implicit approval by the Government, and this is far from being a formality. The Government is sometimes opposed, either temporarily or altogether, to the consecration of a given bishop whom it considers undesirable. A careful examination of the biographies of the bishops shows that, as a general rule and as far as possible, bishops are appointed to the dioceses where they were born or where they have lived for a long period.[8] This tendency to appoint a bishop to the region which he knows and where he is known, is, in the absence of elections, the only way of making the bishop the real representative of his flock and not an administrator imposed from above.

Unfortunately, however, the unity between the bishop and his diocese is precarious. It is most exceptional for a bishop to remain the head of the diocese to which he was consecrated. In the Orthodox Church, bishops are, in principle, irremovable. But in the Russian Church, from the time of Peter the Great, the frequent translations of bishops had become – for political, rather than religious reasons – an established custom. This provided the civil power with an opportunity to display its supreme power over the Church whose direct influence on the people it feared – paradoxical as that may seem. The Council of 1917 took action against this abuse and solemnly reaffirmed the irremovability of bishops. At the same time, it accepted the fact that 'in exceptional circumstances and for the good of the Church', the Patriarch has the right, granted the consent of the person concerned, to remove a bishop. Circumstances have also played their part in persuading the Church to return to a practice she had lately condemned. We have seen that the removal of Joseph, the Metropolitan of Leningrad, was the cause of a revolt against the Patriarchal authority.[9] Later on, changes effected simply by a decree of the Synod became general. The incumbents of certain greater sees (the Exarch of the Ukraine, the Metropolitan of Krutitsy) and

The Clergy

some few prelates alone escaped these changes. On 1st July 1962, Mgr Onesimus of Vladimir and Mgr Anthony of Stavropol, bishops appointed in 1944–5, managed to remain in their dioceses. One bishop is moved on account of his health, another for the good of the Church. But most of the changes are concerned either with forestalling a dispute which is always latent between the bishop and the local communist authority, or with preventing it from becoming acute. Some striking examples will prove the point: in 1949 the Soviet newspapers raised a storm of protest because, during the Epiphany procession at Saratov, hundreds had thrown themselves into the ice-cold waters of the Volga: Mgr Boris, the bishop of the place, was immediately translated.[10] In 1950, Bishop Sergius of Berlin, who had suspended an unworthy priest, a member of the political police, was forthwith summoned to Moscow to receive an imperative and immediate assignment to Kazan, without being given the chance to say good-bye to his flock or his relatives.[11] More recently, following some attacks in the Soviet national papers, various prelates, among whom were Mgr Michael of Smolensk and Mgr Sergius of Astrakhan, were immediately transferred to distant dioceses. In 1960–1, crucial years in the latest persecutions, this was just like a game of episcopal musical chairs: more than half the acting prelates were given new appointments.[12] Some prelates appear to have attracted particular attention; Mgr Donatus Shchegolev, for example, has received six different appointments within five years: from Biysk in Siberia he was moved in 1957 to Sverdlovsk in the Urals, and then in the same year to Velikie Luki, not far from Moscow; in 1958 he was transferred to Balta, near Odessa, and then again to Siberia, this time to Novosibirsk; as the result of giving evidence in support of an incriminated Christian he was transferred from there to Kostroma in northern Russia, and he was prevented, moreover, from taking up that post.[13]

THE BISHOPS' SPHERE OF ACTION. These things afford a sufficient indication of the extent to which a bishop's activity is

143

limited by State control; in addition to the threat of translation, there is the further and more serious danger of dismissal or arrest. The danger of being deported was only too real during the last years of Stalin's life: between 1947 and 1951, Mgr Basil Ratmirov, Archbishop of Minsk; Mgr Antony Marchenko, Archbishop of Tula; Mgr Benedict Plyaskin, Bishop of Petrozavodsk; Mgr Manuel Lemeshevsky, of Orenburg; Mgr Daniel Yuzvyuk, of Pinsk; Mgr Nestor Anissimov, the Exarch of Eastern Asia, all disappeared one after another. The first two have given no further sign of life. The others were pardoned in 1955, but only Mgr Manuel and Mgr Nestor have been allowed to resume their duties. Since 1960, after an interruption of seven years, arrests have begun again.

The bishop's task is made more difficult by the huge size of their dioceses. As a general rule, the diocesan territories, seventy-three in number, coincide with the administrative divisions into regions or republics. But some dioceses have been formed so as to include several administrative regions, for example Odessa and Kherson, Saratov and Volgograd, Irkutsk and Chita, etc.; that of Central Asia includes four republics in its jurisdiction (Turkmenistan, Uzbekistan, Tadjikistan and Kirghizia); that of Kazakhstan is four times as large as France; the whole of Siberia has only three dioceses with their own bishops. Several dioceses are permanently vacant (Pinsk, Petrozavodsk, Khabarovsk, Lugansk, etc.); others remain so for long intervals during which they are entrusted to bishops of neighbouring dioceses. Suffragan bishops are few; only Metropolitan Sees are regularly provided with them. Consequently, bishops have vast territories to administer, and this moves them to delegate much of their authority to priest-deans whose work is rather similar to that of a bishop.

The bishop's field of action was even more enormous in the years immediately after the war when the dioceses had to be reconstructed, often from scratch. Since that time – and in view of the fact that any extra-liturgical activity is illegal – a bishop's main activity can consist only of the supervision of his clergy, ordinations to the priesthood and diocesan visitations. Some bishops do not even take advantage of these latter opportunities, officiate infrequently, and live apart from the people. Others – these are often the same persons – behave like princes of the Church, lead a life of luxury, and organize banquets and receptions throughout the year[14]. The Patriarch complains that many recently consecrated bishops demand summer holidays and spend them lounging at ease in seaside resorts. He contrasts them with the bishops of former days who, even at a great age, over eighty, never missed an opportunity of Divine service with their own people around them.[15]

The visitation of his diocese seems to offer the best opportunities for a bishop to fulfil his duties as chief pastor. But any visitation that involves over-much display, or attracts very large crowds, is in danger of the laws against religious propaganda and may have fateful consequences for the visitor. In June 1955 Mgr Theodocius Kornevitsky, Bishop of Arkhangelsk, left his cathedral city for a diocesan visitation of a month and a half:

Having reached Kotlos by boat on 18th June, he held a service and celebrated the Eucharist in the Church of the town. The people wept for joy as they listened to the bishop's sermon. He spoke to them about the Russian saints and especially about St Stephen of Perm who set out from Kotlos in order to evangelize the tribes of the Koni. After a visit to Yamskoe, a parish far from the railway or any centre of population, the bishop reached Syktykvar on 24th June. This is a region of impassable forests and great lakes, of deep rivers and wide prairies, of nature in the wild and of entrancing silence. Several of its parishes had not heard the bells ring out to proclaim the coming of a bishop for more than eighty years. The expressions of deep feeling, joy, affection and gratitude which accompanied the welcome given him, can therefore be readily appreciated. In many places his path was strewn with the modest but sweet-smelling flowers of the north. Often the people greeted him on their knees. And everywhere – in bustling Murmansk, in austere Kola, in the new industrial town of Kirovsk and in the ancient Solvychegodsk – dense crowds could be seen and words of welcome heard. And, often, tears were shed. And the churches were always filled to overflowing. Seldom could Bishop Theodosius travel without danger. Generally he went by the waterways; the White Sea, the northern River Dvina, the Vychegda, the Onega. His means of travel varied; a modern steamship, an old paddle-boat, or even an ordinary fishing vessel.[16]

Pastoral zeal of this quality could not be permitted, even during this period of toleration and thaw. Some months later, the Holy Synod ordered Bishop Theodosius's retirement 'on grounds of health'. But he is well enough to celebrate regularly with the Patriarch in the churches of Moscow.[17]

BISHOPS AND THEIR FLOCKS. In Russia, a bishop has always been, and continues to be, the centre of popular affection and reverence which has no counterpart in the West.[18] A bishop is held to be the abode of God's grace, as Christ's representative on earth. His arrival in a parish never fails to draw large crowds who hail him as Christ coming into Jerusalem. This popular affection is displayed with intensity during visitations of the dioceses, or when a bishop dies. Here is a description of a visitation in a diocese of Asiatic Russia, given by one who took part in it:

We have been overwhelmed by the kindness and love of the people: you can see how greatly our Orthodox people love their bishops: in the towns through which we passed, the people spread their garments in the bishop's path, and then kissed the places where his feet had trod. . . .

'To thy Name be the glory', our bishop said, his eyes filled with tears.

How eagerly the people 'drank in' his words; how devoutly they received his blessing. And everywhere and always it is like this when we are visiting the diocese.[19]

The Clergy

In a parish in the province of Orenburg, almost all the people living in the road leading to the village, swept their doorsteps and brought out tables covered with cloths. Soon a long line of white and coloured cloths on which icons, bread and salt (traditional symbols of hospitality) and flowers indicated the route which the bishop was to follow. Bishop Manuel came up to each table, blessed it and greeted the people.[20] In an industrial town of the same province:

At four in the afternoon, the bus took the bishop to the Lenin section, where a new church, near the Nickel factory, was to be consecrated. When he arrived, the church could not hold all the people, and a dense crowd assembled around the building. As he approached, this immense crowd knelt down like one man.[21] In a little town in the province of Perm, 'the road along which the bishop was to pass was entirely covered with flowers'.[22] In Siberia, in the church of the town of Tulun, Archbishop Palladius was welcomed by the light of hundreds of candles that the people held in their hands.[23]

But it is when a bishop dies that the populace shows the full intensity of this love for the successors of the apostles. At Novosibirsk, two or three hours after the news of the death of the aged Metropolitan Bartholomew, 'it was difficult to make one's way to the Archbishop's house. For several nights the people filed past the body of their pastor. At the funeral, the great cathedral could not hold more than a small fraction of the people, most of whom had to be content to stand in the courtyard or in streets near by. Thousands upon thousands came to pay homage for the last time before the mortal remains of the dead archbishop'.[24]

There was a similar sight in Leningrad when tens of thousands filled the cathedral at the requiem of the Metropolitan Gregory, and again in Alma-Ata, where the news of the death of the Metropolitan Nicholas Mogilevsky shook the whole town and where 'tens of thousands followed his mortal remains in procession from the cathedral to the cemetery, a distance of five miles'.[25] In a personal letter in my possession, there is a description, with less administrative detail, but more immediate and moving, of the funeral of an esteemed prelate, Mgr Nicon Petin, Archbishop of Odessa, who died on 16th April 1956:

The clergy numbered about two hundred. As for the people, there were so many of them in the procession or watching it along the route that a guard and its auxiliaries a thousand men strong had to be formed to maintain order. Cantors, seminarists in dalmatics and nuns from the convent,[26] headed the procession; after them came the clergy, and then followed the coffin, borne by priests, hung with brocade, open as is customary, without a lid but partially covered by the *mandya* (a full-bodied, sleeveless cloak with a train, worn by monks) of episcopal purple. All along the route, the crowd, estimated at several thousand (counting the procession and the spectators there were some hundreds of thousands present) sang the canticles for the dead. Several times there were brief stations at which litanies were intoned and passages from the Gospels were read by each bishop in turn. Preceding the seminarists came another throng led by Bishop Innocent. The aged Metropolitan John was waiting in the cathedral. The procession lasted for almost four hours, during which time all the traffic was held up in the central part of the town. Not for a long time, perhaps never before, had Odessa witnessed so impressive a sight. The late prelate had preached frequently and abundantly, occasionally even three or four times at one service; but such a powerful sermon as this funeral of his, such a proof, of the common faith and of our people's love for its pastors, it was never given him to deliver, eminent preacher though he was.

Day and night, for nearly a week, a long line of people stretched far into the adjacent streets, waiting to say farewell once more to the dead man. These pilgrims moved slowly forward, orderly and reverently, went into the cathedral and, when they had bowed down to the coffin, left by other doors. Throughout the day, *panikhidy*, brief commemorative services, were continually recited by the prelates and clergy. Mgr Boris celebrated the midnight service, according to a special rite, with an exceptional emphasis and great spiritual fervour. The sight of the people kneeling, while every light in the cathedral was extinguished except the candles and the lamps before the icons; the sound of the soft, poignant chanting of the words – 'Behold the Bridegroom cometh in the middle of the night; blessed is that servant whom he shall find watching' – all this combined to produce an indelible impression. On the eve of his death, the bishop had summoned his companions and asked them to sing this chant at midnight. It is difficult to express the fervour of those days. . . . Finally, there came the day of the funeral which drew an innumerable crowd of the faithful. Although the Eucharist and the funeral service went on for hours on end, no one seemed to notice how long they were. Then, at last, our bishop made his final procession around his cathedral. Throughout the whole service, the clergy stood in four lines on each side of the coffin. When this was lifted on to the shoulders of the bearers to be carried out of the cathedral, there were such sounds of lamentation, it was as if the very walls were weeping.[27]

It need hardly be said that a display of devotion such as this would have been unthinkable a few years before, either in Stalin's day, or a few years later.

SELECTED PORTRAITS. It now remains for us to draw a little closer to some of these bishops who arouse such profound veneration on the part of the people. It is a veneration that is frequently independent of a bishop's personal qualities, and is addressed primarily to the objective grace of God with which he is endowed. It is difficult to imagine an episcopate of more mixed composition; it contains the oldest and the youngest bishops in the world, the learned and the uneducated, saints and great nobles, confessors of the faith and advocates of compromise at any cost. . . . I shall not dwell on the mediocrities, but try briefly to depict some of the great figures of the post-war episcopate, and those also whose life has been a long and painful witness to the faith; and lastly, some of their young successors, who are the future of the Church.

A GREAT ADMINISTRATOR. With Mgr Bartholomew, the Metropolitan of Siberia, the Metropolitan Gregory Chukov was one of the most striking figures of the episcopate in the transitional period when the Church called upon elderly married priests to fill up her depleted ranks.

Nicholas Chukov was born in 1870, the son of a peasant. He left college deliberately in order to attend lectures at the seminary and afterwards at the theological academy in Petersburg. In 1895 he was appointed Inspector of Parochial Schools in the province of Olonets. For fifteen years he travelled the length and breadth of this region, on horse and on foot, by sleigh, in sailing boats and steamships. He succeeded in doubling the number of schools, and in establishing 308 libraries including some in the remotest parts of provinces. He raised the standard of the teachers by organizing congresses, lectures and retreats for them. In reward for these productive labours he was appointed Rector of the Seminary of Petrozavodsk. Driven from this post at the Revolution, he became Rector of the Cathedral of Kazan and coadjutor to the Metropolitan Benjamin. All religious educational establishments had been closed. Thanks to his determination he managed to establish an institute of theology and became its rector. But in 1922 he was arrested with the Metropolitan Benjamin, and condemned to death. This penalty was, however, reduced to ten years imprisonment. On his release, in spite of every obstacle, he organized a new theological school, although this too succumbed in the persecutions of 1928–9. Meanwhile he found time to defend a thesis for the doctorial degree on Jewish Messianic ideas in the *Targum of Jonathan ben Uziel*. At this point in his official biography there is the customary omission: according to trustworthy sources, he spent the next ten years in 'retirement'. In the war, we find him at Saratov, a long way from Leningrad, a widower, having lost his wife and also three of his children during the siege of Leningrad. On 15th October 1942, at the age of seventy-two, he was consecrated Archbishop. In 1944 this man, who had formerly been condemned to death, was appointed to the see of Leningrad, with which was combined the administration of five dioceses. His main work – at the age of seventy-five – was the organization of a network of seminaries, and his greatest success was the foundation of the Leningrad Academy and Seminary. His personal integrity, in spite of a few conformist utterances, is beyond dispute. In ten years he made eight official visits abroad. The last of these, during which he took part in the canonization of the new saints of the Rumanian Church, proved fatal. He died soon after his return (5th November 1955). His grave became a place of pilgrimage.[28]

SURGEON, ARCHBISHOP; HOLDER OF THE STALIN PRIZE. The career of Mgr Luke Voino-Yasenetsky, Archbishop of Simferopol and the Crimea, who died on 11th June 1961 at the age of eighty-two, has points which remind one of Albert Schweitzer. Born in the Crimea in 1877, in a cultured family in easy circumstances, he at first took the fine arts for his higher studies, but the desire to alleviate human suffering soon impelled him to turn to medicine. I shall leave it to him to give his own account of his extraordinary career:

> I should not like you to think that I am boasting in what I am going to tell you. I assure you in all sincerity that I am not seeking my own glory, but the glory of the One who sent me. In the book of Tobias we read these important words: 'It is proper to keep the king's secret, but it is also proper to reveal and proclaim the works that God has done.'
>
> It is precisely about the great works that God has shown forth in my life that I want to talk to you. I know there are very many people who wonder how, after winning fame as

a scholar and as a great surgeon, I was able to give up science and surgery to become a preacher of the Gospel of Christ. But those who entertain such reflections make a great mistake, by thinking that science and religion cannot be reconciled. This is an entirely erroneous opinion: we learn from the history of science that even scientists of genius such as Galileo, Newton, Copernicus, Pasteur and our own great physiologist Pavlov, were deeply religious men. Among our own contemporary professors, I know that there are many who believe; they even ask my blessing. But we shall never manage to make those who reproach me for having become a priest and a bishop understand this. Let us leave them in peace.

I must, however, tell you that I myself find what God has made of me amazing and inconceivable. Yet, looking back on my past life, I can clearly see how, without my being aware of it, the Lord was, from my earliest youth, leading me to the priesthood, to which I had never given a thought, for surgery was my great love and I was devoted to it with my whole soul. This profession wholly satisfied the aspiration I had always had to serve the poor and the suffering, and to devote all my energy to alleviate their pain and supply their needs.

I am dumbfounded when I reflect on what happened to me sixty years ago. I was leaving college, and at the farewell ceremony I received from the president my bachelor's certificate enclosed in a copy of the New Testament. It had been my custom to read it regularly, but now I reread it from cover to cover. I noted whatever impressed me most. Nothing made a greater impact upon me than those words of Jesus Christ to his apostles at the sight of a field of ripe corn: 'The harvest is plentiful, but the labourers are few: pray therefore the Lord of the harvest that he will send labourers unto the harvest.'

These words thrilled me to the heart, and within myself I

cried: 'How is it, Lord, that there are so few labourers in your field?' And I have remembered these words all my life. Several years passed. For my thesis on local anaesthesia I was awarded the degree of doctor of medicine and also a prize of considerable value. I became a doctor in one of the provinces; I healed peasants and workmen and I found this deeply satisfying. After some years I wanted to write a book on the surgery of purulent wounds. When I had finished the introduction, I was suddenly struck by a strange and persistent idea: by the time this book is completed, I said to myself, it will bear the name of a bishop. But why? Who could it be? What bishop? Let me say again: I never had thought of the priesthood, nor of the dignity of being a bishop. And yet a few years later, this strange and vague idea became a reality. I had intended that my book – it became famous later – should appear in two parts. [It was, in fact, published in 1934 and is still the 'indispensable manual for every surgeon' – *The Greater Medical Encyclopaedia*, Vol. v, Moscow, 1958.] When I had completed the first part, I wrote on the cover: *Bishop Luke, A Study of the Surgery of Purulent Wounds*, because I was then a bishop. And I became one in a way that I had least expected, by an obvious call from God. At Tashkent, where I was then chief medical officer and superintendent of the municipal hospital, a diocesan assembly was being held; I took part in it and spoke at length and enthusiastically on a subject of great importance.

At the end of this meeting, Archbishop Innocent, taking me by the hand, led me along the path that surrounds the cathedral and spoke about the deep impression produced by my speech. Then he stopped abruptly, and looking straight at me, said: 'Doctor, you must become a priest.' Although this idea was far from being mine, I gladly accepted the call to the priesthood coming from an archbishop as a call from God, and without a moment's reflection I answered: 'All right, my lord, I will.' On the following Sunday I was ordained deacon, and a week later, priest. In 1921 I became one of the curates of the cathedral. Immediately I found considerable work as a preacher and I presided over theological debates. In discussions with the godless I won decisive victories.

Two years and four months later I became a bishop, and it was as a bishop that the Lord led me [Bishop Luke was deported] to a distant town, Yenisseysk. All the priests of this town, with its great number of churches, as well as those of Krasnoyarsk, the capital of the province, were adherents of the Living Church and represented a section of that innovating body. I was therefore obliged to celebrate the liturgy, in company with three other priests, in my flat. One day when I was about to enter the room and begin the service, I noticed an aged monk standing at the door. Seeing me, he was evidently petrified, and did not even greet me. And this is why. The Orthodox laity of Krasnoyarsk, unwilling to pray with the schismatic clergy, had chosen this monk and sent him to Minussinsk, south of Krasnoyarsk, to be ordained priest by the Orthodox bishop of the place. But some unknown impulse had driven him not south, but north, to Yenisseysk, where I was staying. He told me the reason for his startled amazement on seeing me. Ten years previously, at the time when I was living in central Russia, he had seen himself in a dream, being ordained priest by an archbishop whom he did not know, but had recognized when he saw me.

Thus ten years previously, while I was only a surgeon in the hospital at Pereslavl-Zalesk, I was already recognized by God as an archbishop. You will see, therefore, how, for ten years, the Lord was unfailingly leading me to the post of archbishop, at a time when the Church was in difficulties.[29]

In 1941, Mgr Luke, who was never authorized to return to his see of Tashkent, was made superintendent of the military hospital of Krasnoyarsk; the following year he was appointed archbishop of the same town. He was then transferred to Tambov and finally, in 1946, to the Crimea, and at the same time was awarded the Stalin Prize for his life's work as a surgeon. Those who remember his inflexible courage during the persecutions were saddened to see appeals for vengeance over his signature at the time of the Nuremberg trials[30] and articles advocating the Peace Movement that contained abuse of the 'Western imperialists'.[31] Had his character been distorted by his trials? But his great reputation as a pastor remained untarnished. His life was devoted to both the healing of bodies and the salvation of souls. As a preacher he was tireless and he was engaged in writing a treatise, *Spirit, Soul and Body*. In 1956 he became completely blind, but he continued to administer his diocese and was always immensely popular. An 'enormous' crowd attended his funeral.[32]

A COMMITTED MAN: THE METROPOLITAN NICHOLAS. Who has not heard of Mgr Nicholas, the Metropolitan of Krutitsy? This indefatigable preacher and demagogue travelled several times round the world in order to proclaim the virtues of the *pax Sovietica* and castigate the misdeeds of the imperialists. Applauded and even revered by some people, as another Chrysostom, he was disliked by others as a 'red bishop' and a 'Chekist in a cassock'. He was for long the living image of the ambiguous alliance between Church and State, until the day when that unnatural alliance was broken and he became the first victim of the new persecutions.

He had always shone. Boris Yarushevish (Father Nicholas in religion) was born in 1892 in the family of the Rector of the Cathedral of Kovno. Having finished his secular secondary studies, he came first in the entrance examination for the Petersburg Ecclesiastical Academy. After four years of serious and rewarding studies, he received the monastic habit in 1914 from the Metropolitan Anastasius, later head of the synodal Church of the Emigration. In 1917, aged twenty-five, he defended his thesis for the master's degree and became the youngest lecturer in the academy. In 1919 he was made head of one of the most renowned monasteries in Russia, the Laura of St Alexander-Nevsky. Finally, on 25th March 1922, shortly before the arrest of the Metropolitan Benjamin, the Archimandrite Nicholas was consecrated Bishop of Peterhof, and thus became one of the two vicars of the Metropolitan (the other being Bishop Alexis Simansky, the future Patriarch). He was barely thirty! Although he was not directly involved in the trial of Mgr Benjamin, he was almost immediately exiled to Oust-Sysolsk.[33] He returned to Leningrad about 1926 and distinguished himself in the conflict with the Josephites. The rest of his biography contains few incidents of importance. Until 1940 he remained Bishop of Peterhof and seems to have escaped all the purges. At any rate, just before the war, he was a member of the little group of bishops spared by the persecutions. He was then sent to White Russia where he was born, in order to reconcile the Churches of the eastern provinces of Poland, annexed by the USSR, with the Moscow Patriarchate. For the success of this mission he was promoted to the rank of Metropolitan. After a moment's hesitation when the war began, he entered wholeheartedly and with his customary enthusiasm into national and patriotic activity, which he led for twenty years until he was recalled. He was then given his first government medal, 'For the defence of Moscow'. In 1943–4 the entire publishing work of the Patriarchate was entrusted to him, and also the department of external relations. He was appointed Metropolitan of Krutitsy and became the second important dignitary in the Church and the Patriarch's chief adviser. The part he played in the government of the Church was decisive. In his political speeches he did not stop half-way, as the following example, taken from a thousand, will show:

American aggressors in Korea have covered themselves with everlasting shame. Their monstrous deeds awake feelings of horror in every right-thinking man, and bring a shudder to the mind and heart. These people who are aiming at the mastery of the world are possessed by the spirit of Hitler! The torture and extermination of the civil population of

Korea, the destruction of historical monuments, temples and homes – all this has not assuaged the thirst of these imitators of Hitler. . . .[34]

However, in his sermons – moral rather than theological – he carefully avoided any reference to politics. He was more personal and authoritarian, and although loaded with honours (his medals and his diplomas *honoris causa* were counted by dozens) in human relationships he was always affable and even gentle. His charm cannot be denied. People loved him for his preaching which was frank, vivid, direct, and appealed more to the soul than to the intellect. The significance of his political pleading was not realized and would have hardly astonished the faithful who for the most part were genuinely convinced of the aggressive nature of the Anglo-Americans, the only imperialists in the world.

Mgr Nicholas adapted himself admirably to the 'thaw' and allowed it to be understood that too much importance should not be attached to past invective. In 1955 he was awarded his second decoration from the Government, the order of the Red Star of Labour. He was the master-builder of the new policy of the Patriarchate and prepared the way for the entry of the Russian Church into the World Council of Churches.

His fall was as sudden as it was unexpected. He was dismissed from all his official posts and put under arrest. His death was something more than a mystery and it gave the people the opportunity of demonstrating their love for their pastor. The bishop died as a martyr, and his career symbolized the tragic position of the Church in the USSR.[35]

CONFESSORS OF THE FAITH. Apart from the very young and recently consecrated, there is not a single bishop of the present episcopate who has not been obliged to suffer for the faith between 1917 and 1944. Some, after their first ordeal, decided to follow the way of compromise. Others were broken: this seems to have been the case with Bishop Photius Tapiro (d. 1951), sent to Paris in 1945 in order to effect a reconciliation between the Churches of the emigration and Moscow. Physically exhausted – his body was fearfully marked by the ill-treatment he had undergone during his many years of imprisonment – he looked more like a ghost than a man of this world. To some, again, it was given to emerge triumphant from the inhuman ordeals they had to endure, as we read, for instance, in the biography of Mgr Manuel Lemeshevsky, Metropolitan of Kuibyshev from 1960 to 1965.

Born in 1885, in the family of a Petersburg engineer, the future bishop first studied law, and then, when he was twenty-two, entered holy orders against his parents' wishes.[36] He began his theological studies in 1916, but the Revolution prevented his completing them. During the Revolution he was a member of the confraternity of St Alexander Nevsky, whose principal aim was to alleviate the wretchedness of the people. Between 1921 and 1923 he taught the Old Testament in the theological courses in Petrograd. In 1923, he was consecrated Bishop of Luga and became vicar of the diocese of Petrograd, where, after the assassination of Mgr Benjamin and the deportation of Mgr Nicholas Yarushevich, most of the Churches went over to the Renewed Church. The radiance and eloquence of the young bishop worked wonders: one after another the schismatics did penance and the undecided returned to the Church. On 3rd February 1924, Mgr Manuel was arrested with his brother and was sentenced to three years exile in the Solovki Islands. He did not come back until the spring of 1928, and since he was not allowed to live in Leningrad, he was appointed Bishop of Serpukhov. Disapproving of the Josephites, but having no desire to become involved in the dispute, he asked to be relieved of his charge, and devoted his spare time to writing a treatise on the 'Jesus prayer'. On 1st May 1930 he was again arrested and deported for three years to the Tomsk region of Siberia. He was released in 1936, but was no longer allowed to take public services. In order to be usefully occupied, he compiled a dictionary of Soviet abbreviations. He seemed to his friends to have become an old man, broken by his ordeals; in reality, he was only half-way through his life's work.

In 1940 he was arrested once more and was sentenced to ten years hard labour in the region of Krasnoyarsk. He wrote from there: 'I work as a night-watchman. I have become quite old and here they call me grandfather. If you are not afraid of being connected with me, then send me a reply. I am only allowed to write letters very rarely. . . .' But this man, who was thought to have gone for ever, was soon to reappear: he was released in 1945 and appointed Bishop of Orenburg, where he displayed inexhaustible activity, summoning diocesan meetings, establishing churches in the new industrial cities, etc.[37] In 1948, a further ordeal. After taking part in a session of the Synod, he was arrested for the fourth time and sent to a concentration camp. This last exile was to be his longest; it lasted until the amnesty of 1955. Yet even now, after a total of almost twenty years in the camps, he did not give up the fight. He was appointed to the See of the Chuvak republic, and in 1960 to the more important See of Kuibyshev, and continues to serve the Church with indomitable energy. He is the author of a whole series of historical works; including a catalogue of all Russian bishops of the previous sixty years (1897–1957) and an essay on the schisms that affected the Church from 1917–44.[38] In 1965 Mgr Manuel resigned his office; whether it was on account of his advanced years or, once more, at the request of the civil authorities, is unknown.

Mgr Manuel is not an isolated example. In 1960 he was called to preside at the consecration of a bishop whose life had borne a strange resemblance to his own. Mgr Nicholas Feodosiev, born in 1893, and a priest since 1921, has spent the best part of his life in prison. In the sermon he preached at his consecration he gave an account, in veiled terms, of the misfortunes he had suffered, which is worthy of a place in an anthology of Orthodox spirituality.[39]

There are moments in a Christian's life when he is suddenly visited by God's grace, bringing him a unique joy, a joy not of this world, joy in the Holy Spirit (Rom. xiv. 17). When the Lord called me to the apostolic ministry, he graciously granted this joy even to me, a sinner.

Beloved archbishops, pastors and children of the Church, I beg you all, on this day of God so filled with meaning for me, to join me in this joy; to share the joy of the Lord's passover that is truly illuminating my heart. From where did it come, this sudden joy? Whence has it come to me? In the evening of my life, after thirty-nine years of the priesthood, I could think of little but the near approach of death. I could not help wondering how I was going to present myself before the Lord at his dread judgement seat. I begged God, sincerely and with all my heart, for a Christian end, and a good account to give before the redoubtable judgement of Christ.

And now, suddenly, by God's grace, I have been called to the episcopate. Am I worthy of it? It is true that I come from an ancient priestly family. For seven generations my ancestors, the sons following their fathers, have been priests. My father, who was a priest for more than fifty years, loved our Lord and Saviour with all his heart and soul, and this was shown throughout his pastoral labours. My mother never allowed herself to be left behind; wholeheartedly, she spent herself helping, in Christ's name, the poor, the unfortunate, the reprobate, the orphans and the widows. My parents, whose own faith was so deep, taught me to have faith in Christ. Knowing their prayers, I made up my mind to become a priest, to serve the Lord God in silence and humility, somewhere in a village, and to follow in the faith and good deeds of my parents. The Lord blessed me by giving me a happy Christian family, and I thought I should continue to live like this until the end of my days. . . .

But it pleased the Lord to dispose of my sinful self in a different way. At the beginning of my priesthood the Lord called my wife to eternal life, and he put me to the test by many sufferings, many privations, dangers and misfortunes. Days of bitterness came upon me, days when one had to carry the cross. During this period I twice suffered from terrible illnesses [a euphemism common in the USSR and suggested by the context as a whole, to indicate deportation]. The doctors gave me up as a hopeless case under sentence of death. . . . But in fact, 'although the Lord punished me again and again, he did not deliver my soul to death'.

Trembling, I asked the Lord: 'Why have you let me live? Who needs me?' Today I have the answer: 'You are needed for the apostolic ministry'.

During the time of my cruel ordeal my faith did not wither; it grew stronger. Throughout my trials I continued to cry out to the Lord: 'Thou art my support, O Lord, my strength, my God, my joy.' And now that the days of the divine ordeal are over, I have come to understand the depth of the words: 'Christ is my strength, my God and my Lord.' And so, strengthened in the faith, I accept my appointment as a bishop today. . . .

Beloved archbishops, pastors and children of Christ's Church! At this point of time, you are the representatives of the Church which Christ founded with his most pure blood. His words assure us that the gates of hell shall not prevail against this Church of God. It will last until time ends, for Christ said: 'I am with you always until the end of the world.'

May Christ grant me to serve him with a hallowed zeal; with all my heart, with all my soul and with all my mind, to love the spiritual children entrusted to me as myself, and, if needs be, give my life for them. Amen.

THE NEW RECRUITS. The re-established ecclesiastical academies trained the men who, from 1953 onwards, were successively called to replace the prelates of the older generation. This tendency to rely on younger men has become much more pronounced during the last five years. Here are a few sketches of the bishops upon whom the future of the Church depends.

A FORMER TEACHER OF MODERN LANGUAGES. Michael Chub, born in 1912, at Tsarkoe Selo, in a priest's family, was the first graduate of the new ecclesiastical academy to accede to the episcopate.[40] Before the war he studied at the Institute of Meteorology, and then at the Correspondence School of Languages. Beginning in 1932, although a priest's son, he taught foreign Western languages in various schools. After the war he went straight into the academy without first attending the seminary. In 1950, he was appointed Professor of the General History of the Church and was ordained priest, while remaining a celibate. He continued to teach in the academy and worked at a thesis on Methodius of Patara. When he was consecrated Bishop of Luga he thanked the Synod for granting him the opportunity to carry on his scholarly work. Between 1953 and 1958, he published in the *Review of the Patriarchate* a series of articles which illustrate his breadth of outlook and learning: two studies, based on the results of Western scholarship, of the Dead Sea Scrolls[41] (these were violently criticized in *Science and Religion*); a long article on Sylvanus, the *starets* (elder) of Mount Athos;[42] a description of the shroud in the Cathedral of Smolensk.[43]

He was appointed to the see of Smolensk, and came to be regarded as the hope of Russian theology. He was also a pioneer in the establishment of ecumenical relations. In 1956 he was one of the delegates at the meeting between Russian and Anglican theologians at Lambeth.[44] In August 1958, he took part in the first official conference with the leaders of the Ecumenical Movement in Utrecht.[45] On the fourteenth anniversary of the restoration of the Patriarchate he was appointed one of the principal speakers.[46] He carried out all these duties conscientiously, as an impartial theologian seeking an equitable solution. Was it this attitude that brought him into disgrace? Mgr Michael was one of the first victims of the Soviet Government's offensive against the Church. He was sharply attacked by the Press, although it could only produce the vaguest accusations against him, and in March 1959 he was moved to one of the most remote and least important dioceses in Russia, that of the republic of Udmurt.[47]

The *Review of the Patriarchate* no longer published his articles. His Ecumenical activity had no future. But in 1961 he was transferred to the See of Tambov, and in 1962 to the even more important See of Stavropol, and this may indicate some restoration to favour. In 1962, his name again appeared in the *Review of the Patriarchate*.[48]

At a meeting of bishops in July 1961, he made a speech, rich in patristic quotations, earnestly supporting the entry of the Russian Church into the World Council of Churches.[49] But he was not a member of the delegation to New Delhi, though this included four bishops, as well as Archbishop Nicodemus.

A FORMER ARCHAEOLOGIST. Sergius Golubtsev, born in 1906, son of a professor of Church history in the former Ecclesiastical Academy of Moscow, has spent his life at Zagorsk, under the shadow of the Monastery of the Trinity-St-Sergius. Between the two wars he specialized in archaeology and in works of restoration. Throughout the war he fought in the ranks of the Soviet army and afterwards, in 1947, began his theological studies. When these were completed he was appointed lecturer in Hebrew and the Old Testament. Being a monk he was charged, under his vow of obedience, with the entertainment of the foreign visitors. In 1955 he was consecrated bishop and was soon appointed to Novgorod because of the artistic value of the churches in that diocese. Mgr Sergius, a modest person who seldom gets himself talked about, is a living example of the continuity, preserved by family life, between the old and new theological schools.[50]

A FORMER DOCTOR. More of a public figure is Mgr Leonid Polykov, the present Bishop of Perm.[51] He was born in 1913, the son of a Petersburg doctor, and his first decision was to be a doctor himself. He specialized in chemistry and children's diseases. In the Finnish campaign and in the Second World War he served as a doctor, and was awarded three medals; the military medal, the medal for the defence of Leningrad and the war medal, and was decorated with the Order of the Fatherland War. In 1949 he was ordained priest and began his theological studies. Priest-doctors are numerous in the annals of the Russian clergy of the twentieth century. The extraordinary personality of Mgr Luke, bishop and doctor, has been described above. In March 1961, Mgr Nicholas Muravyev-Uralsky, a former throat, ear, and nose specialist, died[52] at Uglitch, after twenty years of deportation. Mgr Stephen Nikitin, Bishop of Mozhaisk from 1960–62, had specialized in neurology.[53] Mgr Antony Bloom, Bishop of Suroj, now living in London, is a graduate of the Faculty of Medicine of Paris.[54]

Father Leonid was given a lectureship in the Ecclesiastical Academy of Leningrad. In 1957 he was appointed Vice-Rector of the Moscow Academy where he taught homiletics. In 1958 he presented his thesis for the doctorate on the famous monk of Mount Athos, Paissy Velichkovsky. Some extracts from this work – enough to demonstrate its worth – were published in the *Review of the Patriarchate*.[55] In 1959 he was consecrated Bishop of Kursk, in 1963 he was appointed to Jaroslav and in the following year translated to the remote diocese of Perm.[56]

A FORMER GEOLOGIST. Mgr John Wendland was born in Petersburg in 1909. His family was Orthodox, but indifferent to the faith. He completed his secondary studies in 1925, and at the mining Institute in 1930. He practised as a geologist and petrologist for almost six years, but in 1938, realizing that 'on his own he was nothing, but with the Church he would obtain salvation', the young geologist became a monk. His official biography is silent on the course of his life between that date and 1946. It is more than probable, and his toothless mouth suggests it, that he experienced in his body the harsh realities of deportation – though he may simply have returned to his occupation in civil life. In 1946, we discover him far from his native town, as secretary to the Bishop of Tashkent. In 1953, he was appointed rector of the Cathedral of Saratov, and in 1956, he completed his theological studies by a correspondence course at the Leningrad Academy. In 1959, he was consecrated a bishop. He was first appointed representative of the Patriarch of Moscow in Damascus; then he became Exarch in North America. He is a member of the central committee of the World Council of Churches. At Ecumenical meetings he is noted for inopportune and partisan pronouncements of a political nature.[57]

A FORMER ARCHITECT. Seraphim (Vladimir) Nikitin, born in Petersburg in 1905 of working-class parents, completed his studies at the Architectural Institute in 1928. He spent the war at the front and returned with several decorations. He again took up his work as an architect and only decided to be ordained in 1951. In 1959 he obtained the diploma in theology from the Leningrad Academy whose courses he had followed by correspondence. On 14th June 1962,[58] he was consecrated Bishop of Kursk, in the land of St Seraphim whose name he took.

A FORMER ENGINEER. Nikon (Nicholas) Fomichev, like the three previous bishops, comes from Petersburg where he was born in 1910 to a working-class family. As a railway engineer he remained during the blockade in Leningrad where his professional knowledge was of use. His conduct during the siege earned him two medals. Shortly after victory he was ordained and in 1950 completed his higher theological studies. He followed his priestly calling in various dioceses, at Olonetz, Jitomir, and Velikie Luki. On 25th August he was consecrated Bishop of Luga and almost at once translated to the see of Riga.[59]

A MONK. Mgr Pimen Izvekov, consecrated bishop in 1957, at forty-seven, had experienced all the vicissitudes of clerical life in the years between 1929 and 1940. He was born in Moscow and became a monk in 1927 at seventeen. In 1932 he was ordained priest, but until 1935 – probably because he was prevented from carrying out his duties – he was simply a choir-master. There is a blank in his biographical data between 1935 and 1945. At this latter date he was appointed to the Cathedral of Murom. There is every reason to believe that, like most of his colleagues, he was deported or imprisoned. After the war, Father Pimen had a number of appointments. Steward of the Monastery of Odessa; Secretary to the Archbishop of Rostov-on-Don; Superior of the Monastery of Pskov, and afterwards of the Trinity-St-Sergius Monastery.

He was consecrated bishop and became the Vicar of the Metropolitan of Odessa, then he was moved to Dimitrov and given control of the affairs of the Patriarchate. But this did not terminate his career. After a short spell as Bishop of Tula, he was promoted to the position of Metropolitan of Leningrad, then in 1963 Metropolitan of Krutitsy. This appointment puts him in the line of succession to Patriarch Alexis. The *Review of the Patriarchate* has published some of his sermons; which are more remarkable for monastic piety than for theological depth.[60]

THOSE UNDER THIRTY-FIVE. The lightning career of Mgr Nicodemus Rotov who, at thirty-two, holds most of the key positions in the Church, has not failed to intrigue observers. He was born in 1929, in a village in the province of Ryazan (his family's social status is not known). He intended to become a schoolmaster. In 1947, however, when he was eighteen, he took the monk's habit in the diocese of Yaroslavl. When he was twenty he was ordained and became a village priest. But in the following year he was already dean of the region of Uglich. Two years later, on the staff of Yaroslavl Cathedral, he was acting as secretary to Archbishop Dimitri Gradussov, and in the meantime was taking correspondence courses at the Seminary and Academy of Leningrad. In 1955 he concluded his studies by submitting a thesis for his degree on the Russian mission to Jerusalem. It was probably this work that led to his membership of that mission in 1956. A year later he became its head. From Jerusalem he sent the *Review of the Patriarchate* some short articles on details of the life of the mission; modest contributions which illustrate his interest in liturgical details. This temporary connection with the mission equipped him with some knowledge of Greek and Arabic. In March 1959, Patriarch Alexis summoned him to Moscow and appointed him Administrator of the Patriarchal Chancellery. In June of that year he succeeded Metropolitan Nicholas as President of the Office for External Affairs, and at the close of 1960 he was consecrated bishop. In his sermon on that occasion he said: 'I should like to exclaim with God's holy prophet Jeremiah, when the Lord spoke to him and he was called to the prophetic ministry, "Ah! Lord God, I cannot speak, I am a child." And yet I also remember the answer to that cry; the Lord said: "Do not say, I am a child, but go to all those to whom I shall send you, and speak whatever I shall command you. Have no fear . . . for I am with you" (Jeremiah 1. 6–8). Great is the prophetic ministry, but the episcopal ministry is greater, for a bishop is the channel of the grace of the New Testament.'[61]

In spite of his youth Mgr Nicodemus was given additional responsibilities. He was appointed head of the editorial board of the *Review of the Patriarchate* and of *Theological Studies*; he became a permanent member of the Synod, Archbishop of Yaroslavl and in September 1963, at the age of thirty-four, Metropolitan of Leningrad.

Such an avalanche of honours and responsibilities descending upon the shoulders of a man so young and without any outstanding qualities, could not fail to arouse surprise and in some minds disquiet.

How are we to explain this staggering rise to power of so young a bishop when many other stars were passing into oblivion? Is his ulterior motive the Church's welfare? Is he the victim of a policy of compromise with the State? Is he wildly ambitious? 'The Church alone is my pillar and foundation, my protector and my refuge.' Were these words which he spoke at his consecration merely farcical, did they express what he really felt, or were they the despairing cry of a man committed to duplicity? Questions which as yet can be given no final answer.

THE SON OF A PRIEST. The episcopal consecration of a young priest of thirty-two by an archbishop of the same age as officiant, is surely unique in the modern world. Alexis Ridiger, consecrated on 3rd September 1961, Bishop of Tallin by Mgr Nicodemus, was born in 1929 at Tallin. His father, a member of the Christian Action of Russian students, became a priest in 1940. The young Ridiger had acted as a cantor from his boyhood, and entered the Leningrad Seminary as soon as he had reached the regulation age of eighteen. During his first year at the academy, in 1950, he was ordained priest. He married the daughter of the Archbishop of Tallin, but the marriage was later annulled by the Patriarch on the grounds of non-consummation. He became the priest of the church of a small Esthonian town close to Leningrad, and in 1953 completed his studies with a degree thesis on the dogmatic teaching of Philaret of Moscow. His progress to the episcopal bench began with his appointment as a priest in the Cathedral of Tartu in 1957; in 1958 he became archpriest; and in 1959 dean of the district of Tartu. Some weeks after his appointment as bishop Mgr Alexis was called to be a member of the pan-Orthodox conference in Rhodes. He became Mgr Nicodemus's coadjutor in the department of foreign affairs, and as such took part in all the ecumenical meetings. As a member of the Central Committee of the World Council of Churches he entirely submerges his own personality in that of his superior, Mgr Nicodemus. While his meteoric career has caused concern among some Russian Christians abroad, the impression he has made has varied between the belief that he is a deeply religious man and that he is much too young for the office he holds.[62]

A WORKMAN'S SON. Mgr Philaret Denissenko was also born in 1929, a year decidedly productive of young bishops. His family was an ordinary mining family in the region of the River Donets. In his eighteenth year he entered the Seminary of Odessa and continued his studies at the Moscow Academy. Meanwhile, in 1960 he became a monk. His thesis for his degree dealt with a dogmatic subject: the doctrine of redemption in the Fathers of the fourth century. In 1952 he began to teach the Old and New Testaments in the Moscow Seminary and Academy. In 1956 he was appointed vice-rector of the seminary in Saratov, and later of Kiev. When the latter was closed he became the head of the chancellery of the Exarchate of the Ukraine. In May 1961 he was sent to the Russian colony in Alexandria and, at the request of Mgr Nicodemus, he undertook a long journey into north Africa from west to east. Previously he had travelled twice to England, and he formed part of the Patriarch Alexis's suite in his journey through the Middle East. In January 1962 he was consecrated Coadjutor Bishop of Luga, shortly afterwards he was appointed Bishop of Vienne,[63] in 1964 rector of the Moscow theological schools and in 1966 Exarch of the Ukraine.

A PEASANT'S SON, Leo Gudimov was also born in the Ukraine, but his family were peasants from the region of Sumy. He is a year older than Mgr Philaret. At the age of fourteen, in 1942, during the German occupation, he was accepted as a novice in 'the desert' of Glinsk, one of the most austere monasteries in Russia. There he was ordained deacon in 1948 and appointed to the Cathedral of Ismail. He was ordained priest in 1951. Between 1953 and 1957 he studied theology at the ecclesiastical Academy of Moscow. He was appointed professor in the Seminary of Odessa and became its rector after a period as Superior of the Monastery of the Assumption in that place. On 21st December 1961, he was consecrated as Coadjutor Bishop of Podolsk and sent to Damascus to represent the Moscow Patriarchate.[64] In 1964 he returned to Russia.

As these examples show, 'the bishops of the sixties', as the Soviet press calls them, receive a training similar to that of the traditional type of bishop in the pre-revolutionary era, a brief monastic formation, a theological degree, a short period as rector or vice-rector of a seminary, or as the superior of a monastery. The youngest bishops seem destined to deal with foreign affairs and to represent the Church abroad. This phenomenon may be explained in two ways: either these young bishops are in the confidence of the Government, or else the Church considers that they lack sufficient experience to be put at once at the head of a diocese. In the USSR they are regarded with a certain amount of suspicion because their promotion occurred during the time of persecution. But there is justification for believing that by these consecrations the Church primarily intends to guarantee her future.

2. *The lower clergy*

Our information about the lower clergy is more fragmentary; nothing like a clear picture emerges. Officially, the number of officiating priests is estimated at 30,000. This is the figure given by the ecclesiastical authorities in 1945 and again in 1961, as though there had been no change, which is hardly likely. If, for example, we look at the diocese of Kazan, we find that in 1950 it was provided with priests who were nearly all very old. Logically, this would have meant an acute shortage in the immediate future. And in fact we learn from the same source that there was already such a shortage in the neighbouring dioceses.[65] The new theological schools could not have released their first graduates before 1949, and even then their numbers were – and remained – derisory in view of the ever-growing needs. In 1957, the Dean of the Kherson region (at a time when the seminaries were working to capacity) wrote that 'since the Seminary of Odessa could not fill the ranks, the clergy must be recruited from other sources, for example, from the *psalomshchiki*', and given a practical preparation. A *psalomshchik* is a man who reads aloud the parts of the service which are not reserved for priests or deacons, and, when necessary, takes the place of the choir. He has a good deal to do, and to do it well he must have a real liking for religious services and even some liturgical knowledge.[66] Although priests recruited from this source will have proved their attachment to the Church, their moral probity, and their ability to conduct public worship, they find themselves in difficulties when it comes to preaching, or explaining the content of the faith to the people, and are ill prepared for spiritual direction. It seems, however, that most of the rural clergy were previously *psalomshchiki*.

The original priestly caste was shattered by the persecutions. Few survived. Many of them, prohibited by the civil authorities from carrying out their duties, or anxious not to be exiled, have had to give up their priestly work for several years (some from 1928 to 1944). When, after the war, they returned to their priestly work, they found it difficult to resume their task after so long an interruption. In 1949, Mgr Gregory Chukov, the Metropolitan of Leningrad even said: 'The whip is indispensable when dealing with the undisciplined clerical caste'.[67]

It seems that some of the former clergy, especially in the large towns, 'had fallen for the lures of the world and lost their spiritual authority over their flock'.[68] One example was Mgr Gregory's own secretary, who after a series of escapades had to leave the ranks of the clergy and return to his former occupation as a bank clerk.[69]

The fact is that although the Orthodox clergy are allowed to marry, heavy demands are made upon them. Speaking to the seminarists in 1949, Patriarch Alexis said:

A pastor has two sacred duties: prayer and the spirit of sacrifice, which are like two wings which raise him to the heavenly realm. It is with prayers that he accompanies all the sacred rites he performs in Church: it is by prayer that he prepares himself at home for the celebration of divine service. The more profound and fervent that private prayer, the more faithful will be his fulfilment of the Church's precepts, and the more fruitful the worship which he celebrates. . . .

Sacrifice is a priest's life-long companion. A pastor must give himself completely to his exalted task, he must observe the rules and regulations of holy Church with scrupulous fidelity; he must strictly keep the fasts prescribed by the Church and thereby set an example to his flock. [In the Orthodox Church fasting is severe. For more than half the year the Church prescribes complete abstinence from meat, fish, eggs and all milk products.] It is through sacrifice that a pastor's long journey must be hallowed. He must learn to live not for himself, nor even for his family, but for his flock. You will say that such a renunciation of the world, such an addiction to sacrifice, is almost monastic. And it is true that the priesthood and monasticism are twins; their paths coincide; both demand self-detachment and unending self-sacrifice. Holy Church allows a priest to have a family, but simply in order that amid his multifarious activities as a pastor he may have a stay and a support. He comes home from Church and is greeted by the tranquil life of his family and its concern for him. If he can raise his family to the peaks of the spiritual life and make his home the nucleus of the Church, then he may think himself blessed. But woe to the priest who turns to the world for distractions and who draws his family in the same direction; he will soon experience the danger of such entanglements.[70]

It is not so much the bishops but the laity who keep an eye on the discipline and spiritual integrity of their pastors:

The Russian Orthodox laity have a keen sense and a sound appreciation of what makes a true pastor. They are not deceived or led into error by the precious stones shining on mitres and crucifixes of many of the priests of today; they want to see their pastors clothed with the shining virtues of the soul; they want to see in their pastor a man of a high

spiritual value. Russian people long to see in their pastor a
father, lovingly concerned with the needs of his flock. They
come to their priests in order to hear the word of salvation:
how will his soul be saved, how must a man live if he is
to attract the Lord's grace, how is he to overcome life's
difficulties, come to an end of his afflictions, of his weaknesses, his evils, how can he keep himself from falling into
sin?

The laity will forgive many a pastor some degree of dryness,
or a kind of roughness, to which some characters are liable;
but what the Russian Orthodox man will never forgive is a
pastor without belief, or one who carries out his pastoral
ministry without piety, in a negligent, superficial and external
manner. They know quickly enough whether a pastor is
praying when he recites a prayer, or giving merely formal
utterance to what is in the books.

If nevertheless they receive sacraments and benedictions
from a pastor they cannot respect, this only shows the
humility of our Russian people, how deep and loyal is their
sense of the grace of priesthood. They understand, but at
the same time they suffer.[71]

We can quote a concrete example of this attitude of the people
towards their pastors: at Kherson, Father B., a priest previously
living in Paris who had come back to the USSR, was obliged
to give up frequenting the cinema despite his great desire to do
so, because his parishioners looked askance at such worldliness
on the part of a priest.[72]

The theological schools have provided young and comparatively educated ministers. Their numbers are, of course, limited;
two to three thousand at the most.[73] These priests, trained and
educated entirely in a Soviet world, are opening a new chapter
in the annals of the Russian clergy. Any judgement about their
quality is necessarily premature. In the descriptions given by such
Soviet writers as V. Tendryakov, S. Aleshin, C. Fedin, the young
priest appears as a well-fed personage, lacking spontaneity,

excessively cautious, accustomed to deceit, always on the defensive. But some chance encounters with these priests lead one to believe that this account is, to say the least of it, biased. Among the young clergy there is no lack of men who are wholeheartedly devoted to their mission, men of prayer, filled with the spirit of sacrifice. At any rate, after having known comfort, these priests seem to come through the ordeal of persecution victoriously. Out of a hundred recent apostasies, one can count only five from the ranks of the new recruits.[74] On the other hand, it is from their ranks that came for the first time for forty years the Solovki note – a bold protest against the harassment of the Russian Church.[75]

CHAPTER IX

THE PEOPLE OF GOD

The Russian people are Christian, not only on account of the orthodoxy of their beliefs, but also because of something even more inward than belief. They are Christian because of their capacity for renunciation and sacrifice which is like the basic structure of their moral nature.

F. Tiuchev

IN 1943, when the Communist Government agreed to a settlement with the Church, it did so because it had to reckon with 'the people of God', with that very large proportion of the Soviet population for whom religious interests remained of primary importance, and who still, when they had been plunged into darkness, lived in the hope of seeing 'the great light' shine forth again. Earlier in this book we have seen the people of God at work during the war, reconstructing their churches from nothing, maintaining public worship, welcoming the missionary priests wholeheartedly and assisting them in their pastoral ministry.

Let us now see what this people of God amounts to in Russia today, forty-five years after the Revolution, twenty years after the war, from the threefold point of view of statistics, sociology, and as a religious phenomenon: their numerical importance, their geographical and social distribution, and how they exhibit and express their religious faith.

Their numerical importance

It is useless to search in Soviet publications for indications of the number of Orthodox Christians in the USSR. When the relevant departments of the Patriarchate are asked about this, they always reply that the parishes no longer keep registers of births, marriages and deaths, which would be the only means of estimating the number of believers. The anti-religious articles say no more than that religious belief still has an 'important minority' of the population in its grip. This lack of information, aided and approved of by the authorities, extends also to many other aspects of the moral character of the country. Soviet Russia is a country ignorant about itself. Fairly definite economic and demographic statistics have been available for some years, although even these must be accepted with caution.[1] But upon the extent of social evils such as alcoholism, divorce, crime, accidents on the roads or at work, the silence is complete. The reason for this deliberate secrecy is obvious: in a communist society, social evils are survivals from the past which are disappearing. Any detailed and numerical study of such evils might prove dangerously compromising to the Soviet system, for it would probably show that these evils are no less widespread in the USSR – where, theoretically, they should not exist – than in capitalist countries which are presumed to create them.

Religion is one of these social evils, one of these survivals from capitalism whose days are numbered. The watchword therefore, observed equally in the *Review of the Patriarchate* and in the anti-religious press, is to avoid so far as possible the publication of any definite statistics of the practising members of the Orthodox Church. To obtain some idea of the real number of these members, it is necessary to approach the problem in a roundabout way and form estimates that can only be roughly approximate.[2]

The population of Orthodox origin must amount to about one hundred and sixty millions. Nearly two-thirds of this theoretical number may definitely be said to be baptized, that is, there are about one hundred million baptized persons. Until 1928, almost all the newly born continued to receive baptism; atheism had not yet penetrated the masses and the Church was still a physically present reality. From this it follows that the vast mass of Soviet citizens over thirty-five belong, at least nominally, to the Church. But the generation born between 1928 and 1944 experienced the worst effects of the physical annihilation of the Church, and it is among young people from twenty-eight to thirty-five that the fewest baptized persons are to be found. Even so, those who were in the occupied territories received baptism during the war. A Soviet sociologist, A. Zalesky, went so far as to say that under the German occupation the people were made to baptize children who were ten to fifteen years old.[3] After 1941 in the occupied territories, and in 1945 throughout Russia, baptism was administered on a massive scale, especially to the newly born. Contrary to what might have been expected, it was not only believing parents who wanted their children baptized, but also doubters and even unbelievers. A study in religious sociology, significant, but of course without numerical details, was carried out in 1955 among a group of Kolkhoz in White Russia, in a marshy region difficult to approach and under the control of partisans during the war (the Soviet rural area of Zagalie in the district of Liuban). This showed that almost all the young children were baptized. And yet the nearest church open for worship was eighteen miles away; and the region seemed to have no transport apart from the cars for the official use of the Kolkhoz. A priest visited these villages only rarely, two or three times a year, and the villagers do not seem to have been very convinced believers. Parents waited sometimes for several months, sometimes for several years, before having their children baptized, but in the end they did so. A. Zalesky, the author of this study, mentions as a fact deserving attention that a child who had been born in the spring was not baptized by the end of the summer. It would appear that he had not come across any child of more than four years who was not baptized, and those who had not been were, according to their parents' statements, going to be.[4] Another inquiry, less detailed, conducted in the regions of Kostroma and Gorky in 1960 led to the same results: the great majority of children were baptized.[5] At Premysl, in the west of the Ukraine, eight out of ten children were baptized.[6] In the towns the position is less favourable to the Church. At Sverdlovsk, for example, in 1953, only thirty per cent of the children had received baptism. In Moscow the percentage was as high as fifty.[7] The apostate priest, A. Ossipov, calculated that 'in some regions baptisms were in the neighbourhood of fifty to sixty per cent.'[8] The persecutions may have increased the rate of baptisms. The *Journal of the Young Communists* protested that at Vladimir there were more baptisms in 1961 than in 1960. This might indicate that parents were afraid that in the near future it might be impossible to have their children baptized at all.[9]

Today, with fluctuations between one hundred per cent in some rural areas and thirty to fifty per cent in the towns, the average rate of baptisms must approach seventy per cent. Even if this hypothesis is too optimistic, it still remains a fact that the majority of Soviet children continue to be baptized. This paradox may be explained in several ways. According to A. Zalesky, the peasants cannot give up baptism because they consider that although their children may be able to solve all the religious problems later for themselves, it is incumbent on the parents to make sure they are baptized, so that they may not draw down their children's reproaches upon themselves in the future. This argument has a curious resemblance to that used by unbelievers and opponents of dogma in the West. But national tradition also plays its part. A letter from a Ukrainian workman contains the complaint that his workmates urge him to have his child baptized 'because a true Russian can only be an Orthodox Christian'.[10] This is a peculiarly Russian point of view; it illustrates, for example, the extent to which, even in our time, nationality and religion are combined in the spirit of the people.

Finally, the Soviet press lays great stress on the influence of the grandmother, who is the financial and moral support of young households. The *Komsomolskaia Pravda*, which periodically deplores the fact that young communists agree to have their children baptized, describes the following dilemma: 'To have the child baptized involves the risk of social embarrassment. But it may be kept secret and there will be no argument. Supposing, however, that in the end it becomes known, I shall certainly be blamed, but not killed. And besides, I could always say that it was my mother-in-law's decision. . . . No baptism, and one's mother-in-law is upset. She will not actually curse us, but her wrath will be long lasting. Many wrangles ahead, and inconveniences also. We shall no longer be able to send the kid to the country, and then my wife will side with her mother – a fresh source of upset.'[11]

Whatever the explanation may be, the vitality of baptism is an undoubted fact. Great numbers are baptized, but how many of them continue to be loyal to the Church? This question is even more difficult to answer, for loyalty to the Church largely depends upon the Church's actual existence in society, on her material presence. It seems reasonable therefore, to calculate the approximate number of believers by taking into account the number of churches that were open for worship (before 1959).

Estimates as to the number of such churches have varied. A. Sergeenko reported to Moscow that the Patriarchate included 25,000 churches and 3,500 chapels.[12] In 1954, Archbishop Hermogenes Kojine reduced this number to 22,000.[13] The report sent to the World Council of Churches in 1960, speaks only of 20,000 churches.[14]

It is also known that the churches were full to bursting point, not only on feastdays, but on Sundays also. The German pastor Herbert Mochalsky, who visited the USSR in 1954, estimated that on Sundays the small churches had congregations of 2,000–3,000, while cathedrals or large churches were filled with crowds numbering 5,000–7,000.[15] These impressions have been corroborated by reports from various sources. In White Russia, the anti-religious propagandists were dismayed to observe the Cathedral of Minsk and regional churches filled to overflowing.[16] The Easter liturgy in the Cathedral of Alma-Ata (Kazakhstan) in 1950 was attended, according to the most modest estimates, by more than 20,000 people.[17]. When the bishop came to the village church of Roujany in the diocese of Zhitomir, 3,000 peasants gathered to meet him.[18] And it can be stated, without fear of mistake, that every church open for worship incorporated, on an average, a community of 2,000. If we multiply the number of churches open for worship before 1960 – say, 20,000 – by the probable number of believers attached to each church, we reach the minimum, but impressive figure of forty million practising Orthodox Christians, or twenty-five per cent of the population that is Orthodox in origin, and more than a third of those baptized.[19] This number is a theoretical minimum below which it would not be reasonable to go. Mgr Nicholas of Krutitsy considered, not without probability, that the number of believers amounted to fifty millions,[20] while Mgr Antony of Suroj gives thirty to thirty-five millions of believers who are present at worship.

The geographical distribution of the Church

These forty to fifty million practising Orthodox Christians are very unequally distributed. In the USSR the Church's material presence is not the result of a corporate and preconceived plan; it is the result either of historical circumstances (the annexation of territories in the West, the German occupation) or of local conditions (churches miraculously left open, or spared from revolutionary vandalism; or of the exceptionally successful activity of a bishop or a group of parishioners). The distribution of churches open for worship varies according to the different regions and towns. Generally speaking, it may be said that as one moves from the south-west towards the north-east and east, the Church's presence becomes less and less observable. It is weakest in the large industrial cities, the mushroom towns, the recently colonized regions, that is, wherever Soviet Russia has created a new society. It would appear that the one region where the Church has failed to establish herself at all is the province of

Kaliningrad (the former East Prussia). This western outpost of the USSR is populated by 60,000 Ukrainian and Bielgorod peasants who have no place of worship at all. If they are to fulfil their religious duties they must travel to Kaunas in Lithuania, a distance of 110 miles, and even there only two churches are functioning. On the other hand, the central and southern border-lands conquered from Poland, Czechoslovakia and Rumania, Orthodox by tradition, are those in which the number of churches, until the recent persecutions, was as great as that of a normal Christian country. The frontier town of Ismail (Transnistria), with less than 50,000 people, had five churches.[21] Moldavia had fourteen monasteries,[22] and calvaries are landmarks along its roads. The diocese of Lvov-Ternopol (with 3,192,000 people) had 1,800 churches; that of Vinnitza 700; the province of Kherson 97.[23] The Ukraine could be regarded as the great religious reservoir: within its own borders it had 8,500 churches served by 6,800 priests, for its population of 40,600,000; about 40 monasteries out of 67, and three seminaries out of eight. This meant that its parishes amounted to one for every 5,000 people. Its large cities were in a definitely better position than those of the east: Kiev, with its million inhabitants, had 22 churches and five monasteries, that is, approximately one church for every 40,000 inhabitants. This proportion was even higher in Odessa (22 churches for 607,000 inhabitants; that is, one for every 30,000 inhabitants); Lvov (22 churches for 387,000 inhabitants, that is, one for every 20,000 inhabitants).[24] Only Kharkov seems to have been an exception: it had only three churches for 900,000 people.

White Russia, vast (about 80,000 square miles) but not so thickly populated because little industrialized, also occupied a favourable position from a religious point of view: before 1959 it had 700 churches for a population of 8 millions, that is, one for every 12,000 people. In the Baltic countries also, in which the Orthodox are everywhere in a minority, there was no shortage of churches: the diocese of Tallin (Esthonia) had 132 parishes for 213,000

Orthodox Christians, that is, one church for every 2,000 inhabitants.[25]

There is insufficient information for a definite geographical map of the material establishment of the Church in Russia proper. There can be no doubt that the regions which experienced the German occupation, even if only for a short while, were able to restore a network of churches more numerous than in the other regions. In 1954,[26] the diocese of Kuban had 230 churches, whereas in 1947, that of Orenburg had only 35.[27] Even if we allow that additional churches may have been reopened since 1947, the disproportion remains flagrant.

From an analysis of the rare reports of diocesan visitations, and by relating their data to the map, one gains the general impression that in the rural districts there must have been a church open every 16 to 26 miles.[28]

We are better informed about the urban areas and for some of them it has been possible to discover the exact number of churches. In them also the material establishment of the Church varies and depends on local factors. Moscow, for example, the capital and a useful example, only has 38 churches open for worship for its some five million inhabitants (not all of whom are Orthodox), that is, one parish for every 125,000 people.[29] These churches differ in the numbers they can hold, and it is not surprising that they are overcrowded. Their distribution is also far from uniform. There are none at all in the centre, while the north-eastern neighbourhoods are well equipped.[30] The district of Kuibyshev which incorporates the neighbourhoods of Sokolniki, Cherkizovo and Preobrajenskoe, has 10 'religious associations' for 300,000 people, a proportion comparable to that of Paris, and which, seemingly, makes the progress of atheism difficult. In the new southern neighbourhoods, however, there are none, and their people have to fall back on the little Church of the Trinity, on the heights of Lenin, which now delivers more baptisms than any other Moscow church.[31] Before 1960, there were 14 churches in Leningrad, that is, one for every 160,000 inhabitants. It was here, in 1957, that the Church gained one of her great victories: the restoration for worship of the huge Cathedral of the Trinity, which can hold 10,000 people.

The visible presence of the Church is weak and practically non-existent in the great industrial cities of the central and eastern regions of Russia and Siberia, especially in those which owe their phenomenal extension to the war. Perhaps the most striking example is that of Yaroslavl which has 407,000 inhabitants and only one Orthodox church. Five cities with more than 500,000 people have only two churches: Kuibyshev (760,000); Novosibirsk (131,000); Sverdlovsk (707,000); Cheliabinsk (612,000); Kazan (565,000). Voronej with 400,000 people, has three churches. Towns of medium importance are better off: at Yjevsk (252,000) there are two churches; at Orsk (157,000) three; at Michurinsk (70,000) two. The 276,000 inhabitants of Astrakhan, at the mouth of the Volga, have four churches in the town and two in its immediate neighbourhood, that is, one church for every 50,000 people, a reasonable proportion in comparison with those in the cities of central Russia. In Siberia, the large towns have two or three churches each, but the rural areas appear to be pretty barren. The dioceses are immense. That of Yrkutsk, for example, extends to Yakutie in the north and to Vladivostok in the east, that is, it covers more than 3,500,000 square miles.

The Church is not absent from the Mohammedan Republics of Central Asia where the Russian minorities are important and Ukrainian colonists and exiles from all parts are neighbours. Kazakhstan, where Russians are even in the majority, had for its head, from 1945–55, the Metropolitan Nicholas Mogilevsky, an aged bishop of great ability, who combined personal holiness with remarkable organizing power and succeeded in restoring a flourishing religious life. The capital, Alma-Ata, has three churches for 430,000 inhabitants, only half of whom are Orthodox by birth. The town of Chimkent also has three, although its population is only 130,000. The vast diocese which incorporates the four Mohammedan Republics, Turkmenia, Uzbekistan,

Kirghizia and Tadjikistan, and thus extends from the Caspian Sea to China, has about seventy churches mainly in urban areas where the Russian population amounts to fifty per cent. This seems to be the diocese in which the greatest number of new churches has been built: at Frunze, for example, in 1944; at Samarkand, in 1946; at Tokmak, in 1956. The Cathedral of Tachkent was entirely rebuilt and enlarged. In 1957 a great church was built at Achkabad to replace the one destroyed in an earthquake in 1948. One of the last churches to be opened for worship, before the resumption of persecution, was that of Tiup, a small rural district of Kirghiziz.[32]

Sociology

All observers agree that most of those who fill the churches are women. Estimates naturally vary when it comes to settling percentages. It seems that the approximate figure can be settled at seventy to eighty per cent according to the different regions and parishes.

This predominance of the feminine element is not exclusive to the USSR – it is a universal phenomenon. Woman, less intellectual than man, more attentive to the heart than to the mind, is 'naturally' religious. This statement is particularly true of Russia. In the nineteenth century, for example, women were those who, faced by the apostasy of the intelligentsia, upheld and proclaimed the faith. Pushkin contrasts the mocking scepticism of Onegin with the deep religious sense of Tatiana. Kireevsky, the Slavophil, a disciple of Shelling, was introduced to the Fathers of the Church by his wife Natalia. The wife of the citizen-poet, Nakrassov, was converted to the Baptists. Nearer to our own day, the wife of the famous physiologist, Pavlov, was well known for her devotion to the Church; in 1947 she well deserved the solemn funeral accorded to her. It is symptomatic that in the anti-religious review, *Science and Religion*, there are practically no women contributors. In Soviet Russia, women cannot be reckoned as the atheists of the future. But there are also demographic and sociological reasons which must not be forgotten in considering this question of the predominance of women in worship. As the combined result of the war and the purges, there has been a significant excess of women over men in the USSR: according to the census of 1959 there were 94,000,000 men and 114,800,000 women.[33] And this disproportion is borne precisely by that part of the population which is over thirty-two, that is, those who can be seen in the churches. Theoretically, men and women are equal in the USSR but, in practice, women occupy subordinate positions. There are indeed many women doctors (seventy per cent of the whole medical profession) and also women teachers, but in the bureaucratic hierarchy they are limited to the lower positions. So, having less to lose, a woman who attends church is risking less than her husband.

Observers also agree that for the most part believers are well on in years. This, of course, is bound to be a subjective impression, not easily expressed in numbers. Soviet women, forced to take part in the harshest form of work, their health impaired by a monotonous and often illbalanced diet, age more quickly than women in the West. Draped in her head-scarf, a Soviet woman, after thirty, ceases to be of identifiable age.[34] It is also true that this predominance of older people in the churches is another universal phenomenon. G. le Bras has shown, with the help of statistics, that in the churches of France, young women disappear, but come back at about forty, when their children have grown up and when family life is less absorbing. But in the USSR where this phenomenon is definitely more pronounced, it is largely due to ideological and social pressures, not to mention that of the police. No member of the Soviet armed forces (numbering more than three million), no member of the komsomol or of the Party (more than 25 million), no student, no teacher, not even a man or woman holding any position of the least responsibility, can attend church without incurring the most grievous consequences (dismissal, loss of employment, etc.). In these circumstances it is hardly surprising that the main body of church worshippers should be composed of those who have nothing to lose, that is, as the *Teachers' Gazette* informs us, of the retired, housewives and the sick. In the USSR the people of God are mainly recruited from the aged, the 'simple', and the afflicted.

These remarks refer, of course, only to the majority. All the same, there would seem to be something like twenty to thirty per cent of men who are members of the parishes. According to L. Ilichev, thirty per cent of believers are under forty. In the churches the proportion of young people is rarely more than ten per cent. Until the recent measures came into force children were more numerous: 'On Sundays and feastdays we have observed as many as a hundred children of primary school age attending church at Chernigov'.[35] In Leningrad at St Vladimir's Cathedral in 1961 there was a group of little girls all of whom went to Communion, at a weekday liturgy.[36]

A people still attached to their traditions

Russian religion finds expression among the ordinary people in different ways. As in the countries of the West, there is traditional religion that confines itself to the observance of the major festivals and religious customs, that have been more or less emptied of their essential meaning. And there is personal religion, expressed in prayer and active charity, which finds its full expression in receiving the sacraments.

The first type of religion is still widespread, especially in the countryside (fifty-two per cent of the population) as we have seen in connection with baptism. The vast majority of peasants continue to show their loyalty to the ancient traditions. This seems a paradox, but it can easily be understood. To a Soviet peasant, Communism in the form introduced by Stalin, has been an essentially destructive force. Collectivization (1928–33) meant not only millions of victims,[37] but also the destruction of the peasants' age-old way of life. It completely deprived work on the land of personal interest and aesthetic attraction. The peasant's creative work was replaced by the obligatory enforcement of theoretical and inhuman rules. In spite of some degree of mechanization in agriculture and of the more or less complete elimination of illiteracy, the Soviet countryside, in both its material and cultural aspects, has receded not only from what it ought to be, but also from what it was in 1928, and even in 1914.[38] These gloomy estimates of peasant life have not been invented by the author: they are the inevitable conclusion from the permanent state of agricultural crisis. Soviet writers, taking advantage of the slackening of the censorship, have lifted the veil concealing what peasant life is really like in Russia today. Efim Doroche, for example, says that they live 'in bleak misery without hope'.[39] Material and spiritual wretchedness go hand in hand. Men abandon the countryside, and work in the fields shows the same proportion of women as in the churches.[40] Communism has contributed practically nothing to the culture and traditions of the peasants. This is the reason why the peasant has continued to be attached to the ancient customs. Members of the kolkhoz of Zagaliea have, as we noted above, a very loose attachment to the Church, and yet every one of its homes has its icons, for, they say, 'this is the custom'. These icons are sometimes hidden by pictures or a wireless set to avoid observation by the authorities, but the fact of their hidden presence is even more significant. Chombart de Lauwe who visited some kolkhoz in the Moscow region, reports that in all the izbas he entered, he saw icons 'with the little oil lamp whose flame burnt impressively'.[41] In the Province of Riazan 'there is no rural homestead without its icon, and often there are several of them'.[42]

Both believers and unbelievers in the countryside, celebrate with holidays and drinking parties, not only the great festivals of the years, but also the patronal festivals of the different parishes of the district, and, what is still more astonishing, even when there have been no churches open in these parishes for several years.[43] The Soviet papers are always complaining about the absenteeism of the peasants on feastdays. In the Leningrad district the peasants keep as many as seventy-two festivals a year; in that of Gorky they celebrate sixty-six patronal festivals and observe them as holidays. In 1959, in the Province of Kostroma, the villagers of Yakovleskoe (in the Boniesk district) spent from 2nd to 6th August in the village of Ivanichevo to celebrate its feast of St Elijah, and then from 6th August the villagers of Ivanichevo paid a return visit to Yakovleskoe for its feast of SS Boris and Gleb.[44] In Mordovia, in the village of Novly (in the Inser district), on the feast of St Peter and that of Our Lady of Kazan, 190 kolkhozians out of 215, stopped work for four or five days.[45] There is no point in quoting other instances. Those already given are sufficient to indicate that this is a general phenomenon. The Church herself is concerned with the problem: Mgr Onesimus, Bishop of Vladimir, has exhorted his people to take part in the religious solemnities (patronal and others), but without prejudice to their duties as citizens.[46]

The most illuminating and complete account of the vitality of religious traditions in the countryside has been given by the writer E. Doroche in his *Country Journal*. He describes a number of kolkhoz some sixty miles from Moscow. He preferred to give them fictitious names:

It is the feast of St Elijah; a harsh, shrill song echoes through the sleeping village. . . . It is girls who are singing; they have just been to the patronal feast at Urskol. The President of the kolkhoz, Nicholas Leontievich, has gone to Urskol to urge the kolkhozians of the local labour force to resume work. Today, obviously, they will not go to work, but tomorrow the combine harvester will begin work over there. . . .

In the evening, Nicholas Leontievich went to his mother's house in Vekcha, where the patronal feast of the Transfiguration is being celebrated. Ivan Feodosievich – another President of the kolkhoz, a communist of the strictest principles – would, of course, not take part in it. Poor Ivan

Feodosievich, this is going to deprive him of labour for at least three days. .... Fashionably dressed townspeople, on foot and on bicycles, pass us by on the slope of the hill, on the way to Urskol. They are going to the village of Vasilievskoe, whose patronal feast is also being celebrated. What a quantity of bread, hay and vegetables will be lost to the district, the region, the whole country as the result of this feast! What utter lack of any social sense! If they at least believed in God, but they do not even know how to say their prayers, and practically none of them knows what the Transfiguration is. And yet they consider that to work today would be a sin.

I talked about it to a peasant woman, Nathalia Kuzminicna. She said to me: 'I do not know exactly what this feast is, but it is certainly a great one, and to work during it is sinful.' I replied: 'You probably never go to church and confession; heaven knows when you last went. Is this honestly a feast for you? It will soon be 7th October; that is the time for you to celebrate.' She laughed, and naturally I could not convince her. In this place, it is a question not of religion, but of custom. It is also due to the fact that these workers are worn out by harsh toil, live without joy, have no distractions and no culture, whereas rest and diversion are natural human needs.

The Party representative felt himself to be isolated in the village:

On religious festivals, Ivan Feodosievich did not stay at home. There will be drinking in the village, and people may come and say insistently: 'Drink with us, then.' It would be impossible to refuse: the peasants would be offended.

The President of the kolkhoz cannot, however, withdraw completely from the peasant community. He may have to sit at the same table as the priest and even collaborate with him:

While we were having tea, people came in several times to invite Ivan Feodosievich to the *pominki* (funeral meal). A boy of sixteen was to be buried; he had been killed some

189

days previously in a drunken brawl. And the President was now asked to honour the dead lad's memory. But he steadfastly refused, for a number of reasons, as he told me. First of all, he did not like drinking; secondly, it was the burial of a drunken good-for-nothing; thirdly, it served no useful purpose for a President of the kolkhoz to sit at the same table as the priest. . . . But Ivan Feodosievich recalled that at the death of an old woman, an expert milker, he had of course, attended her funeral and the *pominki*. She was of course buried with the assistance of the priest. Before the service, the *batiouchka* [little father, a deferential title for a priest that had completely disappeared from Soviet literature] declared that he would wait in case the civil president wished to speak. And the President gave a farewell address to the deceased milkmaid. It was only after this that the priest began the burial service. At the funeral meal, at the priest's suggestion, it was the President who spoke first.[47]

The *Komsomolskaia Pravda* recently complained that 'a foolish custom prevails in the villages. On the wedding day, the couple about to be married go round the village carrying an icon. When they enter the bride's house, they kiss the icon. V . . . was a komsomol. He had gained full marks in dialectical materialism, not with the aim of getting better paid work, but from conviction. He refused to adopt this custom. Since his fiancée's family insisted, the engagement was broken off'.[48]

A Western tourist, herself an Orthodox Christian, has reported an incident similar to that described by Doroche. Happening to be on a cruise in the Black Sea on the feast of the Transfiguration, she mentioned it to one of the ship's stewardesses. She thanked her warmly and went off to convey the news to her fellow workers so that they might stop work, for 'to work would be a great sin'. But she admitted that she knew nothing about the feast.

Nor are religious festivals forgotten in the towns. In a Ukrainian town, without a church and where ignorance of religious matters seems to be complete, religious festivals are marked in exactly the same way as civil festivals, by heavy drinking.⁴⁹

Soviet writers deny that in general there is any religious significance in the observance of these traditions. But this is certainly a tendentious point of view, for it is hard to believe that attachment to religious customs, harshly opposed by the authority, can be maintained without the support of faith. A priest of Kherson describes the attachment of the Ukrainians to traditions whose religious significance is beyond doubt:

Here in the Ukraine there is still great fidelity to a custom, already forgotten in the north, according to which a priest must visit his parishioners during Advent and Lent and hold a short service in their homes. . . . Aged priests, especially in the villages, must go from house to house to hold this service of penitential prayer, and people feel themselves wronged if they are not called on 'to sanctify Lent' in their homes. . . . On Christmas Eve, after Vespers, the youngsters pay a visit to the members of their family, and to their godfathers and godmothers and take them *vecheria* (cakes made of rice and preserved fruit) and receive from them in return a few delicacies. I myself have been given these *vecheria*. On New Year's Day, the boys come to sing Christmas carols before the icons, and to scatter wheat in every corner so that the coming year may be one of plenty. After the festivals the parishioners must again be visited. Everyone gives you a joyful welcome, and considers the priest's visit as a special blessing. Those who are kept from home by their daily work, often ask their neighbours to see that when the priest comes for this service, he does not fail to visit their dwelling even in their absence.⁵⁰

A people who pray

What endows the witness of the Russian Church with universal significance is the extraordinary fervour of its peoples' prayer.

The conditions imposed by the State upon the Church practically confine the religious life to its unalloyed expression, which is prayer. The people of God are essentially 'a people who pray'. They can fully show their faith only during worship in Church. Orthodox Christianity is more favourable to the contemplative life than either Roman Catholicism or Protestantism. The Byzantine liturgy, in the words of Fr Louis Bouyer[51] is, if not the greatest creation, at least one of the greatest of Christian civilization. From day to day, Sunday to Sunday, feast to feast, it enables Orthodox Christians to relive the life of Christ and that of his Church. It is an immense lyrical and dramatic poem, shot through with biblical images, expressed in the language of Plato, and it provides people with an anticipation of the coming Kingdom, a vision of the Transfiguration, like that which the apostles experienced on Thabor, in which it is 'good to stay and put up one's tent'. The Orthodox liturgy, with its hymns of venerable antiquity, profound thought and perfect style, with its icons and wall paintings which cause the Church of the Old and New Testaments to share in the Eucharist offered by the people, is *heaven brought down to earth*.[52] It is this which explains why, in spite of the length of the services and the custom of remaining standing, people feel no fatigue and are in no hurry to leave 'heaven' and turn back again to earth. By its sharing in the divine mysteries, in those of the Trinity, the Incarnation, the outpouring of the Holy Spirit, the hallowing of time, the Orthodox liturgy provides a complete catechism for the faithful and at the same time demands their active personal participation. These characteristic features of Orthodox piety have acquired a special emphasis in Soviet Russia where, since action in and on the world is forbidden, religion can have no other outlet than in prayer.

The testimony of all those who have been privileged to share in public worship in the USSR is unanimous: nowhere else have they seen such fervour, such intense prayer and contemplation. On Saturday evenings, Sunday mornings, the eves of great feasts, on the feastdays themselves and their octaves, the churches are full to overflowing. The services are celebrated according to the full monastic rite, whereas before the Revolution, they had been considerably shortened. The Saturday evening vigils last at least three hours; those before feastdays, practically five hours; the Eucharistic liturgy, from two to three hours. Apart from the worship prescribed by the canons, extra-liturgical services are often introduced, especially the singing of the extremely popular Acathistus hymn. In most parishes the liturgy is celebrated three or four times a week, Wednesdays, Fridays, Saturdays and Sundays. In the large towns it is offered daily. The Orthodox canons, anxious to safeguard the unity of the Eucharist – one priest, one altar, a single Eucharistic assembly – prohibit more than one celebration a day at the same altar and also forbid a priest to celebrate twice on the same day. But a large number of churches have two or three altars (rarely more) and several priests; this enables several celebrations to be held on Sundays. In those towns where there are too few churches, the evening services (the vigils) are duplicated.

The people pray together as a community and individually as persons. Every face is spiritually withdrawn, lips are gently murmuring: a human person is speaking to the personal God. And then, during the litanies, the doxologies, and the more important moments of the canon of the Eucharist, all make the sign of the Cross and bow deeply. This creates a rhythm of adoration. But this rhythm is no hindrance to a wide freedom of personal behaviour. It does not prevent the worshipper from feeling at home in God's house. He takes his candle to it, he venerates its icons. He is free to make signs of personal humility, like the old man in a Moscow church who, prostrating himself before the congregation, said: 'My brothers, forgive me.' And the all-embracing Eucharistic prayer does not forget the world: during the liturgy unending lists of names pass from hand to hand up to the priest, to make sure that he will pray for relations, the sick, the erring, and the dead.[53]

The communal nature of the services is strengthened by the part taken by the people in the liturgical chant. Everywhere they sing the Creed and the Lord's Prayer; in some parishes they sing a large part of the service. The Acathistus hymn is always sung in unison.

The prayer of the individual members of the congregation is audible; sighs and tears and exclamations accompany it. Heartfelt sobbing sometimes echoes through the church. There are always many infirm, sick and neurotic present, and consequently scenes of *Klikouchestvo*, that is, of mystical hysteria, occur from time to time among the women, causing them to cry out, especially during the sweet and harmonious singing of the cherubikon which opens the second part of the Eucharist: 'the Mass of the faithful'. It is sung while the Eucharistic elements are being carried to the altar. This phenomenon was to be found before the Revolution, and is described by Dostoievsky in *The Brothers Karamazov*, but it seems to have become more frequent now.

One of the most important elements in the life of worship is that of frequent Communion. This is something new, unknown before the Revolution. Before 1914, Fr John of Kronstadt was the only one to preach the necessity of regular Communion. Today it is well established; weekly Communion is normal, and there are many communicants even during the week.

This increase in the number of communicants means that confession also has in most cases become frequent. The prayers of contrition and absolution are read out for all those who are preparing for Communion. Then each individual goes up to the priest and may whisper some particular sin to him. But private confession has not disappeared, especially in grave matters, and where it is physically possible. The *Review of the Moscow Patriarchate* even mentions the case of a priest collapsing with a heart-attack while hearing a confession in a private house.

Preaching, as part of the life of worship, is another novelty in comparison with the pre-revolutionary period. Preaching is prescribed by the canons, but many priests used to omit it. As it

is now the only form of Christian catechism that is permitted –
and even then, only under certain conditions – there may as a
result be three sermons during a service, and a sermon is also
preached at the administration of every sacrament. The people
listen to these sermons, which are often rather dull, with an almost
religious attention: they absorb the preacher's words, and express
their approval or their gratitude aloud.

Parishes in the large towns present one aspect which a Westerner
would find strange; they are, in effect, admirably organized for
mass-production of the sacraments. On Sundays, after two or
three celebrations of the Eucharist in the morning, one or more
priests remain on duty. In one corner of the church, children are
being baptized in rotation, and some adults behind a screen; at
the same time, two or three marriages are being solemnized in
another corner; and elsewhere funerals are being held in the
presence of open coffins. And so it goes on from midday to the
beginning of vespers at six o'clock in the evening.

These are the main characteristics of parochial life. Let us now
try to draw still nearer to these people of God and see how their
fervour is expressed throughout the liturgical year.

In the Orthodox Church, Easter is the festival above all festivals. The people look forward to it all through the year; it is
prepared for by the forty-two days of Lent, followed by a Holy
Week of beautiful and profound liturgies twice every day.
Nowhere in the world is Easter celebrated with such splendour,
fervour and joy, as in Russia.[54] On Easter night, the churches can
only manage to accommodate a tiny fraction of the people.

A parishioner writes that 'in Moscow by seven to eight o'clock
in the evening, all the churches are full and overflowing. The
people wait there until 11.30 p.m. which is the time that the midnight service begins; this is followed by matins for Easter, and
then by the Eucharist. Human feeling goes by the board; half-
dead and dropping with fatigue, this throng is the living witness
of the resurrection of Christ. The people's Communion becomes
a physical impossibility, so great is the crush around the chalice.

The service ends at about four or five in the morning; at the end of the liturgy at dawn, there are as many present as when matins began, at midnight. . . . When all is over, the priests resume the blessing of Easter cakes, the *koulich* (a kind of sponge-cake, made of flour), the *pashka* (a cheese-cake), and painted eggs'.[55]

Here is a description of the picturesque ceremony of the blessing of the cakes as it took place in the principal church of Kherson: 'The crowd stood in a double file around the church and, using both hands, we gave the blessing to the left and to the right. Meanwhile, our aged priest was doing the same inside the church. We went all round the church three times and each time another row of people was there with their cakes. At last' (as the completely exhausted priest relates), 'I went to bed, and immediately slept like a log. Ten minutes later, there was a knock on the door. I got up and said: "What is it?" "Batiouchka, we have come for our cakes to be blessed." "Yes, but why were you not there at the proper time?" "We were on the night-shift." So I had to get up and go to the church, where sixty people were already present. I gave the blessings and went back to bed. Ten minutes later, I was again awakened. And so it went on from five until half past seven. Four times I went to bed, fell asleep and was awakened. The folk on night-shift went home to collect their cakes; they had not been able to take part in the night service, but at least they wanted to celebrate with a blest cake. By seven-thirty I gave up and went back to bed no more.'[56]

The Easter festivities last for several days. Again at Kherson: 'On Easter Monday, after a liturgy celebrated late in the morning, there was again a procession, and once more the congregation overflowed. On the fourth day of the festival, there was still, morning and evening, a great crowd present'.[57] In Moscow on the second day of the festival: 'there is always the same crowd, a crowd that becomes something elemental'. At the resumption of the festival on the day before the eve of the Ascension, there is a congregation of like proportions; in Moscow, the people sang the whole of the Easter canon by heart for the last time. 'When the service was over, no one wanted to go away . . . The priest, sitting at the ambo, started to bless each person individually. Line after line of people kept coming into the church, and long afterwards, people were standing at the doors, at the windows.'[58]

In a Siberian town, throughout Holy Week, many of the faithful had to be content to follow the services from the outside. 'On Easter night, the shining of countless candles lit up the darkness . . .'[59]

Several times during the year, there is a specially solemn commemoration of the dead. One of them occurs in Eastertide, usually on the Tuesday following the first Sunday after Easter. It is called *Radonitsy* (from the word *radost*, 'joy') because the Church then proclaims the great joy of the resurrection with special emphasis. In the Ukraine, it is called the *Provody* (Farewells). A priest has given a description of it. 'It begins on the Sunday and lasts three days. The liturgy, celebrated at an early hour, is followed by a service for the dead. At this service there are a great number of bowls, each containing a *kolivo* [a cake made of rice and honey and preserved fruits, eaten after the prayers for the dead] . . . I hired a truck and, with our bags and vestments, I climbed in with all my priests, the nuns [from the former convent of Kherson] and the cantors, and we set off for the cemetery. Having arrived there, we all scrambled out and at seven in the evening the truck took the whole team back to the church. I was given so many cakes and eggs that we could have lived on them until the Ascension.'[60]

The piety of the faithful towards the dead seems to be heartfelt. During Lent, weekdays are aliturgical (that is, there is no Eucharist) and this deprives them of their daily commemoration of the dead. But they do not resign themselves to this and they 'bring their *gramotki*, that is, their lists of the dead and large Lenten candles. Twice daily after the service, an absolution is chanted, during which all the names are read out. In practice, the procedure is as follows: as soon as the officiating priest begins the "little hours" or Compline, the priest on duty begins to read the list of names in front of a table crowded with lighted candles and jars of honey, and often he has not finished reading them before the end of the service, when the celebrant, having finished vespers or matins, comes up to pronounce the absolution. This is done, morning and evening, throughout Lent. The table is covered with hundreds of lighted candles, and, especially in the evening, the effect is most impressive'.[61]

The second day of the feast of the Transfiguration is also devoted to prayer for the dead: on this day, in a church on the east coast of the Black Sea 'there were many sick among the people; it was a most friendly and moving congregation. When the service is over, one man picks up his plate of rice decorated with preserved fruits, one his *pirojkis* (little pies), another his biscuits, and the church becomes a scene of affectionate brotherly exchanges. Each one offers his neighbour a little rice in a spoon, mentioning the name of the dead person he is commemorating. And each one accepts it in the hollow of his hand or on a scrap of paper; sometimes he eats it at once, but in every case with the response: "May his soul be with God." '[62]

At Pentecost, in the countryside, the custom of renovating the outside of houses or at least of giving them a thorough cleaning, has been retained; for Pentecost signifies a renewal of creation.

The Transfiguration, a feast of secondary importance in the West, is one of the most popular of all in the Orthodox Church. The faithful come to church, carrying fruit, for the Transfiguration is the feast of the Creation. 'The Cathedral of the Assumption of the Trinity-St-Sergius was crammed to bursting on that day: at the signal for Communion it was an extraordinary sight. A bishop and four priests came out to administer Communion; the response was frightening, like the rush hour on the underground. I was hemmed in on every side until I could scarcely breathe.'[63]

On the feast of the Assumption a huge congregation assembles. From a town in Central Asia, a priest writes: 'I went into the church at seven-thirty in the morning and I had no chance to take off my vestments until five-thirty in the afternoon. At six in the evening the vigils of the burial of the Mother of God began, and did not end until one o'clock in the morning.'[64]

Christmas is kept with no less solemnity than Easter. Matins and the Eucharist are celebrated during the night, and are repeated at dawn. The Epiphany, twelve days later – in the Byzantine rite this feast is primarily a commemoration of our Lord's baptism – also attracts a huge crowd. In the Orthodox Church, it has been the custom, from as early as the fourth century, to bless the 'living waters'. This procession, 'the Jordan procession', as it is called, was authorized afresh in the years immediately after the war. In 1949, for example, several thousand parishioners of the town of Saratov, led by their bishop, went in procession along the banks of the Volga. After the blessing of the waters, accompanied by a salvo of gunfire and the release of a number of pigeons symbolizing the descent of the Holy Spirit upon Christ, 'several hundred' people stripped and plunged into openings made in the ice. The Soviet authorities were enraged; the bishop was removed, and 'Jordan processions' prohibited throughout the region.[65] Since then, the blessing of the waters has been celebrated in the courtyard of the church: 'I joined the huge procession, their banners waving, that had assembled for the blessing of the waters. It is hard to express the tumult of feelings that swept through me then: the people sang, the bells clanged mightily, a white pigeon was released which soared into the sky. Then, for ever so long, we went in procession around the church, blessing the water on the way. The custom here is as follows: everyone brings with him a bottle and a basin and, after the blessing, the priests go among the people and pour a little of the water that has just been blessed into each receptacle, and in this way they bless everybody's water. Otherwise, they would have to bless not only buckets but great vats.'[66]

Since the State has appointed certain Sundays to be 'Working Sundays', in order to exceed the norms of its plans for productivity, the faithful have sometimes – admittedly not very often – organized 'Working Saturdays'. In the courtyard of one church 'they built a coach-house and a garage. Peasants, old and young, and of both sexes, laboured for the glory of God. They first made a framework of wood, and then built the walls of interlaced reeds, plastered with clay. Some kneaded the clay, others brought water, and still others threaded the reeds. And all this they did while singing the Lord's Prayer to a melody well-known in this country (the Ukraine). The words "Our Father" are repeated at the beginning and end of each phrase:

"Our Father who art in heaven, Our Father . . .

"Our Father, hallowed be thy name, Our Father . . ."

And so on. It was very moving'.[67]

Pilgrimages

Throughout their history, Russian Christians have been addicted to pilgrimages of the most various forms: parochial processions of several miles; pilgrimages to the holy places of Palestine, Mount Athos, and Russia; and the never-ending pilgrimage from one monastery to another. People used to travel in order to take part in the monastic liturgy, to consult a *starets* (a spiritual director), to venerate miraculous icons or relics.[68]

As we have seen, every patronal festival is a kind of pilgrimage, and entails a large-scale movement of the people. The same thing occurs on those rare occasions when a church is consecrated; for example, when the church of the village of Kachkarova (in the Province of Kherson) had been rebuilt, its consecration drew crowds beyond number; some came in pony-carts, some in *arbas* (long four-wheeled carts used in south Russia); others made the forty-six mile journey on foot.[69] Similarly, when Archbishop Manuel visited a remote village in Chuvachia, pilgrims came on foot from dozens of miles away through rain and bad weather.[70]

There are now far fewer places of pilgrimage than before the Revolution. The Monasteries of Optino, Valaam and Sarov, for instance, no longer exist. Those of the Solovki Islands have been changed into a concentration camp for the clergy. Until 1960,

The People of God

four holy places were still nationally important: people thronged to them from all parts. These were the Trinity-St-Sergius at Zagorsk, some forty-five miles from Moscow – a place both of pilgrimage and of international tourism; the Monastery of Pskov-Pechory; the Laura of Pochaev in Volhynia; and the Monastery of the Grottoes in Kiev (closed in 1960).

Zagorsk, on account of the relics of St Sergius of Radonej, and its central position in Russia and proximity to the capital, seems to be the most frequented. The greatest crowds arrive during the days when the feast of St Sergius is celebrated, in the summer on 18th July, and in the autumn on 8th October. But Pentecost (which, in the Orthodox Church, is also the feast of the Trinity) and the Assumption, to which the two Cathedrals of the Laura are dedicated, and the major feasts in general, also attract large gatherings.

On the evening before the feast of St Sergius a vast concourse of people will already have assembled around the walls and in the huge courtyard of the Laura. Vigils in the Cathedral of the Trinity begin at six in the evening, and are not over before eleven o'clock. In the refectory church, the Acathistus hymn and the pilgrim's prayer continue without a break throughout the night. But the night is short. At four in the morning the first liturgy is celebrated, and it is followed by five others in the various churches of the monastery. After a solemn pontifical Eucharist, the people come out of the churches and chapels, and a service of thanksgiving is sung in the courtyard before a massive icon; the people sing in unison the refrain: 'Our holy father Sergius, pray to God for us.' While this is going on, and throughout the day, a patient queue lines up in front of the well discovered by St Sergius which is said to be miraculous; one by one they fill their flasks. C. de Grünwald, who took part in the festivities in 1960, calculated that about fifteen thousand pilgrims from all parts of Russia were present.[71] A. Kazem-Bek speaks of ten thousand people filling the churches on the eve of the feast, and to these must be added all those who had to stay outside. He says that it was impossible to count the number of communicants.[72] Pilgrims for Pentecost throng in for days before the feast, as soon as the Ascension is over. Many of them, unable to obtain lodgings in hotels and private houses, spend several nights sleeping on the grass.[73] Among the crowd there are many beggars, outcasts and sick people: the Trinity-St-Sergius Monastery has been called a veritable 'court of miracles'.

At Glinka, not far from Zagorsk, another holy well is a magnet for pilgrims. The Journal *Science and Religion* which inveighs against the practice, describes women washing in this well in mid-winter. The tree that rises above it is also an object of veneration: pilgrims take away pieces of its bark, and hang their icons on its trunk.[74]

In the north-west, within the boundaries of Esthonia as it existed between the two wars, there stands the huge Monastery of the Grottoes of Pskov, founded in 1473. The dedication festival of this monastery coincides with the Assumption. The vigils are celebrated outside in the monastic courtyard before the icon of the Mother of God which stands aloft above the multitude gathering there, while the pilgrims hold lighted candles in their hands. When the troparion of the Assumption is sung, the icon is carried in procession. The service ends at one in the morning. The morning liturgy is celebrated in two languages, Russian and Esthonian. At the pontifical liturgy, almost twenty thousand were already estimated to be present. At two o'clock this crowd begins to move in solemn procession round the walls of the monastery, while the bells ring out. Many Esthonians are wearing national dress with necklaces and head-dresses. The more zealous pilgrims stay on for one more day in order to take part in the night service of the entombment of the Mother of God, held according to the ancient rite of Jerusalem.[75] Such were the impressions reported by a student of the faculty of theology in Leningrad, and they are corroborated, although admittedly in a very different style, by the correspondent of the Journal *Science and Religion*. On 28th August 1960, many thousands of believers and spectators assembled at Pechory to celebrate the Assumption. The cathedral, the five churches of the monastery and the parochial churches, were so crammed that the services had to be held outside. A number of booths were doing a busy trade. Baptismal crosses, holy pictures, icons, the publications of the Moscow Patriarchate, holy water, were all on sale. Monks were coming and going with bundles of candles and baskets of blessed bread. Believers streamed unendingly towards the miraculous icon. The writer of these lines comments, with righteous indignation, on the 'massive' number of communicants and expresses astonishment that not only the old but the young also are among them.[76]

The Laura of Pochaev is situated in western Volhynia. Another correspondent of the Journal *Science and Religion* reports that 'every Sunday buses from Kremenets take many pilgrims, organized in companies with their guides; these are not only the local inhabitants; they come from various parts of the Ukraine and even from central Russia. The striking thing is the number of beggars around the church. . . . At Pochaev beggars seem to be held in honour'.[77]

The great feast of the Laura – the finding of the relics of St Job, the protector and wonder-worker of Pochaev – is celebrated with especial splendour. People begin to flow in even from the most distant parts of Russia three days before the feast begins. The solemnities start at two o'clock on 27th August; the saint's reliquary is carried from the Grottoes to the Cathedral of the Assumption. The procession is headed by many banners and icons, the choir, long lines of monks and secular clergy advancing two by two, then come priests in their vestments and the bishops, and after them a human sea of several thousand persons. As at Zagorsk, the vigils last until midnight and at five in the morning begin the celebrations of the Eucharist. The churches are crowded to the doors, and most of those present receive Communion. The saint's reliquary is then carried in procession round the cathedral, and afterwards taken back to the Church of the Crypts. This ceremony also is attended by many thousands.[78]

Until very recent years, the Laura of the Grottoes of Kiev, the cradle of the Russian piety, was a centre of pilgrimage comparable to that of Zagorsk. According to *Pravda*, it was visited in 1955 by 200,000 pilgrims – as many as in 1860.[79] 'I waited, sitting at the entrance to the distant Grottoes,' a spectator reports, 'to listen to what the pilgrims had to say about their pilgrimages: some came from the Donets basin, others from Rostov, others from Alma-Ata and even from Vladivostok, that is, from every district in our vast country.'[80] This Kievan pilgrimage had several objectives. The pilgrims did not confine themselves to visiting the Grottoes where the relics of the founders of the Laura and those of the 118 disciples repose; they went on to the Cathedral of St Andrew (also closed in 1960) in order to venerate the relics of St Barbara, and visited convents and other places of religious interest.

Besides these four great national centres of pilgrimage, there exist – or, more accurately, there existed until quite recently – a certain number of local pilgrimages. At the Smolensky cemetery of Leningrad, for example, in and around the chapel that enshrines the body of the blessed Xenia, who was a 'fool for Christ's sake' of the eighteenth century, there used to be abundant activity.

'Strange sights can be seen there,' wrote a correspondent of the Journal *Science and Religion*:

A young woman makes the sign of the cross several times and then kisses the chapel wall. Another is waiting impatiently for the moment when she too will press her lips against the chilly stones. The chapel is crammed and stifling. . . . Old women with quiet voices stand around recounting the miracles that have happened at the Saint's grave. Witnesses of 'miraculous cures' come forward. Young and old listen to these tales, and kiss the chapel walls with all the more devotion. It is chiefly women who come to beg for grace. . . . They bring little notes to Xenia which contain their prayers: 'Xenia, Servant of God, help us to find new rooms, graciously help us.' 'Dear Xenia, cure my little Peter who is very ill.' 'Xenia, grant that in living with my husband I may avoid conception.' 'Nina and Ludmilla, two girl students at the technical college, beg you, Xenia, Servant of God, to grant them success in their studies.'[81] All day long people file past the tomb, and these are not only the inhabitants of Leningrad, but pilgrims from every part of the USSR.

The chapel of Xenia, whose closure is clamorously demanded, is not the only holy place in the cemetery. In the family vault of the Prokhorov family, there is a mosaic of Christ. Some years ago a rumour spread that this Christ had wept. Many pilgrims were immediately drawn to the vault, and miraculous cures occurred. Elsewhere, aged women point out a common grave, known as the grave of the forty martyrs, and they tell its story:

It was in the days of the conflict with the followers of Trotsky. . . . Forty priests are buried here. They were dragged out of the churches during worship, brought here and buried alive, still clothed in their priestly vestments. To this day, my friends, moanings are heard at night. And on the anniversary of their martyrdom, a pillar of fire ascends from their grave to the sky and shines out in splendour. . . .[82]

At Leningrad there are other centres of pilgrimage, less spectacular in character, such as the Church of the Saviour, built on the spot where the Tsar Alexander II was assassinated (the Griboiedov canal), and called for that reason the Church of the 'Saviour over the blood'. This church which, during 1927–8, became the centre of the Josephite schism, was secularized in 1929, but it continues to attract the faithful. Every morning devout women come and put flowers in it, which the *militsionery* (guardians of the peace) promptly remove. 'A woman approaches the church and whilst endlessly exclaiming "Lord, have mercy", lets herself be wetted by the drops which fall from the roof, soaking her neck and scarf. Another woman is asking the passers-by to pray: "Kneel down and he will reward you. All things are his; wealth and health and sickness; all things are in his hands";

yet another is kneeling down and kissing the crumbling flag-stones on which the great deeds of the Tsar Alexander were formerly engraved.'[83]

The authorities boarded up and then filled in with concrete the window of the secularized Monastery of St John, from which the body of John of Kronstadt could be seen; but in vain. The people tore down the planks and scraped out the concrete. It was necessary to exhume the coffin of the famous priest and destroy it by fire. In spite of this women and children can be seen kneeling on the pavement facing the site where his tomb once was.[84]

On the way to Kiev, pilgrims could stop first at Kharkov, in the spacious cathedral, to venerate the relics of St Athanasius, Patriarch of Constantinople and those of St Meletius, Bishop of Kharkov. They could go on to Chernigov, where on 22nd September the anniversary of the canonization of the holy Bishop Theodosius, was celebrated with great pomp (on this day the service continued throughout the night); and, lastly, they could take part in the procession at Kursk, immortalized in the nineteenth century by the painting of Repin which retains all its popularity. 'Twice a year an uninterrupted flow of people moves in the direction of the church. In the autumn, waiting for the icon to be brought out, believers stay for days and nights in the rain. Many strip and, trembling with cold, plunge into the hallowed waters of the little river Tuskoi. The young also take part in these processions.'[85]

In the eastern regions there are no great pilgrimages, but local pilgrimages are not lacking. One, for instance, to the village of Velikoretskoe, in the Province of Kirov (Viatka), has been in existence for three centuries. According to the *Literaturnaia Gazeta*, pilgrims are still so numerous that it is a real calamity for the neighbouring Kolkhoz. 'Like locusts, they trample over pastures and cornfields, corrupt the peasants and spread disease, and all for a so-called miraculous icon of St Nicholas which vanished from the village years ago.' Here also the people bathe in the icy waters of the river, and leave some of their clothes behind in it.[86] Mount St Nicholas, in the village of Surskoe, in the Province of Ulianovsk (Simbirsk) has been a source of attraction since the days of Ivan the Terrible; in 1959 it needed 650 volunteers to turn back the crowd of pilgrims who were still making the journey. They had come from Vladimir, in the Province of Tambov.[87]

Although people in Russia are not free to live where they choose, wanderers, perpetual pilgrims, who travel from monastery to monastery, and have neither hearth nor home, have not completely disappeared from Russian life. An Orthodox girl student from France met one of these wandering women at the approaches to the Cathedral of St Andrew in Kiev, and gives this suggestive and picturesque description of her:

Kiev, 6th August, 1959

In front of the church of St Andrew, a *vanka-stanka* (this is an egg-shaped doll, which always stands upright again from any position in which it is placed) from Odessa, carrying all her wardrobe on her back, welcomed us with the words of the Gospel: 'They shall come from Samaria, Spain and Italy, and you must receive them. They will have to travel throughout the world.'

She drew a rosary of black cord from her neck, its cross was like one of those Rintintins that we make out of wool. Then she began to tell us how to use the rosary. Her fingers moved down the beads while she recited some prayers. Evidently, we had failed to understand her theoretical explanations, so she now passed on to action, but she said so many, many things, that we were a trifle lost. One must begin by saying: 'God have mercy on us', and then go on to the creed: the Devil then begins to be afraid. If this is not enough, go on to the Lord's Prayer – oh! and if you then say a prayer to the Virgin, he runs away, very frightened.

7th August

We have come back to St Andrew's, our favourite church, both to see it and, perhaps unconsciously, with the hope of seeing J. again. She was there, and her gaze was of a paler blue and even more penetrating than yesterday, as though it too had been brightened by the rain.

'I was soaked again by last night's rain. Yes, I fell asleep. That is the reason why I keep all my clothes with me, and I stay like this throughout the year, winter included. I sleep out of doors and eat what I am given. I mustn't take milk or bread, or my temperature goes up to 104. I feed on cabbages, tomatoes. . . .'

Seeing that we marvelled exceedingly, she decided, with the same simplicity, to tell us her story: 'I was as tiny as that, and I was paralysed; I couldn't walk. While I was asleep, I had a vision of the Virgin, and the next day, when the doctor asked me who had taught me to walk, I replied that it was Mary; they then drove me away from the hospital. . . . Myself, I'm from Odessa, but I have lived here by the walls of the church for eight years. It is the Virgin who has told me what I must do; she told me how long I would have to endure my illness, and it happened just as she said.'

The Virgin's commands, as J. pronounced them, sounded like a prayer: 'Endure, endure, from the beginning to the end. You will not live in a convent. You will live on what is given to you. No roof shall cover you. . . .

'Personally, I am so happy that I do not know how to thank our Lord for the life he has chosen for me. There is nothing sweeter, nothing more powerful than my beloved Lord. Even life in a convent is too luxurious for me, convents have beds and all kinds of comfortable things, and what do I want with a bed? My little knapsack under my head, and away to God! No one, no one at all, is as happy as I am, no one lives as well as I do, not even K. But today those who believe in God suffer because Christ suffers; many do not believe, but that is why we must endure, endure to the end. I tell you, I myself, that the time of Christ's return is drawing near; we must be patient; it will not be long. I do not live in a convent,

and yet I am a nun and a wanderer, and there are many like
me. . . . And now, little girls, go to church. Tell me your
Christian names; I shall remember them, and pray for you.
My own name is J.'

Inside the church on the right are the relics of St Barbara.
Many pilgrims come in and bow. An old man enters; he is
carrying his icons in a bag beneath his waistcoat, like a
kangaroo, and he has come to have them hallowed in this
place. Near the entrance a very old priest is saying his rosary
and making the sign of the cross with his left hand; he is a
sick man. A small, very young man in blue overalls comes
in, and distributes little gifts: three biscuits to one old woman,
three to another, three to an old man, three to the sick priest.
Three soldiers enter, having respectfully taken off their caps.
'Members of the tank corps,' comments one of the old
women at the entrance.

An Acathistus is being sung to St Barbara.

8th August

A seller of mauve everlasting flowers neatly tied with
strands of ivy tried to sell me some, at first without success.
Then he had a sudden inspiration: 'You will put them before
an icon, and that will be like a prayer. Come, come, buy my
everlasting flowers.'

J. was really J. but almost unrecognizable, for she had
taken advantage of the sun and taken off seven or eight of
her garments to let them dry. She was wearing a gown of
marine blue and a loose woollen jacket that had been so
stretched that it came down well below her hips. On a railing,
near the tap where she washes, her large gown of black
homespun was hanging, the others were already folded and
arranged alongside or inside her knapsacks and bundles. She
was radiant, and extremely pleased with the apples and everlasting flowers we brought her. But no, she would not eat
the apples just now, not until the feast of the Transfiguration.
We apologized and asked her whether there was any other

person present who would eat them. She surveyed all her 'wandering' companions, who were sitting motionless or half-asleep against the wall of the church: 'No, no one here will eat them. No one, because the Transfiguration is on the 6th August (according to the old calendar).' Our apples were finally bestowed upon an aged woman who was engaged in introducing a little tidiness into the church and who lived with a heap of grandchildren and nephews. But J. was careful to make it clear that these apples had been brought to her 'as presents' and her words rippled joyfully like a child's.

She talked to us at length about her life, about modern life and luxury. 'We may not say that life is less good today. If things go wrong, we may not blame it on the Government. We live the way we do, because it is God's will. If we have evils to endure, this may be on account of our sins. We do not know; our task is simply to bear it. Now indeed, for one thing, there is an attack on the faith and against those who believe; and that is something . . .'

She decided to offer us a cross and we were a long while disentangling from her lap the strings attached to all the treasures she wore round her neck. She brought them out from under several layers of clothes: St Nicholas the Wonder-worker, an icon of Christ, an icon of St Barbara, medals of the Virgin, a large wooden cross, and little crosses like the one I am now wearing, the one that J. gave me.

Then we told her we should like to take a photo of her with us. She spruced herself up and asked our advice: should she wear her green gown lined with fur, or the black home-spun? Some old women who had gathered round when she produced the crosses for us said with a gentle smile: 'But you will be too hot.' J. answered: 'It isn't I who will be too hot: the only one who'll be too hot will be the devil.'

J. did not just hand us the cross; with a look of concentrated tenderness, she first blessed us with it.

How could we arrange for the photos to reach her? . . .

In no case should we send them. They would never reach her. The priests had already begun to drive her away from here; they didn't like her and treated her as a simpleton, but that didn't matter; it was good for the soul: 'You see, little ones, that helps the soul enormously.'

N. was present when we met yesterday. She was about to pray when we arrived. She was quite young (barely twenty-five); she wore a white scarf and a gown of grey twill. She came from Samarkand. Six months in hospital had brought no improvement. She was suffering from hallucinations, at least this was the scientific name for them. J. interrupted: 'In the Gospel this is called possession by the devil. That is what she is suffering from.' N. then continued: 'I have been trying to pray for three years. Prayer alone is any help to me, but you must realize that it is not easy; I have no fixed abode; I shelter sometimes under one church, sometimes under another. I must wash my linen and the effort to do this uses up my last ounce of strength. When I have finished, I no longer have any strength to pray, and then my illness begins again. This is because my illness demands much prayer. And in order that my prayer may increase, I have to live as the Scriptures ordain; do you realize what that means? It means to be full of good feeling towards other people. It means, for example, that I must love everybody I meet as I love myself; it means that I must speak no evil of anyone, nor give way to anger. Then things go better.'

Just now, while she was listening to us, she began to pray in an undertone, crossing herself frequently. At first she had been afraid to pray in public, just as she did not want to go to school when she was little, because she was afraid she wouldn't be able to work as well as the others.

Extraordinary little N. If only we had a tenth of her implicit faith! . . .

9th August.

Eucharist at 7 a.m. at St Andrew's. We found J. with her

feet in the gutter. It had not rained during the night, but she had stayed in the same position as if it had. 'It is a good thing to suffer for the Lord.' I asked her to lend me a headscarf – I had forgotten mine. She chose the finest, washed and folded the evening before, and after she had sent us to church – 'Go and pray, my little ones, I shall be coming along presently' – she added, when we were some way off, 'If you like the headscarf, keep it in memory of me.'

There were only a few people in church. The priest was devout and gave the words of the service their full meaning. When J. learnt that I meant to receive Communion she was overjoyed and wanted to take steps that Andrée also might receive Communion. At their first meeting, on being told that Andrée was a Catholic, she gave her a broad smile and said: 'Yes, I know. The differences between us are marginal.' After I had received Communion I took a piece of blessed bread for Andrée, and another for J. who accepted the bread and her first question was: 'Did you give Andrée some of it?' Only when I said that I had, did she make the sign of the cross and eat the bread in the Orthodox way, hollowing her hand so that no fragment should be lost.

Before we finally said good-bye, she wanted to provide us with holy pictures. Once more, she drew from her bosom little cloth bags, one inside the other, and we joined her in venerating all the saints who were her companions: Lazarus, her leader; J. her patroness; St Anne, St Nicholas, and all the living Church.[88]

The anti-religious press has also, in its own style, given us some brief sketches of these twentieth-century wanderers: 'Boris received grace when he was adolescent. In response to inspirations as yet unconscious, he took up the life of a wanderer. Year after year, he journeyed from one church to another, from town to town. Saratov and Grozny, Mozdok and Gudermess, Orenburg, Orsk, Kiev, Sverdlovsk (Ekaterinenburg) had received the young wanderer within their walls before he arrived at Yjevsk. There he could be seen in the porch of the church, barefoot, half-clad even in the worst weather, praying for sinners, concerned with their future, proclaiming the end of the world. Wherever he stayed he was fed and clothed by charitable people who gave him a lodging and money. . . .' The career of this strange being ended, of course, in the lock-up.[89]

Some militant layfolk

Although most of the faithful confine themselves to prayer alone, from time to time one hears of layfolk devoting themselves body and soul to the Church and, in defiance of Soviet laws, proclaiming the Word of God to nonbelievers. Of course their work is hidden, and only comes to light in a distorting mirror when the Soviet police succeed in suppressing it.

The Russian authors' Journal *Literatura i Jizn* (Literature and Life) announced that Sergius Kazeev, a young electrician of twenty-four, was arrested for having organized the secret publication of prayer books. To ensure the success of his effort, he obtained the assistance of a number of employees of a technical publishing house who, unknown to its directors, printed the religious texts. This clandestine firm – its title was *Alleluia* – sold a little book of prayers for five roubles. The Journal asserts that the culprits were unable to withstand the temptation of money. But we may well believe that this illegal and severely repressed activity was rather the work of Christians anxious to provide believers with the prayer books which are so cruelly lacking.

Vadim Chavrov, a former Soviet Naval officer, a theological graduate of the Odessa Seminary, thirty-five years old, is carrying out a real apostolate among the young. This young theologian has written a treatise of apologetics, inscribed with Pascal's famous *pensée*, 'A little knowledge separates one from God; great learning draws one nearer to him', as its motto; this is an autobiographical work in which he gives an account of his conversion. His writing succeeded in bringing to Christ a number of girls, members of the *komsomol*. Chavrov and several women take care of children whose parents go out to work; in this way they have managed to form several groups of schoolboys who are able to regularly act as servers in the Moscow churches. In a private chapel, he and his circle gather groups of young people to whom they read the lives of the saints and of the first martyr of the Roman Church, Vladimir, the Metropolitan of Kiev. Vadim Chavrov's activity extends to a number of provincial towns and seems to be encouraged by ecclesiastics in high position. The author of the article describing these young apostles of modern Russia loudly denounced their guilt.[90]

A Western tourist provides a sketch of a naïve and moving scene of Christian witness in the Moscow streets:

Near the church doors, among the pigeons pecking for crumbs, a hairy old man and an old woman in a grey scarf were calling out to the passers-by, 'Wednesday is Christmas Day.'

There were varying responses: 'Yes, yes, I know,' came from a man with an aristocratic face and a disdainful shrug.

'It can't be! O thank you, I might have forgotten!' The bulky matron crossed herself several times and went on her way. . . . Another man had passed on without understanding such language, he had looked at the old woman with amazement.

A minute's pause: our friends made up the reckoning. 'That first one, now; she really did not know; you saw that?' – 'Yes, and it is true of most of them, they seem really to have forgotten.'

'Get along with you!' The hairy one made a sign to the old woman that there was someone coming. It was as though he said: That's enough gossip; we are not here for *that*. 'Wednesday is Christmas Day,' they cried out in unison.[91]

'Nicodemuses', in great number

More numerous than the militants, and this for obvious reasons, are the secret Christians, known in Russia as midnight Christians, the Nicodemuses.

They are believers, but their safety matters to them, they wish to preserve their social status, and avoid any public manifestation of their belief. Among Christians of this kind there are, of course, differences in degree, and many who go to church, take care to do so without needlessly arousing the curiosity of others. We hear, for example, of a parish priest whose priesthood is unknown to those in the adjoining flats;[92] of a Moscow lecturer who prudently goes to a different church each time; of a Soviet colonel in Berlin who asked the Orthodox bishop to baptize him by night and with the utmost secrecy.[93] Children, from their earliest years, learn to keep their religious beliefs a close secret.[94] A Soviet youth told an interpreter in the French Exhibition in Moscow that after years of close relationship he had found out, by accident, that his best friend was a Christian like himself.

In a sense, every Christian in the Soviet Union has a Nicodemus as his double. But there are also those who deliberately sever all connection with organized religion, turn some corner of their house into an oratory, and allow nothing of their convictions to transpire.

Here are some typical sketches of these midnight Christians:

Alexander Turkin, a pupil of the Moscow School no. 147, was about to become a member of the local komsomol. Shortly before the vote, a comrade said to him, jokingly:

'I expect you believe in God?'

But Alexander replied in an undertone:

'Yes, I believe.'

An embarrassed silence followed. Was it possible that this Alexander who so convincingly propounded on the blackboard the theories of Darwin and the hypothesis of Schmidt, could be a believer in God? He had friends in the school. But an invisible frontier divided them – the inner world of each man was sealed off from his fellows. When the section met, Turkin's case naturally came up, and he was asked:

'Do you go to Church?'

'No.'

'Do you wear a cross?'

'No.'

The komsomols were reassured, and took no action against Turkin, because his belief was not expressed by outward signs.[95]

An officer in the Soviet army, a Party member, tolerated the possession of icons by his wife. They were living in a garrison, far from any church, and he made no attempt to oppose his wife's religious attitude; he simply said: 'Pray to God, but let no one know it', and he did his utmost to conceal her oratory from the eyes of the curious. His flat was really ruled like a fortress. The family isolated itself and no longer received guests. . . . In the end, an employee of the management of the flats denounced them: 'I have always told my wife,' the officer explained, 'that this would all end by becoming known and that I should land up in trouble.'[96]

A mathematics master in a secondary school, formerly a militant anti-religionist, led a secluded life, unnoticed by anybody, until one day a zealot of the komsomol broke in like a burglar and found out his teacher's convictions.

'He tried to bar the way into his room, but I managed to get in. On his table I saw his students' papers, and on the wall . . . The whole wall was covered with icons. . . . He never went to church, and observed his devotions at home, so as not to get into trouble, and he received no one into his home.'

The day after this discovery, the head of the school came to see his colleague whom he had known and appreciated for ten years. 'Yes,' admitted the teacher defensively, 'I am a believer; I have prayed for many years; yes, with my heart and soul, I believe in God. But this is a purely personal matter; the private property of my soul, if you like. I have not communicated it to anyone, and I have no intention of doing so. What oath could I take that would be solemn enough to convince you that I have not allowed the slightest reference to the faith to cross my lips in class?'

'God on the one side, and on the other, co-operation in work with those who deny him. Such duplicity is impossible to understand,' the head replied.

'But what else could I have done? I teach mathematics, and I have no other special subject. I am not a Don Quixote, to live without any means of livelihood. If I have said nothing in class in favour of belief in God, nor have I said anything against it. I live and hold my peace, content if people will only leave me alone and not come rummaging into my soul.'

'I was confronted,' said the head, 'by a new kind of hermit; not an old man with a patriarchal beard, not an ascetic, worn out by prayer and fasting, and clothed in rags and a hair-shirt, but a man, properly dressed, complete with shirt and tie, a man who goes regularly to the cinema, rubs against his fellows every day, and yet was living apart from them, in fact as a hermit. To live with people and yet be a stranger to them, is more fearful than to withdraw into the wilderness. . . . To have constantly present to one's mind that other people do not share your opinions, opinions that must be hidden, and about which one must be silent. . . .'[97]

But this is how Christians in the USSR have to live.

CHAPTER X

ON THE FRINGE OF THE CHURCH:
SCHISMS AND SECTS

New sects, coming into existence every year, prove that the Russian people are far from indifferent to the religious problem.

Vladimir Soloviev, Sunday letters, XXII, 1898

IF THERE IS A SPHERE in which Soviet Russia has no need to envy the United States, it is that of its sects. Today, more than ever, an impressive number of sects or schismatic groups, some of which go back several centuries, while others originated only a few years ago, live parasitically upon the body of the Orthodox Church. Anti-religious propaganda pays special attention to them. In the symposium *We have broken with religion* (Moscow, 1960) twice as many pages are devoted to the sects as to the Orthodox Church. And yet in terms of real numbers, the membership of the sects is but a small percentage of the huge number of the Orthodox.[1]

The disproportion between the size of the sects and the attention given them by official propaganda, is due partly to their multiplication and their growth, but also to their dynamism and to their suspicious or negative attitude towards the new social system. They are active minorities, difficult to keep track of, and even more so to hunt down. Outwardly they merge into the contemporary world, yet they are profoundly alien to it.

The world of the sects, as it appears today, is infinitely varied and complex. To shed a little light on this matter, which is still hardly studied, it seems helpful to classify the sects and schismatic bodies according to their origins: first, the traditional sects of Russia: Old Believers, Men of God, Spiritual Christians, etc.; then the sects imported from the West, Protestant by derivation, introduced into Russia recently and particularly active today; and, lastly, the new schisms and sects that have appeared in Russia since the Revolution and were provoked by it.

Study of the sects is made difficult by the absence of reliable documentation. Articles in journals and pamphlets abound, but they lack precision: the ideas of the sects are described in a summary or confused manner; details about the number of their adherents, and their geographical distribution are often missing. In 1959 the historical section of the Academy of Sciences sent an important sociological expedition into the province of Tambov to study the sects that it contained, but the conclusions reached were strictly local and in no way took into account the important movements of population which have affected this region since the Revolution.[2]

The traditional Russian sects

I. THE OLD BELIEVERS. Shortly after its appearance, the schism of the Old Believers[3] found itself short of bishops and split into two main bodies (1692-4).

A. The *Bezpopovtsy* or priestless, arguing that the entire hierarchy had died out, were logically led to give up both priesthood and sacraments, with the exception of baptism which can be validly administered by the laity.

B. The *Popovtsy* (literally, 'presbyterians') who, being anxious to preserve the essentials of the Christian way of life, searched the world over to find an authentic bishop and regain the apostolic succession, meanwhile resigned themselves to receiving fugitive priests who had been expelled from the Church for misconduct, or came to the Old Believers for money. Later, the *Popovtsy* split into several bodies: the *Edinoviertsy* who, while retaining the ancient ritual, submitted canonically to the Church (1811); the followers of the 'Austrian hierarchy' who were themselves divided into several sections; and lastly, the pure or *Bieglopopovtsy* who continue to recruit their clergy from fugitive priests.

The priestless, in their turn, gave rise to a swarm of minor sects, most of which have lasted on until our day.

The hierarchy of Bielokrinitsa or Austrian hierarchy. In the middle of the nineteenth century, a monk of the Old Believers set off to the Middle East to try to find a bishop who had kept the ancient faith in its integrity. After travelling through the Balkan countries, Egypt and Syria, he at last succeeded in convincing a Greek Metropolitan, whom the Turks had deposed, to accept the faith of the Old Believers. This abjuration by the Metropolitan Ambrose, and the consecration of the first Old Believer bishop, occurred in a Bukovine monastery of Old Believers in the Austrian territory of Belaiakrinitsa – the White Waters. The so-called Austrian hierarchy had its origin in this event. It quickly became the predominant branch of the Old Believers. In spite of frequent internal disputes within the schism, 'the Austrians' continued to develop, and in 1926, on the eve of the persecutions, they had twenty-one bishops.

Today, the Archbishopric of the Old Believers, recognized by the State, includes only five dioceses (Kishinev, Odessa, and Chernovitsy for the south-west; Donets – Don – Caucasus for the south and south-east; Klintsy and Novozybkov in White Russia, Gorky and Moscow) and three hundred parishes incorporating about a million people. In Moscow and its region there are thirteen parishes and some fifty thousand people. The spiritual centre of this Church, the Cathedral of the Virgin's Intercession in the Rozoj cemetery, can hold ten thousand and is often full. Visitors will appreciate its icons of great beauty and the impressively austere and almost monastic chanting during the services.

The Church is governed – theoretically at least – by the Councils, and in the intervals by the Council of the Archbishopric, the present head of which is Joseph Morzhakov, Archbishop of

Moscow and all Russia, elected in 1960. As far as is known this Church is the only juridical corporation in the USSR to own a private printing press; which shows the reluctance of the Old Believers to entrust the printing of their books to atheist or, even worse, to Orthodox printers. But their publishing is very limited. Since 1945 they have issued an ecclesiastical calendar. Those of 1947 and 1948 gave valuable information about the organization and present position of this Church.[4] In 1951 the publication of these calendars ceased, and was not resumed until 1955. The more recent calendars are limited to the printing of prayers used by the Old Believers. In 1957 the archbishopric published an important volume of reproductions of icons, but the quality of the printing was much inferior to what it had been before the Revolution.

The Old Believers seem to remain firmly established in their traditional provinces: Nijny-Novgorod and Kostroma. A few dozen miles from this latter town, C. de Grünwald had the privilege of visiting the village of Strelnikovo, mainly inhabited by Old Believers; all the men, old and young, were bearded; many wore the ancient style of dress, with long *caftans* and flat caps.[5]

In 1953, the village of Chupoleika, north of Nijny, with 260 dwellings, had fifteen hermitages of Old Believers and only one communist club. The smaller village of Podlesovka could boast of five hermitages and no communist meeting-place at all. Lake Svetloiar, in which, according to the legend, the holy city Kitej was engulfed, still draws many pilgrims, as in the past. Young schoolgirls can be seen moving round the shores of the lake on their knees; old women with their ears to the ground listening to the bells of the vanished churches, and preachers proclaiming the end of the world.[6]

The Bieglopopovtsy took advantage of the troubled period following the Revolution to re-establish one, if not several hierarchies. Thus in 1923, a bishop with the strange Christian name of

Distaphia, allowed the formation of a 'Church of Orthodox Old-Christians', with State recognition.[7] In 1952, the head of this Church, one John, with the high-sounding title of Archbishop of Moscow and all Russia, took part in the conference for the maintenance of peace, held by all churches and religious bodies, in Zagorsk.[8] In December 1948 three priests of this group rejoined the Orthodox Church. One of them addressed his former colleagues in these words: 'Because your bishops do not possess the grace of the Holy Spirit, they are clowns and do not belong to the true, holy, Catholic and apostolic Church of Christ. This is the reason why their communities are quite literally sects, who have neither charismatic bishops nor priests, and are simply clowns.'[9]

Another hierarchy re-established by the *Bieglopopovtsy* has its centre at Kuibyshev (Samara). Its head is Epiphanius, Archbishop of Kuibyshev and all Russia. Almost nothing is known about this branch, except that it has communities in the region of Perm, with bishop Eusebius at their head. In Kuibyshev itself, if we accept atheist propaganda, the Cathedral of the Old Believers is attended only by about fifty old women.[10]

The 'Priestless' have disintegrated into a sand-heap of sects. Their apple of discord was marriage. Must the invalid marriage of the official Church be accepted, or given up altogether?

Three main groups recognized by the State, took part in the inter-denominational conference for the maintenance of peace at Zagorsk in 1952. These were:

A. The 'Old Pomorians', Old Believers of the Transfiguration. This body drew its name from the maritime region of Pomoria, in north Russia, the common place of origin of all the 'priestless', and from the *Preobzazhenskoe Kladbishche* cemetery, which from 1771 had become the centre of the *fedoseevtsy*, the main branch of the 'priestless', established in Poland in 1706 by one Theodosius. The Old Pomorians have always had the cemetery of the Transfiguration as their centre. Their number is unknown. A former member of the sect who has become an atheist, describes their present position as follows:

The sect depends for its existence upon the members of the old generation, who had reached maturity before the Revolution. The middle-aged, whose schooling took place after it, hesitate between religion and atheism. The young who, although they have experienced the influence of the Old Believers' way of life, now no longer practise it. But they try to avoid disputes about it with their elders, and do not raise any objections to their observance of the rites. For their part, the old have become more conciliatory. They say their prayers in the kitchen or in some secluded place where the young will not see them. The young intermarry with the 'Niconians', that is, the Orthodox, or even with the atheists, but they allow grandparents to baptize their grandchildren, and to give them religious instruction. The elderly Pomors make no attempt to propagate their faith, but obdurately resist anti-religious propaganda.[11]

B. The *grebenschiki* community of Old Believers, another branch of the *fedoseevtsy*, in order to satisfy the authorities, have resigned themselves to celebrating a simulated form of marriage. Before 1941, this sect had 107,000 adherents in Latvia, that is, a fifth of the total population of that country. Eleven thousand of them lived in the capital, Riga, but the majority were inhabitants of the villages of the province of Latgal, not far from the Russian frontier.[12] In 1952, they still had a number of parishes distributed among the kolkhoz and towns of the Republic of Latvia.[13] The Orthodox bishop of Latvia maintains friendly relations with the *grebenschiki*.[14]

C. The Old Believers of Lithuania also form part of the *fedoseevtsy*. They number about thirty-five thousand.[15] On 27th January 1952, thirty-eight of their spiritual directors held a congress in Vilnius on the struggle for peace.[16]

Apart from these three main bodies, isolated groups are to be found in the forgotten regions of Asiatic Russia, such as the Old

Believers of Bukhtama in the Altai mountains; the Uraltsy, who were transported by the Tsarist Government between 1875 and 1877 from the Urals to Central Asia, and were rediscovered in 1945 by an ethnographical expedition in the Republic of Karakalpak; and the Old Believers of Ussuri, on the Chinese frontier.[17] Lastly, in quite recent times (October 1962), 1000 *Nekrassovtsy* Old Believers (so named from Nekrassov, their leader), who had left Russia under Peter the Great and established themselves in Turkey, returned to the Soviet Union.[18]

The survival of several minor branches of the 'priestless' is similarly attested:

1. The *Filipovtsy*, or disciples of a certain Philip, who in 1738, refused to restore the prayers for the imperial family.

2. The *Denisovtsy*, or disciples of a certain Denis, about whom nothing is known.

3. The *Netovtsy* (from *niet*, 'no'), refusers or nihilists who reject all contact with the world.[19]

4. The *Yovtsy*, or adherents of a certain Job, have been observed in the region of Mariupol.[20]

To complete the account, we should mention the existence in 1939 of the *Dyrniki* (from *dyra*: a hole) who, if they have no icon dating before the schism, make a hole in the roof of their *izba*, for the purpose of praying to God; and the *Skrytniki* who distrust the authorities to the point of refusing to give their names.[21]

The *Sputnik Ateista* affirms that the Old Believers, unlike other denominations and sects, make little attempt to propagate their doctrine. The growth of this sect takes place only within that of the families of Old Believers, which makes atheist propaganda to individuals difficult.

Their anti-social tendencies are passive, and untainted by any political standpoint. The Old Believers continue to live in the same way as their ancestors, they shun modern dress, do not shave, drink no coffee, do not attend places of entertainment. The most fanatical among them will never eat from a vessel that has been touched by the lips of a man of a different faith.[22]

2. THE 'MEN OF GOD', OR KHLYSTY. This is one of the most ancient sects of Russia; it originated towards the end of the seventeenth century, at the same time as the Old Believers. It is both rationalist and mystical in outlook. It rejects all the fundamental beliefs of Christianity (Church, hierarchy and sacraments) and believes that the Christ may become incarnate in more than one person. They despise the body, and hold marriage in contempt, but their ecstatic prayers sometimes degenerate into orgies. Children born outside marriage are called 'little Christs' (*khristosiki*). The sect is divided into two communities, with less and more intensity of ritual practice: (A) 'the old Israel', with sobriety in its rites, and (B) 'the new Israel' who practise flagellation and much leaping and jumping. Cathechumens are not allowed in the general meetings until their loyalty to the sect and their ability to propagate its doctrines without compromising their brethren has been tested. When a neophyte is finally admitted, he swears that he will renounce all this world's goods and live for the community alone. The sect is admitted to be remarkably stable. The Men of God are impenitent individualists, and yet they have remained numerous. In the province of Tambov, for example, it had 500 adherents before the Revolution, and even now has 250. They keep clear of the kolkhoz and on their individual scraps of land they cultivate potatoes, although they do not eat them, for, in their view, potatoes are 'the devil's fruit'.[23]

Their life is extremely ascetic, and they eat no meat, some even sacrifice their lives to God. In 1957, for instance, at Orenburg, an important centre of these 'men of God' was discovered. On 7th September 1955, a young member of the sect, with the Christian name of Galina, let herself die voluntarily, as an expiatory victim. Now the whole sect observes the day of Galina's death with a fast. At Kuibyshev there are groups of *khlysty* whose leader, thirty-five years old, has passed altogether thirty years as a prisoner,[24] among the miners of the Donets basin,[25] in Kazakhstan where the 'men of God' of the village of Yvanovka (Semipalatinsk province), convinced that the end of the world was imminent, burnt everything they possessed.[26] This sect is not recognized by the State.

3. THE SKOPTSY (CASTRATI).[27] The *Skoptsy* had their origin in the *khlysty* and carried the latter's teaching to its most extreme conclusions. In their view only castration could win the victory in the conflict with the flesh. They were cruelly persecuted during the thirties, and the *Sputnik Ateista* claimed that they had ceased to exist.[28] But this statement is contradicted by A. Erichev[29] in the *Great Soviet Encyclopaedia*,[30] and by the Journal *Science and Religion* which notes the existence of active groups of the *Skoptsy* in Orel and in the province of Kursk. The latter tend to substitute abstinence or 'spiritual castration' for physical mutilation.[31]

4. SUBBOTNIKI (SABBATARIANS). The sect of the *Subbotniki* (not to be confused with that of the Adventists whom the people call by the same name) also seems to be derived from the *khlysty*. Evidence for its existence first appears at the end of the seventeenth century. It is characterized by emphatically Jewish tendencies: it rejects the Trinity, and the divinity of Christ and observes Jewish practices and rites. It is divided into two bodies: (a) the *Beschapochniki*, who pray with their heads uncovered, and (b) the *Chapochniki* who pray with a hat on, and observe Jewish customs with greater strictness. Just before the Second World War, more or less important groups of Sabbatarians were to exist in Siberia (Staraia Zima); in the Caucasus (Prochladnensk) and in Kazakhstan.[32] In the province where the sect originated, it appears to be passing away, before the Revolution 2,300 of its members lived there; now there are only 60.[33] They are refractory to the system of collectivization, and were probably dispersed all over Russia when this was put into operation.

5. SPIRITUAL CHRISTIANS: DUKHOBORS AND MOLOKANES.
Two distinct but very similar sects appeared in the eighteenth
century: the *Dukhobors* and the *Molokanes*, also called 'Spiritual
Christians' (*Dukhovrnye liudi*).

The *Dukhobors* – those who fight for the spirit – (from *Dukh*,
'spirit', and *borotsia*, 'to fight') are supposed to have been founded
by a foreign Quaker living in the Kharkov region, but their real
development is due to Sylvanus Kolesnikov, a learned disciple
of Eckartshausen and Saint Martin, who lived from 1750 to 1775
in the Ekaterinoslav region. They reject the Church and its
institutions; they discard everything in the Bible that seems to
them useless; they believe in the pre-existence and transmigration
of souls, including that of Christ, who, they say, was simply a
human being. To this rationalistic spiritualism they add the cults
of the saints and of the Mother of God which they have taken
over from Orthodoxy. They are contemptuous of 'the letter',
that is, of everything written or printed, and they shun all written
fixation of their doctrine. They are socially active and profess
Christian community of goods. In 1826 they were authorized to
occupy the banks of the Molotchnaia river, where they established
very prosperous communities. But in 1837 the *Dukhobors*, who
refused to accept military service and to obey the laws, were
transported to Transcaucasia. Thence, 8,000 of them emigrated
to Canada. Few of those who remained in Russia escaped the
persecutions of the thirties: the 4,000 members of the community
of Salsk suffered especially. In 1939, many villages of the Bog-
da___ region of Georgia were still inhabited by *Dukhobors*, of
___od numbe_ ar_ged to escape collectivization and still
___backs up v form of modern civilization.[34] The
___ecognize State. Recent anti-religious pam-
___ver, whi g that the sect continues, are careful
no___ck it, probab__ __ause they do not wish to offend the
Canadian *Dukhobors*, some of whom, in 1958, were thinking of
being repatriated to the USSR.

The sect of the *Molokanes*, an offshoot from the *Dukhobors*, was founded in the second half of the eighteenth century by Simeon Uklein, a peasant from the province of Tambov. From the start it was strongly influenced by Protestantism. The name (from *moloko* 'milk') was assigned to it in 1765 by the consistory of Tambov, because its members drank only milk during Lent. The *Molokanes* give a different explanation of their name: they say that it is due to the fact that their doctrine is that 'spiritual milk' of which the Scriptures speak (1 Cor. 3. 2). But the name that they themselves prefer is that of 'Spiritual Christians'. They reject the Church (hierarchy and sacraments) but accept the Bible in its totality. Their Christology is coloured by Monophysitism. They are fundamentally pacifist, but in 1929, under pressure from the authorities, they were compelled to accept military service.

The sect is recognized by the State. In 1952 it was represented at the conference of Zagorsk. According to their spokesman, the *Molokanes* have 'tens of thousands of members in Azerbaidjan alone, and especially in Baku', and a number of communities in Moldavia and the Far East.[35] They originated in the province of Tambov, but there they are now becoming extinct; there were 8,000 before the Revolution, and at present only 330.[36] What the sect loses in numbers, the Baptists seem to gain. The chief leaders of the Baptists are former Molokanes.[37]

The Soviet press is constantly grumbling about the activity of this sect in Transcaucasia. 'In the villages of the Schemachin region inhabited by the Molokanes the members of the sect are especially active. At Khilim every marriage, without exception, is celebrated with a religious ceremony; even the Communists do not refuse to join in the procession through the village to the monotonous chanting of the hymns. . . . The clergy catch the young in their nets and, under their influence, the latter sometimes break with the komsomol. Even in the new socialist towns, Sumgait and Mingechaur, the Molokanes have succeeded in opening chapels and disseminate their poisonous ideas among the young. The number of places of worship is not decreasing; the reverse is true, even though in Azerbaidjan only one religious community, that of Baku, is officially registered. Does not freedom of worship encourage both those who make a profit from religion and those elements hostile to the Soviet Union who feel comfortably settled in their illegal chapels?'[38] This scarcely veiled threat hints of dark days ahead for the sect of the Molokanes. Even so, in 1961, 2,000 Russian Molokanes who had been living in the Kars region of Turkey, were repatriated to the USSR.[39]

6. PRYGUNY (JUMPERS, from *prygat*: to jump). This sect was founded by Lucien Petrov, a Molokane 'Christ', in the first half of the nineteenth century. Petrov believed that in the word 'hyssop' in Ps. 50. 7, he could discern a noun derived from the Russian verb *sopet*: to blow through the nose, and he ordered his followers to blow in this way on each other, so as to obtain forgiveness of sins. The sect has been influenced by the *khlysty* from whom it adopted ecstatic dancing, and also by the *Subbotniki* (observance of the Sabbath and the feast of Tabernacles).

In 1926, the Pryguny held a congress at Nikitino in Armenia, but they could not agree on the attitude to be taken to the civil power.[40] In the Fioletovo–Lermontova district of Azerbaidjan, however (the home of David Rudomiotkin, a direct descendant of the celebrated nineteenth-century *prygun* Maxim Rudomiotkin) the sect still shows a certain vitality.[41]

7. IMIASLAVTSY (GLORIFIERS OF THE NAME, from *imia*: a name, and *slavit*: to glorify). The 'Glorifiers of the Name' originated shortly before the First World War in the Russian monasteries of Mount Athos. They represent an extreme deviation from the *Hesychast* tradition. The Holy Synod promptly condemned these over-zealous *Hesychasts* as heretical and appealed to the secular arm to expel them from Mount Athos and return them to Russia. The sect increased rapidly in the Caucasus and on the eastern shore of the Black Sea, but it was harshly attacked by the Soviet Government. Most of its leaders had been Tsarist officers: they were condemned to death and executed in 1930.[42]

But even though the sect practises great austerity and is opposed to the new social system, it has managed to survive. In 1947, it was reported as existing in Maikop, where it bears the name of *Solianovtsy* (from *sol*: salt).[43] More recently, in 1960, a Soviet journal declared that the *Imiaslavtsy* were firmly established in several villages of North Caucasus, still sullenly opposing collectivization and the Soviet way of life.[44]

8. JOANNITES. In the early years of the twentieth century some fanatical admirers of the famous missionary priest John (Sergeev) of Kronstadt became convinced that he was a new incarnation of Christ, and founded the sect of the Joannites. Although it was cruelly persecuted it survived in several places. In 1938 it was reported from Dniepropetrovsk, Viatka (Kirov), Tver (Kalmin), in the Caucasus; from Tartary and Udmurtia.[45] Quite recently, an important nucleus of Joannites was discovered in the province and town of Cherkassy. Mitrophan Koval, their leader, was condemned to imprisonment for anti-social activities. So great was his influence that the anti-religious propagandists considered it necessary to produce a film specially designed to unmask the activities of 'Father Mitrophan'.[46] The *Pravda Vostoka* was disturbed to find that Joannite writings were still circulating in the Caucasus.[47] Small groups of them exist in Kazakhstan.

9. INNOKENTIEVTSY. This sect, local in character, was founded in 1908 by Innocent Levizor, a monk of the monastery of Balta in Moldavia, who gave himself out to be an incarnation of the Holy Spirit. The adherents of the sect proclaim the imminent end of the world and so reject marriage and recourse to doctors, and practise a special devotion to the Holy Spirit. The sect is monarchist in tendency, and lives in the deepest secrecy in underground places, where children have been found who had never seen the sun, and who believed they had been begotten by the Holy Spirit. The anti-religious press declares that the sect practises human sacrifices, some members letting themselves be buried

alive. Some 'death chambers' have been found in the town of Beltsy, and in the villages of Rychkany, Novaia Syngeria and Berlintsy. A film about them has been produced. There may be several hundreds or even thousands of these *Innokentievtsy*.[48]

Sects of Western origin

1. MENNONITES. The Mennonites are one of the oldest Protestant sects. It was founded in Germany by Simon Mennon (1499–1561) a Catholic country priest, and has close affinities with Anabaptism. At the end of the eighteenth century the Russian Government encouraged the immigration of Mennonite families who settled in the region of Ekaterinoslav (the present Dniepropetrovsk) and colonies were later established in Central Asia, Siberia, the Caucasus and on the Volga. They are convinced pacifists, and in 1874 they were exempted from military service and attached to the forestry service. When the Soviets came to power, the Mennonites inevitably clashed with them, and very many emigrated. Those that remained were harshly persecuted and deported. Their journal *Unser Blatt* was suppressed and most of their churches shut. In 1928 a Congress of the sect was constrained to accept the principle of obligatory military service for its members. In the Ukraine, during the last war, thirty-five thousand of them took advantage of the German occupation and left the country. Nothing further was heard of them in Russia until 1956 when two of their American leaders rediscovered some of them in the Altai and Kazakhstan regions of Siberia. About one hundred and twenty-five Mennonite villages with a population of fifteen to twenty thousand are said to exist in these regions, one thousand of them in the town of Karaganda.[49] The total number of Mennonites in Russia today must be forty-five thousand, almost as many as at the last century. (In the whole world, there are supposed to be four hundred thousand.) In spite of difficulties, the Mennonites are increasing. Every member tries to make Christ known through personal conversation with those

around him.[50] Originally the sect was German speaking; it is rapidly adopting Russian.

2. THE BAPTIST AND EVANGELICAL CHRISTIAN UNION. This powerful Christian body, one of the most important after the Orthodox Church, was formed during a combined Congress (26th–29th October 1944) through the union of two separate branches of liberal Protestantism: the Evangelical Christians or *Pashkovtsy* (so called from Colonel of the Guard, Pashkov, who introduced the sect into Russian aristocratic circles at the end of the nineteenth century) and the Baptists, who began to develop in the same period, but among the peasants of the Ukraine. Until the first Five-Year-Plan, the Baptists benefited from the encouragement of the authorities; they were even asked to set an example of collective work and living. Christian kolkhoz were created with such names as Bethany, Gethsemane, etc., but this did not survive the radical attack on the kulaks. For several years a more or less secret *khristomol* (Christian youth) movement tried to compete with the komsomol. Government toleration also enabled them to publish a complete Bible in 1926 in Leningrad (25,000 copies), a selection from the Bible in 1927 in Kiev (10,000 copies), a New Testament (25,000 copies), and, in 1928, even a biblical concordance (10,000 copies). Their publishing activity was, however, ended by the persecutions, and in 1929 their three periodicals were suppressed. A number of prosecutions decimated the sect.[51]

It was their experience of brotherhood under persecution which, in 1944, led to the union of the Baptists and the Evangelicals. In 1945, this Union included 'Gospel Christians' or Pentecostals, at least those of them who were willing to give up ecstatic forms of prayer. Many Pentecostal communities, however, preferred to keep their freedom and disowned the Union (see below, under Pentecostals). Conversely, some Evangelical Christians and 'authentic' Baptists (*istinnye*), anxious about the integrity of their doctrine, were disinclined to unite with the

Pentecostals and left the Union. Also, in the western regions of the Ukraine, outside the Union there still remain some groups of reformist and stricter Baptists.[52]

The Union is administered by a 'Pan-Unionist Council of Evangelical Christians and Baptists', composed of 12 members (5 from Moscow; 3 from Kiev; 1 from Riga; 1 from Revel). Its present head is J. Jidkov, born in 1888. The Union forms part of the Baptist Universal Alliance. Since 1954 it has maintained regular relations with the Protestant world (reciprocal visits; 5 Baptist students sent to study theology in England, etc.). In August 1962 this friendly intercourse was crowned by the entry of the Union into the World Council of Churches. The Union's journal is the 70-page review *Bratsky Vestnik* (The Fraternal Messenger), which has been published since 1946. At present 5,000 copies are issued. This absurdly small number does not even equal the number of existing communities (5,400). Between 1955 and 1958, the Baptists were authorized to publish the Psalter, the Bible (10,000 copies) and a collection of Spiritual Hymns (15,000 copies). The communities are administered by 45–60 'superintendents', whose duties are to ordain pastors, inspect them and submit reports to the Council of the Union. Their function, therefore, is similar to that of bishops. The communities themselves elect their pastors or 'presbyters', but these are ordained only after a preliminary period of one or two years.

Five times a year – at Easter, Pentecost, the Harvest Festival on the last Sunday of September, the festival of Unity between Baptists and Evangelicals on the last Sunday of October, and at Christmas – a collection is taken in all the communities in aid of the central organization.[53]

In 1960 the total number of the baptized rose to 540,000, and until the fresh persecutions, 15,000 baptisms were registered every year. Making allowance for the number of deaths, the sect could count on a regular yearly increase of 7,000 members. (We should remember that, in conformity with their doctrine, they confer baptism only upon adults whose faith has been tested by a long catechumenate.) The number of those reached by Baptist preaching is reckoned to be between two and three millions.[54]

The Baptists are scattered throughout all the regions of the USSR, but principally in the Ukraine, the Baltic countries and the Far East. In the province of Kharkov there are 56 communities (that of Kharkov itself is 1,650 strong); in Kiev, 170 (4 in Kiev itself); 72 in Chernigov; 73 in the Donets basin, etc.[55] In the large towns of the Kuban and the Caucasus the communities have a membership of 500–800. The numbers are even greater in the towns of Central Asia and the Far East (for example, 1,300 in Tachkent; 1,000 in Novosibirsk). The Moscow community numbers 4,500, and registers 200 baptisms yearly; that of Leningrad, 2,000, with 100 baptisms yearly. In Russia proper their numbers are few, but they are gradually infiltrating into provinces where they were previously unknown.[56]

The strength of the Baptists lies in their method of propaganda. Each member must bring one or two unbelievers to Christ every year, must take an active part in the prayer meetings, and see that their 'brothers and sisters' keep a firm hold on their faith. Religious services are held three times a week; on Wednesday, Saturday and Sunday. One odd feature of their worship is its acceptance of the Orthodox retention of the Julian calendar. They have also retained most of the Orthodox festivals, including the Annunciation. 'Evenings of divine charity' (*vechera liubvi*), are organized for the young, during which hymns are studied or episodes acted from biblical history. Baptist leaders in Tachkent arrange classes in Bible study for the young, but in 1961 they paid for this by being condemned to 'punishment which they richly deserved'.[57] In Leningrad a young Baptist workman distributed religious literature by dropping it in letter boxes.[58] The communities maintain a fund for mutual help.

The anti-religious press unanimously agrees that the Baptists have a real influence on the young. 'I went into the Baptist church in Khabarovsk,' a journalist remarks, 'to see what was going on. I was exceedingly surprised to observe that besides the elderly there were some twenty young people.'[59] A young Moscow communist declares, 'This was the first time I had seen believers, and the strange thing is that they were young.'[60] The Baptist church in Kuibyshev attracts not only the aged; children, school-boys and students are also to be found there.[61] In Tachkent, fifty boys in the highest class received baptism.[62]

Converts to the Baptists are no longer confined to the un-lettered; at least in the provinces, the sect is influential in cultured circles. At Kuibyshev, for instance, they are proud of having two professors, several engineers, a surgeon and an agriculturalist among their members.[63]

According to press reports, what attracts youth to baptism is the tangible, efficacious nature of Christian morality, and the rule of brotherhood between members of the sect.

At Kuibyshev recently, Inna Tikhaia, history mistress in school No. 144, resigned from the komsomol. Asked why she had taken this unusual step, 'this frail young woman stood up, gripped the back of her chair with both hands and, with a proud glance at those present, said in tones of calculated tranquillity, "I am a Christian. . . , I believe that the only way of leading men to live rightly is to lead them to follow the teaching of Christ. Some of those who are now Baptists were formerly regarded as social outcasts, belief in Christ has made them new men. . . . Everyone needs an ideal, and the ideal cannot consist in the possession of material goods alone; but above all in having good moral values."

"Does that mean," the secretary of the komsomol retorted, "that we communists do not profess any lofty ideas, do not fight for them, do not create new men?"

"If the communist faith," the young Christian answered, "succeeded in creating new men before the coming of material prosperity, then I would agree. But at present I see no evidence of this. . . . In places, however, where Baptists are in a majority, those laws about which you communists can only dream, are already a practical reality. In the province of Orenburg there is a Baptist village in which communism is almost a reality. No door is locked and yet there are no thieves. Every man shares his goods with his neighbours.'''

Conversion from the communist to the Baptist faith is made all the easier for the young because the komsomol proclaims the same virtues, but with less appreciation of what they imply and therefore with less efficacy.[64]

'It seems to me,' remarked a twenty-two year old Baptist, 'that there are many points in common between the komsomol and the Baptist faith; both aim at the development of the moral virtues in men. But the communists have no fear of God, whereas the Baptists have, and that explains their greater success.'[65]

The communist Krainov, who has been in contact with the Baptist community in Moscow, adds definition and depth to these remarks:

'It would appear that the young people who come to the meetings are seeking spiritual communion with each other. Why should we try to hide the fact that among ourselves, in scientific undertakings and institutes, everywhere, in the collective life as well as in the specialized groups, there are people living in spiritual isolation. But the young are genuinely looking for love, friendship and mutual respect. And how difficult it is for them to find an attitude of this kind in komsomol circles, or at work, or in the clubs.'[66]

Baptists forbid their members to smoke, drink and swear. Their attitude to Soviet civilization is quite flexible, and their taboos are not absolute. Their ideal is to renounce worldly entertainments (theatres, cinemas, etc.) and to live for God alone. But they do not make this an absolute condition for admission to the sect. Some pastors, however, are stricter and forbid their people to read newspapers, listen to the radio, send their children to school, etc.[67] Baptist teaching lays great emphasis on sanctification through work.

Its leaders have adopted the same policy of explicit loyalty towards the Soviet Government as that of the Orthodox Church. The recent persecutions, however, have fallen as heavily on them as on the other religious denominations. There have been prosecutions in Leningrad, Tachkent, and Chigi-Tul (Kazakhstan).[68]

3. THE PENTECOSTALS. The sect of the Pentecostals was founded in 1907 in America. It believes in special revelations of the Holy Ghost, similar to the descent of the tongues of fire at Pentecost, and it practises 'speaking with tongues'. It was introduced into the USSR by American evangelists about 1921. It increased considerably, and gave rise to several distinct branches.

The Tremblers. The popular name for those Pentecostals who had refused to join the Baptist Union is *Triasuny*, the Tremblers (from *triastis*, to tremble), because during their prayers in common the most inspired among them shook and trembled and began to prophesy. Being prohibited by law, they have no fixed places of worship, but meet, with the utmost secrecy, in little groups, in the homes of their members. In the province of Gomel, they meet three times a week. (In order to prevent any leakage, ordinary members must know nothing of each other.) Among their rites, the breaking of bread and the mutual washing of feet, would appear to be reserved to the initiated. One of their peculiar features is the adoption of the tunes from popular or revolutionary songs for their hymns.[69] In the summer, they hold their meetings out of doors, in the woods. The most zealous of the tremblers graduate by degrees to the title of 'prophet', with one, two or three 'crowns'. The sect forbids its members to take any part in the social and cultural life of the nation.

It is a dynamic body and every member is an active propagandist. The Pentecostals have been reported in various provinces of European Russia: Smolensk, Tula, Kazan, Sverdlovsk, Saratov, Riazan, etc.,[70] in Siberia, the Far East, Altai, and in most of the republics of Central Asia. The community of Briansk has fifty members.[71] The port of Nakhodka has become the rallying point for the Tremblers of Siberia and Asia: whole families, from Kirghizia and the province of Barnaul have moved to Nakhodka, hoping to find there an ark, specially let down from heaven to save the true believers from the imminent destruction of the world. The Pentecostals as a whole tend to be somewhat nomadic, and seldom stay for more than a year or two in the same place.[72]

The sect appears to have some kind of fascination for youth; it is subject to cruel persecution.

The Smorodinsty (followers of Smorodin) or 'The Evangelical faith in the spirit of the apostles'. This branch of the Pentecostals was founded in 1932 by Nicholas Smorodin, among the Catholic population of Polish Volhynia. With the arrival of the Soviet troops in 1939, the leaders of the sect were tried and sentenced, but the sect survived. It appears to be particularly extreme in its refusal to accept Soviet institutions; its members prefer to go into the streets as little as possible to avoid meeting unbelievers. Centres of this sect, in which the young are predominant, are reported from Odessa, Nicolaiev and in some other places on the Black Sea coast.

Mourashkovtsy (followers of Mourashko). This sect was founded by a former Pentecostal from the region of Brest–Litovsk in about 1920. His teaching, about which little is known, is a curious amalgam of paganism, Judaism and Protestant rationalism. It also seems to have been influenced by the Anabaptists and the *khlysty*, and its most conspicuous social characteristics recall those of the spiritual Christians. Between the two wars, the followers of Mourashko in Poland sold all their possessions in order to establish a settlement with the name of Sion, and with Mourashko as its 'father'. When the Soviet army arrived, Mourashko emigrated to the Argentine, but this did not lead to the disappearance of the sect.

Its rites of initiation represent a return to paganism. On the body of each neophyte 'seven seals' are cut. The blood which flows from these incisions, cruciform in shape, is mixed with wine, and then given to the members of the sect as communion.

It is said that some gallons of this communion 'wine' were recently discovered hidden away. Prayer meetings are held in the greatest secrecy, in the woods, at night. They are accompanied by ritualistic dances and, according to the *Sputnik Ateista*, end with scenes of general debauchery.

After the Second World War, the sect greatly increased, but it appears to be confined to White Russia (the provinces of Brest and Pinsk), Moldavia, the Ukraine (Rovno, Volhynia, Odessa) and Kazakhstan.[73] It has a youth organization, entitled 'the army of Christ'.[74] Its present leader is Liubov Uchenko, repatriated from the Argentine in 1947. Quite recently members from Moldavia and Odessa made an attempt to win over Georgia where they believed a New Sion could be founded.[75] The sect is strongly opposed to the Soviet régime and all its ways. It forbids its members to work in the kolkhoz or serve in the army. The Soviet authorities keep a watchful eye on the sect.

4. THE SEVENTH DAY ADVENTISTS. This sect is American in origin and derives from the Adventists who were founded in New York in 1833, by W. Müller. On the strength of the book of Daniel, he foretold the end of the world for 1843, and later, for 1847. These prophecies remaining unfulfilled, his disciples, after his death in 1849, founded the sect of the Seventh Day Adventists or Sabbatarians. They await the end of the world in the near future, but without giving a precise date. Their tenets emphasize the sacredness of Saturday, baptism by immersion, and abstinence from tobacco, alcohol, and pork.

In Russia, where they are usually called *subbotniki*, they were few in number before the Revolution (4,000 in 1911) but under the Soviet régime they have increased considerably. In 1928 the sect had 13,404 members and published three reviews, in Russian, Ukrainian, and German. Today they have State recognition, were represented at the Zagorsk Conference, and have 300 communities scattered throughout the country, but they are mainly concentrated in the Ukraine in which it is estimated that there are 115 communities.[76] The total number of professed Adventists is reported as only 26,000 (9,000 of them in the Ukraine) but there are grounds for believing that their real number is far higher.[77] Important groups have been reported from the Donets basin – one of the most religious regions of the USSR – the province of Rostov in the Crimea, Bashkiria, Siberia, the Far East, Kazakhstan and the republics of Central Asia.[78] In Tadzhikistan, the sect is said to include medical and university students and engineers.[79] In Kazakhstan, the Saturday services are attended by young peasants.[80]

Officially, the Seventh Day Adventists profess complete loyalty to the State. But their observance of Saturday involves frequent conflicts with the local authorities. Moreover, their expectation of the imminent end of the world produces at times a complete alienation from the things of this world. In the sub-Carpathian region of the Ukraine, some peasants who had absorbed the preaching of a local Adventist, thought that the end of the world was at hand and, wearing white trousers, stretched themselves out on tables to await the great cataclysm.[81] Similar incidents occurred in two villages of White Russia.[82]

W. Kolarz believes that the little sect of the 'Ascensionists' owes its origin to Adventist preaching. In 1949, some kolkhozians of the village of Kitaievskoe (in the province of Stavropol) disciples of a man called Belimov, became convinced that they were about to be carried off to heaven. At the beginning of May they sold all their possessions, shut up their homes and, in an enclosure shaded by acacias, awaited their ascension, which it had been foretold would take place between 25th May and 15th June. Adolescents, pale with fright, kissed the earth as a parting gesture.[83] But it is not so certain that they were related to the Adventists; a number of sects share these apocalyptic ideas (*fiodorovtsy, khlysty,* etc.).

5. JEHOVAH'S WITNESSES (YEGOVITSY). Dozens of articles in newspapers and reviews and a number of pamphlets illustrate

the importance of the Jehovah's Witnesses in the USSR. We must first note that in Russia today the sect is marked by two distinct trends, one of them purely Russian, the other of American origin.

The *Yegovisty–Yliintsy* (Jehovists–followers of Iliin) were founded by Captain Nicholas Iliin in about 1850. Their doctrine is a rather crude form of Manicheism (the opposition between Jehovah–Christ and Lucifer, Jehovah's rebellious son). The sect survived all the vicissitudes of the Revolution. *Voiovnichy ateist* reports its presence in the Donets basin (8, 1961, pp. 18–20).

The Jehovah's Witnesses originated in America after a schism among the Adventists. In its present form, the sect no longer has anything in common with Christianity. Its doctrine is a strange mixture of theocratic and eschatological hopes. They believe that after a world war, Armageddon, God–Jehovah will destroy all existing States, and in their place will institute a theocracy in which only members of the sect will have a place. In the USSR where the Press deliberately fosters a psychosis about atomic war, this teaching of the Jehovah's Witnesses found a natural home.

The sect came into the USSR at the time of the Second World War, and made its entry by way of the western regions that had been annexed. In 1949, on the request of Corvington, Knorr's assistant at the Brooklyn world centre, a delegation of the regional committee of the sect visited Moscow to ask that all the Jehovah's Witnesses might be co-ordinated as a unity. Stalin gave a point-blank refusal. Most of the members of the regional committee as well as a great number of other members were arrested and deported in 1952.[84] The Witnesses reckon that 7,000 were deported at this time.[85] The massive deportation which was followed in 1954 by a fairly inclusive amnesty, enabled the sect to extend its field of work considerably. It is very active, but it works in secret. Its basic unit is a cell of fifteen to twenty members. Several cells constitute a group; the union of groups forms the *stref* which receives orders from the regional committee.

Catechumens must take a course of 'theocratic studies', held in meetings in which publications from America are read and pondered. These are sent through the agency of the 'peoples' democracies or in food parcels, and reproduced in Russian and Ukrainian on arrival. The type for printing is stolen from the State presses by Witnesses who become printers solely for this purpose. By this means the sect manages to print the reviews *Bashnia Strajy* (Russian editions) and *Vartova Bashnia* (Ukrainian edition) as well as other publications.

Jehovah's Witnesses are chiefly recruited from the unlettered and from victims of the régime. (Cultured members could be counted on the fingers). The sect's propaganda has proved very successful in the concentration camps. Its present numbers are not known. In 1959, as the result of prosecutions and pressures of various kinds, 500 members left the sect, a figure that suggests that its total membership must run into thousands (10–20,000?).

Its converts come from the ranks of the young. At Usolia-Sibirskoe the active members were workers from thirty-one to fifty years of age. Some Witnesses have earned the reputation of being superlative workers. A preacher named Burlak, for example, is working in Moldavia as a carpenter, and regularly exceeds the normal output. Or there is Sagin, forty years old, who, if he had not belonged to the sect, would have received Kruschev's heartiest recognition. He discovered new ways of cultivating maize and obtained excellent yields. His fame extends beyond the boundaries of the province of Tomsk where he works. And in the kolkhoz of Frunze (in the province of Tomsk) there is a member named Kuku who is its best shepherd, and an enthusiast for his work.[86]

Active members are persistently harried by the State police; prosecutions of Jehovah's Witnesses have in recent years been made in Kazakhstan (secret cells were discovered in Ust-Kamenogorsk, Tekeli, Karaganda, etc.),[87] in the Moldavian province of Nikolaiev;[88] in that of Tomsk (in Assino the study group had seventy-five members); in Vorkuta (Inte, Ukhta); in the Altai, at Ordzhonikidze (north Ossetia); at Makhachkala, etc.[89] This list shows that the sect is particularly numerous in Siberia, in the far north (the area of deportation), and in the western Ukraine. But cells have been reported from central Russia, in Mtsensk (in the province of Orel), Kalinin and at Krasnodar in south Russia.

The anti-religious press depicts the Jehovah's Witnesses as paid agents from the United States. But, during the prosecutions, the accused denied that they had anything to do with politics, and asserted that they acted solely in the religious sphere.[90]

Schisms and sects that have sprung up since the Revolution

The Soviet régime, far from arresting the growth of sects, created an atmosphere favourable to their proliferation. The religious persecutions and the social upheavals caused a great number of new ones to appear. On the eve of the war twelve recently formed sects were reported from the Ukraine alone.[91] Nor is this process over; the latest arrival, according to my information, was in 1957. It appeared in the Crimea and was called 'Christ's Last Link'. It was immediately suppressed. Unfortunately, I have no information about its teaching.[92]

I. CHURIKOVTSY (*followers of Churikov*). The *Churikovtsy* (also called the *Trezvenniki* – the Temperate) is one of the very few new sects whose hostility to the Government is not pronounced. It was founded during the twenties by Ivan Churikov, a peasant from the province of Samara, who declared that the coming of the Kingdom of Heaven depended upon the complete disappearance of alcohol and that since diseases were sent by God, no attempt should be made to cure them. The sect met with some success in the Leningrad region where it had about 4,000 members.[93] It was long thought to have disappeared, but recently a Soviet journal announced that it had come to light again in the Leningrad region. It has proved unexpectedly attractive to the young. It continues to practise temperance and to refuse medical aid.[94]

2. SECTS OF THE RED DRAGON. Soviet controversialists have given the name of *Krasnodrakonovtsy* to a whole group of anti-government sects who identify the Soviet Government with the dragon of the Apocalypse and exhort their members to resist the socialization of life either actively or passively. To judge by the *Great Encyclopedia* of 1948, the sect had not then wholly disappeared.

Before the Second World War the most important sect hostile to the Government was that of the *Fiodorovtsy* Crusaders, so called from its founder Fiodor Rybalkin.[95] In 1923 these sectaries appeared at Novo Liman, in the Donets basin. They identified Communism with anti-Christ, and awaited the *Parousia* which, in their view, will be the collective ascent of the members of the sect. They are ultra-ascetic, and hold the cross in especial veneration. On many of their houses the first verse of Psalm 1 was engraved: 'Blessed is the man that hath not walked in the counsel of the ungodly'; or, alternatively, the first verse of Psalm 67: 'Let God arise, let his enemies be scattered.' They are fiercely opposed to collectivization, and shun all intercourse with the kolkhozians whom they consider to be great sinners.[96] Before 1930, the sect had many members in the Donets basin, at Voronej, Kiev, on the banks of the Don and in the northern Caucasus. In 1930, a massive public prosecution of the sect was held at Voronej. It was decimated, yet in 1938 its reappearance was reported from the Donets basin.[97] A fraction of the sect bears the name of *Enokhovtsty* (Enochians) on account of its ascensionist beliefs. Little groups of the *Krasnodrakonovtsy*, *Fiodorovtsy* and *Enochovtsty* were reported from Kazakhstan in 1961.[98]

Cherdashniki (the name derives from *cherdak*: a loft) was a sect which aimed at replacing the Soviet régime by the laws and institutions of the Gospel. Khalikev, its head, was held by his disciples to be a Christ; the members of the sect were called 'apostles', and the area of their apostolate, Palestine. Dressed in long black robes, they went from village to village proclaiming the triumph of God's justice on earth. In their prayers they beg God to grant a collective ascent to heaven – hence the probable origin of their name.[99]

The *Chernokhristovtsy* or followers of the Black Christ are widespread in the Ukraine. They will have no contact at all with the Soviet system, and if they find Soviet papers or money they quickly throw them out without touching them. Their hatred of planning leads some of them to banish all idea of number from their lives (*liudi ne znaiushchie chisla*).[100]

Lastly, various sects of the red dragon are known to us by their names alone, such as the *Apokaliptiki*, the *Ostrijniki*, the *Krestovatiki*, etc.[101] Today all the sects of the red dragon have been swallowed up or eclipsed by two large groups which, to some extent they have influenced: the True Orthodox Church and the True Orthodox Christians.

3. THE TRUE ORTHODOX CHURCH. For a time it seemed likely that the right wing opposition to the Patriarchal Church had not survived the persecutions. A brief article in the *Review of the Moscow Patriarchate*, published in 1948, did indeed note the existence of a group of Orthodox Christians in the Tambov region, who would not accept the authority of the Patriarch Alexis, and described themselves as the only 'true Orthodox Christians.'[102] But only after Stalin's death was it learnt that this 'group' was really a movement, or rather, two movements, organized and widespread in several regions.

The *True Orthodox Church* (*Istinnaia Pravoslavnaia Tserkov*, I. P. Tse. for short), unlike the *True Orthodox Christians*, cannot be classed as a sect, but is, rather, a schism or, more accurately, the logical climax of the right-wing schism of 1928. In central Russia, where its members are particularly numerous, it is in the direct line of descent from Alexis Bui, the Bishop of Voronej, one of the fiercest opponents of the Metropolitan Sergius.[103] The

True Church has its own clergy, ordained either outside the Patriarchal Church or before the schism, but whether it still has any bishops is not known. In some places where it has no priests, its communities are directed by laymen. It has no churches, and its members, in this respect like the 'Nicodemuses', cover the walls of their rooms with icons. Their prayer-meetings are held in complete secrecy with at most twenty present. Some sacraments, such as confession, are practised at a distance, by means of couriers who carry written confessions from individuals to a priest. Among the sins that are enumerated in the sect's special list is any concession to the Soviet régime (work in the kolkhoz, membership of the syndicates, etc). Among their members there are many monks and nuns who gather in little secret hermitages. In the town of Michurinsk, for example, there were forty-five nuns out of ninety-eight active members.

Between 1946 and 1950 they tried to re-establish 'a single centralized organism', but it seems that the police frustrated their plans. A great effort was made to attract the young by evening meetings and youth groups. In 1950, the ages of the members of the Michurinsk community were as follows: out of sixty-five people whose ages were known, eight were less than forty; thirty-two were between forty and sixty; and twenty-nine were over sixty. This is not a picture of a set of aged crones about to disappear.

The religious appeal of the True Church is due to its proclamation of the imminent end of the world and its identification of the Government with anti-Christ. In 1948 there was an earthquake at Ashkhabad – incidentally, this was never mentioned in the Soviet press until after Stalin's death – and the True Church seized the opportunity to declare that Moscow was soon to be 'swallowed up'. Between 1948–9 the activity of the True Church was considerable, but after Stalin's death and the consequent liberalization of the régime, its development may have been retarded.

In 1950 most of its leaders were tried and condemned. Very little is now known of its geographical distribution. At Temir-

Tau in Kazakhstan, there used to be a monastery of the sect; it was reconstituted by nuns who had been pardoned in 1954, but in 1960 they were compelled to join the labour camps once again.[104] In the Crimea this Church once had some attraction for the young. But in the Tambov region only a few little groups of members remain. It may be that the recent persecutions are drawing them closer to the Patriarchal Church. If this does not happen this Church may soon either be reduced to a sect or else become submerged in the various sects to which it has given rise. Even now it is being supplanted by the True Orthodox Christians.

4. THE TRUE ORTHODOX CHRISTIANS. During the Second World War, the 'True Orthodox Church' gave birth to a body entitled the True Orthodox Christians. (Their name indicates that they no longer claim to be a Church.) They were numerous in the Tambov region; their prayer-meetings are held in the open air, near wells or stones or trees that are considered to be sacred. These meetings, which used to draw crowds, took place in an atmosphere of mystical exaltation: exorcists could be seen at them, and women crouched over water, looking for the face of the Mother of God to appear on its surface, preachers, young and old, who spoke in whispers or in a voice of thunder, the unfortunate of all kinds, the blind, the lame, 'fools for Christ's sake', seers and prophets. The 'True Orthodox Christians' are genuinely concerned with the sick: for example (still in the region of Tambov), a poor paralysed idiot, with six fingers, whose only method of communication was a horrifying roar, was drawn in a carriage by a team of these people. They are said to express frankly monarchist views and to have spread the rumour that some members of the imperial family miraculously escaped from the massacre of Ekaterinenburg. Admission into the sect is allowed only if the applicant agrees to leave the kolkhoz, the syndicate or the factory. The children of its adherents must be withdrawn from the schools at the end of their fourth year. All official documents must be destroyed.[105]

A young member of the sect, twenty-three years old, one Bobzovsky, was summoned to the military recruiting tribunal. He came into its office and made the sign of the cross. He had burnt his military pass and his identity card, and had no wish to replace them.

'May God save me from it, I shall never accept papers from the devil.'

'And yet you are liable for military service?' asks the commandant.

'I am a Christian.'

'But you are also a citizen of the USSR?'

'No, I belong to God.'[106]

When a 'True Christian' is asked 'Who are you?' he usually replies, 'God's servant'. If he is asked his name he simply says: 'God knows it.'

One of the young members has given an account of the atmosphere of mystical exaltation prevailing in the sect.

'My belief in God began at the wells when I was sixteen. There you can see many who are possessed; they fling themselves down, foaming at the mouth, but this only happens when they have come close to the wells. Young people also flock to them, and the meetings were so intense that they set one's heart on fire for God. It was at these wells that I learnt what "God" means; I experienced a kind of fear. The people I met there had seen visions in their youth. About forty of us assembled for a discussion. We all prayed. A woman, one of the possessed, occasionally visited us; she went up to each person and explained how he or she had personally sinned, and her statement was correct. She was between thirty and thirty-five. My brother was a student of the Scriptures, he told others what he had found in them, and they believed. My own work was the production of the metal casing for icons. I read the *Lives of the Saints*, and I was particularly drawn to the career of the man of God, Alexis. . . . I read all of the Gospels and the Bible, particularly the prophets, and these too spoke of the last days. The parables moved me deeply. I know the

Sermon on the Mount by heart. I learnt a trade, the production of the casing for icons, and I earned a great deal of money. . . . . It is a general rule in our society that no one should work, but if it is for oneself or to help the other believers, it is allowed. At this time I still wanted to run the streets. But God was stronger even than the streets. My parents brought me up strictly. They were God fearing; persons in distress turned to them, and they adopted two orphans to bring them up in godly living.'[107]

This body of extremists is almost exclusively recruited from the young. In the Tambov region, for example, in 1952, out of eighty-three active members, forty-four were less than thirty; twenty-seven were between thirty and fifty and only twelve had been born before the October Revolution. The sect is said to exist in several regions of Russia: Suma, Lugansk, Voronej, Saratov, Riazan, Kirov, Perm, Novosibirsk, Alma-Ata, Chimkent, Cheboksary, Mordovia, etc. In the Altai entire villages are populated by its members.[108] Some lead a wandering life, others are solitaries.

In 1955 the sect is said to have split and its divisions to have turned in opposite directions. Some members gave up their radical opposition to the régime and abandoning their extreme asceticism, returned to normal family life: 'Our heroism has been without result.' But others have intensified their isolation and formed groups of 'the silent ones' (*molchalniki*). These reject all contact not only with the world, but also with those who have not made the vow of silence. They are to be found in the northern districts of Tambov. In 1959 there were seventy-one 'silent ones' in this province of Tambov, a significant number for so radical a sect and one, moreover, prohibited by the law. This body was composed of thirty per cent of men and seventy per cent of women. It included twelve young persons of less than twenty-five years. These 'silent ones' are able to exist through the help of the members of their families who have not taken the vow of silence and who work. The poorest of them are helped by neighbours who are often members of the Patriarchal Church.[109] The sect is harshly persecuted, and the children of its members are taken away from their families and placed in boarding schools.[110]

5. LEONTIEVTSY. The True Orthodox Church, founded by Leontius Gritsan in the southern part of the province of Rovno, after the Second World War, does not appear to be very different from some bodies described above. It is opposed both to the Soviet régime and to the Patriarchal Church. Its founder was deported,[111] but the sect survived. He is respected as a martyr and a saint. Like the True Christians, they destroy all official documents, and condemn themselves to live as wanderers, and they are thus enabled to spread their faith. They have gained recruits from the numerous pilgrims who come to the Laura of Pochaev; where they benefit from the sympathy of some of the monks.[112]

6. BOJZHII DETI (*Children of God*). This sect, of recent formation and purely local (it is confined to north Kazakhstan), presents characteristics similar to those of the True Orthodox Christians. It held regular meetings 'in order to converse with God'. Its attitude was completely negative, and its members even destroyed musical instruments. They refused to speak to 'unbelievers', and, in view of the imminent end of the world, went so far as to plan the burning down of the Ivanovka kolkhoz in the region of Semipalatinsk. In 1958 its leaders were prosecuted and received severe sentences.[113]

We have now rapidly surveyed some forty sects which are at present active in the USSR. Some of these have a membership of several hundred thousand, or even more than one million (Old Believers, Baptists); others number several thousand only. The total membership of those who are 'on the edge of the Church', is difficult to assess; it may amount to five million.

The development of these sects is far from being uniform. Of the traditional Russian sects, only the Old Believers and the Khlysty are holding their ground; the rest seem to be decreasing.

On the other hand, sects of Western origin are showing a remarkable vitality and may well become a new and important religious minority, of Protestant character, among the millions of Russia. Latterly, the Revolution has provoked, in the Orthodox Church, schisms productive of new sectarian movements favoured by the apocalyptic events of our time.

Geographically, the sects are distributed all over the Soviet Union. A town like Kuibyshev has an Orthodox bishopric, an Old Believer bishopric, Baptist communities, Jehovah's Witnesses, True Christian communities, etc. But the sectaries are concentrated in certain definite areas: the Ukraine (especially in its western provinces, and the Donets basin); the far north and the far east; in the Altai, Kazakhstan, and the republics of Central Asia (the last five regions being the principal reception areas for deported persons). In Russia proper, only the Old Believers in the north and in the region of Kostroma and Nijny–Novgorod where they originated, appear to exist in significant numbers.

At first sight the survival of the older sects and the success of new ones or of those from the West, may seem surprising; but there are a number of reasons that account for this:

A. The Orthodox Church is still by far the largest body, but the persecutions have left it weakened. It is far from being present in every locality, and in some towns and rural areas there are no Orthodox churches at all. This religious void, which the civilizing efforts of communism do nothing to fill, creates conditions favourable to the growth of sects. On the other hand, the Orthodox Church is deprived of every means of explaining and spreading its teaching by means of the printed word; the religious instinct has to seek means of expression wherever and however it can.

B. The too numerous Orthodox communities, with their absorption in the activities of public worship, do not always enable the young to develop their personal religion. The individual is lost in the crowd and condemned to a passive religious life. But in the small communities of the sects, in which everyone has some part to play, even if only in spreading the faith, the young find the spiritual atmosphere, the mutual affection and the sense of responsibility so lacking in the communist organizations.

c. The Orthodox Church has been too conciliatory in its attitude towards the Soviet régime. The unifying factor in these sects which are otherwise so diverse, is their common opposition to the various aspects of the Soviet system. Since there are no political parties, it is the sects that attract the opponents of the régime.

The recent persecutions, though they have fallen also upon the sects, cannot but benefit them in the end. They are less organized and less visible than the Orthodox Church, and therefore not so vulnerable.

CHAPTER XI

NEIGHBOURING CHURCHES

APART FROM the Orthodox Church and the numerous sects which compete with it, most of the great Christian denominations are represented in the USSR by minority Churches on the borders of the country, in the neighbouring areas that were annexed to Russia at a comparatively late period, Churches that have retained their own beliefs or their own ecclesiastical organization.

1. The Orthodox Church of Georgia

Georgia has been a Christian country since the fourth century. Unlike the neighbouring Persian and Armenian Churches, it did not reject the Council of Chalcedon, but kept in unbroken communion with the Orthodox Church, both before and after the schism of 1054. Originally it was subject to the jurisdiction of the Patriarchate of Antioch, but in the sixth century (553) it became autonomous, and in the eighth century, autocephalous. At the beginning of the nineteenth century, Georgia asked to be incorporated in the Russian Empire. The Church was the loser by it: it lost its independence in 1811, when its last Catholicos, Antony II, was exiled to Russia and replaced by an Exarch, a member of the Russian Synod. Only the first of these Exarchs was a Georgian; all his sixteen successors until 1917 were of Russian origin; and their progressive Russification of the Georgian Church was as clumsy as it was unjustified. Understandably, therefore, in 1917, this Church took advantage of the Revolution and resumed its autocephalous status – a unilateral action which the Russian

Church refused to accept for thirty-seven years, that is, not until 1943. In the meanwhile the Georgian Church had endured the persecutions. In 1924, its Catholicos, Ambrose Chelai, was sentenced to eight years' imprisonment. In some mountainous districts the almost total closure of the churches led to the re-surgence of pagan cults.[1]

Georgia does not appear to have shared in the religious renais-sance of post-war Russia. Of the 2,455 parishes before the Revolu-tion only eighty were re-established – and this for a population of four millions. Its Church has seven bishops, one hundred and five priests, two monasteries and two convents, and it publishes a liturgical calendar. It has no seminary, but lectures in pastoral theology seem to be more or less regularly delivered.[2] First-hand information suggests that the Georgian rejection of religion is fairly widespread: the members of its Church are mainly recruited from the important Russian minority which may amount to a million. Three of the eleven churches of Tiflis, the capital (with 635,000 inhabitants) are Russian. Since February 1960, the head of the Georgian Church has been the Catholicos Ephrem, unani-mously elected at a secret ballot, in succession to the Catholicos Melchisedech who had died. Mgr Ephrem Sidamanidze, born in 1896, is a graduate of the Tiflis Seminary (1918), and of the Faculty of Letters in the same city (1923). He has written a mono-graph on St Maximus, the confessor. At the reception given after his enthronement, representatives of the Georgian intelligentsia, including the poet G. Leonidze, were present.[3] The Church continues to form an essential feature of the nation.

It maintains friendly relations with the Russian Church which are expressed in mutual visits and in a common front in the struggle for the preservation of peace. It was invited to the Pan-Orthodox Conference in Rhodes, but it did not attend. Nevertheless, in August 1962, it was admitted to the World Council of Churches. The Patriarch went in person to Paris to support his Church's candidature; all were impressed by his sincerity and modesty.

2. The Armenian or Gregorian Church

The Armenian Church is even older than that of Georgia, but since it rejected the decisions of the Council of Chalcedon it was separated from the Great Undivided Church at the end of the fifth century. Even today it belongs to that body of Eastern Churches, nominally Monophysite, which claim to be Orthodox even though not in communion with the Byzantine Orthodox Churches. Throughout the centuries the Armenians have suffered cruelly from their Persian and Turkish neighbours; during the Second World War, for instance, the Armenian minority in Turkey was practically exterminated. In all these trials the Church has been the refuge and symbol of the nation's personality. The Armenian Church, more than any other, is the Church of a people and a nation.

Since the fifteenth century, it has been divided into two bodies, each with its own Catholicos; the Catholicos of Echmiadzin in what is now Soviet Armenia; and that of Cilicia who, since 1916, has resided in Antileas, near Beirut. These two centres are independent and have equal rights, but the Catholicos of Echmiadzin has a primacy of spiritual honour over that of the Great House of Cilicia, whose jurisdiction does not, in theory, go beyond the boundaries of the Middle East. The Catholicos of Echmiadzin has the title of Catholicos of all the Armenians; his jurisdiction extends not only over the Soviet Armenians (3,100,000), but also over the other three-quarters of the Armenians of the diaspora (1,400,000). Thus Echmiadzin is the international religious centre of the Armenians. The Soviet Government, by acting through the Church, is able to exert its influence over the foreign Armenian communities, whose economic and political significance is not negligible. Although the Church has suffered greatly in the persecutions – the number of parishes had fallen from 1,446 to a mere 89 in 1954 – Echmiadzin still retains its right to certain privileges. In 1932, for example, the Soviet authorities, though denying the Russian Church the right to assemble in Council allowed a national Council of the Armenian Church to elect a new Catholicos. The latter, Khoren I, gave tangible evidence of his loyalty to the régime, but this did not prevent him from being assassinated in 1938. Only after the war did a more or less normal religious life again become possible. The community of the Monastery of Echmiadzin which, *ceteris paribus*, plays the part of the Roman Curia in the Armenian Church, became reduced to a dozen members and was forced to appeal to the secular clergy in order to replenish its ranks (fifty-five members in 1960). An institute of theology was opened in 1945; between 1953-4 it had thirty-four students, and in 1960 there were forty. Both the students and the professors included Armenians from abroad. Professors Ararat and Garibian Arakel Arakalian, from the Armenian Universities, teach in the institute of theology, and are also members of the Supreme Religious Council. This is a feature which distinguishes the Armenian Church from the other religious bodies in the USSR; it is due to its fundamentally national character. The Monastery of Echmiadzin produces a review (five or six numbers a year) and a yearly calendar.

The international influence of Echmiadzin increased after the death of the Catholicos George (Guevork) VI (11th May 1954) which coincided with a period of diminishing intransigence in Soviet foreign policy. The national Council of the Church which included ninety-eight delegates from the Soviet Union and thirty-nine from foreign countries elected, on 29th September 1955, Vazgen Palkian, a young Armenian bishop from Rumania, to the office of Catholicos. He was forty-seven, and well-known for his work for peace. One of the first acts of the new Catholicos, who was at once given Soviet nationality, was to visit Beirut – an event without precedence in the history of the Armenian Church – to take part in the election of the new Catholicos of the House of Cilicia. His real purpose, however, was to prevent the election of an independent Catholicos and to bring the Cilician Church under the control of Echmiadzin. The intrigue failed; the Council elected Mgr Zarch (d. 1963), the candidate of the *dachmak* party (independent, anti-communist). Vazgen found it prudent to leave Beirut before the elections. From Cairo he proceeded, unsuccessfully, to dispute their validity.

Some of the Churches of the diaspora, realizing the dependence of Echmiadzin upon the State, have turned to the House of Cilicia. In 1958, the three dioceses of Iran and also one in North America, spontaneously placed themselves under its jurisdiction. In order to forestall similar defections, Vazgen undertook a four-months' journey, in 1960, through Europe and America.

In 1962, at the meeting of the Central Committee of the World Council of Churches, the two divisions of the Armenian Church were admitted to the Council. They took the opportunity of explaining in a common statement that their individual requests for admission must not be interpreted as representing the candidature of two different Churches. Relations with the Moscow Patriarchate are friendly, and find expression in mutual visits and in common statements on the maintenance of peace.

Practically nothing is known about this Church's inner life. As with the Russian Church, that of Armenia enjoyed a period of comparative expansion during the years 1956–9. Some of its buildings were restored to it by the State. We do not know whether it was struck by the recent wave of persecution.[4]

3. *The Roman Catholic Church*

After the eighteenth century Roman Catholicism became one of the Churches on the periphery of Russia. Previously, it had been regarded by Russians as the militant and hostile Church of their dangerous neighbours in the West. The various attempts made by Rome to encroach upon the Orthodox Church, first by military campaigns (for example, the attacks of the Teutonic Knights in the thirteenth century) and by the more or less compulsory unions enforced upon Orthodox dioceses then under the authority of the Polish crown, all made an unfavourable impression on the Russian people, and indeed sometimes produced a deep hatred of the 'Latin heresy'. Nevertheless, the imposing structure of the Roman Church did succeed in attracting some members of the very Westernized Russian aristocracy. After the edict of toleration of 1905 the Roman Church gained complete freedom of action, but its intense propaganda met with little success.

Within the boundaries of the Russia of 1921, the Catholic Church represented no more than a comparatively unimportant minority: about one million six hundred thousand members centred in the western provinces of Mohilev, Minsk, Volhynia, and Kamenets-Podolsk. The persecution soon dealt with this minority Church which, as the following table shows, ceased to have any visible existence:[5]

	1917	1934
Archdioceses and dioceses	7	none
Bishops and apostolic administrators	21	none
Churches and chapels	980	3
Priests and men of religion	912	10
Religious institutions and houses	200	none
Schools and social undertakings	300	none
Seminaries	4	none
Publications	10	none

On the other hand, in 1939, and especially in 1945, the annexation of the eastern half of Poland, of the three Baltic countries and of sub-Carpathian Russia, made the Roman Church, some twelve million strong, the most numerous Christian denomination after the Orthodox Church. The Soviet Government which saw in the Vatican and the 'Catholic international', one of the greatest obstacles to the spread of communism in the world, and which could not tolerate the existence of a foreign authority, even though it were spiritual, on its own territory, took energetic measures to restrict the activities and influence of the Catholic Church.

The Latin dioceses in the former Polish territories, which incorporated 3,500,000 Catholics, saw most of their churches and institutions closed. The Archbishop of Vilnius, Mgr Miecislas Reinys, was arrested in May 1947; the Bishop of Lutsk, Mgr Adolf Szelazck, died in exile in 1950; the Latin Archbishop of Lvov, Mgr Eugene Baziak, alone seems to have been spared. In 1939 there had been 270 churches and 246 priests. In 1952 only 5 churches and 3 priests remained.[6]

In Lithuania, where the population is about eighty-five per cent Catholic (about two million five hundred thousand members) the Soviet Government has succeeded in disrupting the hierarchy, but not in destroying the Church and the religious instincts of the people. Mgr Matulionis, Bishop of Kaisedorys, who had had two previous experiences of communist prisons, was again arrested in 1946. He was pardoned nine years later, when he was eighty-two. In the same way Mgr Ramanauskas, Auxiliary Bishop of Telsiai, arrested in 1946, appeared again in Lithuania in 1956, but only to die soon afterwards. Mgr Borisevicius, Titular Bishop of Telsiai, was condemned to death on 3rd January 1947; there has been no further mention of him. Only one bishop, Mgr Poltorakas of Panevezys, managed to remain in office until his death in 1957.

The clergy have decreased by half. In 1947 there were 1,470 priests; in 1954 there were 741 serving 688 churches. The Seminary of Kaunas provided training for replacements; in 1947, the number of its students rose to 300, but the Soviet Government ordered them to be reduced to 75, and then to a mere fifty. Even so, large sections of the population have remained devoted to their religion: on 11th September 1955, 15,000 people attended the consecration of two new Lithuanian churches; and a crowd of 20,000 was present at the opening of a church in the port of Klaipeda. The Cathedrals of Vilnius and Kaunas have huge congregations. The pilgrimage of Kalvarya, near Lake Platyalyai, was attracting so many that, in 1959, the communist authorities organized a secular counter-pilgrimage.[7] In 1961, Fr Balciunas, a priest of the diocese of Telsai, was condemned to twenty-five years imprisonment for having organized a journey for some young Catholics for whose religious training he was responsible.[8]

In 1962, two priests of Klaipeda, were also given a prison sentence for having tried to build a new church in their town.[9]

In Latvia, Catholics form only a quarter of the population (479,000 out of 2,000,000). In 1945, only the aged Archbishop, Anthony Springovics (1867–1958) escaped arrest. In June 1947, he was able to consecrate two bishops, one of whom, Peter Strods, is now his successor; the other, Mgr Casimir Dulbinskis, was arrested soon after his consecration. There still seem to be 126 priests serving 170 parishes. Quite recently the pilgrimage to Our Lady of Aglona attracted several thousand people.[10]

4. The Uniate Churches

The other important body of Catholics was formed by the so-called Uniate, or Greek-Catholics: about four million in Galicia (ex-Polish territory) and almost five hundred thousand in sub-Carpathian Russia (a former province of Czechoslovakia). In 1596, as the result of pressures of various kinds, Michael Rogoza, the Metropolitan of Kiev, and most of the bishops, in spite of protests and opposition from the laity, signed an act of union with Rome at Brest. The Churches that were thus joined to the Vatican retained the Byzantine rite, at least in part, and the Slavonic language. In 1839, after the partition of Poland, a section of the Uniates returned to Orthodoxy, but the Church as a whole, being within the Austrian dominions, remained loyal to Rome.

In 1944 when Galicia was restored to the Soviet Union, the Uniate Church was not at first disturbed. Its Metropolitan, the eminent prelate Andrew Szepticky, who died on 1st November 1944, was given a solemn funeral. Among other dignitaries present was Nikita Kruschev, then secretary of the Communist Party in the Ukraine. Mgr Szepticky's successor, Mgr Joseph Slipyii, sent a delegation to Moscow and thanked the Patriarch Alexis for the hospitality he had bestowed upon it.[11] But soon the attitude of the Soviet Government changed entirely: on 11th April 1945, all the bishops of the Uniate Church were arrested and deported:

(Mgr Slipyii, the Metropolitan of Lvov, reported to be in the concentration camp of Vorkuta in 1959; Mgr Nicholas Budka, his Auxiliary, Mgr Gregory Khomyzzin, Bishop of Stanislav; his Auxiliary, Mgr Latysevsky; Mgr Czarnecky, etc.). The two last named came back to Galicia after the amnesty of 1955. But they came back to die; the former in 1957, the latter in 1959.[12] Mgr Slipyii was pardoned in 1955, again arrested in 1957, freed at the beginning of 1963, and allowed to withdraw to the Vatican.

These arrests were admitted by the *Review of the Moscow Patriarchate*, but it was careful to add that 'no other ecclesiastical arrests had occurred', and that 'reports on this matter that have appeared in the West are erroneous'.[13] Immediately after these tragic events a 'Committee to promote the transference of Greco-Catholics to the Orthodox Church', was set up at Lvov, under the direction of three Uniate priests, Gabriel Kostelnik, Michael Melnik, and Antony Pelvetsky. This Committee issued an appeal to the Greco-Catholic clergy, asking them to complete the 'territorial unification of the Ukraine' by its religious unification through incorporation in the Orthodox Church. At the same time, the Committee sent a note to the Soviet of the Peoples' Commissars of the RSS in the Ukraine, which contained the important ruling: 'No immediate transformation of the Uniate Church into Orthodoxy should be thought of. For this,' the note continued, 'time is needed, so that the honour of the clergy may be respected, and the people made familiar with the idea and calmed. . . . It must be done in such a way that no one will oppose it.'[14] In its reply to this note, the Soviet recognized the Committee as being the 'sole juridico-ecclesiastical organ that has the right to govern the Greco-Catholic parishes without qualification' and ordered it to send a list of deans, priests or monastic superiors who refused to accept its authority. A protest sent by a number of Uniate priests to Molotov was disregarded.

On 20th February 1946, a group of Greco-Catholic priests, led by Fr Kostelnik, were officially received into the Orthodox

Church at Kiev. On 24th and 25th February, two of them, Melnik and Pelvetsky, were given episcopal consecration to the sees of Sambor and Stanislav.[15]

On their return from Lvov, a Council, held from the 28th February to 10th March, in the Cathedral of St George, and composed of 216 Uniate priests (out of the 1,270 who belonged to these dioceses) and 19 laymen, renounced 'the Latin errors', and asked to be reunited to the Orthodox Church. Shortly afterwards, Fr Kostelnik, who had been made Proto-Presbyter – the highest distinction for a married priest – two bishops and a delegation of priests, were received in Moscow by the Patriarch Alexis (5th April). Since this date the Uniate Dioceses of Galicia have formed an integral part of the Orthodox Exarchate of the Ukraine.[16]

The precarious nature of this reunion, due to the initiative of the Soviet Government and assisted by its police, was made plain by a series of tragic incidents. On 20th September 1948, Fr Kostelnik was assassinated in the streets of Lvov. This murder was depicted as an act of revenge instigated by the Vatican, but the murderers were never discovered, and no one was prosecuted. W. Kolarz does not rule out the possibility of the Soviet police being implicated.[17] When Fr Kostelnik was in Moscow he had uttered the gravest accusations against the Vatican, but at Lvov he had opposed a too hasty transference of the Uniates to Orthodoxy.[18]

In October 1955, another tragic event occurred, and so far it has not been explained. A delegation of ex-Uniate clergy, led by Mgr Michael Melnik, set out on 7th October, on the invitation of the Patriarch Alexis, to visit Kiev, Moscow and Leningrad. Between Lvov and Kiev (400 miles), on 8th October, Fr Vladimir Kunovsky, the bishop's secretary, died in mysterious circumstances. No explanation of this sudden death was offered. The next day, Mgr Michael himself – he was only fifty-two – also died suddenly. His body was taken to Dorogobouj, while the delegation continued on its journey as though nothing had happened. In an article entitled – not without a certain sardonic

humour – 'an unforgettable journey', the members of the delegation made no mention of Fr Kunovsky's funeral.[19] In fact, according to a private source, difficult to check, Fr Kunovsky quite
simply disappeared in the hands of the police. The same source
alleges that Mgr Michael and his secretary not only sheltered a
Uniate priest who had come back from the concentration camps
after the amnesty, but had encouraged and arranged his flight to
the West – 'a crime' which would account for their assassination.[20]
Whatever the explanation, the death of Mgr Michael and his
secretary, with only a day's interval between them, and in such
circumstances, can hardly be put down to natural causes. Fifteen
months later, Bishop Anthony Pelvetsky also died suddenly.
But he was sixty, and there is no reason to doubt that his was a
natural death. All the same, ten years after the Council of Lvov,
the three leading members of the Committee for promoting the
transference of Greco-Catholics to Orthodoxy, were no longer
in this world.

In 1949, the Uniate Church of sub-Carpathian Russia, which
incorporated in the diocese of Mukachevo, 461,500 layfolk, 281
parishes, 374 priests, and a dozen monasteries, was liquidated in
practically the same way as that of Galicia. When Mgr Macarius,
the Orthodox Archbishop of Lvov, visited that country in 1947,
only one priest rallied to Orthodoxy, and the prospects for union
'seemed almost desperate'.[21] On 1st November 1947, the young
Uniate bishop Romza, aged thirty-six, died in a mysterious car
accident.[22] In August 1949, the end of the Uniate Church was
solemnly proclaimed during a Council at Uzhgorod, about which
we know practically nothing. All this suggests that here, even
more than in Galicia, reunion with Orthodoxy was the work of
the Soviet police.[23] It should be added that Mgr Kherie, the
Uniate Bishop who was arrested in 1948 and pardoned in 1955,
died in 1958 in circumstances which it would be an understate-
ment to call mysterious.[24]

The Rumanian and Czechoslovak Uniates were likewise reunited to Orthodoxy; the former in 1948; the latter in 1950.

'Those who have been divided by force will be reunited by love.' Before the Revolution this was the attitude of the Orthodox Church to the Uniates. But history has taken a different view. The Uniates were returned to the fold by force and through the secular arm of an atheist government. The attachment of the Uniates brought about under such conditions can only be precarious. Many ex-Uniate priests have been assassinated by Ukrainian partisans.[25] On two occasions, in 1950 and in 1952, the bishops of the ex-Uniate dioceses have ordered their priests to give up Uniate customs (low Masses, the omission of Vespers and Matins, etc.) and to observe the Byzantine rite in all its features.[26] The amnesty of 1955 freed a number of Uniate priests who were carrying out their ministry in semi-secrecy.[27] *Pravoslavnyi Visnik* admitted that in 1957 there were still hundreds of parishes not attached to the Patriarchate of Moscow.[28] In 1963 three secret convents (belonging to the Servants of the Immaculate Virgin, the Sisters of Saint Vincent de Paul and the Basilian Sisters) were discovered at Lvov. As can be seen, the loyalty to Rome and to Uniate customs has not entirely vanished, not least because nothing, or practically nothing, beyond a Ukrainian Review published at Lvov, has been done to educate the clergy and the faithful in their new faith. Perhaps the recent persecutions will prove to be a unifying factor in the relations between the Orthodox and ex-Uniate communities. In Stanislav, for example, the closure of the town's second church has obliged the traditional Orthodox believers to join forces with the ex-Uniate community.[29]

5. The Lutheran Church

Lutheranism is represented in the USSR by two important Churches near its borders and by a great number of Baltic and German people who have been uprooted and deported to Siberia.

The Lutheran Church of Latvia, with Archbishop Gustav Turs at its head, now has 500,000 active members and 115 pastors.

Before 1940, it had 1,070,000 members and 240 pastors. Theological lectures appear to be given in Riga where twenty students are preparing for the ministry. In 1954, this Church published a book of hymns (5,000 copies) and in 1960 a volume of Psalms (1,500 copies). Recently it was granted permission to publish the New Testament. In 1962, during the August session of the Central Committee of the World Council of Churches, the Lutheran Church of Latvia was admitted to the Council.[30]

The Lutheran Church of Esthonia is less numerous. It is headed by Archbishop John Kiivit and has 350,000 members, 448 parishes, and 114 pastors and 25 deacons and lay preachers.[31] This Church also was admitted to the World Council of Churches in August 1962.

The number of German-speaking people living in Siberia is estimated to be a million. Many of these may well have remained faithful to Lutheranism. The Lutheran Church of Russia was officially dissolved in 1938, and nothing more has been heard of it. But the amnesty of 1955 restored their civic liberties to thousands of Germans who had been deported to Siberia at different times, and who were thus given the opportunity to re-establish their religious life on a legal basis. At the beginning of 1956 a letter reached Germany from a pastor in Siberia, asking for 10,000 confirmation certificates. Churches have been built – at Akmolinsk, for instance, where Pastor Eugene Bachmann has been officially approved by the State.[32] But as a general rule, owing to the lack of pastors, Bible reading and services are conducted by lay preachers. The Lutheran World Federation has tried in vain to obtain permission for a delegation to visit these isolated Lutheran communities.[33]

6. *The Reformed Church*

The Reformed Church is represented in the USSR by the Hungarian community of sub-Carpathian Ukraine. In this region it has now 120,000 members who, at their own request, have been incorporated in the Reformed faith. Such persons must be over eighteen and have signed the Church's statement of belief. They also promise to provide for the material needs of the Church. They are distributed among 91 parishes served by 67 pastors. In the future it is hoped to send candidates for the ministry to do their theological studies in Hungary or Czechoslovakia. The greater part of this community is Hungarian in language and tradition; ninety per cent of its professed members are regular attendants at worship, and their generosity is most praiseworthy.[34]

7. *The Methodist Church*

The Methodist Church has survived in Esthonia where it numbers 3,000 members divided among twelve communities under the direction of three pastors. It is recognized by the State.

CHAPTER XII

THE PROPAGANDA AGAINST RELIGION

In its essence, the religious instinct will not succumb to any argument
or to any form of atheism.

Dostoevsky, *The Idiot*, 1867

AT THE BEGINNING OF THE WAR the *League of Atheists* was
dissolved. Its President, E. Yaroslavsky, died opportunely in 1943
and anti-religious propaganda was entirely suspended. A French
journalist, Eve Curie, who had travelled through the length and
breadth of Russia in 1942, felt able to state that religion was dead:
'Twenty-five years after the Revolution of 1917 the Soviets
perhaps are no longer in need of anti-religious propaganda, since
their youth is now beyond the influence of the Church. If the
battle against the Church has been won, the victors can indulge in
the luxury of an armistice'.[1]

Twenty years later, the facts belied this hasty conclusion:
atheist propaganda which, some years after the war, had hesi-
tantly begun to lift its head again, was unleashed once more, and
loudly demanded either the reconstitution of the League of
Atheists, or at least a great organization to centralize the increasing
energies needed for ideological struggle against what survived of
religion.[2] In 1962, we were back again at the starting point,
unexpectedly confronted by the demands of 1925.

The development of the attack against religion

The summer of 1947 marked the first occasion since the war when

267

the Press again mentioned the need to resume the conflict with religious superstitions and prejudices, especially in the ranks of youth. The *Komsomolsky Rabotnik* (The Komsomol Worker) carried a reminder that anti-religious action must form part of communist education. 'The members of the komsomol must not only be convinced atheists, opposed to every form of superstition, but are also under an obligation to take a lively part in the struggle against the spread of superstition and prejudice among the young.'[3]

The *Komsomolskaia Pravda* itself stressed the radical incompatibility between the two ideologies: 'A young man cannot be a communist unless he has shed every religious conviction.'[4] At this time the *Society for the spread of Scientific and Political Knowledge* was founded; some were premature in seeing this as the *League of Atheists* come to life again. F. Oleschuk, the former right-hand man of Yaroslavsky, correctly pointed out that 'atheist propaganda is the duty of all members of the Society,'[5] but in fact it was concerned with much wider issues than those of the League. Indeed it tended to neglect the religious struggle, and in 1951, Oleschuk himself complained that both its anti-religious pamphlets and meetings were insufficient in number and quality.[6] In 1951, the January number of the Society's monthly review *Nauka i Jizn* (Science and Life) announced that henceforth, at the request of numerous readers, it would publish a regular series of articles 'denouncing the reactionary activities of the various religious denominations'. In the following number, a writer, named Manuilov, gave an account of the anti-religious pamphlets published in 1950; the March number contained an attack on the 'religious moral code'; and that was all. Until March 1955 the promise of the editorial board remained a dead letter. Articles and pamphlets against religion could be counted on the fingers and they were restricted to attacks on the Vatican and summaries of the essential principles of atheism. During the last years of Stalin's life, propaganda against religion assumed mainly a negative character; instead of attacking religion directly, it confined itself to omitting anything favourable to it. This was the reason why Dostoevsky, Leskov, the historians Soloviev and Kliuchevsky, and a poet of the calibre of Essenine, not to mention other thinkers and philosophers, were banned.

After Stalin's death a violent assault on religion was begun, but did not last. The editorial in *Pravda* on 24th July repeated its complaints against the persistence of religious prejudices and the inertia of those whose duty it was to oppose them. On 12th August 1954, Radio Moscow announced that a new periodical *Science and Religion*, about to be published, would specialize in the fight against God. The newspapers carried articles belabouring believers and their beliefs. But in November, by a resolution of the Central Committee of the Soviet Communist Party, Nikita Kruschev put an end to this probably factitious campaign. While emphasizing the need for an increase and improvement in the ideological conflict with religion, this resolution condemned attempts at administrative interference in the life of religious communities and the ill-mannered attitude to the clergy.[7] It resulted in a relaxation of anti-religious propaganda; the publication of the periodical *Science and Religion* was postponed, and in its place a section of a dozen pages was inserted in the review *Science and Life*. Pamphlets against religion continued to decrease in number; in 1955 there were 187; in 1956 they declined to 145, and in 1957 to 102.[8]

But in 1956 the position abruptly altered, when a fresh attack against religion was secretly planned. In September 1959, the *Society for the spread of Scientific and Political Knowledge* at last produced the anti-religious periodical. New magazines and reviews allotted ample room for the description of the misdeeds of believers and the triumphs achieved by atheists. Atheist pamphlets flooded the book market. Emilien Yaroslavsky and his works were rescued from oblivion. Radio, television, the cinema and the theatre were all enlisted in the struggle against the opium of the people.

In short, anti-religious propaganda, incorporated in a huge

campaign of restrictive measures, was revived on a scale worthy of the first years of the Communist régime.

Examples

In theory anti-religious propaganda is aimed at Soviet man from his earliest moments and does not relax until he dies. The means put at its disposal by the State are unlimited. The law demands that both parents go out to work, and atheist education begins before school-age in the day nurseries to which they are obliged to send their children.[9] But school is considered to be the best opportunity to 'plug the gaps through which religion still seeps in'.

'Communist education has for its principal task the elimination of the surviving elements of religion, the demonstration to pupils that science, the real and concrete reflection of the world as it objectively exists in the consciousness of the people, is fundamentally incompatible with religion which is an unreal, distorted, and consequently harmful reflection of the world'.[10] The duty of every teacher is not only 'to be an unbeliever, but also to show himself an active propagandist of atheism, a carrier of the militant atheism of the proletariate.[11] There are still families – and not a few – in which children are brought up with a religious mentality. These deficiencies in family education must be corrected by the school.'[12] According to Soviet specialists 'an adult becomes religious only exceptionally, whereas children between seven and eight years old are peculiarly receptive to the influence of religion'.[13] Militant atheists complain that sociological inquiries are no longer conducted among pupils in order to estimate the importance of the surviving religious elements, to classify them according to their different features, and to combat them.[14] In the few schools where an inquiry of this kind had in fact been held, it was found that half the pupils were infected with the religious virus. In the village of Maksim, for example (in the Chernigov region of the Ukraine), out of twenty-two first-year pupils (seven years old) ten could make the sign of the cross, three could say their prayers, but only one attended church services. In the village of Kreshchatik, fifteen out of twenty-five second-year pupils had been given a religious education in their family.[15]

In February 1959, E. Afanassiev, the Minister of National Education, took measures to ensure that atheist propaganda should be conducted systematically; a circular drew the attention of headmasters and school inspectors to the need for developing the anti-religious education of schoolchildren. In 1960 a further note recommended that all subjects should be directed to this end, but that physics, chemistry and biology should be especially devoted to providing an atheistic explanation of the world. At the same time a new subject, the origin of political ideas, was introduced into the top classes. This subject included instruction in atheism.[16] To supplement the deficiencies of the school books, the Minister ordered the publication of several series of articles by teachers who, in their respective subjects, were trying to train their pupils in the spirit of dialectical materialism and scientific atheism.[17] In some schools the teachers not only add attacks against religion to their lessons, but even organize atheist groups among their pupils. In Chernigov, for example, in School no. 9, the pupils formed a society that was named 'The young Atheist'. The rules of this society permit every member of the five upper classes to belong to it, providing each of them is worthy and known for his social activity and agrees to conduct atheist propaganda, in a persistent and systematic way, in the schools and among the people. It must hold at least two anti-religious meetings a month. This local society of atheists publishes an aggressive magazine, *The Godless*, and maintains a small museum, etc.[18]

Theoretically, teachers also have the duty of expounding atheism outside the classroom; they should arrange parties and excursions on days when religious feasts are celebrated, and make searching inquiries into those parents whose attitude is suspect. In reality, however, many teachers find the destruction of the idea of God in

the minds of the young a distasteful occupation and confine themselves to explaining the theory of 'non-religious' education. 'There
are many who hold that it is useless and even harmful to raise
these problems in school, because, they say, their pupils are not
interested in them, and to discuss them might well arouse un-
healthy curiosity about religious matters.'[19] Some even go so far
as to say that explicitly anti-religious instruction may become 'an
indirect way of propagating religious ideas, information and
images'.[20] A good many schools are content to conform with the
regulations of the administration simply by arranging for anti-
religious talks only twice a year, at Easter and Christmas.[21] The
theory of non-religious education has been widely disseminated
among the various training colleges that specialize in training
teachers for the secondary schools. Professors Chimbirev and
Ogorodnikov published a manual of pedagogy in 1954 – it
remains a standard work – in which atheist education is not
mentioned. There is a similar omission in the *Teachers' Manual* by
professors Ossipova and Goncharova. The review *Sovietskaia
Pedagogika* maintains the same theory; during six years it has
published only three four-page articles on atheistic subjects.[22] In
fact, education in Soviet schools today does not correspond with
what was expected of it, that is, 'not to allow religion to seep into
the future'.[23] But it must be recognized that during the coming
years special attention will be paid to this subject, particularly in
view of the fact that, to put a stop to family education, the
Government is setting up a network of boarding schools to house
the whole of the school population.

Youth organizations

The fight against God in the souls of the young is not entrusted to
teachers alone. 'The anti-religious ideas which pupils receive in
the classroom are later consolidated . . . in the organizations of the
Pioneers and of the Komsomol (Communist Youth), and thus
become firm convictions.'[24]

Practically the whole of Soviet youth is regimented in these two organizations which in 1954 numbered 18 million children from nine to fourteen and almost 19 million adolescents and young people from fourteen to twenty-five.[25]

Information about the atheist education provided by the Pioneers is sparse. It is not very active, but its hidden presence is real enough. When parents forbid their children to join the Pioneers, it is always for religious reasons.[26] The red scarf, the badge of the Pioneers, is incompatible with the cross. Children who do not wear it are in a minority. They have to endure the gibes of their comrades, and are the subject of particular attention by atheist propaganda.[27] In Moldavia, meetings of the Pioneers are sometimes organized in the homes of children whose parents are known to be confirmed upholders of religious belief.[28]

By definition, a young communist is a militant atheist: the statutes of the Komsomol decree that every member's duty 'is to combat drunkenness, debauchery, the survival of religious superstitions, and the absence of a friendly relationship with women'.[29] The religious struggle, squeezed in between debauchery and the failure to respect the dignity of women was thus, until very recent times, the Komsomol's weak point. In 1954, A. Shelepin, the secretary of the VLKSM (the Komsomol's full title is: *The Panunionist, Leninist and Communist Union of Youth*) disclosed the fact that atheist propaganda had become most ineffective and in some places had ceased altogether.[30] The young communists were carrying out the programme in order to conform with the statutes and avoid trouble, but they treated it as an embarrassing task, imposed from above. One of them remarked that 'Our activity is practically reduced to this: in God's name do not believe in God'.[31] Komsomols who were believers and who attended church were not uncommon. In the Kuibyshev region, Nicholas Sentsov, the Director of a Komsomol club, had dismissed two girls from the local organization, because they went to church, but some months later, at the request of his fiancée, he himself was married in church. The married couple were in their turn, 'unanimously' dismissed from the Komsomol, but among the girls who had voted for their expulsion were some who had been seen in church on Sundays.[32] This is not an isolated example, for to belong to the Komsomol is less a matter of conviction than a necessity, a routine affair. It does not imply an inner adhesion to communist doctrine and its missionary commands. In any case, for a young man this doctrine often amounts to little more than good behaviour and a keen devotion to work. A distinguished worker is naturally anxious to become a member of the Komsomol; should he be rejected, his career might be endangered. The *Komsomolskaia Pravda* of 30th May 1958, published an account of Lida Vikhrova, a seventeen-year-old peasant girl, a member of the Komsomol's District Committee, and a competitor for the improvement of milk production (the cows entrusted to her produced a great quantity of milk of exceptional quality), who made no difficulty about being married in church, wearing the customary white dress and holding a candle.

Since 1958, concerted effort has been made to intensify the atheistic education of young communists and to spur them on to resume the fight against religion. Almost everywhere the regional committees have held special sessions for the development and strengthening of anti-religious propaganda. Hostels and clubs were established in big cities for young atheists, to serve as training grounds for future instructors. In several regions real universities of atheism are in action. But personal propaganda aimed at believers is naturally entrusted to the Komsomols. At the fourteenth Congress of the organization (April 1962), its Secretary, S. Pavlov, gave an account of some of the great victories won by communist youth on the anti-religious front, especially the closing of a monastery in Moldavia.[33] But even more recently a leading article in *Science and Religion* lamented the fact that an important section of youth was still unconcerned about the fight against religion.[34]

The activity of the youth organizations is completed by that of the army in whose ranks the whole of Soviet youth, with the exception of students, spend on an average three years. Recent reports issued by the Ministry of War show that a great effort has been made to destroy the faith of believers during their military service.

Adults

It is not possible to obtain as clear a view of the situation of adults as that of youth. Theoretically, the *Society for the spread of Scientific and Political Knowledge* is responsible for their education. It is an administrative machine for the delivery of lectures and the publication of pamphlets of popularized information, but it is not very combative. It is, however, in its name that the militantly anti-religious periodical *Science and Religion* is published.

In practice, when atheistic propaganda is conducted on a large scale, it is the combined work of the local committees of the Party, the Komsomol and the Society. Up to now, the co-ordination of the work of these different bodies has been entrusted to the agencies of the Party. But the propagandists are increasingly feeling the need for the creation of a new body specifically concerned with the fight against religion. If we may believe the statements made in November 1961, the establishment of this body will not be long delayed: 'All the cultural organizations should find their precise position within a single system of atheist education which should include all sections of the population. The Society will devote itself to the preparation of qualified teams (discussion groups in the schools and universities of atheism) and to educational work among the doubtful and unbelieving. Those who work in the day nurseries will be responsible for children of pre-school age. Teachers, who are members of the Society, must work wholeheartedly in the schools. Within a single organization of atheists everyone will have his own position . . . the doctor, the writer, the artist. . . . Of course when people abroad hear that a Society of atheists is to be created, there will be abuse in plenty. But their objections cannot be sustained, for we shall patiently explain that the intensification of anti-religious propaganda has nothing in common with persecution.'[35]

The means employed

While awaiting this unification of the attacks on religion, the various bodies at present in charge of them, are using the classical means of spreading ideas – the press, books, discussion groups, clubs, cinemas, theatres, museums, etc. – which have been put entirely at their disposal by the Government.

The Press: No daily or weekly anti-religious paper is at present published, and there is only one monthly anti-religious review in Russian, *Nauka i Religia* (Science and Religion). This review consists of a hundred pages and more than 100,000 copies are always printed; 112,000 copies in 1960; 132,280 copies in 1961; 126,000 at the beginning of 1962; 140,000 at the beginning of 1963. (For the sake of comparison we may note that the two great literary reviews, *Novyi Mir* and *Oktiabr* only print 110,000 and 130,000 copies respectively.) This review is unpretentious in its set-up, and its scope appears to be limited: 'No believer will pick it up. . . . For whom then are you writing this review?' asks the writer Pomerantsev; 'Doubtless for yourselves, and yet the propagandists have enough publications apart from this one.'[36]

Another monthly review *Voiovnichy Ateist* (The Militant Atheist) has been produced since 1961 at Kiev in Ukrainian. It consists of sixty pages; 47,000 copies are printed.

Although there is no specialized daily, the national and local papers often provide space in their columns for anti-religious diatribes that are either purely speculative or else denounce some scandal or some excessive display of religious feeling. The frequency of such articles is hard to determine; they vary according to regions and seasons.

Books: Until 1957 anti-religious books were non-existent, that is, if we except first the monumental series of collected articles published annually by the Academy of Science: *Problems in the History of Religion and of Atheism*, of which ten volumes have already appeared (the number printed has steadily declined; 10,000 for the first two; 3,500 for the sixth; 2,700 for the ninth); and secondly, the *Annual Report of the Museum of the History of Religion and Atheism* which has appeared since 1957; its clientele is even more restricted; only 1,700 copies are printed.

The production of anti-religious books on a vast scale only began in 1959. A start was made by unearthing the classics: *The Bible for Believers and Unbelievers*, by E. Yaroslavsky, a crudely frivolous treatment of some of the themes of the Old Testament; *Considerations on Religion* by the same author (150,000 copies of each of these were printed); *The Origin of our God*, by the early Bolshevik writer Skvortsov-Stepanov; then came the voluminous manual of atheism, *Sputnik Ateista* (2nd edn, 1961, 526 pages, with illustrations; 180,000 copies); the *Foundations of Scientific Atheism* (1961, 455 pages; 100,000 copies), etc. In order to prop up the fragile structure of the arguments in the Russian works, translations were made from the French of the 'fundamental' book by Charles Hainchelin, *Les Origines de la Religion* and of the collective work by A. Denis, R. Garaudy, G. Cogniot and C. Besse: *Des Marxistes Répondent à leurs Critiques*.

Anti-religious pamphlets, issued by various State publishers (Znamia, The Young Guard, Army Publications, etc.) are legion. The number of copies printed varies between 8,000 (Ju. Krianov, *On the Opposition between Christian Ideology and Scientific Communism*, Moscow, 1961) and 300,000 (A. Rakitov, *Why is Religious Morality Harmful in Socialist Society?* Moscow, 1960, p. 48).

The subjects dealt with in these pamphlets vary considerably; some of their titles may serve as examples: *What is Atheism?* (Moscow, 1961, 300,000 copies); *On the Devil and on Miracles* (Moscow, 1959, 100 pages, 100,000 copies); *Unmasked* (Moscow, 1960, 108 pages, 150,000 copies); *Religion and Women* (Moscow, 1960, 50 pages, 50,000 copies); *Relics* (Moscow, 1961, 113 pages,

100,000 copies); *I take a look at Believers* (Moscow, 1961, 113 pages, 85,000 copies); *The Fanatics* (Moscow, 1961, 54 pages, 175,000 copies); *We were Baptists* (Moscow, 1960, 110 pages, 100,000 copies); *Before the Judgement Seat of Science* (Moscow, 1960, 64 pages, 178,000 copies); *Religion and Daily Life*; *Attempts to modernize Religion*; *The Proceedings of the Holy Fathers of the Vatican*; *God and the conquest of Space*; *Men, Idols and God*; *God, Adam and Society*; *The Story of a Former Priest*; *In Search of the Biblical Hell*; *Did Christ Exist?*; *The Myth of the Immortality of the Soul*; *The Origin of Life*; *War and Religion*, etc.

In 1962 the number of books and pamphlets produced increased to 355 titles with a total circulation of 5,422,000, three times more than in 1954 (119 titles and 1,944,000 copies) and twice as much as in 1930, the year when anti-religious propaganda was at its most intense.[37]

These countless publications supply materials for the no less numerous lectures which are still the basic source of anti-religious propaganda, in spite of the constant criticisms made of them: repetitious and monotonous in tone, standardized talks, delivered without conviction, etc.

Films: These lectures do not as a rule attract many people. They are usually accompanied by film shows, which though on the increase, are still considered to be insufficient in number. Scientific documentaries are comparatively numerous, but they do not necessarily attack religion. Films of any length are the exception; in fact there have been only four (*The Miraculous Icon*, from the story by Tendriakov; *Clouds above Borsk*; *Deceived*; *Ivanna*). In addition there are short films which portray the depravity of believers: for example, *Beyond the Darkness* which assembles every possible and imaginable extravagance in religious behaviour: an Orthodox priest condemned to fifteen days forced labour for drunkenness, a victim burnt at the stake by the *khlysty*, a member of a sect crucified by fanatics, the snatching of a child from its parents, etc.[38]

Radio and Television: Lectures and films are repeated in broadcasts and on television. In three years, the main channel has sent out 200 anti-religious broadcasts, that is, between one and two lectures a week. This modest output is however accepted as a maximum simply because of a scarcity of lecturers. Regional stations, however, seem to be more active and mordant, they concentrate upon vigorous attacks on the clergy. Anti-religious propaganda on television is only just beginning. A televised news reel, 'The Truth about Religion', is a regular feature, and viewers are given the privilege of seeing the personal appearance of the apostate, A. Ossipov, etc. A study circle is soon to be specially devoted to the examination of the position rightfully belonging to television in the fight against religion.[39]

Theatre: Anti-religious ideas are invading the theatre. In the Ukrainian Republic alone, between 1959 and 1964, twenty anti-religious plays were put on. But they attack the clergy rather than religious ideas.[40] In 1961, the famous marionette theatre of Obraztsov showed, to young and old, the *Divine Comedy*, a parody of the creation of the world by Isidore Stok who derived his ideas from the caricatures of John Effel.

Museums: Before the war anti-religious museums were one of the favourite weapons of militant atheism; every town possessed its own. In 1941, almost all of them were either closed or else changed into ordinary historical museums. At present there is only one specialized museum that contains a very considerable collection of features illustrating the religions of the whole world and the fight of the peoples of the world for the 'triumph of atheism'. This is the famous *Museum of the History of Religion and Atheism* in Leningrad which, since 1932, has been installed in the former Cathedral of the Virgin of Kazan. Especially since 1947, when it received the essential contents of the central anti-religious Museum of Moscow which had been closed, it has become the depositary of extensive collections. At present it has a library of 200,000 volumes including many manuscripts and incunabula; and 300,000 items of the most varied nature. These latter are divided into historical sections and each section is split up among a number of stands. The most important sections are those of the history of Orthodoxy and of Russian Atheism (57 stands) and those of the history of the Papacy and of the Inquisition (90 stands). The Museum attracts a host of visitors; atheists, mere sightseers and even believers. In 1956, 256,633 visitors were recorded; in 1960, there were more than 500,000. This increase was due to the growing number of people who came in groups; 5,430 in 1959; 6,083 in 1960. Besides this, the Museum acts as a nursery for atheism in the Leningrad region; it arranges lectures (367 in 1958; 595 in 1959), talks on Sundays, and trains future instructors.[41]

Houses of Atheism: These are comparatively recent institutions, but they already exist in most large towns. Their function is similar to that of the anti-religious Museum in Leningrad; the concentration of anti-religious forces; the establishment of varied programmes suited to particular audiences (the young, intellectuals, women, etc.); the training of propagandists; the provision of a permanent consultative centre; the organization of travelling exhibitions, etc. One of the principal hostels is that of Odessa; its activities extend beyond the boundaries of the region, and even beyond the Ukraine.[42]

Manpower

Anti-religious propaganda is well supplied with material equipment and heavily financed by the State, but it is weak in manpower. This is its Achilles' heel: 'The circle of those engaged in atheistic activity is still a very narrow one. Only those who have been especially assigned to this work – "the atheists", as they are called, as though the rest were not also atheists – are constantly occupied by it. And yet propaganda for atheism ought to be the concern of the whole community. Yet our work scarcely interests scholars, writers, dramatists, and film producers.'[43] The review *Science and Religion* cannot boast of having distinguished contributors. Scholars will certainly grant interviews on request, but their statements do not go beyond generalities and are not necessarily directed against religion.

The almost complete absence of literary men from atheist propaganda is significant from this point of view. Representatives of the labour corps recently addressed an open letter, in the form of an editorial, in *Science and Religion*, which called upon these 'fashioners of human souls' to take up the work. 'Among all these books, pamphlets and newspaper articles, there is scarcely anything of literary value. The militant section of our *intelligentsia*, especially the workers [*sic*] in literature and the cinema, fail to realize that the fight against religion is one of their most important tasks.[44] The days when a writer of the calibre of Maiakovsky contributed his talent to the fight against God, seem to be over. Among the writers of the old guard willing to shoulder the responsibility of anti-religious propaganda, there is only Nicholas Asseev, who had his hour of fame as a futurist poet, but ended in the most banal form of insipid conformity, and Constantine Simonov. Among the young we may note A. Bezymensky, a not very able poet, and V. Tendryakov, a prose writer of great promise. His novel, *The Miraculous Icon* has been praised by official criticism as the literary masterpiece of atheism, and its reading forms part of many atheist study-circles. It is cleverly written, and describes the conflict between family education and the school, and the difficult position of a priest in such a conflict. But in this novel there is no frontal attack on the idea of God or on belief.[45]

Tendriakov's second anti-religious novel was published in small print in *Science and Religion*. The small print was understandable, because the book is more a criticism of the methods of atheist propaganda and of the dogmatism and intolerance of the Party organs, than of religion. Watchful Komsomols discover in their school a believing pupil and a mathematics master who is also a believer. The former ends by losing his faith, marries and becomes a satisfactory member of the lower middle class. The latter, in spite of protests from the head, is dismissed from the school, and is at last enabled to profess his religious convictions openly. By way of conclusion the author bitterly criticizes the methods of the fight against religion which will admit no opposition and no free discussion: 'I should have preferred people who believe in God, but who think', and, addressing himself to the communist authorities, he remarks: 'Blessed are the poor in spirit . . . for they know not what they do.'[46]

Subjects

Although the means employed by anti-religious propaganda vary, its subject-matter does not. The narrow dogmatism of this propaganda, its utterly negative approach, has meant that from one book to another, from one discussion to another, exactly the same statements reappear, expressed in the same way. Soviet atheism is a science without development; such as it was in 1925, so it remains today.

Anti-religious literature as a whole revolves round two principal themes:

1. The radical incompatibility between science and religion, from which it follows that all religion, and Christianity above all, is essentially anti-historical in character and purely fanciful.

2. The no less radical opposition between communist morality and religious morality (the clergy as the flunkeys of religion, believers as depraved).

1. Religion contradicts scientific truth and is openly hostile to it. Conversely, science has demonstrated that religion is essentially an illusion, a deceit, and a transitory phenomenon. In the words of Engels – monotonously repeated in all the anti-religious writings – religion is 'no more than an imaginative reflection in human minds of the external forces that rule them in their daily lives, a reflection in which these real forces take on the aspect of unreal beings'.[47]

Science – in this case, archaeology [*sic!*] – 'has demonstrated' that religion appeared on the scene only during a comparatively recent period, probably during that of neanderthal man. For hundreds of millions of years, pithecanthropus and sinanthropus were entirely without religion. Its origin was due to social causes – fear in face of the forces of nature – and also to epistemological causes; religion is a product of knowledge. When society came to be divided into classes, religious beliefs reflected the apparent powerlessness of the workers in the grip of social forces, and served as an instrument in the hands of their exploiters. Originating in fear, manipulated for their own benefit by the exploiters, religion is fundamentally unreal and evil; it is destined to disappear with the causes that produced it. Moreover, it is one of the forms of philosophical idealism; as such, it denies the material reality upon which existence depends, it denies that being and matter are antecedent to consciousness; that matter is a single uniform reality, eternal in character, dependent upon no other reality than itself; that the laws of the universe are absolute, unchangeable, and knowable, and therefore enable man to dominate the world. Thus the anti-scientific and reactionary aspects of religion are complementary.

All the sciences are laid under contribution to this thesis. The researches of O. Schmidt on the formation of the stars out of stellar dust and the hypotheses of Oparine on the part played by albumen in the production of life, are alleged to prove that the world was not created, but has always existed. In the realm of physics, however, atheist propaganda is at present on the defensive and confines itself to combating the hypotheses of 'bourgeois' science. In psychology, on the other hand, it is claimed that Pavlov's theories on reflexes have disposed of the idealist notion of the soul once and for all.

Christianity is entirely without historical foundation. Not only Jesus, but also the apostles (the twelve, as well as the seventy) and including the apostle Paul, are merely mythological figures. Historical science has proved this time and again.[48] The anti-religious pamphlets have taken over – without ever giving their reasons – a more or less common account of the dates when the sacred books were written. On this view, the earliest Christian document is the Apocalypse, dating from A.D. 68; following it come the Epistles to the Romans, Corinthians and Galatians (beginning of the second century A.D.); the catholic Epistles and some fragments of the Gospel (first half of the second century); the Epistles of the captivity (late second century); the pastoral Epistles and the canonical Gospels (the third quarter of the second century); and finally, the Acts of the Apostles (the last quarter of the second century). This description of the facts, 'irrefutably demonstrated by science', goes to show that the claim of Christianity to be historically true was a late invention. It began as a myth, and the historical details were added afterwards.

Being purely fictitious, a perversion of history,[49] Christianity is an amalgam of elements taken from earlier religions: one from animism (Communion), an element from Egyptian religion (the myth of death and resurrection); elements from Roman religion and Judaism. Anti-religious propaganda is determined to deny at all costs that there is anything original in Christianity.

The practical sciences add their own contribution to the demonstration of the unreality of religion. The crop increases obtained by the agriculturist Michurin and his disciples are considered to have an important bearing upon atheism.

Today, the conclusive argument is drawn from the Soviet space flights. *Science and Religion* gives wide publicity to the exploits of the cosmonauts. The sputniks and their pilots have not come across God in the sky, nor on the hidden sides of the moon.[50] The dogs used in these flights figure prominently in the illustrations to the Manual of Atheism.[51]

In contradiction to science, religion is its sworn enemy. Atheist propaganda publicizes (with exaggerations) the various conflicts that have occurred in history between scholars and the Church: the murder of Hypatia, the imprisonment of Roger Bacon (the fact that he was a friar is not mentioned), the execution of Giordano Bruno (without reference, however, to his philosophy of religion), and of Vanini and Servetus, the condemnation of Galileo, etc. The propagandists are reluctantly compelled to admit that some 'bourgeois' scholars (for example, Einstein) have held religious beliefs, but they try to save Russian and other Soviet scholars from the same pitfall. Many thinkers and scientists are wrongly said to be materialists and atheists (Lomonosov, Herzen, Vernadsky, etc).[52] One of the most burning and controversial topics in this sphere is whether or not Pavlov believed in God.[53]

Since religion is unreal and obscurantist it is essentially reactionary. But assertions on this point have become more discreet, because the propagandists are speaking to Christians living in the USSR where the Church has ceased to be a political power and professes obedience to the State. It is admitted that the baptism of Russia was originally a factor that made for progress. It was only later that the Church put herself at the disposal of feudalism and was transformed into an instrument of exploitation and reaction. But even in a socialist society, religion is harmful, because it is anti-scientific. Denying that society can be transformed by revolutionary methods, teaching that everything depends upon God, religion is a brake upon the progress of Communism. Great stress is laid on the damage done to the socialist economy by the observance of religious festivals, and on the unhygienic nature of some religious ceremonies (group baptisms, Holy Communion, etc).

The extent of the conflicts between Christianity and the Russian State is minimized. The only persecutions mentioned are those of the second half of the third century, and even in these, Christians are depicted as pusillanimous. *Sputnik Ateista* is completely silent about the clashes between the Russian Church and State between 1917 and 1940.[54]

2. In anti-religious propaganda the hostility between science and religion claims the lion's share. The propagandists run into serious difficulties over the second topic, the opposition between

communist and religious morality. Radio Moscow recently had to abandon a talk on the subject, because it could not find any speaker willing to give it.[55]

These difficulties arise because communist ethics are as yet undeveloped, and also because the 'personality cult has discredited communist moral teaching among great numbers of people'.[56] It has also borrowed so much from Christian terminology that whole passages in communist treatises might well find a place in Christian catechisms: 'The moral code of the builders of communism presupposes that men will strive for moral perfection to be reached through moral and self-education. . . . A communist must do everything that is possible and necessary to found a unified and stable family.'[57] The essential difference however, lies in the fact that 'the guiding principle of the communist moral code is that only those actions and devices which contribute most to the building up of communism have a genuinely moral value'.[58] But this is obviously only an interim ethic which is bound to give way to another, as yet undefined, when the time of communism's definitive establishment has arrived.

In order to show the incompatibility between communist and religious morality, the anti-religious propagandists have been obliged to present a completely distorted version of the latter. 'Just as religion declares that every attempt to alter and transform the world is an offence against God, so religious morality refuses to ascribe ethical value to any active, creative and conscious human approach to life. When it declares that everything in man's environment is vanity, it makes men indifferent to the future of their race and to their government.'[59] The Christian commandments are abstract and lead to results that are the very opposite of what they prescribe. 'Christian morality must be judged not by its words, but by its deeds.'[60] Christian misdeeds, throughout history and in our own time, and those of the clergy especially, are adduced as crushing proofs of the harmfulness of religious morality. The clergy do not believe in God; they deceive the people simply to acquire money: they are crude, greedy, inclined

to drink and fornication. *Sputnik Ateista* contrasts the commandment 'Thou shalt not kill' with the blessing given by Pius XII to
Hitler and Mussolini, and with an infanticide perpetrated in 1959
by a fanatical couple who sacrificed their child to God. The
commandment 'Thou shall not steal' is quoted against the inroads
made upon church funds by Bishop Sergius of Astrakhan (now
Bishop of Perm) and the systematic thefts of a Christian cashier
in a large Moscow store.[61] The most popular saints are subjected
to regular denigration; St Seraphim of Sarov, for example, is
depicted as an idler who spent his life exploiting the people,
etc.[62]

Unreal, unmasked by science, purveyed by the knavish and
corrupt, noxious, reactionary and non-moral – such is the image
of religion. If to this we add the attempts made to show that the
Russian people have never been religious, we are left wondering
how it is that religion can still have any hold whatever upon the
'millions' of Soviet citizens. Survival of the religious instinct in
countries where the social causes to which it owed its origin have
disappeared, is a problem that greatly perplexes the theorists of
Marxism. Their usual explanation is that changes of consciousness
occur slowly compared with social transformation. But since such
a time-lag arouses disquieting thoughts, the persistence of the
religious instinct is also attributed to capitalist encirclement.[63]

Anyone can see that this propaganda against religion is flagrantly
crude and one-sided, and its naïveté is not unnoticed by the
leaders of the movement. 'Anyone reading us would gather that
religion is nothing but a monstrous absurdity.' 'Our propaganda
is insipid and boring,' remarked the writer, S. Mikhalkov,
recently.[64]

Militant atheism is, in fact, trapped in a service of contradictions
from which it is difficult to see how it can escape.

1. Atheism claims to be the one true science, and yet through
its completely dogmatic attitude, it turns its back on science. A
Soviet atheist has given an excellent account of this inherent
contradiction in scientific atheism:

What impresses me . . . is that atheism today seems to have given up the search for truth; facts and arguments which tell against it, are dismissed in silence. It claims to solve every problem, but, finding that it cannot do so, conceals its powerlessness. The impossibility of proving the reality of a *perpetuum mobile* has been scientifically demonstrated. The atheists alone dispute it. They hold that the structure of the universe, depending upon the principle of the *perpetuum mobile*, has always been in movement, and has never received any addition of energy. True, we do not know which of the two, science or the atheists, is in the wrong; and there may even be a third solution. But it is incontestable that this question is unresolved. If the atheists hold on to their conviction, they are proclaiming their belief in spite of science and logic; their position seems to me to be like that of Tertullian: *credo quia absurdum*, and they ought not to parade their belief in the absurd as if it were science.[65]

As Henri Chambre has shown, this degradation of Marxism into bogus science and positivism is a betrayal of the thought of Marx himself.[66]

The dogmatic attitude of the anti-religious propaganda leaves no room for a dialectic or for any intellectual development. Its outlook is so narrow that its propagandists have had to avoid any form of controversial meeting or discussion which might put the Church in a more advantageous position than atheism. It is also a major hindrance to the training of officials for the movement; any serious study of religion and the Bible might prove dangerous to budding atheists, and propagandists are usually ignorant of the things they are fighting against.[67] The propaganda is conducted as though the least doubt, the slightest questioning, would be a mortal danger for the entire anti-religious system.

2. On the one hand, believers are described as depraved in spite of the rules of their religion. This implies only a contradictory proposition that proves nothing: a religion which preaches

the good produces depraved believers. On the other hand, it is affirmed that although religion is intrinsically evil, its adherents are decent people and honest workers. This is an intrinsically contradictory proposition; it affirms that religion, an evil reality, is the source of virtuous disciples; and it also contradicts the previous proposition.

3. The third contradiction follows from the first and the second, and belongs to the sphere of action. Propaganda against religion only succeeds when it is accompanied by 'administrative measures', that is, in plain language by coercion, in even plainer language, by persecution.

'Two extremes can frequently be observed in the scientific practice of atheism. Either there is an absence of enthusiasm in unmasking religion; it is done haphazardly, without incisiveness, zest, or real pugnacity. Or else, on the pretext of fidelity to principle, false methods are used which violate the freedom of religious worship guaranteed by the constitution.'[68]

These fundamental contradictions inherent in Soviet atheism are by no means embarrassing to its leaders. The measures taken in January 1964 make provision for an unprecedented extension of anti-religious propaganda and for the setting up of a veritable army of propagandists supported by an imposing bureaucratic system (Committees, Soviets, Editorial services, etc). The introduction of atheism as an obligatory subject in teachers' training colleges, medical and agricultural schools makes it, more than ever, an official doctrine. Atheism can only triumph when imposed by force. Surely that is an admission of its weakness.

CHAPTER XIII

FRESH TRIALS

The academician Dronov to Father Seraphim: 'If the soul is surrendered to you, you will take the whole man.'
S. Aleshin, *All Things Belong to Man*, 1962.

IN 1959, quite without warning, the Party and the Soviet Government launched their fourth general attack against the Church. This new wave of violent persecution, like those of the years 1928-32 and 1937-40, began after a short but clearly defined period of religious toleration.

As the reader will have observed in the course of the chapters on the various aspects of religious life, freedom of worship, theoretically guaranteed by the Constitution of 1936, became a practical reality between 1954 and 1958. The Church herself benefited from the relaxation of police control, from the amnesty, and from the temporary liberalization of some of the machinery of State. Bishops, priests and many layfolk came back from exile. Faces that had vanished long years ago were seen again. In a sermon preached on the feast of the icon of Our Lady of Unexpected Joy, Mgr Nicholas of Krutitsy exclaimed: 'We are finding this joy in what is happening today. A man disappeared: nothing was heard of him for years; his relations believed him dead, and then suddenly we hear from him, or he appears in person. This too is a gracious act of God! An unexpected joy!'[1]

The poetess Olga Bergholz – her husband had died in exile – made this sad comment during the same period:

That year (1954) is etched deep
in my memory
My memory has engraved it for ever.
When from the depths of the seas, the waterways, the forests, our friends suddenly came
back to their homes.
But why should we pretend? For few in fact
returned. . . .
Seventeen years – these constitute an epoch.[2]

The following dignitaries were now to be seen again: Mgr
Gabriel Abalymov, Bishop of Ostachkovo, who had been exiled
in the Solovki Islands since 1923 (d. 1958);[3] Mgr Athanasius,
Bishop of Kovrov, whom the historian and poet Vostokov had
met in a concentration camp in Moldavia in 1951; even then he
had spent twenty of the thirty years of his episcopate in detention;[4]
Mgr Nicholas Muraviev-Apostol (d. 1961), who had disappeared
in 1937; Mgr Joseph Chernov, Bishop of Taganrog; Mgr Benjamin Novitsky, Bishop of Poltava, arrested in 1944; Mgr
Benedict Pliaskin; Mgr Daniel Yuzvyuk (d. 1965); the Metropolitan Nestor Anissimov (d. 1962). These last five had disappeared
during the post-war years.

At the first signs of the 'thaw', the laity began to attend public
worship in great numbers, and to restore, adorn and sometimes
even build churches. In 1954, in the diocese of Chernovtsy alone,
seventy-two churches were being restored.[5] The *Review of the
Moscow Patriarchate* devoted a new section to describing 'the
building and restoration of churches'. Many buildings were given
back for public worship. The same review reported that seven
churches were consecrated in 1956, and ten in 1958, but these
figures are in no way complete.[6] In the play *All Things Belong
to Man*, by the Soviet writer S. Aleshin, Father Seraphim remarks:
'I was given one parish, then a second, then a third, and now still
more . . .'[7]

Although no theological school and no new monastery could
be opened – projects for both were however discussed – new

buildings were added to those already existing, to meet the ever-growing number of postulants.[8] In September 1956, the relics of St Nicetas of Novgorod (1096–1108) on their restoration to the Church were solemnly transferred to the Cathedral of St Nicholas of Novgorod.[9] In 1957, the Church regained the use of the great Cathedral of the Trinity in the Laura of St Alexander Nevsky in Leningrad.[10]

Diocesan visitations became more frequent and systematic. For the first time since the Revolution, the Government gave the Orthodox Church permission to publish the whole Bible (but only 25,000 copies) and the New Testament (about the same number), a prayer book, and a theological review.

The best evidence, however, for the reality of the religious revival in the USSR is afforded by the great increase in church attendance. The *Review of the Patriarchate* was continually reporting 'vast crowds', 'never have so many people been seen', etc. In 1957, P. B. de Kherson observed that 'there were far more people present during the services of Holy Week this year than last'.[11] In the province of Riazan, where between 1955 and 1958 more than half of the churches had been restored and refurnished, religious practice increased twofold or even threefold.[12] In 1959, S. Khudiakov, one of the foremost leaders of the propaganda against religion, admitted in words that display his embarrassment, that 'together with the general stabilization of the present position of atheism and of its growth in the future, the activity of the religious organizations during these last three or four years has visibly grown stronger: a number of believers have shown an increasing concern with religious problems, and religious observance has become more frequent. . . .'[13]

Preparations for further persecution

But this period of relative expansion for the Church was not to last long. The Communist Party was putting the finishing touches to the twenty-years plan for the complete establishment of communism and could not tolerate such a contradiction between the extinction of the religious sense which was envisaged, and the facts indicating the contrary. In addition, the ideological fervour of the young communists needed rekindling; they needed a battle-cry and a battlefield. Making the Church a scape-goat may have been intended as a reply to the accusations of 'revisionism' levelled from all quarters at the new ruling team in the USSR.

It would appear that the decision to alter policy was settled or at least discussed as early as August 1957, at a big secret Congress in Moscow at which 350 atheist theorists and militants were present.[14] According to a report that has reached the West, M. B. Mitin, the President of the *Society for the Spread of Scientific and Political Knowledge,* had declared at this Congress that the position on the religious front 'was grave'. 'The influence of religion,' he said, 'is still making itself felt today . . . among an important section of the people of the USSR. In many places there is an increase in the number of believers. . . . Girls and youths are falling under the influence of religion. There are Komsomols that not only admit that they are believers, but also have the audacity to proclaim their belief, and local committees are showing a culpable tolerance towards such *komsomoltsy-bogomoltsy* (young communists who pray to God).' The members of the Congress admitted these shocking facts. Some, like Ramm (a specialist in matters concerning the Roman Church) and Priadko, declared that the evil was irreparable and were re-proached for their fatalistic pessimism.[15]

It is difficult to say exactly when the first direct measures were taken against the Church. The year 1958 was chiefly devoted to mobilizing the anti-religious forces which were still on the alert, and to preparing an intensive campaign for atheism, through the press and books, but also through individual action in regard to priests and lay people who seemed likely to give up religion.

In order to minimize the unfavourable impression which the resumption of persecution might produce in the West, and still more in the countries of Asia and Africa, the Soviet Government resorted to a subtle stratagem: it authorized the Moscow Patriarchate to publish a sumptuous book in seven different editions (English, French, Russian, Spanish, Italian, German, Arabic), a publication which, in detail and with plenty of photographs, depicted the situation of the Church in the USSR as brilliant.[16]

The campaign in the USSR was still only in its preparatory stage when, in Rumania, where the Orthodox Church had long enjoyed a privileged position, violent persecution had already broken out. Several hundred monks were thrown into prison, and even the Patriarch Justinian was put under house arrest. In 1958, when the head of the Rumanian Church sent his Christmas greetings to the Patriarch Alexis, he alluded, in words that could hardly be mistaken, to the fate of his Church: 'This festival moves us to join in loving union with the humble, the wretched, the persecuted and the oppressed. In the days when the Lord Jesus dwelt on this earth, the friendship of the kings and great ones of this world was not bestowed either on himself or on the holy Church which he founded. His disciples came from the ranks of the persecuted, from the company of poor fishermen and shepherds. It was for them that he preached the Sermon on the Mount.'[17]

The first restrictions provoked a series of public apostasies. On 11th February, Paul Darmansky, a forty-year old priest, with a degree in theology and attached to a church in Leningrad, made a spectacular break with the Church.[18] On 10th September his example was followed by Alexis Yakushevich who announced his secularization in *Zaporojskaia Pravda*. (Taken prisoner in 1941, he had escaped and had become a priest to evade the German – or Soviet – police.) On 25th December, Nicholas Teliatnikov, another priest of the Melitopol district, forsook his duties.[19]

The general assault

The signal for the general assault was given in 1959; the authorities began a systematic attack on churches, the clergy, monasteries, and even the laity.

'In 1959,' states a petition from parishioners addressed to the Eastern Patriarchs, 'Anti-Christ raised up a terrible persecution against the Orthodox Church.'[20] This fresh, and fifth, wave of violent persecution has lasted for upwards of five years; and it can now be said that it is one of the longest and most implacable persecutions suffered by the Church. Although it began in a concealed and anonymous manner it was, so to say, made official in January 1964 by the publication of the Iliichev report.[21] Unlike the persecution under Stalin, which combined legal cunning with cruel repression, the new persecution avoided so far as possible the shedding of blood. Paradoxical as it may appear, its favourite weapon is legality, and its arsenal is to be found in the body of Soviet legislation, past and present, and in certain new laws enacted for the occasion.[22] The tactics employed are the literal and savage interpretation and application of these laws. But this is legality only in name. Passports to the interior, work permits, enabling a residence permit to be obtained, the deliberate ambiguities in the legislation, the identity in nature and outlook between the executive function of the Party and the legislative and policy-making function of the Government – all these provide ways and means for the establishment of arbitrary rule under the guise of legality.

As a last refinement, the Church was even accused of infringing the law in concerted and systematic fashion.[23] In the Iliichev report repressive measures were termed a return to legality. In fact, the decree of 1929, adopted in the thick of Stalin's persecution and, contrary to Iliichev's assertion, not 'Leninist' at all, had been allowed to lapse: the tacit concordat of 1943 and the ensuing normal relations between Church and State had rendered many of the decree's clauses obsolete. Now its strict application was called for. But Stalin's legislation was soon seen to be insufficient and in its place crude administrative devices (*administrirovanie*) were adopted; in other words, sheer arbitrary rule reigned supreme. These arbitrary measures were regretted, indeed they were condemned,[24] but the authorities appear to have neither the power nor any real desire to put an end to them. It all seems as if the central authorities let the local authorities act in this way, rebuking them mildly after the event while profiting by the results of their action.

Already several stages can be discerned in this wave of persecution. The first onslaught was the most brutal: the authorities endeavoured to close in record time the greatest possible number of churches (1959–61). Then, by tightening up the anti-religious legislation (1961–2), they tried to reduce to a state of suspended animation, or progressively to stifle, what still subsisted; finally, in the third stage (1963–4), an assault was made on the inmost bastions of faith: an attempt was made to destroy Christian families, to isolate children completely from the pernicious influence of religion and to root out religious belief from the inmost conscience of the individual.

Closing of the churches

The only means of aiming a blow at the freedom of worship, guaranteed by the constitution of 1936, was to reduce to a minimum the already insufficient number of places of worship. All possible legal and semi-legal methods were brought into play to obtain the closing of churches. Thus a fifteen-year-old decree was revived under which all arrangements on Soviet territory made by the armies of occupation were null and void. This decree, although quite legitimate, had become obsolete by prescription, yet it was applied in full severity to the religious buildings made over to the faithful under agreements entered into with the occupying forces. This legal trick enabled hundreds of churches to be disaffected in the western regions of the USSR, chiefly in the Ukraine and White Russia.[25]

Another decree, legal because based on the regulations controlling work and places of residence, forbade priests to administer several parishes together. The churches thus deprived of their ministers were declared unusable and closed. This procedure was rapid but geographically limited. Recourse was had therefore to an old trick, which had already proved successful in previous persecutions,[26] whereby the parishes were stamped out by financial measures. The priests, hitherto treated on the same basis as the workers, were subjected to the severe tax which, to prevent them existing, is exacted from the last vestiges of the liberal professions; it amounts to 83 per cent of incomes (Article 19 of the Finance Law).[27] It was even given retro-active effect. To prevent avoidance of tax, in 1962 the authorities, through the agency of the Patriarchate, required that priests should henceforward be paid a fixed monthly stipend (previously the remuneration of the clergy was derived principally from the contributions of the faithful). This reform was not effected without opposition.[28] Tax inspectors were ordered to track down the slightest infraction of these regulations. Several priests, as a result, were sent to prison. Indeed they were faced with a dilemma: either they could resign their office or else they must endeavour to outwit the law. Recently the *Literary Gazette* reported on three priests of the diocese of Orenburg sentenced for having bribed tax officials:

'Three upstanding old men with beards. They it was who bribed several income tax officials. The latter decreased the amount of taxes to be paid and carried out other financial services not provided for by the law. In future there will be three vacant places in the diocese. Is that too many for a diocese which includes no more than ten parishes?'[29]

Parish incomes also came under attack. The profit made from the sale of candles (revealed, with supporting figures, by apostate priests)[30] was declared an illegal form of trade and treated as speculation. The Church was accused of battening on the faithful by thus imposing on them involuntary contributions forbidden by law. In future candles must be sold at cost price.[31] According to the careful calculations of the review *Science and Religion* parishes thus lost 75 per cent of their incomes.[32] In White Russia collections in churches have been forbidden and the faithful must put their offerings into alms boxes. Finally, parish resources are automatically burdened with a heavy contribution to government funds for peace.[33]

Inspection commissions can at any time issue certificates stating that religious buildings are dilapidated and requiring their complete restoration immediately. This is legal but unjust. Parishes that cannot raise the high costs involved are obliged to ask the authorities to close them down. For this reason one of the two churches in the city of Stanislav was closed.[34] It is true that very often the proverbial generosity of the faithful makes it possible to counter this financial strangle-hold. But the authorities have other ways of bringing pressure to bear. For example, the existence of churches and cathedrals may be held to contravene Soviet law: a church too close to a school constitutes a danger to the secularism of the teaching: it is a mute but eloquent witness to the faith[35] (it is a frequent occurrence, for the State schools have taken over the premises of the former parochial schools). Another church will be classified as a historical monument and so must belong to all Soviet citizens and not to believers only; in this way St Nicholas's Cathedral in Novgorod was taken away from the faithful (it was the only church open for worship in the city; in compensation the small Church of St Philip in the suburbs was allowed to be used). A cathedral, like that of Perm, attracts large crowds and is held to be an obstacle to the free movement of traffic.[36] Paradoxically enough, to attract great crowds is more dangerous for a church than for it to be comparatively deserted. Trades unions and Komsomols are alerted and collect thousands of signatures from peaceful and hardworking citizens calling for the disappearance of these relics of the past. As in 1930 the churches are then closed by the wish of the unbelieving majority without regard for the faithful, whatever their number. In another place the overriding needs of town-planning are invoked. This was the pretext recently urged for the destruction of the Patriarchal Cathedral of the Epiphany in Moscow.[37] If this threat had been carried out (at the moment the Cathedral has only been spared out of regard for the Patriarch) a serious blow would have befallen the Church. For the Patriarchal Cathedral possesses a great symbolical importance for the faithful. It is one of the rare churches of Moscow which safely weathered the storm of the persecutions under Stalin. It was there that the Metropolitan Sergius preached his historic sermon calling on the people to rise in defence of their country. It is there that his body lies.

Often, in order to close a church the Government delegates have recourse to a particularly treacherous method. On some pretext or other the priest's registration is cancelled or he is silenced. The delegate requires the parish to elect a new committee of twenty. A general meeting of the parish cannot be summoned without the permission of the Rural Soviet or the Executive Committee of the local Party. These authorities categorically refuse to grant the necessary permission for they have been warned that the church in question is to be closed. The parishioners then appeal to the Government delegate who takes cover behind the decision of the local Soviet or Executive Committee of the Party. There is thus a vicious circle. If the parishioners take it on themselves to meet they are accused of breaking the law. Meanwhile, time passes and the parish is still without a minister, for priests have not the right to celebrate in a church whose committee of twenty has not been confirmed in its powers by the authorities. At the end of a certain time (about six months) the Government delegate orders the keys of the church to be given up to the local Soviet under the pretext that the church is not being used. Thus it is the Government delegate himself who deprives the priest, withdraws from the committee of twenty its right to registration and, through the local Executive Committee, gives the order to close the church.[38]

Encouraged by the Government the closing of churches became a matter of competition between the local authorities and took on a massive and brutal turn for the worse, at least in certain districts.[39] The papers published gloating reports of success: 180 churches closed in Volhynia,[40] 68 in the Province of Jitomir, 43 in that of Poltava, 40 in that of Cherkassy, 18 out of 25 in the single district of Lipkan in Moldavia, 6 out of 14 in the district of Kotov[41], 1 in 6 on an average in the Diocese of Perm.[42] Twelve parishes were put out of action in the Diocese of Novgorod, several in the Urals, in the Diocese of Kuibyshev and in Altai.[43]

Western tourists have managed to gather some striking details on the spot: in Kiev, only 8 out of 25 churches remain: in Odessa, 9 out of 23; in Ismail, 1 out of 5; in Rostov on the Don, 4 out of 12. The Cathedrals of Orel, Briansk, Chernigov, Riga, Kaunas, etc., have been withdrawn from public worship. In Orel, the relics of St Tikhon of Zadonsk were desecrated for the second time, and probably destroyed.[44] In 1960, 600 churches were disaffected in the Ukraine, 300 in White Russia. According to N. Yudin, the author of a well-informed anti-religious pamphlet, at the beginning of 1962 there remained only 11,500 Orthodox churches in use out of the 20 or 22,000 in existence before 1959.[45] Thus less than three years after the beginning of the persecution nearly 10,000 churches had been closed to worship. Since then the closing of churches has continued; in the first months of 1964 a further 2,000 were shut.

After the event – and again adopting the methods of the persecution in 1930 – the official press admitted that many churches had been closed merely by administrative action and recalled the conditions required by the law for putting an end to a church's existence. In theory, a church can only be closed and its community dispersed if the number of people willing to support it becomes inadequate. (This explains the need for crushing taxes that would eliminate both the number and the generosity of the faithful.) But a church may also be closed and demolished for reasons of town planning, when, for instance, a neighbourhood has to be rebuilt, or a locality becomes obsolete. (Here, also, arbitrary decisions are possible, for it is the Party organs that decide whether a locality is obsolete or a neighbourhood needs rebuilding.) In the latter case, however, the religious association is not dissolved and it can ask for the lease of other premises, but in view of the great shortage of premises it is difficult to see the State agreeing to any such request.

'The closing of churches solely by administrative action must at all costs be prevented.'[46] This was the somewhat tardy conclusion of the review *Science and Religion*. The fact is that excessive zeal had led to a number of local conflicts. At Murmansk, for example, the militant anti-religious faction rushed to close the only church in the town; this aroused such violent protests from believers that in the end the church was given back to them.[47]

Of course, all church building or extension has been forbidden for the future. Restorations which provided opportunities for 'improper enlargement' (the provision of side-chapels) were in some cases ordered, and in others severely restricted, and occasionally both at once.

'As yet we lack a sufficient number of flats in the towns. . . . In some places, the cellars are being used as dwellings; in some schools for want of room, classes have to be given in rotation (in three sessions, morning, afternoon and evening). As yet we have too few General and Maternity Hospitals and Day Nurseries. It is therefore indispensable to oppose restorations that can wait,' said N. Kruschev. 'The fact that these works are done at the Church's expense is no excuse. Building materials and machines do not fall from heaven, but have to be withdrawn from urgent earthly tasks.'[48]

The destruction of churches which had never been discontinued (on 1st June 1956, the Cathedral of Ufa, dating from the sixteenth century, the oldest building in the town, was blown up),[49] has been resumed on a grand scale. The writer, Victor Nekrassov, was present in 1962 at a meeting whose purpose was to reduce by half the list of monuments under State protection. 'Some of those upon whom the fate of monuments depends consider that a church or an icon is primarily opium for the people and only secondarily a work of art.' Nekrassov went on to say that an influential daily paper of Kiev published an article which demanded the destruction of churches and synagogues of the eleventh and twelfth centuries, on the grounds that they disfigure the landscape.[50] *Science and Religion* informs us that a whole series of churches have been withdrawn from State protection to be destroyed or left to crumble.[51] Vandalism does not spare the most ancient monuments: in 1961, a twelfth-century church at Vitebsk and an eighteenth-century cathedral in Leningrad were destroyed.[52]

The closing of a church and its destruction often go together. At Minsk the church at the archbishop's residence and that in Kozyrevskaia street were closed and destroyed; seven miles from Pochaev, not content with destroying the church, the authorities blew up the rock on which it had been built.[53] At Kiev the churches disappeared one after another with unheard-of brutality. At Darnitsa (a suburb of Kiev) on 5th July 1963, a mechanical excavator was used to dig a large hole beside the church. It was blown up during the night and shovelled into the hole prepared for it. In the morning those who came to pray were astonished; where the church had stood men were planting flowers. The previous evening, the priest who said Vespers guessed that preparations were being made to destroy the church and asked permission to remove the Antimension (equivalent to the Corporal in the West) and other objects pertaining to worship; by way of answer he was seized and shut up in the police station while the fate of the church was settled.[54] At the same period the destruction of two churches in Novosibirsk was reported. Destruction of churches has spread to Moscow; on 15th July 1964, the Cathedral of the Transfiguration, where Nicholas Krutitsy, the Metropolitan, had his throne, was suddenly closed to the faithful. Despite their protests, on the next day the Cathedral was demolished to its foundations to enable an entrance to the underground railway to be made.[55]

The Laura of the Grottoes of Kiev – the cradle of Russian piety – was officially closed on account of a landslide. But apparently the danger threatened only the monks, for the civilians who took over the monastery are continuing to live in it.[56] Some religious houses, the convent of nuns at Odessa for example, have been brutally closed in a single night: a cordon of militiamen arrives, surrounds the monastery and expels the monks or nuns. Those who have homes are told to return to them; those with nowhere to go are taken to mental homes. When morning comes the people find their monastery closed. Others were suppressed by the steady application of vexatious economic or psychological measures: frequent medical inspections (particularly dreaded by nuns), in one case, the installation of a loudspeaker at a monastery window which poured out a ceaseless flood of profanity and propaganda against religion, etc.[57] In such circumstances, it is understandable that some monks preferred to carry out their vocation in the outside world. In this way the following monasteries in Moldavia have been closed: Khirov, Rechoul, Varsarekht, Tabor (more than 300 nuns were transferred to industrial production), Gerbovets, Balta, Dobruj, etc.; most of the Transcarpathian monasteries; the nunneries of Odessa, Dnepropetrovsk, Chernigov, Grodno, Rovno, the Presentation of the Virgin in Kiev, the 'desert' (*poustyn*) of Glinsk, renowned for the high standard of its monastic life. The closing of monasteries was a much easier matter, because there was no law sanctioning their existence. In the space of four years their numbers fell from sixty-seven to 'about thirty' and in 1964 no more then ten remained.[58]

The numerous methods used to compel monasteries to capitulate and to ask for their own closure (always this same concern for legality) have recently been disclosed in detail, through two petitions addressed by the Christians of the region of Pochaev, one of them to the 'President of External Ecclesiastical Relations of the USA' and the other to N. Kruschev himself. Written in artless and popular Russian, tinged with Ukrainian idioms, the two petitions aim at forestalling the closure of the famous Laura of Pochaev, the spiritual centre of the Western marches of Russia.

It seems worthwhile giving the essential content of these documents here, for they enable us to see how the mechanism of religious persecution actually works. It is a grotesque and tragic combination in inhuman and tragic actions, and a merely formal concern for legality:

The monks are deprived of the right to possess anything produced by the State, and with this as an excuse, the local authorities have made a clean sweep of everything owned by the abbey under the Polish republic, not to mention what it acquired later. They have confiscated all buildings erected within the abbey's enclosure, even those indispensable to it, like the cemetery, the Holy Doors, the water–pumping system, the electricity generator, and all the offices. They have also confiscated the lorries and carts, as well as all the material for buildings and repairs (sheet-iron for covering roofs and walls, marble and metal plating, non-ferrous metals and other materials), and they have taken over the flower and kitchen gardens, so that the monks have nowhere to walk.

But the authorities are not satisfied with things connected with the buildings; they are also trying to lay hold of objects used for specifically religious purposes; articles used in worship, the library, the chapels and cells of the monks, have all been placed on the list of items to be withdrawn – the first step to their seizure.

No decree for the closure of the abbey has been issued, but the method used is to continue to drive out groups of monks until not one will be left to welcome the people. These expulsions are put into execution with the help of brutal and inhuman methods: every day for the last two years monks have been summoned to the offices of the Minister of the Interior and of the Committee of Public Safety. There they are insulted, abused with filthy expressions, tortured, beaten, and ordered to leave the abbey. Last year, for instance, Isidore Lichchiniouk, the Monastic Guardian of the abbey, was beaten; Gregory Unka was tortured to death in prison; the monk Stankevich and others were also beaten. Even so, most of them accepted these sufferings and refused to leave the abbey until their death. 'They may torture us,' they said, 'but we will not go away.' The authorities then resorted to a method less easy to oppose: the young monks, after being re-adjudicated by the Council of Revision, are declared fit for military service by doctors acting on the instructions of the KGB. They are then enlisted, even though some of them are complete invalids. By these methods, Likitenko and Piletsky, for example, were driven from the abbey. Since they were quite unable to carry out their service, their cases were reconsidered, but they were absolutely forbidden to return to the abbey, and even to settle in Pochaev or in the Ternopol region.

The older monks are treated differently. They are continually being brought before Medical Boards and these attribute every sort of illness to them, and then compel them to enter hospital. Last year, for instance, a group of monks (Golovanov, Khvoruk, Nikitenko, Mirchukitz) were detained for a lengthy period in the Pochaev Mental Hospital, although they were of perfectly sound mind and had never suffered from any mental trouble. They were put among the inmates of the asylum and given very painful injections that left them nearly dead.

A further examination was arranged in order to discover cases of dysentery, and again, men in good health were shut up in hospital for more than two months. They were ordered to give up all thought of the abbey, and they remained in hospital until the Department of Public Health in Moscow intervened and they were released.

Those who were more stubborn and who refused such treatment were prosecuted and their passports confiscated. This was the case with Vassily Ivanovich Solomka who, to the general indignation, was condemned to a year's imprisonment for refusing to have the injections because there was nothing wrong with his health. The passports of those monks who were summoned to the courts were also confiscated. Ten of them, of different ages and positions in the community, from the prior to an ordinary lay brother, were dealt with in this way.

All Orthodox Christians were greatly disturbed by these actions. There was a general protest, but the authorities of Pochaev and the Ternopol region took no notice. On the contrary, they came to the decision that the abbey should now be completely liquidated and proceeded to take the following violent measure:

On 31st August 1962, officials of the KGB (the Committee for the security of the State) attached to the Militia of Pochaev and Ternopol, notably Commandant Bocharev, Captains Ostapenko and Maximov, together with twelve men, entered the abbey enclosure and broke open the door of the cell of seventy-year-old Fr Joseph. They beat him up, gagged him and dragged him away to a mental home. Since then he has not been heard of. It is rumoured that he was killed. This demonstration of force proved acceptable to the higher authorities of the region, and two days later, a more important group of KGB officials arrived. They were led by Colonel Korochenko, and the civilian N. A. Kolomatskin, the official responsible, under the Council of Ministers of the Ukraine, for matters connected with the Orthodox Church in the Ternopol region. They came with a motorized column, from which they took five lorries. They forced their way into the abbey and arrested ten of its inmates and dragged them into the lorries. Anyone who protested was beaten; the monks' hair was torn out and their arms twisted. On the colonel's order, one of them was hand-cuffed.

When they had them safely in the lorries, they drove them off in different directions to places as far as 150 miles away and left them there. They were told that if they went back to Pochaev, they would be given up to five years' imprisonment.

This bestiality stirred up indignation; but the Government's representatives remained deaf to the protests of monks and parishioners; on the contrary, they intensified their repressive measures. The monks, confronted by this unwarrantable infringement of the law, shut themselves up in the Abbey church and continued to celebrate the offices in it. But on 3rd October, the same group of officials with a body of men now increased to a hundred, broke into the church, having first smashed its door, as well as those of the cells, in which they found no monks.

In the church they heaped insults upon the monks, tore out their hair, beat them and dragged them to the lorries, as they had done the others. A large crowd had gathered and protested. It was dispersed with hoses.

As the result of these methods, employed in 1961 and 1962, the number of monks at the abbey was reduced to such an extent by the activity of the KGB that out of 150 monks, only 36 now (Autumn 1962) remain. And these latter are destined to the same fate, for the latest Medical Board, that met on 24th August, declared that twenty-three of them were ill and 'in urgent need of treatment in a clinic'. All of them, however, were, in reality, in good health, and were carrying out their duties in the Abbey, and not one of them had the slightest wish for medical treatment. In spite of this, they are in no less danger of suffering like the others, and of being forcibly removed from the abbey.

All these restrictions are known to the Patriarch, and especially to Gregory, the present Bishop of Lvov and Ternopol. But they are powerless and there is no way for them to intervene. Indeed, they have given way to the threats of the KGB and have ratified the appointment of weak and unstable characters to positions of ecclesiastical importance, as, for instance, the Prior Vladislav, dean of the abbey, who has had no experience of monastic life and who assists the illegal actions of the local authorities that lead to the expulsion of the monks.

In view of this acquiescence on the part of the religious authorities, the civil authorities have taken over all ecclesiastical government and completely control the local Church Council, just as they do the local Militia, in accordance with the instructions of the KGB.

They summon meetings of the Church Council, and in these all the leaders of the district and of its Party Executive Committee, as well as Representatives of the Party organizations, take part. They take decisions acceptable to themselves and impose these on the Church Council and compel its members to sign. This is an open interference in the internal affairs of the Church.

All Orthodox believers in our country are outraged by the reign of tyranny thus instituted by the Party organization. Protests from every quarter have reached Kruschev, Brejnev, the Editorial Board of *Izvestia*, etc. But all of these have been forwarded to Ternopol and remain without effect, or, if there is any effect, it is an increase in persecution.

We are all sunk in despair, and we beg you to put an end to all these inhuman and shameful deeds with which we believers are afflicted, and also to make it possible for us to preserve our holy abbey.[59]

The tenacity of the faithful, the effect of these petitions in the West, brought results. In 1965 the Laura was still in existence, despite further incidents of which a few examples are here given:

Fr S., at the age of ninety-seven, came to live at the abbey on the orders of the Patriarch; he was intercepted by the police and interrogated for a whole week, after which he was asked to leave Pochaev; the superior, Fr V., was even unwilling to receive this monk of nearly a hundred years of age who had spent forty years of his life at Pochaev.

On 31st July 1963, the local court at Pochaev sentenced a seventy-two-year-old monk, Fr M., for 'vagabondage', but in reality because he desired to live in the abbey. For a whole year Fr M. had negotiated to obtain his residence permit at Pochaev, explaining to the authorities that he had given to the service of the State the whole of his working life and that now he wanted to end his days in penance. The officials confined themselves to tearing up his requests and fining him for illegal residence and threatening him with expulsion. But Fr M. answered them that he would never leave Pochaev. He was therefore tried and sentenced under article 196* for contravention of the passport regulations. Many monks have been taken away by force, others have been sent to parishes which have been subsequently closed, and those who have refused to leave the abbey have been sentenced and imprisoned. At the expiration of their sentence they have returned to Pochaev but the authorities refuse them a residence permit and threaten to imprison them again with an increased sentence. Our hearts are torn to see the wandering life led by the monks of Pochaev who do not know where to find shelter for the night.

To obtain the closure of the abbey the authorities also make use of other methods. It is forbidden, for example, for fuel to be brought to the abbey and in winter the monks are dying of cold.

This last piece of information is corroborated by an article appearing in *Krokodil* which jeers at the monks of Pochaev because 'the icy temperature of the cells prevents communication with Most High'. The article describes the unfortunate adventure of a monk looking for wood to heat the abbey who ends by falling into the hands of a patrol of the People's Militia.[60] In January 1964,

---

* Of the penal code of the Ukrainian Republic, Article 196 is concerned with deliberate and repeated infringement of the passport regulations. Such infringements are liable to imprisonment up to two years, or a fine of fifty roubles.

several monks of Pochaev were once more sentenced to prison:
Fr Appelius Stankevich to two years (third sentence), Fr Andrew
Schur to three years (second-sentence) etc.[61]

The fate of the seminaries

The methods used to liquidate the seminaries differ little from
those used for the monasteries. In order to give a semblance of
legality for their closure, the authorities artificially provoked a
decrease in their membership. Unlike other Soviet students,
seminarists were not exempted from military service, but they
were able to postpone it, and since priests were not bound to
serve, seminarists applied for ordination shortly before the conclusion of their studies. But in 1959, this postponement was no
longer granted and priests, like everyone else, were liable for
military service. The application of this measure enabled the
seminaries to be emptied – legally.[62] Additional measures were,
however, necessary: authorizations of residence for students
whose home was elsewhere than the town in which the seminary
was established, were withdrawn; priests who gave recommendations for requests to be admitted to a seminary were now prosecuted. The Patriarchate was obliged to alter the formalities for
admission in order to free the lower clergy from responsibility:
a recommendation from a priest must henceforth be endorsed
by the local dean and presented to the seminary by the diocesan
bishop.[63] Applications for admission are regularly intercepted
and candidates for the seminary are sought out, subjected to
propaganda and threatened.[64]

The consequences of these measures were not long in manifesting themselves. Before the summer of 1960, the authorities seized
the buildings used for the Seminaries of Saratov, Stavropol, Kiev
and Odessa.[65] The Seminary of Odessa alone managed to survive
by taking refuge in the Monastery of the Assumption, spared
because it is the summer residence of the Patriarch.[66] The seminary
at Minsk, which had been emptied of its students by various

measures, struggled valiantly for four years. At the beginning of 1964 the professors refused to leave and the authorities were obliged to take measures for their expulsion.[67] Yet 120 applications for admission had been sent in to the seminary. The seminary at Wolhynia held out until 1965. There, too, the applications for admission were numerous but the authorities disregarded the fact. In 1962 there were no first-year students.[68] At the Leningrad Seminary the position is scarcely better; in 1961 there were no more than eight first-year students against sixteen in 1960 and thirty-seven in 1959.[69] The fine correspondence course seems to have disappeared; it was to be replaced by one established in connection with the Moscow Academy.[70] As this example shows, the Moscow Theological Schools appear to be in a better position, but there too admissions are limited in number. Every year several of the accepted candidates find that they are refused the necessary residence permit for Zagorsk.[71] The *Review of the Patriarchate* continues to call for vocations to the priesthood; it even goes so far as to state that if the candidate, owing to the closing of his parish, is unable to furnish a recommendation from his priest, that circumstance need not be an obstacle to his candidacy.[72]

The higher clergy and the persecution

The higher clergy principally have been limited in their activity. Most administrative matters seem to have been taken over by the regional delegates of the Council for Orthodox Affairs, leaving to the bishops the direction of public worship. 'It is for us to govern, for you to hold services.' At least, that is the story told by the laity in the USSR. In many cities the bishop's residence has been seized (for example, in Ismail, in Leningrad where the authorities have taken possession of the residence of the Metropolitan which had for long been that of the Patriarch Alexis,[73] and in Stavropol whose bishop was obliged to take refuge in a neighbouring diocese). In almost every diocese the bishop has been moved.[74] In a number of cases retirement has been enforced. The Archbishop of Tachkent, Hermogenes, who by means of pastoral letters had tried to answer calumnies against himself in the press, was suspended for a year.[75] A bishop in the Ukraine was declared undesirable;[76] another was refused the right to preach and to celebrate the liturgy.[77] It is clear that the authorities are anxious not to create new martyrs. Nevertheless, some arrests have been made. In 1960, for example, Job Kressovich, Archbishop of Kazan, was sentenced to three years' imprisonment for an impressive series of the most varied financial, political and religious offences: he was accused of having withheld large sums of money from the taxes; of having sown discord among the nations by the restoration of a feast in commemoration of St Goury, a missionary to the Tartars in the time of Ivan the Terrible, of having refused to order an appeal supporting the Peace Movement to be read in churches and, lastly, of making too frequent visits to the clergy of his diocese.[78] In 1961, Archbishop Andrew Sukhenko, who had previously been imprisoned as a priest, was declared guilty of deceiving the taxation authorities and of corruption of youth.[79] This time the sentence was more severe, eight years' imprisonment. In the same year, Benjamin Novitsky, the aged Archbishop of Irkutsk, who had spent the ten years 1944–54 in a concentration camp, was prosecuted for 'having bought some stolen vaseline' [*sic*].[80]

The disgrace and death of the Metropolitan Nicholas

The most tragic victim of these new persecutions, however, has been the famous Metropolitan, Nicholas of Krutitsy, well known throughout the world for his active and even enthusiastic part in the International Peace Movement, and as the Patriarch's chief adviser and Chairman of the Department of the Church's External Relations.

From sources that are completely reliable but which we may be forgiven for not indicating more clearly, it can be stated that he was not only dismissed and kept under surveillance but, without doubt, was assassinated.

For a proper understanding of his fall it must be placed in the context of the first two years of the persecution. Such an abrupt change in policy was bound to involve the disappearance of the leading figures in both camps. G. Karpov, the President of the Government Council for the affairs of the Orthodox Church, who had honourably carried out his duties since 1943 (the year when this body was set up) was replaced by V. Kuroiedov whose zest in promoting the new policy has been described above. The change corresponds to the development of the situation : the man responsible for the Concordat could not act as ring-leader in the persecution. The Metropolitan Nicholas, on the other hand, was the Church's strong man. He had been the Patriarch's Benjamin for fifteen years, and was his most probable successor. His political competency, his manifold connections with foreign personalities and institutions, made his presence an embarrassment at a time when the State was about to resume its desperate struggle with the Church.[81]

This was particularly true in his case, because it was believed that he was an advocate of a hardening of the Church's attitude to the State. He was behind the Holy Synod's decision to excommunicate apostates publicly,[82] and the Patriarch's courageous speech, in February 1960,[83] at the Conference of the Soviet Social Organizations for Peace. In this speech, which was punctuated by noisy outbursts from those present, the Patriarch praised the services rendered by the Church throughout history and denounced the unjust deeds of which she was the victim. Mgr Nicholas's fall came close on these two events which revealed the vitality and worth of a Church believed to be for ever servile and passive.

'Since 19th September 1960,' Mgr Nicholas wrote to one of the leaders of the Peace Movement, 'I have been in a state of forced inaction as unexpected as it is incomprehensible. Thank God, I am in good health, but it is clear that I shall no longer be able to take part in any activity, or celebrate the liturgy or publish anything. After forty years of work, what a startling climax!' But it was true, for on 6th December 1960, even though it was his feastday, he learnt that he would not be allowed to celebrate. At Christmas, he was permitted to concelebrate with the other bishops in the Patriarchal Cathedral, but he had to leave the building immediately after Communion, even before the end of the liturgy. He had to spend Easter night in his room, 'the first time,' he said, 'for forty-seven years'. On the fourth day of Easter week he was allowed to celebrate in the Church of the Trinity-St-Sergius, but care was taken to keep him away from the people. 'Monseigneur wept throughout the service, and when they saw him, all the concelebrants and many of the people wept also, as though they sensed that this was his last celebration. Until mid-November various persons were allowed to visit him. He felt extremely well and seemed to be intellectually alert. Then one day, Valentina Ivanovna, a woman doctor, arrived; she prescribed a cure which he refused to follow. Shortly afterwards he felt ill and was taken to the Botkin hospital where he was under constant observation by the woman doctor.'[84] 'It was impossible to discover the real cause of his illness,' wrote one of his suite. 'All visits, including those of the Patriarchate's representatives, and of his family, were strictly forbidden. The woman doctor (Valentina Ivanovna) let it be known that his position might improve, and yet, eight days before his death, she knew that it was desperate. . . . It was forbidden to pray for him aloud in the churches. He died on 13th December at 4 o'clock in the morning, without having received the sacraments, without knowing why none of his relatives had come to him, and in the presence of Valentina Ivanovna alone.' The congregation of the Cathedral of the Transfiguration expressed the wish to have the body of the man who had been their pastor and their spiritual father, but they were met with a refusal. His naked body was left unattended in the mortuary for more than thirteen hours. At last, in the afternoon, the Patriarchate's representatives came to clothe him in his episcopal vestments. When Mgr Cyprian and Mgr Nicodemus arrived for the placing on the bier, the people who had gathered in great numbers near the mortuary, greeted them with shouts of "murderers". At noon the following day, the bier was taken from the mortuary. In spite of what had been promised, the people were at first not allowed to pay their respects before the bier; the order was given for it to be taken to the hearse. Whereupon the people literally took possession of the bier, placed it in a room in the mortuary, and organized their own processional farewell. It is impossible to describe all that took place on that day. What tears were shed! When the coffin was put into the hearse, some began to kiss the carriage, others knelt in the snow. The weather was appalling, a cutting wind, a whirlwind.'[85]

Although Monseigneur had purchased a piece of ground in the cemetery of the Transfiguration, the order was given to bury him in the Trinity-St-Sergius. Everything was done to prevent the people from expressing their reverence for the Metropolitan. An attempt was made to make the people present in the church go away for the night, but quite in vain, no one left. His death was not announced in any church and the time and place of his funeral was known only to a few. . . . On the morning of the ceremony, several trains for Zagorsk were cancelled. When the Rector Rujitsky, in the course of his panegyric on the dead, declared that Monseigneur had died from overwork, angry cries of protest rang out in the church. When the clergy began to sing the solemn chant for the dead, their sobbing reached such a pitch that they had to stop, and the singing was taken up by the seminarists. I think that there was no one present who had not wept. The people's farewells went on for three hours during the evening before the funeral and for two hours after it. Their grief seemed inconsolable, and their tears never ceased. During the service a crown-shaped ornament fell from the ceiling; by a miracle nobody was hit. . . .'

Mgr Nicholas was buried in the church called 'The Church of the Steeple'. Very shortly afterwards, the church was closed to stop the influx of pilgrims who had come to meditate at his grave. 'Apparently even after his death the authorities found him alarming.'[86]

It is true, of course, that the disturbing facts just mentioned are presumptive evidence and not proof that Mgr Nicholas was murdered. But one thing is certain: the people are convinced that he died a martyr.

The trials of the lower clergy

Like the episcopate, the status of the lower clergy has been diminished, and their activity restricted. We saw above that since 1945 the priest was President of the Executive body of the parish, and that this contradicted the Decree of 1929. By a resolution of the Holy Synod of 18th April 1961, issued on the express request of the Soviet authorities, the Ecclesiastical Regulations of 1945 were brought into line with the legislation on worship: he no longer forms part of the Parochial Council and is to direct the spiritual affairs of his community and nothing more; in other words, he again becomes simply and solely a minister of public worship. This anti-canonical measure, because it modified conciliar decisions, encountered opposition from the bishops and clergy. Since a Council could not be held, a meeting of bishops had to be summoned. The opponents of the resolution were not admitted to it. They had previously been dismissed from their posts. The Holy Synod's decision was ratified without opposition.[87] In this way, the Soviet authorities succeeded in impairing the unity of the parish and in reducing the authority of the priesthood.[88]

Furthermore, the activity of priests is minutely supervised and controlled; an attempt is being made to reduce it to an absolute minimum, to the celebration of public worship. 'Until 1959 the priests of Kassimov (in the Province of Riazan) used to organize excursions to the woods for young people, give them little presents and talks on the meaning of life, on happiness and virtue.'[89] This form of activity, regarded as illegal in conformity with Article 17 of the decree of 1929 is now absolutely forbidden and severely punished. Any form of pastoral zeal runs the risk of being interpreted as an act of religious propaganda. For the periodical *Science and Religion* a priest who distributes chocolate to children commits an offence.[90] To visit parishioners in their homes is regarded as reprehensible, especially if there are atheists in the family.[91] In some cities, priests no longer have access to the hospitals, even when they are requested by the dying. At Anikchai in Lithuania, no priest has possessed the right to enter the hospital since 1961, even at official visiting hours, even to see his own relations.[92] Preachers of any popularity are silenced or deprived of the right to preach and even to celebrate the liturgy. 'Now that I no longer preach,' writes a bishop, 'and keep quiet, the authorities don't bother me any more.'[93] And so the clergy prefer to preach quite inoffensive sermons (but still they do preach) rather than attract the anger and reprisals of the authorities. In 1963, in certain dioceses the priests received the verbal but categoric order to refuse Communion to children.[94] In that case, also, some complied to avoid worse befalling them.

Indeed, hundreds of priests have been deprived of the right of exercising their ministry; as married men, responsible for a family, they have been reduced to begging, for it is hardly possible for them to obtain ordinary employment. A correspondent of *Science and Religion* gives a sarcastic description of the case of a young priest, a former engineer, the father of two children, who was reduced to asking his Diocesan Bishop for a job; meanwhile entirely destitute, he has to live off the parcels sent by his mother-in-law. After experiencing a certain ease, if not affluence, the Russian clergy have again been reduced to poverty.[95]

Scores, even hundreds of priests – the precise number will never be known – have gone to prison. Thus *Science and Religion* informs us that in the Diocese of Orenburg alone, in 1960, twenty-six priests were before the courts.[96] Any pretext is good enough to attack the clergy. Despite the official amnesty wiping out all voluntary or involuntary defections during the war, the past life of the priests is examined with exemplary severity; the slightest suspicion of possible collaboration with the occupying powers leads to their arrest or suspension. Thus Alexander Pospelov, a deacon, accused belatedly of several crimes, was arrested at the end of the liturgy in the Church of SS. Peter and Paul at Kuibyshev;[97] Fr Donetskoi was sentenced to ten years in prison for collaborating with the Germans twenty years previously.[98]

But as a general rule accusations made against the clergy are specifically religious. In the Province of Kalinine, the young parish priest of Likhoslavl was severely punished for 'trying to attract young people to church'.[99] Two Catholic priests were sentenced at Vilnius, one to eight, and the other to four, years in prison for having endeavoured to build a church.[100] The new religious legislation, adopted in 1961 in the Ukraine and a year later in Russia, is aimed especially at the clergy. The new Article 227 of the Penal Code lays down among other things that 'the organization or direction of a group whose activity, exercised under the cover of preaching religious doctrines or performing religious rites, is likely to be harmful to the health of the citizens ... or is accompanied by incitation to refusal of social activities ... together with the enrolment of minors in such a group . . . is punished by imprisonment of up to five years'.[101]

Reading of this article enables us to understand why the parish priest of a village in the Province of Riazan should for several hours have refused to baptize children in his unheated church;[102] in the end he asked the parents to state in writing that they freed him from all responsibility. Indeed there was some precedent for his anxiety; in 1960 A. Scherbatov, a priest of Magnitogorsk, was sentenced to three years in prison after the death of a baby which occurred shortly after its baptism: advantage was taken of this case to close the church.[103] In 1962, a Baptist pastor, Prokofiev, under Article 227 of the Ukrainian code,[104] was sentenced to five years imprisonment followed by banishment for five years for 'having organized illegal baptisms of the young at Kharkov and Jdanov'.[105]

The knowledge that the Minister of Health has declared that the sacrament of Baptism (administered by the Orthodox and the Baptists by immersion), Communion from the chalice by means of a spoon, the veneration of icons and even the fact of kissing a priest's hand, constitute a serious risk of disease and epidemics; the knowledge that social activity is to all intents and purposes obligatory in the USSR and is endowed with an openly atheistic character, and the further knowledge of the threats uttered by L. Iliichev against those who exercise a religious influence over children, will enable us readily to understand what a formidable weapon against the clergy, and even against the faithful, is to be found in the new article of the Penal Code.

After three years of persecution the Orthodox clergy had diminished by half: according to N. Yudine, at the beginning of 1962, there remained only 14,500 priests at work as compared with 30,000 before 1959.[106]

Lastly, the authorities are making a greater effort than ever to corrupt the clergy from within their own ranks by introducing confidential agents and spies among them. Patriarch Alexis has himself admitted that 'at present there are some who, with unbelievable impertinence, are attempting to make their way into the enclosure of the Church with self-seeking, ill-intentioned, and even treacherous aims'.[107] New bishops are asked to be extremely cautious as to the priests whom they ordain.[108]

It is in the light of these facts that we must interpret the numerous apostasies of priests, which never fail to be given wide publicity by the Soviet press. Careful inquiry has revealed that, in most cases, such priests were in some canonically irregular position or had a politically dubious past. It may be some of these who 'have made their way into the Church with a treacherous aim,' and have subsequently unmasked themselves.

Alexander Ossipov, Professor of the Old Testament in the Leningrad Academy – the one person of significance among the apostates – belongs to both categories. A native of the Baltic countries, where he was active in the Russian Students' Christian Action and afterwards in political organizations of the extreme right, as a result of the events of 1940, he was parted from his wife who managed to escape to America. He had become a priest, but in spite of canon law which forbids priests, even if widowers, to make a second marriage, he remarried. The Patriarch put him under an interdict for life, but ordered him – and in his circumstances this was humiliating – to wear the cassock. Since then he has not been satisfied with leaving the Church; he has not only embraced the most inept of the dogmas of anti-religious propaganda, but has joined wholeheartedly in the fight against the Church.[109] The unfrocking of the priest Alexander Chertkov, another native of the Baltic countries and a graduate of the Moscow Academy, is also explicable by his uncanonical position: he had forsaken his family in order to follow a woman who may have been sent with the intention of leading him astray. This is what is rumoured in Moscow, and it is the impression left after reading his confession.[110] According to the former secretary of the Exarchate of the Ukraine, the number of apostates is about one in a hundred and most of them are priests ordained in a hurry during the German occupation and without the proper inquiries being made.[111] This was in fact the case with Yakushevich[112] and Spassky.[113] Out of some 200 apostates, only the names of about thirty are known.[114]

The ordinary faithful are aware that wolves have been introduced into the sheepfold – 'To root out the Orthodox faith and close the churches all the more quickly,' says the petition addressed to the Eastern Patriarchs, 'the Government trains atheists for the priesthood and causes them to be appointed as rectors of cathedrals and even as bishops. Other clergy, of weak character, have become the servants of Anti-Christ.' The problem of members of the Party disguised as priests disturbs unbelievers also. Several letters in this sense have been sent to *Science and Religion* which, of course, answered them by mere denial of the facts.[115]

Fresh Trials

The position of the laity and external hindrances

Everything is arranged to prevent the people from attending church or going on a pilgrimage. In some dioceses, early morning celebrations on weekdays are forbidden. In 1961, it was decided that Easter Sunday should be a working day, and processions round the churches forbidden. A Western tourist who wanted to go into a church in the suburb of Leningrad was informed by a girl at the door that it was shut, whereas in fact it was open. Even in Moscow young Komsomols can be seen near churches accosting people with such words as: 'Eh, grandpa, what are you going to do in church; much better go home!'[116] At Anikchai in Lithuania the school sends fourteen-year-olds to watch the churches and make a note of the names of those they know. The devout people of Anikchai go to other cities to perform their religious exercises.[117]

Places of pilgrimage demand more thorough measures. To stem the tide of pilgrims on their way to the reputedly miraculous hill of St Nicholas (near the village of Surskoie in the Ulianovsk Province) and to turn them back, 650 militiamen and auxiliaries questioned the pilgrims, searched them, scrutinized their papers and 'proposed to take them to the nearest railway station in a lorry'. Purveyors of religious goods and souvenirs were sent to prison. Pilgrimages, therefore, came to an end, and to ensure that this should be permanent, the place was levelled with a bulldozer and turned into a sports ground. As a substitute for the religious festival, the Party organized a mammoth Spring Festival in which 700 singers took part.[118] The pilgrimage of Velikoretskoe, dating from the time of Ivan the Terrible, the procession at Kursk, and the pilgrimage to Lake Svietloiar, were all similarly abolished. A Communist Pioneer camp was set up on the lakeside.[119] The Church of our Saviour's Blood in Leningrad had been withdrawn from public worship, but it was still a place of pilgrimage. An iron grille was then put up to bar the way. For a while the people were satisfied with saying their prayers at a distance, on the farther side of the Griboedov canal. Then some adventurous spirits managed to break through the grille, and it again became possible to kiss the mosaics of the crucifix and the saints that adorned the gates of the church.

On 20th May 1963, a great number of pilgrims from all over Russia gathered at Jirovitsy (Grodno Province) to celebrate the patronal feast of the Apparition of the Icon of the Blessed Virgin. The officials of the Committee for Ecclesiastical Affairs for the Provinces of Minsk and Grodno went to Jirovitsy and forbade the clergy to hold services for the festival.[120]

At Kalvarya, a Catholic pilgrimage in Lithuania, the authorities forbade cars bringing the pilgrims to enter the town. The step was fruitless: the number of pilgrims arriving at their destination was no less than in previous years.[121]

But it is at Pochaev that the struggle for the right to pilgrimages has taken on the most tragic form:

For two years now, the regional services of the Pochaev Militia, with its huge membership and its Auxiliary Volunteers (*Drujinniki*) have issued prohibitions almost daily, forbidding people to come to the abbey to pray. They have set up barriers, and in particular, posted a company of volunteers, at the entrance to the abbey. They stop pilgrims by force, load them on lorries and take them away to the heart of the forests of Brodny, Smyjskoe and other places and leave them there, threatening them that if they should be seen in the neighbourhood of the abbey again, they would be sentenced to five years' imprisonment for vagrancy, a sentence which is in fact carried out.

Pilgrims are not allowed to use public transport. If a driver fails to observe this rule, he loses his employment and sometimes even his freedom. So all pilgrims come on foot, as they did two hundred years ago. But this does not worry them as long as, at the end of so trying a journey, they are enabled to reverence the relics of Pochaev; be blessed on the Holy Mountain, and drink the saving water of the Well of the Footsteps of the Blessed Virgin.

In fact, however, they are prevented from any such approach; their personal possessions and their money are confiscated; filthy expressions of every kind are showered upon them, and they are even beaten.

No peace can be found by day or night, not even for one or two days together. It is as though the people have been afflicted by a plague. Every day, and on festivals twice a day (the second time, during the night), Auxiliary Volunteers led by the Head of the Passport Office search houses to make sure that no incoming pilgrims are lodging in them. If any are discovered, the householder is liable to a fine which may amount to the huge sum of 50 roubles (56 dollars in official currency, about a month's wages for a skilled worker) and he is told that if he repeats the offence he will be evicted. The local people are forbidden to visit the abbey, under the penalty of being dismissed from work and banished from Pochaev.

All these repressive measures are directed to a single end: to deprive the people of the divine grace they receive during their common prayer in the holy Abbey of Pochaev, to deprive the monks of popular support and to drive them away as being of no use to anyone.[122]

'Nevertheless,' reports the petition addressed to the Eastern Patriarchs, 'pilgrims still crowd into Pochaev from all over Russia, even though they have to sleep in the open. On the night of 18th and 19th August 1963, Militiamen brought up lorries to seize the pilgrims, but warned in time, they managed to get away.'[123]

Anti-religious festivals

After some hesitation – for fear of being accused of imitating religion – the atheist authorities decided to draw up a secular ritual to combat the attraction exerted by the religious festivals and individual sacraments. In the country districts where patronal festivals remained very popular, three principal festivals (of Song, of Spring, and of the Harvest) were instituted and certain festivals of lesser importance (as, for example, days in honour of drivers, stock-breeders, etc). In several districts, Meetings of the People decided to give up religious festivals so that their place could be taken by the new ones. For example, the kolkhoz members of the village of Viaski (Porkhov district, Pskov Province) decided to abandon religious festivals and announced the fact in the local newspaper under the headline: 'Do not come for the festival; we are not at home.' The kolkhoz members of the village of Ugol (Sokol district, Vologda Province) not only adopted the festivals of Spring and the Harvest but at the same time ordered the suppression of the festivals of Easter, St Elijah, St Michael, the Transfiguration, the Assumption etc. So it seems that introduction of the new festivals is accompanied by prohibition to observe the old ones – it is a real ritual without religion imposed by the State.

Komsomol marriages, for which in several cities special buildings have been provided, have not furnished the expected results. It is true that in Leningrad, marriages in church have dropped in two years, between 1959 and 1961, from 25 per cent to a quarter of one per cent; but it is difficult to attribute so rapid a fall to the irresistible attraction of the secular rite. At Volsk (Saratov Province), on the other hand, in 1962 fifty-nine religious marriages were recorded as against ten in 1961. Komsomol marriages have quickly lost their special attraction and have become boring occasions. 'I remember,' writes a correspondent of the *Komsomol Journal*, 'what a great occasion were the first weddings in the marriage bureau at Grodno. Nowadays, unfortunately, they have become a pretty routine matter; no one is attracted by the rite and we are unable to refashion it.' It might well be objected that religious marriage has not varied for centuries, but never lost any of its attraction. Some are proposing to go further in the imitation of religious ceremonies by introducing into the fixed secular rite, quasi-sacramental formulas, hymns and processions, which in time might become traditional.[124]

Fresh Trials

Individual propaganda and religious discrimination

Not only are the faithful deprived of the possibility of frequenting their churches, going on pilgrimage and observing the Christian festivals, but an effort is made to take from them their personal faith in God. Individual propaganda – the method is to influence each believer personally – depends on police work and denunciation. The believer is tracked down and followed; he is conditioned by exhortations which go on for a period of several weeks, and then by threats. If he still holds out repressive measures of a social nature are taken against him, amounting to real religious discrimination; these have been applied since 1959.

Although 'previously (about 1954) in the schools no account was taken of the belief of the pupils, and a believer might even belong to the Komsomol with an easy conscience'[125] it is by no means the same today. For the children of believers, particularly those of the clergy, the school forms a real Calvary:

'Previously,' writes the daughter of a priest, 'my life was happy and carefree. Then it all changed. . . . I no longer wanted to go to school, for every day I encountered new difficulties. I gave no sign of the sufferings inflicted on me. Even the Headmistress said of me, "she is proud". And at home every day I used to cry and blame my father – "It's all your fault!" I made up my mind to leave the school and go to live elsewhere at my grandmother's.' But the unfortunate girl was not even allowed to attend the school although she had formally renounced her faith in writing.[126] The children of believers encounter great difficulty in gaining entrance to establishments of more advanced learning.[127]

Science and Religion admitted in 1962 that workers were often dismissed for purely religious reasons. In condemning such excesses it reported that under various pretexts, but always for the same real motive (religious belief), students had even been sent away from universities, even those entirely in order and eminently deserving.[128] But in 1963, the same periodical and other Soviet newspapers described, without much reaction, fresh cases of believers being sent away from their schools or their work.

Science and Religion reports the case of Serge Gorbatov. He was a pupil of the top class of School 648 in Moscow. An active member of the Komsomol he was intelligent, gifted and an excellent chess-player. But he was a believer. When, quite by chance, it was discovered, the whole school protested: a believing Komsomol was unheard of! He must be sent away. Soon Gorbatov himself requested his exclusion from the Communist Youth Organization. The hostility of the teachers increased. For a whole year efforts were made to make him deny his faith. An apostate priest was even sent for. During a lesson in natural science, he was intentionally given a question on the origin of man. 'I can't answer according to the textbook,' he replied. This was his last lesson. A few weeks later he was in the dock and sentenced. Indeed, the correspondent of *Science and Religion* remarked candidly enough, 'he is eighteen and is not a student anywhere'. Unsuccessful in their efforts to wean him from his belief the atheists thought to achieve their ends by dragging him before the courts. Gorbatov's sister, Nina, shared the same fate. An engineer at the Institute of Building Machinery, after being called on several occasions to abandon her belief, in June 1963 she was excluded from her work: 'We are not locking her out; if she likes she can come back. We have already taken trouble enough over her.'[129]

At the University of Rostov-on-Don one Baluev was a student in philosophy and history. It was learnt by chance that he believed in God. A committee, formed at once, gave Baluev ten minutes to make up his mind to reconsider his whole philosophical position and give up his faith. Baluev preferred to leave the university.[130] A similar case occurred at the Teachers' Training College at Rostov where a woman student, Yastrebkova, after a long resistance to atheist indoctrination was categorically called on to apostatize. She, too, preferred to give up her studies.[131]

At Nijny-Taguil, at the Polytechnic Institute of the Urals, a student Bozhkov aroused the suspicions of no one; and then it was learnt that before entering the Institute he had cherished the idea of putting his name down for the seminary at Zagorsk. Students and teachers would not believe his denials. Some demanded a public apostasy, others insisted on more radical measures still. Bozhkov left the Institute of his own accord.[132]

The struggle for the souls of the children

The principal effort in the campaign against religion is now directed towards children and adolescents. The newspapers profess astonishment that 'Soviet laws cannot protect children completely from religious influences. Methods not only of persuasion but of coercion are needed. All religious pressure on a minor must be punished as a crime under the common law'.[133] This idea, which was merely an isolated opinion, was made official by L. Iliichev: 'We cannot and we must not remain indifferent,' he said in his speech before the ideological commission, 'to the fate of the children on whom parents, fanatical believers, are in reality inflicting an act of spiritual violence. We cannot allow blind and ignorant parents to bring up their children like themselves and so deform them.'[134]

Indeed it is now an order that must be carried out: 'To prevent the clergy, groups of believers and individuals from pursuing an illegal activity supervision intended to preserve children and adolescents from clerical influences must be strengthened and parents must not be allowed to require their children to perform religious rites.'[135]

But even before these peremptory and threatening assertions appropriate measures had been taken. Ever since 1962, the administration of baptism has become more difficult. In future, for a child to be baptized the written agreement of both parents and a work certificate or residence certificate provided by the local authorities are necessary. Local authorities which provide these certificates are blamed by the newspapers and the Party organizations and accused of infringing the decree on the separation of Church and State.

A citizen B —, reports *Izvestia*, decided to have her child baptized. At the church she was told that she must produce a certificate in due form, according to the law. The Administrator of Residence Group number 2 of the chemical factory of Tambov made no difficulty about giving her a certificate in the following terms: 'We certify by these presents that citizen B — actually lives at Tambov. Certificate delivered to be shown at the church for the baptism of the child.' The Administrator was at once criticized. Not only had he broken the law, but he had done nothing to dissuade B — from having her child baptized.[136]

Thus all parents desirous of having a child baptized must not only make themselves known to the authorities but lay themselves open to the attempts to dissuade them by the active anti-religious workers.

It does not appear that this flagrant interference in the internal affairs of the Church has borne its promised fruits. In several cities, at Vladimir,[137] Volsk,[138] in the towns of the Province of Riazan,[139] for example, the number of baptisms has increased in 1962 in comparison with 1961. And the village women of Tuma who, on 21st November 1963, waited for several hours in a freezing church, and finally compelled the timid priest to baptize their children, showed once again the depth of the attachment of the Russian people to the sacrament of baptism.[140]

For children of school age the authorities have adopted even more radical methods. At first, by virtue of a law which forbids minors to work in churches, it was prohibited for anyone less than eighteen years of age to serve at the altar.[141] Then, in certain dioceses, they were forbidden even to frequent the church. 'The local government official,' we are informed by a petition of the faithful, 'is stationed at the doors of the Cathedral of Minsk to prevent the children frequenting it. If he sees that children have entered the church he sends the churchwarden of the parish to them; this latter, a servant of anti-Christ, takes the children by the necks and knocks their heads against the wall. . . .'

The headmistress of School 18 at Minsk on several occasions summoned Theodosia Varava in order to dissuade her from letting her children go to church: 'You are deforming your children by bringing them up religiously.' Faced by the mother's steadfastness the headmistress declared that she would be sent for trial and that her children would be placed in a boarding school.[142]

What for Theodosia was only a threat was for others a sorrowful reality. On several occasions parents, who persist in bringing up their children with a religious faith, despite what they are told by the school authorities, have been deprived of their rights as parents. At first, in most of the cases mentioned by the newspapers, the accusation reported only the penalties undergone by the children. But gradually, deprivation of parental rights has been extended to parents whose only crime was the religious education of their children. In some cases Pentecostalists have been deprived of their parental rights because they took their children to worship and forbade them to frequent the cinema, the evening meetings at school or to look at television.[143] In others, Orthodox parents have had their children taken away from them because these latter fasted too much.[144]

At Minsk, during a divorce case, the three children of the couple were entrusted to the drunken and adulterous father and the mother was expelled from the home for the only reason that the latter, an exemplary worker and careful mother, belonged to the Baptist faith.[145]

The Komsomol periodical published the photograph of four kneeling children with the following caption: 'These children have done no harm. It was their Pentecostal parents who obliged them to kneel. We can say at once that this photograph is out of date. The four children whom you see there have been removed from the guardianship of fanatical believers. But they are not the latest victims of religious despotism. Our duty as Komsomols and elder brothers obliges us to guard every child from the attacks of religious fanaticism.'[146]

Among other documents left by the Pentecostalists of Chernogorsk, who took refuge for several hours at the American Embassy, there figured several letters from children taken away from their parents and placed in boarding schools: 'The masters want to make us abjure our faith and beat us to make us stop praying,' wrote a girl of twelve who implored her parents to ask Kruschev for permission to leave the USSR.[147]

Public trials have produced scenes of a harrowing nature: '"My dear Lida, think of your mother who is all alone, come back home." The child's lips trembled, but did not utter the decisive word.'[148]

The Soviet press constantly reports family conflicts provoked by religious persecution. In one case it is a boy who rebels against his mother whom he thinks too devout and writes to her from the boarding school: 'Let me make my way alone.'[149] In another it is a grandmother who denounces her grandson who had the queer idea of becoming a seminarist.[150]

Some children find themselves in impossible situations which they are unable to bear; they are too young to deal with them. The Komsomol periodical reports that a boy of thirteen, brought up in a Pentecostal family at Ussuriisk committed suicide and left his grandmother the following note: 'Grandmother, I am going to be a wicked boy. I have deceived the Lord, I have deceived you, my father, my mother, George and all men. I have asked God to forgive me, but I am full of sins and he has not forgiven me. Kolia.'[151]

Nevertheless, the withdrawal of children from their parents has been elevated by L. Iliichev into a national virtue. Indeed, in his report, Iliichev quotes with admiration the noble action of a young fitter of Leningrad, Robert Malozemov, who after a hard struggle managed to separate from his parents six of his half-brothers and sisters: 'There is an atheist who is really intelligent, we want many like him. . . .'[152] The unhappy mother, who was thus deprived of her offspring, is a war widow who remarried and is perfectly respectable. Her only crime was to be a believer (a Baptist) and to have refused to buy her children a television set.[153] Like Pavlik Morosov, of the earlier period, who denounced his father when collectivization was being carried out, Robert Malozemov is on the way to becoming a national hero.[154]

Reactions by the faithful

The people try to defend their churches and their ministers by signing petitions and appeals. But this needs considerable courage, for it means drawing the attention of the authorities on themselves. The signatures are scrutinized and their authors subjected to extremely unpleasant visits in their homes.[155] Dramatic incidents that even involve bloodshed are not infrequent. For example, when St Andrew's Church in Kiev was closed, about a hundred women shut themselves up inside. At first the authorities let them alone, but after a few days a cordon of Militia sealed off the church and the people were driven out *manu militari*: the young were transported to a part of the country as yet uncultivated, and the old women were shut up in mental homes.[156] Inevitably, the nerves of believers are stretched to breaking point, and snap at any increased strain. A Western tourist in a church near Moscow was mistaken for a spy and was threatened by those present: 'If you have come to cause trouble, we will beat you with pine cones. You will not leave here alive!' These threats became congratulations and embraces when the accused could show his reverence for the holy place.

G. Bachkin, the guardian of the Cathedral of Novosibirsk shot a young man dead under the eaves. According to the indictment, the lad had come with the purpose of stealing pigeons. The murderer was condemned to death. The bishop of the town, Mgr Donat, who had the courage to intervene on behalf of the accused, was at once suspended for five years.[157] At Novgorod an attempt was made to assassinate a renegade priest who had acquired a well-earned reputation as a police-spy and a persecutor.[158] In Udmurtia, an aged peasant, 'dekulakized' in 1930, who had spent most of his life in concentration camps, stabbed a young anti-religious lecturer to death. The murderer was condemned to death and shot.[159]

In Moldavia, in the village of Baraboi, both the priest and the sacristan were found dead in a field. Exasperated Kholkhozians took their revenge by lynching a leading communist whom they believed to be responsible for this double murder. Four of them were shot and the rest condemned to long periods of forced labour.[160]

The most significant crime, and the one about which, thanks to a long article in *Science and Religion*, we have the most information, was committed at Biisk in the Altai, by Vladimir Shchegurov, a thirty-year-old believer. His father had been a communist for very many years. When he came back from his military service, Vladimir became a militant Christian. He was pestered by the leaders of the anti-religious movement and was obliged to change his work repeatedly. But his beliefs were known everywhere, and it was said that each morning he left for work as though on a journey to the scaffold. To him individual propaganda was per-secution, and unfortunately he could not escape from it even in his own home. Bielkov, the occupant of the room next door, was for ever scrutinizing the least thing he did or said, and never stopped urging him to give up praying and attending church, and to take down the icons. And Bielkov did this, as a corres-pondent in *Science and Religion* admits, 'in a most clumsy way'.

Vladimir did not want to vote. 'If the Soviet press, and radio, and the intelligentsia are against God, then I cannot vote for the communists.' On election day, Bielkov, who seems to have been commissioned to make sure that his neighbours voted,[161] arrived early in the morning to persuade Vladimir to come to the polling booth. Vladimir persisted in refusing and shut himself up in his room, 'until the Militia should arrive'. But to his great relief it was not the Militia, but the officials of the polling booth who arrived with the ballot box to secure his vote at all costs. He again refused. Thereafter he lived in terror, a prey to a real and under-standable persecution mania. He thought that he was constantly being watched. He suspected that Bielkov kept the wireless going to prevent him praying – and this may have been no delusion. The very existence of Bielkov became intolerable to him. On 23rd March 1961, he killed him with nine thrusts of a dagger. He then went to church and confessed and allowed himself to be arrested by the police. At his trial the prosecuting counsel tried to explain his crime by the noxious effects of religion. 'His soul was corrupted and laid waste by God.' But Vladimir had no regrets about killing Bielkov – he said it was a crime that rid him of a most heavy burden – and that religion played no part in it. Needless to say he was condemned to death.[162]

These are certainly extreme cases. But the sequence of these crimes – never before has the Soviet press devoted so much space to law reports – provoked by the persecution, shows with un-mistakable clarity, the nervous tension and despair afflicting believers who are subjected to the continual pressure from Party organs, the administration and the police, and who have no one to turn to for help.

Quite different from this uncontrollable despair is the confident prayer of those who include in one act of thanksgiving the fearful and the courageous, the executioners and the martyrs: 'The great golden temples built on the sand of tepidity, of love of money and vanity collapse. Not a hair falls unless it be the will of the heavenly Father – Glory be to God. Martyrs, innocent children are put to death, making their bodies temples of the Holy Spirit – Glory be to God!

'No longer can silver bells be cast or golden altars be put up. Fear not those who kill the body, but cannot kill the soul – Glory be to God. It is possible to give the priest a half of a man's frugal meal – Glory be to God. Glory be to God for everything, for everything!

'Forgive us and bless us all, thieves and samaritans, children, those who fall by the wayside, the priests who pass by on the other side – all are our neighbours: the executioners and their victims, those who curse and those who are accursed, those who rebel against thee and those who prostrate themselves before thy Love. Take us all in thee, holy and righteous Father. And let not our praise cease in thy sight, for our life, for love, for the joy of finding peace in thy will.'[163]

The Church, obliged once more to a secret existence, has withdrawn to the catacombs. In the Kharkov Province the people are burying their icons. Many have ceased to attend church or if they do are more than ever furtive in their approach.[164] Here is a significant event: recently, twenty miles from Vilnius, a religious community was discovered that, in the guise of a Kolkhoz was practising strict monastic observance and running a model farm.[165] Once again the Church has gone underground and retired to the catacombs.[166] The Church no longer tries to furnish any official opposition to the persecution. The time for bold speeches and the public excommunication of apostates, seems to be over, and in fact, these gestures proved too costly for the Church. But from the Patriarch to the least of the faithful, all are vividly aware that they are living the apocalypse. The present time is compared to the dark hours of Gethsemane and the apparent failure of Christ's work. *The gates of hell shall not prevail against her:* this promise of Christ, the truth of which Christians in the USSR had once before experienced, is now again the constant theme in pastoral letters, in sermons, in the articles of the *Review of the Moscow Patriarchate*[167] in the conversation and correspondence of the people.

The Soviet writer, Victor Nekrassov, reports that at the Trinity-St-Sergius 'close to the saint's reliquary, a good-looking, clear-complexioned priest is standing. Slowly, silently, the long queue moves forward. In it there are men, and young men, as well as women. All of them cross themselves and kiss the relics. They hate and despise us; we are unbelieving, faithless dogs!

'We go outside into the courtyard. In the clear autumnal sky the crows circle round and round above the startlingly beautiful domes, and below, close to the white walls of the cathedral, hysterical women (*klikuchy*) parade around a skinny, bloodless simpleton with rolling eyes.

'He prophesies: "There will be no war, no war I tell you. Love in peace and mutual love; yes, love, above all else. And you there, do not stare at me; I will not speak to you, not one word. Your eyes have no message for me: go away. As for the Church it is the end; she is living in the last days. Turn to God and beseech him; for dark days are ahead; war and terrible slaughter are on their way. Life on earth will come to an end. Only the flowers, the leaves and the grass, only the sea and the sky will remain. Ask me no more, no more. From this Sunday onwards I shall be silent . . . for a year, for two years and even three. . . ."'[168]

CONCLUSION

OUR INQUIRY into the position of Christians in the USSR concludes on a sombre note. The Orthodox Church, already gravely weakened, finds her very existence again threatened. What could cause the Soviet Government to change its policy? It is extremely hard to say. The resistance put up by believers? Some serious internal crisis similar to that which moved Kruschev to give way over Cuba? Or pressure from the West?

The West could and should make its solidarity with Russian Christians unmistakably clear. It could and should stir up world opinion, opinion which is more feared by the Soviet Government than might be imagined. For the first time no political reason can be adduced to justify the persecution. The Church has proved her loyalty to the Soviet Government and to Russia, not only by what she has said, but also by what she has done. The present persecution is entirely doctrinaire.

The Government has encouraged the Russian Church to enter into relationship with the outside world, and this has enabled it to neutralize the various Western influences that could have registered a protest on behalf of the Christians of the USSR and made a plea for freedom of conscience in general. The Russian Church is now a member of the World Council of Churches; she has her permanent representative in Geneva, and her trusty servants in the Committee of Information. Geneva has kept silent, and this is because a solemn protest would at once provoke sharp retributory measures against those representatives of the Churches

336

behind the Iron Curtain which have recently been admitted to the Ecumenical Movement. In 1930 the Primate of the Anglican Church organized a colossal meeting of Christians in London as a protest against the persecutions in the USSR. In 1962 this same Primate paid an official visit to Moscow and joked with Anastasius Mikoian. The National Council of the Protestant Churches of America keeps in touch with the Moscow Patriarchate with the naïve belief that some work in common may be initiated. Even the Vatican has reconsidered its attitude of reserve towards Moscow.

The Press in the West has, *experto crede*, shown itself completely, or almost completely, indifferent to the religious situation in the USSR. It needed the desperate move on the part of members of the Evangelical Church in Siberia who, with their wives and children, came to seek refuge in the American Embassy in Moscow, to draw even a modicum of attention from the West to the new religious persecutions.

And yet Russian Christians beg, sometimes with tears in their eyes, those Western tourists whom they meet, to tell those at home what circumstances are really like and to pray for them.

For long, for too long, the West has remained silent. The establishment in Paris in February 1964 of an information committee on the position of Christians in the USSR and the ecumenical meeting held on 11th March at the Palais de la Mutualité are the first signs of some awakening of public opinion. 'Christ is in agony in Moscow, we cannot sleep while it continues.' It is greatly to be hoped that this appeal by François Mauriac will be heard throughthe world.

Belief, however, is not dependent upon the Church's visible existence, or, rather, the Church still exists even though her sanctuaries are closed and her sacramental life has become impossible. For personal belief and prayer then take the place of sacraments. In 1939 the visible Church was destroyed, but belief endured. May not the new persecutions give new strength to this belief? The anti-religious authorities themselves seem to think so, for they say that the measures taken by the administration only strengthen the religious spirit.

Belief still flourishes in the Soviet Union, and its intensity and duration cannot be dismissed as simply a delayed response to social change or as the result of the comparatively feeble encirclement by capitalist countries. The Marxists themselves often explain matters by the material difficulties which the socialist countries are experiencing. The Polish writer, L. Kolakowsky, for instance, has said that Socialism is the régime in which most of the people turn to religion for comfort in their misfortunes, and the opponents of religion have no hesitation in attributing the increase in religious bodies to the material difficulties experienced by the Kolkhoz during the post-war period of reconstruction, and they say the recent successes of atheism are due to the economic progress of these last years. A little more butter in the cabbage soup, they say, that is your best weapon against religion.

It is an explanation that contains some truth, but which cannot convince a Christian conscience. That the Soviet people in 1964 lack bread, meat and butter, does not necessitate the spread of religion; in South America this same phenomenon leads rather to irreligion. In the last resort, the spiritual can be explained only by the spiritual.

Youth in the USSR is at present in the throes of a serious spiritual and intellectual crisis. As yet no serious study of this crisis has been made, but no one can doubt that it exists. The personality cult, the deification of the State in the person of a single man, lasted for thirty-five of the forty-five years in which Communism has been in power. Moreover, it began well before Stalin and to some extent has survived him. It has been imposed by lies and terror and cannot have failed to inflict great psychological damage upon the whole Russian people. Life behind bars, with the mind in chains, followed by the discrediting of the Stalin myth, have together produced a great void in minds and hearts, above all in those of the young. Drunkenness, which on Kruschev's own admission, is causing havoc among the young, the frequency of suicide among students, the flood of poetry expressing their despair, suffering or confusion (cf. the underground reviews *Boomerang, Syntax, Phoenix*), are all indications of this crisis.

Christianity can fill this void only in exceptional cases. For the revolt of the young is often absolute. They then become not only non- but anti-Christian: Stalinism, a religious ersatz, has to their eyes discredited all religion and every dogma. But the revolt is also a susceptibility, and it cannot continue indefinitely without self-destruction.

Schoolboys and robots may believe, and all the more easily because Soviet authorities have fondly repeated it, that God does not exist because neither Gagarin nor Titov have met him. But students and adults generally cannot be satisfied by so naïve a brand of atheism. The crises of life and of human conduct, the enigma of death, presented with such power and penetration in Russian literature during the nineteenth century, are still problems for every individual to resolve. Recent news seems to establish that a wave of conversions is taking place among the students, especially in the provinces, the Church seems to be exerting a certain attraction in circles hitherto closed to her, as, for example, among the Jews. This return to the Church is combined with a lively interest in Russian religious philosophy – Beydaev, Bulgatov, Frank, Chestov are the authors particularly sought after and read avidly.

The great poet Alexander Blok has said that every Russian instinctively shares the outlook of the Church even when he has broken with her. This sense of an indissoluble bond between Christianity and Russia is still very much alive: quite recently a correspondent wrote to the review *Krokodil*: 'All Russians are Christians; they always have been, and always will be.' This belief of the Russians themselves in the perennial survival of their Christianity – which is perhaps no less than the expression of God's presence among them – gives us a right, in spite of everything, to hope.

APPENDICES

HISTORICAL DOCUMENTS CONCERNING THE
RELATIONS BETWEEN CHURCH AND STATE

Document A : Message from Patriarch Tikhon, dated 19th January 1918

From the humble Tikhon, by the grace of God Patriarch of Moscow and all Russia: to all the beloved in the Lord, bishops, pastors and all the faithful children of the Orthodox Church of Russia. 'May the Lord deliver us from this present evil world.' (Epistle to the Galatians I, 4).

It is a hard time that the Holy Church of Christ is now going through in the Russian land. Both the open and secret enemies of the truth of Christ persecute this truth and aim at destroying the work of Christ, and, instead of Christian love, sow everywhere the seeds of evil, of hatred, and of fratricidal struggle. The commandments of Christ – to love one's neighbour, are forgotten and trampled underfoot. Every day, there comes to us news of horrible and cruel massacres, the victims of which are innocent men and even people lying on a bed of pain, guilty only of having accomplished in all honesty their duty towards their country, of having used their strength in the service of the good of the people. And all this is accomplished in our time, not only at night under the cover of darkness, but even in full daylight, with an audacity unknown to this day, and with a cruelty that knows no mercy, without any judgement, and with the trampling underfoot of all right and all law, and all this takes place, almost in all the towns and villages of our country, in the capitals just as in distant border regions (in Petrograd, Moscow, Irkutsk, Sebastopol etc.).

All this makes our hearts overflow with a deep and painful sadness, and forces us to address to these monsters of the human race terrible words of accusation and censure following the injunctions of the holy apostles – 'Then that sin rebuke before all, that others also may fear.' (I Timothy v, 20).

Come to your senses, madmen, stop your bloody massacres! What you are doing is not simply cruelty; it is, indeed, the work of Satan for which you deserve eternal fire after death and the terrifying curse of future generations to come in this life. By the authority given to us by God, we forbid you to come to the Mysteries of Christ, we anathemize you if you still bear Christian names, or even if it is only through your birth that you belong to the Orthodox Church. Whereas you, faithful children of the Orthodox Church of Christ, we entreat you not to enter into any communion whatsoever with such monsters of the human race. 'Put away from among yourselves that wicked person' (I Corinthians v, 13).

The Holy Church of Christ is being equally cruelly persecuted. The sacraments, bearers of grace, whether they sanctify the coming of man into this world, or whether they bless the conjugal union of the Christian family, are openly declared as unnecessary, superfluous: the holy churches are either destroyed by means of bombardment from death-dealing weapons (the holy Cathedral Churches of the Kremlin in Moscow), or else pillaged and desecrated in a sacrilegious manner (the Chapel of the Saviour at Petrograd). The holy monasteries venerated by the faithful (such as the Monasteries of Alexander Nevski and Pochaev) are seized by the atheist masters of the darkness of this century and declared by them to be the so-called property of the people; schools maintained at the expense of the Orthodox Church and preparing pastors for the Orthodox Church and teachers of the faith are considered superfluous and are either converted into schools for atheism or even into breeding grounds of immorality. The property of Orthodox monasteries and churches have been confiscated under the pretext that they are the heritage of the people, without any right and even without any desire to take into account the legitimate will of this people. And finally, the authority which promised to bring order to Russia, justice and truth to guarantee freedom and law, has only shown everywhere the most unbridled self-will and a violence without end to all, and particularly to the Holy Orthodox Church.

Where will these outrages inflicted on the Church of Christ stop? How, and by what means can one put an end to this assault, to which it is subjected by furious enemies?

We call to all of you, the faithful sons of the Church, rise to defend your Holy Mother, which is being outraged and oppressed today! The enemies of the Church have seized power over the Church and its good property through the force of fire. Oppose to them the force of your faith, the loud clamour of all the people, a clamour which will stop the madmen and show them that they have not the right to call themselves the champions of the good of the people, the makers of a new life in accordance with the demands of popular reason, for they act in a manner contrary to the conscience of the people.

But, if one has to suffer for the cause of Christ, we call you all, beloved children of the Church, to suffer with Us, repeating the words of the apostle: 'Who shall separate us from the love of Christ? Shall tribulation? Or distress? Or persecution? Or famine? Or nakedness? Or danger? Or the sword?' (Romans VIII, 35).

And you brothers, bishops and pastors, without relaxing for an instant your religious activities, call your flock to defend with an ardent zeal the rights of the Orthodox Church which are at present being trampled underfoot. Create immediately spiritual unions, invite the faithful to enter, not from necessity, but with good will, into the ranks of spiritual fighters who, against the forces from outside will pit the strength of their sacred zeal; and we are absolutely confident that the enemies of the Church will be humiliated and scattered, dispersed by the force of the Cross of Christ, for the promise of the divine bearer of the Cross is immutable. 'I shall establish my Church and the gates of hell shall not prevail against it.'

19th January 1918   TIKHON
                                     Patriarch of Moscow and all Russia

Document B: Letter from His Holiness Tikhon Patriarch of Moscow and all Russia to the Council of the People's Commissar on the first anniversary of the establishment of Soviet power, 7th November 1918

'For all they that take the sword shall perish with the sword' (Matthew XXVI, 52).

We address this prophecy of our Saviour to you who now decide the destinies of our country, and call yourselves the Commissars of the People. For a whole year now you hold the power of the State and you are already preparing to celebrate the first anniversary of the October Revolution. But the torrents of blood of our brothers slaughtered without pity at your orders cry to heaven, and make it necessary for us to say to you the bitter words of truth.

In usurping power and calling to the people to put confidence in you, what are the promises that you gave (to it) and how have you kept them?

In truth, instead of bread, you have given the people a stone, and, instead of fish, a serpent. To a people exhausted by a bloody war, you have promised 'a peace without annexations or contributions'.

What were the conquests that you could renounce, you who have led Russia to a dishonourable peace, the humiliating conditions of which you did not even dare to make fully public. Instead of annexations and contributions, our great country has been invaded, diminished, dismembered and, in order to pay the tribute which has been imposed on it, you secretly export to Germany gold, which others than you have collected.

You have deprived those who have fought of all that, in the name of which, they formerly fought so valiantly. A short while ago they were full of courage and invincible, and you have taught them to abandon the defence of their country and to flee from the field of battle. You have extinguished in their hearts the thought which inspired their awareness that 'greater love hath no man than this, that a man lay down his life for his friends' (John xv, 13). For a native land you have substituted a soulless International although you know perfectly well that when it is a question of defending the motherland, the proletarians of all countries appear as its faithful sons, and not as traitors.

You have renounced the defence of the motherland against its enemies from outside, and yet you are none the less constantly assembling new armies. Against whom will you lead them?

You have divided the people into enemy camps, and you have thrown it into a fratricidal war of a cruelty that has never been known to this day. The love of Christ you have openly replaced by hatred, and under the guise of peace you have artificially stimulated the class struggle. And one can see no end to the war which you have begun, for your aim is to bring triumph to the spectre of world revolution by the hands of Russian workers and peasants.

Appendix I

It is not Russia who needed the shameful peace which you have concluded with the outside enemy, but you yourselves who decided once and for all to destroy peace inside the country. No one feels safe. Everyone lives in the constant terror of search, pillage, expulsion, arrest, execution. People without any defence are arrested by hundreds. They are left to rot for months on end in prison, they are frequently put to death without court investigations or judgement, not even the simplified form of court procedure which you have instituted. It is not only those who are guilty of anything towards you who are executed; but also those who have nothing to reproach themselves with and who are only taken as 'hostages'. These unfortunates are killed in order to avenge the crimes committed by persons who not only do not even profess the same opinions as they, but who are frequently your followers or who have convictions which are close to yours. Bishops, priests, monks, nuns who are innocent in every way are accused wholesale, in a very general and imprecise way, of counter-revolutionary activity. These inhuman executions are all the more terrible for the Orthodox, because the latter are deprived of the final consolation of the administration of the Last Sacraments, and because the bodies of those who are executed are not returned to their families in order to receive a Christian burial.

Is this not the summit of senseless cruelty on the part of those who say that they are the benefactors of humanity and have themselves suffered a great deal in the past from cruel governments?

But it is not enough for you to have reddened the hands of the Russian people with their brothers' blood. Under cover of different pretexts – contributions, requisitions and nationalization, you have pushed it to the most undisguised and shameless robbery. At your instigation, lands, estates, plants, factories, houses, have been pillaged and cattle, money, personal property, furniture, clothes have been stolen. In the beginning, the rich were robbed as bourgeois and then the richer and more hardworking peasants, as 'kulaks', thereby multiplying the number of those rendered penniless; although you could not but agree that the ruin of a large number of individual citizens destroys national wealth and is the cause of the ruin of the country itself. Having tempted an ignorant and uncouth people by the possibility of getting rich easily and with impunity, you thereby obscured its conscience and blunted its consciousness of sin. But by whatever other actions you may mask your evil actions – murder, violence and

347

pillage will always remain grave sins calling for chastisement from heaven.

You promised freedom. Freedom is an infinitely good thing, if it is correctly understood as freedom from evil, as freedom which does not oppress others, which is not transformed into anarchy and selfwill. But that freedom you have not given. Your freedom consists in encouraging the lowest passions of the crowd, and leaving murder and pillage unpunished.

All manifestation of true public spirit as well as of the greatest spiritual freedom of humanity has been pitilessly oppressed by you. Is it freedom when no one without a special authorization can transport provisions, rent a flat, change their place of residence from one town to another? Is it freedom when families and sometimes even all the inhabitants of a whole house are expulsed, appropriated and their property thrown into the street and when citizens are artificially divided into categories, among which certain categories are left to hunger and to be robbed? Is it freedom when no one dares to voice their opinion openly for fear of being accused of counter-revolutionary activity? Where is the freedom of speech and the freedom of the Press? Where is the freedom of religious preaching? Already many brave preachers of the Church have paid the price with a martyr's blood. The voice of discussion both social and political, as well as of criticism, is smothered and the Press, except for the strictly Bolshevik Press, is completely throttled.

The attacks on freedom in matters of faith are particularly painful and cruel. Not a day passes without the organs of your press publishing the most monstrous slander and heinous blasphemy against the Church of Christ and its servants. You mock the servants of the altar, you force bishops to dig trenches (e.g. Bishop Hermogne of Tobolsk) and you send priests to do low, manual labour. You have laid your hands on the patrimony of the Church which has been amassed by generations of the faithful, and you have not hesitated to act in a manner contrary to their final wish. You have closed a whole series of monasteries and chapels without any pretext or reason. You have forbidden access to the Moscow Kremlin – that sacred patrimony of all the faithful. You are destroying the traditional framework of the ecclesiastical community – the parish. You are closing down brotherhoods and other charity and educational organizations maintained by the Church. You break up diocesan assemblies. You interfere in the internal administration of the Orthodox Church. By excluding all sacred images and forbidding the teaching of the catechism in schools, you deprive children of the spiritual food which is indispensable for their education as Orthodox.

'And what more shall I say? For time would fail me' (Hebrews XI, 32). If I were to tell of all the misfortunes that have fallen on our country. I shall not speak of the ruin of Russia, which once was so great and so powerful, of the complete disorganization of the means of communication, of the unheard-of disorder which reigns in the distribution of food supplies, of hunger and cold which threaten towns with death, of the lack of basic essentials in village husbandry. This is happening before the eyes of all. Yes, indeed, we are living through a terrible epoch of your reign, and it will not be soon erased from the soul of the people, in which the image of God, has been obscured in order to imprint the image of the Beast. The Words of the Prophet are coming to pass 'Their feet run to evil and they make haste to shed innocent blood: their thoughts are thoughts of iniquity. Wasting and destruction are in their parts' (Isaiah LIX, 7).

We know that our accusations will only provoke anger and indignation in you, that you will only seek in them a pretext in order to accuse us of opposition to the authorities. But the greater the pillar of your anger, the more it will witness to the justice of our accusations. It is not for us to judge temporal authority. All power allowed by God would call for our blessing, if indeed it appeared as 'the servant of God', for the good of its subjects, and if it was to be 'feared, not by those who do good, but by those who do evil' (Romans XIII, 34). Today, you who use power in order to persecute your neighbours and to destroy the innocent, we address these words of exhortation to you. Mark the first anniversary of your coming to power by giving back their freedom to those who are in prison, by stopping the shedding of blood, the violence, the pillaging, the persecutions of the faith. Turn your faces not to destruction but to the building of order and law. Give to the people the rest it longs for and which it has deserved after the fratricidal struggle, 'for otherwise you will be asked to account for the blood of all the just men which you have shed' (Luke XI, 51). 'And by the sword shall ye perish, ye that have taken the sword' (Matthew XXVI, 52).

Appendix I

Document C: Excerpt from a message addressed by Patriarch Tikhon to the bishops, clergy and faithful of the Russian Orthodox Church, dated Donskoy Monastery, 28th June 1923, and published in Izvestia the same day

If, during the first year of the existence of the Soviet authorities, I have occasionally allowed myself bitter attacks against them, it was because of the education I have received, and also because of the predominating outlook in the council which was sitting then. But, with time, many things have begun to change and to become clearer in our country. Thus, for example, we are today obliged to ask the Soviet authorities to undertake the defence of the Orthodox persecuted in the regions of Kholm and Grodno, where the Poles are closing Orthodox churches.

On the other hand, I have attempted, since the beginning of 1919, to dissociate the Church from Czarism and from foreign intervention, and, in September of the same year, I addressed to the bishops and priests a message on the non-participation of the Church in all politics and its submission to the dispositions of the Soviet authorities in so far as the latter were not contrary to faith and piety. That is why, when we learned that, at the Council of Karlovci, a majority had declared itself in favour of the restoration of the Romanov dynasty, we sided with the minority which considered this decision out of place. And when, in March 1922, we learned of the steps taken by the Presidium of the Supreme Ecclesiastical Administration abroad, concerning the non-admission of Russian delegates to the Genoa Conference, we ourselves dissolved this Administration which had been organized with the approval of the Patriarch of Constantinople. This shows that I am not as much of an enemy of the Soviet authorities, nor as counter-revolutionary as I have been represented by the Council of the Living Church.

As regards my present attitude to the Soviet authorities, I have already defined it in my declaration addressed to the Supreme Court, in which I appeal for a modification of the sentence passed on me, in other words, that my freedom should be restored. The true author of the crime for which I do recognize myself as being responsible, is that social milieu which impelled me continually, in my function as Head of the Orthodox Church, towards active manifestations directed, in various forms, against the Soviet authorities. From now on I declare clearly to all that their efforts will be absolutely vain and fruitless, for I resolutely

Appendix I

condemn any attempt, wherever it may come from, against the Soviet authorities. May all the monarchists and supporters of the White Army, abroad as well as inside the country, understand that I am not an enemy of the Soviet authorities. I have understood all the falsehood and calumny of which the Soviet authorities are the victims, on the part of its enemies, Russian as well as foreign, and which the latter spread, verbally and in writing, throughout the whole world. I myself have not escaped it. In the newspaper *Novoe Vremya*, 5th May, no. 606, there appeared a story that I had been tortured by electricity in the course of my interrogation by the Cheka. I declare that this is pure falsehood and calumny, and yet another calumny against the Soviet authorities.

Document D: Note addressed by the bishops deported to the Solovki Islands to the Soviet Government, Summer 1926

Despite the basic law of the Soviet Constitution, which guarantees to all believers the freedom of conscience, of religious meetings and preaching, the Russian Orthodox Church, to this day, experiences considerable oppression in all its activities and religious life. It has still not received the permission to open regularly acting organs of central and diocesan administration, it cannot transfer its activity to its historical centre, Moscow, its bishops are either not allowed at all in their diocese, or, if they are allowed to go there, are frequently forced to give up the most basic duties of their service – preaching in churches, visiting various communities which recognize their spiritual authority, sometimes even consecrations. The Patriarchal *locum tenens* and nearly half of the Orthodox bishops are languishing in prisons, in exile, or are performing forced labour. Without denying the reality of these facts, government organs explain them by political reasons, accusing the Orthodox bishops and clergy of anti-revolutionary activities and secret intentions directed at the overthrow of Soviet power and the re-establishment of the old order.

Many times already, the Orthodox Church, first in the person of the late Patriarch Tikhon and then in the person of his successors, has attempted in official addresses and notes to the Government to dispel the atmosphere of distrust which has surrounded it. The lack of success and the sincere desire to put an end to the regrettable misunderstandings between the Church and the Soviet Government, which is very painful for the Church and complicates in vain the execution of its duties for the State has forced the governing body of the Orthodox Church to put forward in all fairness before the Government the principles which govern its attitude to the State.

Those who have signed the present declaration are fully aware of how difficult it is to establish mutually well-intentioned relations between the Church and the State in the conditions of present-day reality and do not consider it possible to remain silent on the subject. It would be a lie that would not correspond to the dignity of the Church, a lie which would be pointless and would not convince anyone, if they tried to assert that between the Orthodox Church and the State of the Soviet Republics there are no differences of opinion. But this difference of opinion does not consist of what political suspicion wishes to see, or what the slander of the enemies of the Church points to. The Church is not concerned with the redistribution of wealth or with this wealth becoming common property, as it has always recognized that this was the right of the State, for the actions of which it is not responsible. Nor is the Church concerned with the political organization of power, for it is loyal to the governments of all those countries within the frontiers of which it has its members. It establishes a *modus vivendi* with all forms of government organization from the eastern despotism of ancient Turkey to the Republic of the North American States. This difference of opinion lies in the impossibility to reconcile the religious teachings of the Church with materialism, the official philosophy of the Communist Party and the Government of the Soviet Republics directed by it. With such an irreconcilable ideological divergence between the Church and the State which is inevitably reflected in the everyday activities of these organizations, a conflict between them in everyday work can only be avoided by a strictly defined law, determining the separation of the Church from the State, according to which the Church must not interfere with the secular government in the organization of the material well-being of the people, nor must the State hamper the Church in its religious and moral activity.

Such a law, one of the first to be published by the Revolutionary Government, formed a part of the constitution of the USSR and could, with a different political system, satisfy both parties to a certain degree. The Church has no religious reasons for not accepting it. Our Lord

Appendix I

Jesus Christ commanded us to render unto Caesar, i.e. all care for the material well-being of the people 'to Caesar', i.e. to State authority and did not leave his followers any commandment to influence the form of a government or to direct its activity. Following this teaching and tradition, the Orthodox Church has always kept apart from politics and has remained obedient to the State in all that did not concern the faith. For this reason, while remaining inwardly alien to the Government of the ancient Roman Empire or recently to that of Turkey, the Church could remain (and did indeed remain) loyal in all that concerned secular civil law. But nor can a modern state, on its side, demand anything more from it. In opposition to former political theories, which have always considered essential for the inner solidarity of the political union, the religious unanimity of all its citizens, it does not recognize the latter as being of any importance in this matter, uncompromisingly declaring that it has no need for the collaboration of the Church in the attainment of the aims it had set itself, and, that it gives its citizens full religious freedom. In the prevailing situation the Church would only wish for a full and consecutive application of the law on the separation of the Church from the State.

Unfortunately, the reality of the situation is far from corresponding to this (desire). The Government, both in the laws it passes, and in the exercise of its functions, does not remain neutral in relation to belief and disbelief, but quite clearly takes up a position on the side of atheism, using all the means of State at its disposal for its establishment, development and spread as a counterweight to all religions. The Church on whom its teaching lays the religious duty of preaching the Gospel to all, including the children of believers, is forbidden by law to fulfil this duty in relation to those persons who have not reached the age of eighteen years, whereas all those who are in schools and youth organizations, children from the youngest age as well as adolescents are energetically indoctrinated with the principles of atheism with all the logical conclusions to be drawn from them. Basic law gives citizens the right to believe whatever they wish, but it is in conflict with the law which deprives a religious body of the right of legal entity and the right, connected with it, to possess any property whatsoever, even objects, which do not represent any material value, but which are dear and sacred to the believer, exclusively through its religious significance. In order to further the aims of anti-religious propaganda, according to this law, the Church has been deprived of the relics of the saints which it venerates and which have been put into museums.

It is government policy to take all measures for the suppression of religion. It uses all pretexts for the closing of churches and their conversion into places of public spectacle, for the closing of monasteries despite the introduction of the principles of labour in them. It subjects the servants of the Church to every conceivable kind of oppression in everyday life, does not allow believers to teach in schools and forbids the lending out from public libraries of books of a religious content, or even expressing simply idealistic trends, and, through the most important representatives of the State, constantly declares that the limited freedom which the Church still *does* enjoy, is only a temporary measure and a concession to the age-old religious habits of the people. Of all the religions experiencing the weight of all above-mentioned forms of oppression, the most oppressed is the Orthodox Church, to which belongs the vast majority of the Russian people and which forms the overwhelming majority in the State. Its position is made still more difficult by the fact that a section of the clergy which has split away from it, and which has founded the schism of the Renewed, has, so to speak, become the State Church which the Soviet authorities, despite the laws passed by it, favour at the expense of the Orthodox Church. In an official act the Government has declared that the only lawful representative of the Orthodox Church which it recognizes within the limits of the USSR, is the Renewed Synod. The schism of the Renewed is in possession of executive organs of higher and diocesan government which are allowed to function unmolested. Its bishops are allowed to go to their diocese, they are allowed to visit communities, and their cathedral churches which have been taken away from the Orthodox, have nearly everywhere been transferred to them and now, as a result of this, are usually empty. The clergy of the schism of the Renewed enjoys to a certain degree even the material support of the Government. Thus, for example, its delegates received free tickets for railway travel to Moscow to their so-called 'sacred Council' of 1923 and free lodging in Moscow, in the third house of the Moscow Soviet. The greater part of the Orthodox bishops, in prison and in exile, have undergone this fate for their successful struggle with the Schism of the Renewed which, according to the law, is their absolute right in the exercise of their functions, but which has been considered as an activity contrary to the aims of the State.

Appendix I

The Orthodox Church cannot, like the members of the schism of the Renewed, witness to the fact that religion within the frontiers of the USSR is not subjected to any oppression, and that there is no other country in which it would enjoy such freedom. It will not announce to the whole world this shameful lie which could only be inspired by their hypocrisy, their servility or their absolute indifference to the fate of religion, which deserves the full condemnation in all its servants. On the contrary, in all justice it must declare that it cannot recognize as just or welcome either the laws which hamper it in the fulfilment of its religious duties, nor the administrative measures which increase many times over the oppression of these laws, nor the patronage given to the schism of the Renewed at its expense. Its own attitude to the State, the Church bases on a full and consecutive application of the principle of separation of Church and State. It does not aim at the overthrow of existing order and does not take part in any actions directed towards this aim. It does not call anyone to arms and political struggle. It obeys all laws and directives of a civil character, but it does wish to keep in full measure its spiritual freedom and independence which have been granted it by the Constitution, and it cannot become the servant of the State. The Soviet Government does not believe in the loyalty of the Orthodox Church. It accuses it of activities which are directed at the overthrow of the new order and the re establishment of the old. We consider it essential to assure the Government that these accusations do not correspond to reality. In the past, it is true, there have been political declarations by the Patriarch, which have given rise to these accusations. But all the acts of such a character published by the Patriarch were directed not against the authorities as such. They apply to those times when the revolution was manifesting itself as an exclusively destructive force, when all social forces were in a state of struggle, when the authorities, in the sense of an organized state. possessing the essential means of government, simply did not exist. At that time, the organs of central government in process of formation, could not hold in check the abuses and anarchy either in the capitals or in other places. Everywhere groups of people who did not inspire any confidence were active, giving themselves out as agents of the Government, whereas in reality they turned out to be confidence tricksters with a criminal past and even more criminal present. They beat up absolutely innocent bishops and priests, broke into houses and hospitals, killed people there, plundered property, robbed churches and then disappeared without leaving a trace. It would be strange if, at a moment when political passions and greed were raging, at a moment of such hatred of some against others, if in such a general struggle the Church alone remained an indifferent witness to all that was happening. Permeated by its national and state traditions, inherited by it from its age-old past, the Church, at that critical moment in the life of the nation, came out in defence of order, seeing in this its duty to the people. And in this too it did not diverge from its teaching, which demands from it obedience to the civil authorities, which use their sword for the good of the people and not in the name of anarchy, which is a national misfortune. But with time, when a definite form of secular power took shape, Patriarch T. made a declaration, in his appeal to his flock, on loyalty to the Soviet Government and definitely abdicated from all influence on the political life of the country. To the end of his life the Patriarch remained faithful to this act. Nor have the Orthodox bishops infringed it. From the moment of its publication one cannot point to a single legal case in the course of which the participation of Orthodox clergy could be proved in actions having as their aim, the overthrow of Soviet power. The bishops and priests who are suffering in such large numbers in exile, in prison or who are doing forced labour, underwent these oppressions, as a result not of legal sentences, but of administrative decisions, without a clearly formulated accusation, without a regular investigation of their case, without a public hearing, without representation or any possible defence, frequently even without an explanation of the causes, which is indisputable proof of the lack of any serious accusatory material against them. The Orthodox hierarchs have been accused of relations with émigrés, whose political activity is directed against the Soviet authorities. This second accusation is as far from the truth as the first. Patriarch T. condemned the declarations of émigré bishops made by them in the name of the Church. The sees occupied by bishops who became émigrés were filled by others. When the Council at Karlovtsy called with his permission, went beyond the bounds of its ecclesiastical powers and passed a resolution of a political character, the Patriarch condemned its activity and dissolved the Synod which had allowed the departure of the Council from its agenda. Although the canonically Orthodox diocese created abroad are under the jurisdiction of the Russian patriarchate, in fact, an administration of them, based on Moscow, and exercised in a fully ecclesiastical sense, is impossible through the absence of any legal form of contact with

Appendix I

them. And this fact absolves the Patriarch and his successors from the responsibility for what happens in them. We can assure the Government that we do not take part in any political activity and do not maintain any contact, either open or secret, with them in political matters. The absence of any facts, showing the Orthodox hierarchs to be in criminal relations with the émigrés, forces the enemies of the Church to have recourse to reprehensible forgeries. Such is the 'document' submitted in October 1925 by Vvedensky, calling himself Metropolitan at the so-called sacred Council of the Renewed Schism. V. was not ashamed to pretend that he had believed the authenticity of this crudely fabricated forgery. Its relation with the civil powers as a result of the law on the separation of the Church from the State, the Church conceives in the following form: The Basic law of our country prevents the Church from taking any part in political life. The servants of the Cult are thus deprived of any active or passive, elective right and they are forbidden to influence the political self-determination of the masses by force of their religious authority. From here, it follows that the Church both in its open activity as well as in its intimate, pastoral action on believers must not criticize or condemn the secular measures of the Government. But, it follows also from this, that it is not incumbent on it to approve them, as not only criticism but approval of the State is interference in politics, and the right of approval presupposes also the right of criticism, or at least the right to withhold approval, which can always be understood as a sign of discontent or disapproval. The Church acts according to this.

We can assure the Government in full sincerity that neither in churches nor in any ecclesiastical institutions, nor at church gatherings is any political propaganda pursued in the name of the Church. In future, bishops and clergy will refrain equally from the discussion of any political questions in their sermons and pastoral appeals. Ecclesiastical institutions, from parish councils to the Patriarchal Synod will consider them as subjects beyond the limits of their competence. Nor will they be included in the agendas of parish meetings. Meetings of clergy charged with administrative duties and diocesan conferences, national All-Russian councils, they will not be touched upon in any way at any such gatherings. In the elections of members to ecclesiastical institutions and representative assemblies, the Church will not take into any account the political views, social position, financial position and party membership of those elected, whoever they may be, and will limit itself exclusively to religious demands and purity of faith, to zeal for the needs of the Church, and to irreproachable personal life and morals.

In a republic, every citizen enjoying full political rights is called to participation in the passing of laws and the government of the country, in the organization of the Government and influence on the composition of this Government according to the forms established by law. And this is not only his right, but his duty as a citizen, in the execution of which no one has the right to hamper him. The Church would be interfering in civil government if, as it were, having given up an open discussion of political questions, it began to influence the direction of affairs by means of pastoral action on individuals, indoctrinating them either with a full non-participation in political activity, or a certain programme which would call for admission to certain political parties and for struggle with others. Every believer has his own mind and his own conscience which must show him the best way to the building of a state. Without refusing to give to those who ask for them a religious evaluation of measures, conflicting with Christian teaching, morals and discipline in questions which are purely political and civil, the Church does not limit their freedom, teaching them only the general principles of morality, calling them to a conscientious fulfilment of their obligations, to actions which are not just in the interest of the individual or which have the despicable aim of seeking favour with the authorities, but in the name of justice and public good. The firm withdrawal of the Church from any interference in the political life of the republic, of necessity involves also its refusal to undertake any supervision of the political reliability of its members. In this lies the profound difference between the Orthodox Church and the Schism of the Renewed, the administrative organs of which, as well as its clergy, as has been seen from their own manifold declarations in print, have taken upon themselves the duty before the Government of supervising the loyalty of its members, to answer, in this respect, for some and to refuse to do so for others. The Orthodox Church considers supervision and political denunciation as being absolutely incompatible with the dignity of a pastor. The State disposes of special organs of supervision, and the members of the Church, its clergy and laity are not distinguished in any way in the eyes of the present government from other citizens, and therefore are subject to political supervision like everyone else. From these same principles stems the impossibility of an ecclesiastical tribunal to deal with the accusation of political crime. The Schism of the Renewed, putting itself back into the position of a State Church, does admit of such a tribunal.

At the so-called Council of the Renewed in 1923, Patriarch Tikhon and the bishops who had gone abroad with the émigrés, as a result of being accused of political crimes, were made subject to ecclesiastical punishment. This punishment was justly annulled by the Orthodox Church. The Orthodox Church does not recognize such a tribunal. Those ecclesiastical civil laws, by which the Church was guided in a Christian State after its fall lose their power, whereas purely ecclesiastical laws, which are the only ones the Church can go by at present, do not foresee a tribunal for judging clergy accused of political crimes and do not as yet contain canons which could lay ecclesiastical punishment upon the faithful for such crimes. As a condition for the legalization of ecclesiastical institutions, representatives of the GPU more than once demanded from Patriarch T. and his successors a proof of their loyalty to the State by the means of a condemnation of the Russian bishops who were acting abroad against the Soviet authorities. Basing ourselves on the principles laid down above, we cannot approve of the transformation of the Church pulpit and Church institutions into a one-sided weapon in the political struggle. All the more so since the political interest of the bishops abroad throws a shadow on the Orthodox Church within the frontiers of the USSR and feeds the distrust of their obedience to the law and interferes with the establishment of normal relations between the Church and the State. None the less, we would be placed in a very difficult situation if it were demanded from us to express our disapproval in any ecclesiastical act of a legal character, as the collection of canonical rules, as has already been said, does not presuppose the existence of a tribunal for political crimes. But even if the Orthodox hierarchy without taking into account this fact, followed the example of the schism of the Renewed and decided to institute such a tribunal it would lead with a whole series of special difficulties which would create insurmountable obstacles for the fully legal framework of the case in which only a definition given by the tribunal can be given absolute canonical authority and be accepted by the Church. The émigré bishops could only be judged by a council of Orthodox bishops, but a fully authoritative council cannot be held if for no other reason, than that almost half the Orthodox bishops are to be found in prison or in exile, and as a result, their dioceses cannot be legally represented at the Council. In accordance with Church rules of ecumenical order the personal presence of the accused is essential before the tribunal and only in the case of their deliberate absence from the tribunal can the case proceed in *absentia*. The émigré bishops, who are serious political criminals in the eyes of the Soviet authorities, were they to come within the frontiers of the USSR, would be deprived of any guarantee of personal safety and therefore their refusal cannot be considered as deliberately evil-intentioned. Every tribunal presupposes a legal investigation. The Orthodox Church does not dispose of organs by means of which she could investigate the case of the political crimes of the Orthodox bishops abroad. But neither could it pass judgement on the basis of that accusatory material which was collected by the State organs, and even if it were submitted to the Council in the case, for example, of an objection to it on the part of the accused, or representation or the submission by them of new data and justificatory documents, the Council would be put to the necessity of revising the results of the Government investigation, which on the part of the Church would be an absolutely inadmissible transgression of civil laws.

The Council of the Renewed of 1923, which experimented with the type of tribunal which is now demanded from us, and which disdained the ecclesiastical laws which do not allow such a tribunal, by the same token rendered its decisions insignificant and deprived them of any recognition on the part of anyone. The law about the separation of the Church from the State is double-edged. It forbids the Church to take part in politics and in civil administration, but it contains also the giving up, abdication on the part of the Government from any interference into the internal affairs of the Church, into its teaching, the celebration of services and administration. Whilst fully submitting itself to this law, the Church hopes that the State too will fulfil in good conscience in relation to the Church those obligations entailing the preservation of its freedom and independence which it took upon itself in passing this law. The Church hopes that it will not be left in that situation of oppression and deprivation of rights in which it finds itself at the present moment, that the laws about the teaching of the catechism to children and the deprivation of religious assemblies, of the rights to legal right, will be revised and changed in a direction favourable to the Church, that the relics of the saints venerated by the church will stop being the object of blasphemous actions and will be returned from the museums to the churches. The Church hopes that it will be given the authorization to organize a diocesan administration, to elect a Patriarch and members of the Holy Synod which will work with the Patriarch, to convoke, when she recognizes this as being necessary, diocesan conferences and an all Russian Orthodox Council. The Church hopes that the Government will refrain from any open or secret influence on the election of members to these conferences and Council and will not hamper the freedom of discussion of religious questions at these meetings, and will not demand any preliminary undertakings which will decide already beforehand the nature of their future resolutions. The Church hopes too that the activity of the ecclesiastical institutions so created will not be placed in a position, where the appointment of bishops to a diocese, the definition of the composition of the Holy Synod and the decisions taken should be subjected to the influence of a State official who would be entrusted in all probability with political supervision over them as well. Submitting the present note to the Government, the Russian Church once again considers it necessary to note that it has put forward before the Soviet authorities with absolute sincerity not only the difficulties which interfere with the establishment of mutually well-intentioned relations between the Church and the State, but also those means by which they could be improved.

Profoundly convinced that relations which are long-lasting and full of trust can only be founded on absolute justice, it has laid forth openly without passing over anything in silence or in a double-edged way, all that it can promise the Soviet authorities, in what it cannot depart from its principles, and what it expects from the Government of the USSR.

If the suggestions of the Church are found to be acceptable, the Church will rejoice in this decision by those on whom it will depend. If its plea is rejected, it is ready for the material deprivations to which it is being subjected to meet the latter calmly, remembering that it is not in the fullness of an external organization that its strength lies, but in the unity of the faith and love of those faithful to it, placing its hope especially in the invincible strength of its Heavenly Founder and His promise of the invincibility of His Creation.[1]

---

[1] Taken from a manuscript of the period which bears the following note in pencil: This was done through the initiative of Bishop Hilarion. No answer has yet been received from the Central Committee of the Communist Party.

Appendix I

Document E: Letter from his Grace, Sergius, Metropolitan of Nijny Novgorod, locum tenens of the Keeper of the Patriarchal Throne to the clergy and faithful of the Patriarchate of Moscow; Moscow, 16th/29th June 1927

The humble Sergius, by the grace of God, Metropolitan of Nijny Novgorod, Locum Tenens of the Keeper of the patriarchal throne and the temporary patriarchal Holy Synod, to the most holy bishops, to the well-loved pastors, to the venerable monks, and all the faithful children of the Holy Orthodox Church of all Russia, 'rejoice in the Lord'. One of the preoccupations of our most holy father, the late Patriarch Tikhon, on the eve of his death, was to establish the correct relations between our Russian Orthodox Church and the Soviet Government, and thus to give the Church the possibility of existing in conditions of absolute peace and law. At the moment of his death, His Holiness used to say that he 'should have lived perhaps some two or three more years'. Thus we can be sure that, if his unexpected end had not interrupted his pastoral labours, he would have taken his work to the desired conclusion. Unfortunately, various circumstances, and above all declarations by enemies of the Soviet state abroad, in which not only the simple faithful of our Church, but also its rulers participated, have provoked a justified distrust on the part of the Government towards the leaders of the Church in general, thus hampering the efforts of His Holiness and thus it was not given to him to see his efforts crowned with success during his lifetime. Today, it has once again fallen on me [the unworthy Metropolitan Sergius] to be the temporary *locum tenens* of our pontiff. By the same token, it is incumbent on me to continue the work of the late Patriarch, and try by all the means at my disposal, to achieve a peaceful organisation of our ecclesiastical affairs. The efforts that I have undertaken in this direction with the support of the Orthodox bishops, seem not to have remained fruitless: with the institution under me of a temporary Patriarchal Holy Synod our hope to achieve a fruitful organization of our ecclesiastical government is strengthened as well as our certitude that it is possible to achieve a peaceful life and activity within the framework of the law.

Now that we have almost arrived at our goal, the activities of outside enemies do not cease; assassinations, fires, attempts on the lives of individuals, explosions and other similar manifestations of an underground struggle are there to be seen by all. All this, by creating an atmosphere of mutual distrust and every kind of suspicion, disrupts

362

the peaceful course of life. Thus it is all the more necessary for our
Church and all the more obligatory for all those who hold dear its
interests, and who desire to put it on the path of a legal and peaceful
existence, to show that we, the leaders of the Church, are not with the
enemies of our Soviet state, nor with the mad, insensate instruments of
their intrigues, but that we are with our people and our government.
And it is in order to testify to this that we send, the Synod and I, this
present letter. In addition to that, we would inform you that in May of
this year, at my invitation and with the permission of the authorities,
a temporary Holy Synod under the *locum tenens* was convened, a
Synod counting among its members the signatories of this letter (they
do not include the Metropolitan of Novgorod, Arseny, who has not
yet arrived, nor the Archbishop of Kostroma, Sebastian, who is absent
through illness). The steps we have undertaken to obtain for the Synod
the authorization to begin to administer the All-Russian Orthodox
Church, has been crowned with success.

From now on, our Orthodox Church in the Soviet Union possesses
a central administrative body which is absolutely legal, not only from
the canonical point of view, but equally in the eyes of civil law, and we
hope that this legalization will spread progressively to all the lower
rungs of ecclesiastical government, diocesan, regional, etc. It is hardly
necessary to explain the importance and all the consequences of the
change which is thus being effected in the position of our Orthodox
Church, of its clergy, all its active leaders and all its institutions. Let us
thus raise prayers of thanksgiving to the Lord who has deigned to act
thus on behalf of our Holy Church. Let us also express publicly our
gratitude to the Soviet Government for the interest which it has
manifested to all the spiritual needs of the Orthodox population, and
at the same time let us assure the Government that we shall not abuse
the confidence that it has shown us.

In undertaking, with the aid of God, our synodical work, we see
clearly all the magnitude of the task which falls not only on us, but on
all the representatives of the Church. We have to demonstrate not by
words, but by our actions that it is not only people who are indifferent
to Orthodoxy, or who have betrayed it, who can show themselves to
be faithful citizens of the Soviet Union, but also the most zealous
supporters of Orthodoxy, for whom, with all its dogmas and traditions,
with all its canonical and liturgical structure it is as dear as truth and
life. We want to be Orthodox and, at the same time, to recognize the

Soviet Union as our civil motherland, joys and successes of which are our joys and our successes and misfortunes of which are our misfortunes. Every blow directed against the Soviet Union, be it war, boycott, or some public misfortune, or even simply a street corner murder, as in Warsaw, is felt by us as though it were directed against us. Whilst remaining Orthodox, we remember our duty to be citizens of the Soviet Union, 'not only for wrath, but also for conscience' sake' (Romans XIII, 5), as the apostle taught us. And we hope that with the help of God and with our mutual collaboration and support, we shall resolve this problem.

There is only one obstacle which might hamper us, which in the first years of the establishment of Soviet authorities has already proved an obstacle to the organization of the life of the Church on a basis of loyalty. And that was an insufficient awareness of all that had taken place in our country. The establishment of Soviet authorities was, in the eyes of many, a misunderstanding, a result of chance, and for this reason was not destined to last. People forgot that for the Christian there is no chance, and that in what is accomplished, there acts, as always and everywhere, the right hand of God which infallibly leads every people to the goal which is assigned to it. To those who do not wish to understand the 'signs of the times', it can seem that one cannot break with the old régime and even with the monarchy, without breaking with Orthodoxy. Such an outlook in certain ecclesiastical circles which has naturally been expressed in words and acts, and which has provoked the distrust of the Soviet authorities, braked the efforts made by the Most Holy Patriarch to establish peaceful relations between the Church and the Soviet Government. It is not in vain that the apostle teaches us that 'we may lead a quiet and peaceable life all godliness and honesty' (I Tim. II, 2) only by submitting to the legitimate authorities, otherwise we must leave society. Only cabinet dreamers can think that a society as vast as our Orthodox Church with all its organization can quietly exist in a state and hide from the eyes of the authorities. Now, that our Patriarchate, in accomplishing the will of our late Patriarch, has in a decisive and irreversible manner engaged on a path of loyalty, the people entertaining such views, must either reform themselves and, leaving at home their political sympathies, only bring their faith to Church, and work with us only in the name of faith, or else, if they cannot reform themselves immediately at least they must abstain for the time being from all activity and thereby not hamper us. We are convinced that they will return to work with us very soon, having convinced themselves that the only thing which has changed is the attitude to the authorities, whereas faith and the Orthodox life remain unshakeable.

There is one question which in the present circumstances is particularly acute, and that is the question of the clergy who have gone abroad with the émigrés. The sharply anti-soviet declarations on the part of certain of our bishops and pastors abroad, which harmed relations between the Soviet Government and the Church to a considerable degree, forced the late Patriarch, as everyone knows, to dissolve the Synod abroad (5th May–22nd April 1922). But the Synod continues to exist without changing its political attitude, and lately by its pretensions to wield power, has even split the Russian Church society abroad into two camps. In order to put an end to this, we demanded from the clergy abroad a written commitment of absolute loyalty to the Soviet authorities in all its public activity. Those who will not have signed such an undertaking, or else who will have infringed it, will be excluded from the cadres of the clergy dependent on the Patriarchate of Moscow. We consider that by separating ourselves in this way, we shall be insured against any unexpected move coming from abroad. On the other hand, our decision will perhaps force a great many to ask themselves whether it is not time to review the question of their attitude to the Soviet authorities in order not to break with their church and their native land.

Another problem, which we consider no less important, is the preparatory work for the convocation and the actual convocation of our second Local Council which will elect a central ecclesiastical administration which will no longer be temporary but permanent, and which will pass a resolution over all who would rise against the ecclesiastical authorities and thus tear the robe of Christ. The terms of reference and the date of the convocation as well as the agenda of the council and other details will be worked out later. We shall limit ourselves for the moment to the expression of our firm conviction that our future Council, after having resolved a great number of the painful questions of our internal ecclesiastical life, will equally give final approbation 'with one reason and one voice' in Council, to the work undertaken by us to establish the correct relations between our Church and the Soviet Government.

In conclusion, we ask you all most emphatically, bishops, pastors, brothers and sisters, to help us, each according to your rank by your collaboration with this godly work, by your devotion and your obedience to the holy Church, and above all by your prayers for us, asking the Lord to grant us the successful accomplishment and, in a way which shall be pleasing to him, the work which has fallen to us to the glory of His Holy name, for the good of our Holy Orthodox Church and our common salvation.

May the grace of our Lord Jesus Christ and the love of God the Father, and the communion of the Holy Ghost be with you all. Amen. For the *locum tenens* of the Patriarch, Sergius, Metropolitan of N.N.; Serafim, Metropolitan of Tver; Silvester, Archbishop of Vologda; Alexis, Archbishop of Hutjin, administrator of the diocese of Novgorod; Anatolia, Archbishop of Samara; Paul, Archbishop of Viatka; Philip, Archbishop of Zvenigorod; administrator of the diocese of Moscow; Konstantin, Bishop of Sumi, administrator of the diocese of Kharkhov and members of the temporary, Patriarchal Holy Synod, the Secretary, Sergius, Bishop of Sezukhovo.

Document F: Speech by M. G. G. Karpov (at Council of 1945)

Reverend bishops, priests and delegates of the faithful of the Russian Orthodox Church!

The Government of the USSR has instructed me to greet in its name this exalted assembly and to convey its wishes for the success of your labours in organizing the higher administration of the Church.

The Soviet Government has also asked me to greet the guests of honour of the local Council, who have come from the Orthodox East – Patriarch Christophoros of Alexandria, Patriarch Alexander III of Antioch, Metropolitan Germanos representing the Ecumenical Patriarch, Archbishop Athenagoras representing the Patriarch of Jerusalem – as well as those who come from our Georgia – Catholicos Callistratos of all-Georgia – and from the Slav nations, our brothers – Metropolitan Joseph representing the Synod of the Serbian Church, and all the bishops and priests who accompany them.

The present local Council, called to elect the Patriarch of Moscow and all the Russias, and to adopt a rule for the administration of the Orthodox Church, will be a landmark in the history of the Russian Orthodox Church.

I am deeply convinced that the decisions of this Council will be of value in strengthening the Church, and will form an important starting point for the further development of its activity in helping the Soviet people to fulfil the major historical tasks which confront them.

The local Council of the Russian Orthodox Church has met at a time when all the nations of our great country, together with all the freedom-loving nations of the world, are fighting a holy war of liberation against the imperialist German bandits and are straining every nerve for victory at the cost of the lives and possessions of millions of people sacrificed on the altar of patriotism.

Throughout the sore trials to which our country has so often been subjected in the past, the Russian Orthodox Church has never broken its links with the people: it has shared their needs, wishes and hopes and contributed its full measure to the common task. It was in its churches and monasteries that learning arose and the earliest chronicles of the life of our country were compiled; the walls of our churches and monasteries have more than once withstood the assault of foreign invaders, and many eminent churchmen have given their lives for their country.

And now, when the Hitlerite bandits have viciously attacked our sacred soil, when all the nations of the Soviet State have risen and surged forward to fight this great patriotic war in defence of their honour, their freedom and their independence, the Russian Orthodox Church has from the first taken the fullest part in defending the country with all the means at its disposal.

Having fully grasped the significance of the events, that eminent churchman, that wise and venerable man who was first Metropolitan, then Patriarch Sergius, bestowed his blessing upon the faithful in their task of participating in the defence of the frontiers of their country. In his many sermons and messages to the Church, he ceaselessly called upon her loyal sons to fight to the death against the barbarous enemy of the Soviet land – Hitler Germany.

Last year, the Patriarch Sergius died to the great loss of the Russian Orthodox Church. In accordance with his testament, the government of the Church passed into the hands of the senior Bishop, Metropolitan of Leningrad and Novgorod, Alexis, an outstanding churchman and an ardent patriot who never once left his post during the 900 days of the siege of Leningrad and who, in total unanimity with the other members of the Holy Synod, has guided the Church from the death of the Patriarch to this day.

The Church has not confined its patriotic action to letters and sermons but has collected funds for building tanks and aeroplanes and for help-ing the sick, the wounded and those crippled or orphaned by the war.

The Soviet Government has shown and continues to show deep interest in the Church's part in the struggle against the enemy.

In our country, the triumph of the new régime, a Socialist régime unprecedented in history and the most righteous in the world, has also brought about a new relationship between Church and State.

The great Socialist October Revolution which liberated our people from slavery and gave them freedom, has also freed the Church from the shackles which impeded its internal activity.

Freedom of conscience, promulgated by the Decree of 23 January 1918, has been consolidated by the basic laws of our country as em-bodied in the Soviet Constitution.

The Council of Church Affairs which, by Government decision, has been created and attached to the Council of People's Commissars of the USSR, forms a link between the Government and the Patriarch of Moscow and all the Russias, and provides liaison in all matters needing government approval.

Without in any way interfering with the spiritual life of the Church, the Council promotes normal relations between Church and State by seeing to the proper and timely application of government laws and decrees concerning the Russian Orthodox Church.

There is no doubt that the normal relations established between the Council and Patriarchate have helped to strengthen the Church admini-stratively; the Council will continue in future to take all necessary steps to remove obstacles of whatever sort which may hinder the Soviet citizen in the exercise of the liberty of conscience granted by the Constitution.

Once again, I sincerely wish the members of the Council success in the task which awaits them.

Document G: Facing new persecution. Speech by the Patriarch Alexis at the Disarmament Conference of the Political and Social Organizations of the USSR, 16th February 1960

The Russian Orthodox Church, with its millions of Orthodox Christians, citizens of our country, speaks to you through me. Accept its greeting and its best wishes.

Appendix I

As history shows, this is the Church that, from the very beginning of the Russian State, helped to establish political and social order in Russia, strengthened by its Christian teaching the legal basis of the family, gave women their legal rights, condemned usury and slavery, trained the people's sense of responsibility and duty, and often, by its laws, made up for the deficiencies of those of the State.

This is the Church that created the masterpieces which have enriched Russian culture and remain a source of national pride for our people.

This same Church, when the country was broken up into separate principalities, helped to reunite Russia by backing the cause of Moscow as a political and religious centre of unity.

This is the Church that, in the harsh days of Mongol rule, interceded with the Khans to spare the Russian people further raids and destruction.

It was this our Church that fortified the spirit of our people in those days, maintaining their faith in their future liberation and their sense of national dignity and of moral strength.

It was this Church that strengthened the nation in its struggle against foreign invaders during the Time of Trouble and the patriotic war of 1812. And during the Second World War, she was again with her people, helping them by every means to victory and peace.

This, briefly, is the Russian Orthodox Church which throughout the centuries has contributed mainly to the moral development of our people, as well as helping to establish the social and political order of the nation in the past.

After the Second World War, this same Church, in agreement with her sister Orthodox Churches abroad, called upon the Christians of the world to become 'the bulwark against all attacks against or threats to peace'. And since 1949 she has, through her representative Metropolitan Nicholas, taken an active part in national and world congresses of the partisans of peace.

As everyone knows, whether in Paris, Stockholm, Berlin, Warsaw, Vienna, Helsinki, Prague or Ceylon, world public opinion has been extremely sensitive to the voice of the Russian Orthodox Church whose attitude to the main problems of our day has been an example to other Christian associations and Churches.

The many appeals, declarations and messages of the Russian Orthodox Church, published in the past few years in the secular, religious and foreign Press, are evidence of the great effort made by this Church to unite Christians throughout the world in a common struggle against the dangers of a new world war.

Here, today, we speak once more for the Russian Orthodox Church, in order to express the peaceful aspirations of our people and to help ward off whatever might serve as cause or pretext for a new armed conflict – because for us, members of the Church, war can only be a gross distortion of our Christian faith and a flagrant violation of the commandment of love given us by Christ our Saviour.

Today as always, our Church condemns all discord, hostility and hatred between nations, sets its face against rearmament and blesses men's intention to suppress all weapons of war – for Christianity, the religion of humility, love and compassion, is a stranger to all violence, above all to violence in the name of God who, as the Holy Evangelist John the Theologian says, is Love (St John IV, 16).

Unshakeable in its hope, the Russian Orthodox Church today once more zealously supports the Soviet government's proposal for complete and general disarmament, taking the view that the recent law' on the reduction of armed forces is proof positive of the peaceful aspirations of our people.

I must say that the proposal for general and complete disarmament fills us Christians with particular joy when we remember the appeal to all the nations of the world to 'turn their swords into ploughshares and their spears into sickles'. These words, which express our Christian conviction, are those of the ancient prophet Isaias (II, 4) whom we Christians call the Evangelist of the Old Testament because he foretold the birth of the Saviour of the world long before the event took place.

Thus we see that the Bible, the Holy Scripture of the Christian Church, is the fountain-head of those ideas of universal peace which today – given the development of more dangerous weapons than ever before – must be regarded as the most important of all for the future of mankind.

It is true that the Church of Christ, whose aim is the good of men, is nevertheless attacked and denounced by these same men, but it will continue to do its duty, to preach the gospel of love and peace to mankind. Indeed, the situation in which it finds itself is a source of comfort to the faithful, for what can all the efforts of rationalism avail against Christianity, when its two thousand years of history speak for themselves and when all the insults and injuries suffered by the Church were foretold by Christ himself who promised that its foundation would be unshakeable and that 'the gates of hell shall not prevail against it'.

We Christians know that we must live to serve mankind and that no circumstances can diminish our love for our neighbour. This is why all men of good will, whatever their beliefs and convictions, can rest assured that, in their struggle for total disarmament, the Russian Orthodox Church is their most faithful ally, just as it is that of the patriotic undertakings of our country.

Out of its centuries of experience, our Church can say: If, to the common good of the world, we all contribute virtuous thoughts, pure feelings, worthy aspirations and righteous acts – then we will have done all that is needed to bring about peace among men and among nations.

Document H: Measures adopted by the Central Committee of the Communist Party of the USSR to promote the atheistic education of the population. January 1964

The Ideological Commission of the Central Committee of the CP of the USSR has worked out 'Measures to promote the atheistic education of the population'. The Central Committee of the CP of the Soviet Union has approved these measures and urges that the Central Party Committees of the Soviet Republics, as well as the Committees of the Autonomous Regions and Provinces should – while taking local conditions into account – plan concrete measures to improve atheistic work and put them into practice.

The measures to promote the atheistic education of the population consist in:

SCIENTIFIC STUDY OF THE PROBLEMS OF ATHEISM AND TRAINING OF SPECIALISTS IN THE STRUGGLE AGAINST RELIGION

It has been decided that the academies of Social Sciences attached to the Central Committee of the CP of the USSR should create an Institute of Scientific Atheism. The task of the institute is to direct and co-ordinate all the scientific work in the field of atheism to be carried out by the Academy of Sciences of the USSR, the higher educational establishments, and the organs of the Ministry of Culture of the USSR;

train highly qualified cadres; organize the detailed study of the topical problems of atheism; and arrange scientific conferences and fruitful courses of study throughout the Union. The Learned Council of the Institute of Scientific Atheism will be composed of representatives of the Ideological Commission of the CC of the CP of the USSR, and of central ideological and scientific organs, as well as of social organizations.

The Presidium of the Academy of Sciences and the Board of the Ministry of Higher and Secondary Technical Education will study the problem of activating the participation of academic institutes and higher educational establishments in the scientific study of the problems of atheism as well as in atheistic propaganda.

Drawing on *Problems of the History of Religion and Atheism*, published by the Academy of Sciences, and on the *Yearbook* of the Leningrad Museum of the history of religion and atheism, the Institute of Scientific Atheism will publish a six-monthly periodical devoted to *Problems of Scientific Atheism*. During the year, the Institute and the all-Union society *Znaniye* [*Learning*] will invite specialists and propagandists of atheism to attend scientific and methodological conferences on the problems raised by the critique of modern religious trends.

Starting in the school year 1964-5, the Ministry of Higher and Secondary Technical Education has decided to introduce specialized training in scientific atheism for some of the students attending the philosophical and historical faculties of the universities and the literary faculties of the higher pedagogical institutes (this will be done by means of regular courses, evening classes and correspondence courses). Chairs of scientific atheism will be created in a number of universities and pedagogical institutes, as well as departments of atheism in the higher training institutes of the universities of Moscow and Kiev.

The ideological sections of the CC of the CP of the USSR and the CCs of the CPs of the Republics of the Union will start regular courses for propagandists of atheism (lecturers, directors of theoretical studies, advisers and others).

Training of atheist cadres. As from the school year 1964-5, obligatory courses on the *principles of scientific atheism* (to be followed by an examination) will be started in universities, higher schools of medicine and agriculture, and high schools; in other educational establishments, these courses will be voluntary. The *principles of scientific atheism* will likewise be taught in training colleges, medical colleges and schools of general culture. The type of student attending the course will be taken into account in preparing programmes and manuals. The plans and schedules will include a compulsory course of practical work, essays, and practical tests in atheism which will count towards the examinations. The atheistic trend of courses in the humanities and natural sciences will be intensified.

During the new school year, correspondence courses on the principles of scientific atheism will be started by the higher Party school of the CC of the CP of the USSR, the higher Party four-year schools, the central school of the Komsomol, and the Soviet Party schools. The programmes of the philosophical courses of two-year Party schools will devote more time to the study of scientific atheism.

Party and Komsomol Committees are invited to make wider use of political education for the training of atheistic cadres. To promote this end, it has been decided that, throughout the country and especially in regions where the popular manifestations of religion are relatively strong, atheistic groups, schools and study-circles shall be founded to enable those who attend them to combine their studies with atheistic work. Programmes for the study of atheism shall be brought up to date with modern requirements; in conjunction with these, manuals of atheism for use in political education shall be prepared for publication at the start of the school year 1964 j.

Study-circles on problems of atheistic education should be organized for Party, Soviet, Komsomol and Trade Union workers and activists, for teachers, doctors, Pioneer leaders, the staffs of kindergartens, colleges and professional and technical schools, cultural workers, journalists, administrative staffs, chairmen and members of womens' soviets, house committees, and soviets of pensioners.

All means of ideological pressure must be used in atheistic education. The All-Union society *Znaniye*, the CC of the All-Union Leninist–Communist League of Youth, and the Ministry of Culture will jointly organize a congress for the study of methods to improve the organization and material of scientific atheistic propaganda through lectures.

Party Committees are invited to study the problem of drawing scientists, teachers, professors, doctors, writers, journalists and undergraduate students of agriculture, medicine and the humanities, into active participation in scientific atheistic propaganda through lectures.

Appendix I

People's universities should be used more widely for the spread of atheistic education.

The Committee of the Council of Ministers in charge of the Cinema plans the yearly production of films on atheistic themes: art films, popular science films, documentaries and cartoons. Atheistic films will be used for television, shown without charge in cultural establishments, and reproduced in small format.

Members of the Ministry of Culture and of the Committee of the Council of Ministers in charge of the Cinema, and the Secretaries of the Boards of Writers' Unions will attend a joint congress to discuss methods of increasing the role played in atheistic propaganda by literature and the arts. Competitions may be organized and prizes offered for the best artistic works on atheistic themes (in literature, drama, cinema and the fine arts). Ways will also be studied of improving the atheistic content of amateur artistic efforts.

Measures are being planned to improve atheist literature, widen its themes, use more varied styles and raise its ideological, political and journalistic level. The Committee in charge of the Press has been asked to work out a joint publishing programme, including larger editions in the national languages of the Union, books for children and adolescents; mass editions of the 'Little Atheist Library'; popular series (philosophical and others) for the use of believers; new editions of the best works of classical atheist literature, and translations of the best Russian and foreign works into the national languages of the USSR.

In order to improve the quality of atheist literature, and to avoid overlapping in its publication, it has been decided to create an editorial committee to advise the Government Press Committee, and the scientific and atheistic departments of the main republican and provincial publishers – though without increasing their existing staff.

In order to step up the publication of atheistic material, special sections will be devoted to it in the following journals: *The Agitator, Political Self-Education, Problems of Philosophy, Problems of History, Science and Life, Learning is Strength, Nature, Health, The Woman Worker, The Peasant Woman, The Work Shift*[1] and in corresponding journals of the federal republics. In order to develop atheistic themes in newspapers, periodicals, books, and radio and television programmes, the government Press, Radio and Television Committees, the Union of Soviet

[1] *Agitator, Polititcheskoe Samovbrazovanie, Voprosy Filosofi, Voprosy Istorii, Nauka i Jizn, Znanie-Sila, Priroda, Zdorovie, Rabotnitsa, Krestianka, Smena.*

Appendix I

Journalists, and their republican and provincial organizations are urged to hold regular seminars for journalists who specialize in problems of atheistic education; to advise them on such problems; to urge the Press to concentrate on unmasking religious ideology and systematizing the practice of atheistic education; and more actively to encourage specialists to take part in this journalistic work.

The radio and television throughout the country, and the republican and provincial radio and television studios, are urged to put out programmes for various categories of listeners and viewers (lectures, newspaper serials, round table discussions, brains trusts) with the collaboration of the best scientists and propagandists of atheism, and to produce films on atheistic themes.

Trade Unions, the Ministry of Culture and the Society *Znaniye* are urged to improve the material and technical basis of atheistic propaganda by means of lectures and the spreading of culture, to stimulate the atheist activity of museums (especially historical and local ones), planetariums and travelling exhibitions and clubs, and put out re-prints of films, etc.

The role played in atheist education by medical workers is to be increased, regular courses on atheism will be started for the staffs of medical institutes, and atheist propaganda will be organized at centres of public assistance, hospitals, maternity clinics, and at medical consultations for women and children.

In order to promote the introduction of a-religious holidays and rites into the life of the Soviet citizen, a congress will be held for Party, Soviet, Komsomol and Trade Union workers, ethnologists, propagandists, and staffs of civic bureaux; in their town-planning, the Soviets of workers' deputies should allow for the construction of Palaces of Happiness; more use should be made of the Houses of Culture, and – while considering local conditions – of the official proceedings connected with the registration of births, the issue of passports, the celebration of marriages, and other important events in the life of the citizen.

Seminars and lectures will be held on the official recommendations regarding individual work with believers. Party, Komsomol and Trade Union committees are urged to study the religious situation in their neighbourhoods. With this in view, they should select workers who are familiar with local conditions and enjoy local prestige, and train them in atheistic work. More propagandists and lecturers must be enlisted, and groups must be organized for individual propaganda to believers in each community. Believers should be urged to attend cultural circles and schools.

Atheistic education of children and adolescents. The atheist trend in school curriculums, particularly in the social sciences, must be intensified. Wider use should be made of extra-mural activities, e.g. young atheists' clubs, lectures, talks, parties, excursions, cultural visits to cinemas and theatres, etc.

The Republican Education Ministries, jointly with the Komsomol Committees and the Academies of Pedagogical Science are urged to run discussion courses for teachers, Pioneer leaders and kindergarten teachers, for the study of the problems of atheistic work among children, young people and parents. Regular courses for such workers will be started in the pedagogical institutes. Peoples' universities and schools for mothers will be used more widely for the atheistic education of parents.

Checking the application of Soviet laws to religious practices. There must be stricter control to prevent illegal activities by clergy, lay groups and individual believers, and to preserve children from the influence of priests, and of parents who may impose religious practices on them.

Measures are being planned to spread the knowledge of Soviet legislation regarding religious practices. The journals *Workers' Deputies' Soviets, Socialist Legality* and *Soviet State and Law* are invited to spread information concerning the law and its application in practice.

District and town executive committees of the Soviets of Workers' Deputies, responsible for checking the application of the law, should intensify their activity.

Organization of atheistic work. Party organizations must appoint Communists who will be responsible for organizing atheistic propaganda, and who will be assisted by groups of Soviet activists in charge of propaganda and of organizing atheistic work in offices, on building sites, in collective and State farms, Civil Service, schools, Pioneer organizations, etc. They must also keep more strictly to the communist requirements, formulated in their statutes, concerning the struggle against the survival of religion.

It may be useful to attach Soviets (or sections) to all the main Party organizations (district committees, Party production committees,

Appendix I

Party town, provincial and autonomous regional committees): these will be responsible for atheist propaganda and will unify and direct the efforts of the committees of the Party, the Trade Unions, the Komsomol and the Society *Znaniye* in cultural educational establishments and schools. Members of the ideological commissions of Party committees should be given a specialized atheistic training, particularly in regions, provinces, towns or districts where popular religious feeling is relatively strong.

Atheist soviets will be created in the central ideological organizations and the editorial offices of newspapers and periodicals.

ADDITIONAL DOCUMENTS:[1]

Statement issued by the Council of the Russian Orthodox Church at a meeting held on 11th November 1917.

Letter from Mgr Sergius to the Peoples' Commission for internal affairs.

Pastoral letter: to the priests and faithful of Christ's Orthodox Church from Mgr Sergius, Metropolitan of Kolomna and of Moscow, head of the Russian Orthodox Church, given to all parishes on 22nd June 1941.

Resolution passed by the Central Committee of the Communist Party of USSR.

Speech made by M. Leonides Iliichev on 25th November 1963 at the meeting between the Ideological Commission and the Central Committee of the Communist Party.

[1] See note on page 418.

APPENDIX II

LEGISLATIVE DOCUMENTS

Document A: Decree of the Council of the People's Commissars (23rd January 1918) concerning the separation of the Church from the State, and schools from the Church

1. The Church is separated from the State.
2. Within the territory of the Republic, it is forbidden to promulgate any laws or local decrees which would hamper or limit freedom of conscience or establish advantages or privileges on the basis of the confessional membership of citizens.
3. Every citizen can practise any religion he wishes, or not practise one at all.

All loss of rights resulting from the practice of any faith or the non-practice of a faith, is repealed.

N.B. All indication of religious membership or non-membership of citizens is deleted from all official acts.

4. The activities of any State or other public, legal or social bodies will not be accompanied by any religious rites or ceremonies.
5. The free practice of religious rites is guaranteed in as far as it does not interfere with public order and is not accompanied by any attempt on the rights of the citizens of the Soviet Republic. Local authorities will be empowered to take all necessary measures in these cases, to protect public order and security.
6. No one may defect from the fulfilment of his public obligations by reason of his religious views.

Exceptions from this resolution, on condition one public duty is replaced by another, are permitted in individual cases, on the decision of a Peoples' Court.

7. Religious oath taking or swearing in is annulled. Where necessary, only a solemn promise will be given.
8. Marriage acts will only be drawn up by the civil authorities: by marriage and birth registration offices.

9. Schools are separated from the Church. The teaching of religious doctrines in all State and public as well as any private educational establishments where general subjects are taught, is prohibited.

Citizens may teach and be taught religion privately.

10. All ecclesiastical and religious societies are subject to the general regulations concerning private societies and associations and do not receive any privileges or subsidies either from the State or its local authorities and self-governing bodies.

11. The enforced gathering of collections and contributions, as well as any measures of enforcement or punishment on the part of these societies against their members is not permitted.

12. No ecclesiastical or religious society has the right to possess property. It does not enjoy any legal rights.

13. All the possessions of ecclesiastical and religious societies existing in Russia are declared to be national property. The buildings and objects specially intended for use in services, are made over, by special decree of the local or central state authority, for the free use of the aforesaid religious societies.

> *Chairman of the Council of People's Commissars,*
> V. Ulianov (Lenin)
>
> *People's Commissars:*
> N. Podvoisky, V. Aglasov, V. Trutovsky,
> A. Shlikhter, P. Proshian, V. Menjinsky,
> A. Shliapnikov, G. Petrovsky
> *Chargé d'affaires:*
> Vl. Bonch-Bruevich
> *Secretary:*
> N. Gorbunov

Document B: Decree of the Central Executive Committee of all Russia and of the Council of People's Commissars on religious associations (8th April 1929).

I

The CEC of all Russia and the Council of People's Commissars of the RSFSR decree that:

1. The decree of the Council of People's Commissars of the RSFSR of 23rd January 1918 on the separation of the Church from the State and

of education from the Church shall apply to churches, religious groups, movements, trends and all other associations for religious worship of whatever denomination.

2. Religious associations of believers of all rites shall be registered as religious societies or as groups of believers. No citizen shall belong to more than one religious or ritual association (society or group).

3. A religious society is a local association of at least twenty believers, having reached the age of eighteen and belonging to the same denomination, rite, movement or trend, for the purpose of satisfying their religious needs in common.

Believers who, because of their small number, cannot form a religious society shall have the right to form a group of believers.

4. Neither a religious society nor a group of believers shall be a person at law.

5. In order to register as a religious society, twenty constituent members shall submit to one of the above-mentioned bodies (Art. 4) an application for registration in the form determined by the Permanent Commission for Religious Affairs of the Presidium of the CEC of the RSFSR.

6. In order to register as a group of believers, their nominated representative (Art. 13) shall submit to one of the above-mentioned bodies (Art. 4) an application for registration in the form determined by the Religious Commission of the Presidium of the CEC of the RSFSR.

7. The above-mentioned bodies (Art. 4) shall, within a month of receiving the application, register the society or group, or inform the applicants that their application is refused.

8. A list of members of the association, of its executive and administrative bodies and of the clergy serving it, shall be communicated to the registering body within the delay and in the form determined by the Permanent Religious Commission of the Presidium of the CEC of the RSFSR.

9. No one shall be listed as a member of a religious association without his express consent.

10. In order to satisfy their religious needs, believers who have formed a religious association shall have the right to enter into an agreement with the local Municipal Council or District CEC, granting them the free use of a religious building and of objects of exclusively ritual use.

They may also hold religious meetings on other premises put at their disposal by individuals or by the local Municipal Council or EC within the terms of the law. Regulations applying to religious buildings under the present decree shall apply equally to these premises. The agreement for the use of such premises shall be made by each believer on his own responsibility. Such premises must also comply to building and sanitary regulations.

No religious society or group of believers shall dispose of more than one set of premises for its prayer meetings.

11. Arrangements connected with the administration and use of religious premises and ritual objects – such as employment of watchmen, delivery of fuel, upkeep of religious buildings and ritual objects, acquisition of goods, effects for use in religious rites, ceremonies, other such acts closely and directly related to the teaching and ritual order of the cult in question, lease of premises for religious meetings – can be made individually by any member of the executive body of the religious society or group of believers empowered by the association.

Such arrangements shall not apply to contractual relations connected with a trade or industry, however closely related to the cult, e.g. lease of premises for a candle factory, a printing press printing books on religion or morals, etc.

12. General meetings of religious societies and groups of believers may be held by permission of the Religious Commission of the Municipal Council in a town and of the District EC in a rural area.

13. The religious association shall, at its general meeting, elect by a show of hands an executive body, consisting of three of its members in the care of a society or of one representative in the care of a group, entrusted with functions connected with the administration and use of religious premises and ritual objects, as well as with representing the association.

14. The registering body shall have the right to exclude certain persons from membership of the executive body of the association.

15. The religious association shall have the right to elect at its general meeting a control commission of not more than three of its members for the control of ritual objects and of sums accruing from members' contributions or from voluntary gifts.

16. The executive body or control commission of a religious association shall have the right to meet (hold its session) without obtaining the permission of government authorities.

17. Religious associations are prohibited from:

    a. creating funds for mutual aid, co-operatives or associations of producers, and from using the effects at their disposal for any purpose other than the satisfaction of their religious needs,

    b. granting material aid to their members,

    c. organizing religious or other meetings specially intended for children, young people or women, or biblical or literary meetings, groups, sections or circles, or meetings for sewing, manual work, religious instruction, etc., or excursions, or playing fields for children, or open libraries, reading rooms, sanatoria, or provide medical aid.

The only books which may be kept in religious buildings on religious premises are those indispensible for the celebration of the cult.

18. No teaching of religious dogmas of any sort shall be tolerated in State or private schools or other educational establishments. Such teaching may only form part of special theological courses which citizens of the USSR have the right to organize by special permission of the Permanent Religious Commission of the CEC of the RSFSR or of the autonomous republic concerned.

19. The activities of priests, preachers, instructors, etc., is restricted to the place of residence of the members of the religious associations which they serve and the place where the religious building used by it is situated.

The activities of priests, preachers and instructors serving two or three religious associations are restricted to the area in which the members of these associations reside.

20. Religious associations may organize meetings or congresses of believers in the district, the RSFSR or the Soviet Union, provided special permission has been obtained individually in each case from:

    a. the Permanent Religious Commission of the Presidium of the CEC of the RSFSR if the meeting is that of believers throughout the RSFSR or the Union, and is held on RSFSR territory, or of believers in two or more districts or regions, or

    b. the regional or district Religious Commission if the congress is a local one.

In the case of a republic-wide meeting or congress in an autonomous republic, permission must be granted by the Religious Commission of the CEC of the Soviet Socialist Autonomous Republic concerned.

21. A local, Russian or All-Union religious meeting or congress may elect from among its members an executive body responsible for the

application of the statutes adopted by the congress. A list of the members of the executive body elected at the congress, as well as the proceedings of the congress shall be communicated in duplicate, in the form determined by the Permanent Religious Commission of the Presidium of the CEC of the RSFSR, to the body which has granted permission for the congress to be held.

22. Neither the congress nor its elected executive body is a person at law, and neither has the right to:

    a. organize a central fund to collect free donations from believers;

    b. levy forced contributions of any sort;

    c. own, lease or purchase ritual objects or premises for religious meetings;

    d. make contracts or agreements of any sort.

23. In dealing with matters of a purely religious character, the executive bodies of religious societies, groups of believers and religious congresses have the right to use stamps, seals and headed paper stating their denomination. Such stamps, seals or letter headings shall not bear any emblem or slogan used by Soviet Government organs or institutions.

24. Religious gatherings, conferences and congresses can be promoted and organized by religious societies, groups of believers and their executive bodies, as well as by the executive bodies of religious congresses.

25. Ritual objects used by believers who have formed a religious association – whether granted by contract or subsequently acquired by or received by them as gifts – are regarded as nationalized property and listed by the Religious Commission of the local Municipal Council or District EC, while remaining at the disposal of the believers for their use.

26. The watchman's hut, whether situated in the grounds or attached to the religious building, shall be put at the disposal of the believers by the same contract as the building itself.

27. The contract granting the use of religious buildings and ritual objects to believers who have formed a religious association shall be concluded by the Religious Commission of the local Municipal Council or District EC in the name of the Municipal Council or District EC.

28. In accordance with the contract, the religious building and the objects which it contained are handed over by a representative of the

Municipal Council or District EC to a minimum of twenty members of the religious society who place them at the disposal of all the believers.

29. Under the terms of the contract between the believers and the Municipal Council or District EC, the persons who have been granted the use of the religious building and ritual objects undertake to:

    a. be responsible for them as government property placed in their charge;

    b. repair the building and cover the costs of upkeep and use, e.g. heating, insurance, watchman's salary, taxes and local dues, etc.;

    c. use the building and objects solely for the satisfaction of their religious needs;

    d. compensate the government for any damage caused by deterioration or loss;

    e. keep a list of all ritual objects used under contract, adding those later acquired (by purchase, gift or transfer from other religious bodies) and – with the knowledge and consent of the contracting MC or District EC – remove those no longer in use;

    f. admit without hindrance, at any moment except during the celebration of religious rites, members of ECs or Municipal or Rural Councils empowered periodically to inspect and check the lists of such objects and premises.

30. Religious buildings of historical, artistic or archaeological importance, within the competence of the People's Commissariat of Education, shall be handed over for the use of believers in the same manner and on the same terms as others, but on condition that the regulations for the safety and control of such buildings are observed.

31. All local inhabitants belonging to the same religious denomination, movement or trend, shall have the right to sign the contract granting them the use of a religious building and of ritual objects, and thereafter to transfer such objects; they thus acquire the right to take part in the administration of such properties on the same terms as the original signatories of the contract.

32. Any signatory of the contract has the right to remove his signature upon application to the bodies listed in Art. 4, but this does not relieve him of his responsibility for the safety of the properties for the period preceding his application.

33. Religious buildings must be insured against fire in the names of the signatories of the contract, in favour of the relevant EC or MC. The insurance money may be used for the reconstruction of the build-

ing or, by order of the relevant EC, to relieve the social and cultural needs of the community, in accordance with the decree of the Presidium of the CEC of the RSFSR of 24th August 1925, concerning the affectation of sums recovered by insurance in the case of burned-down religious buildings (Codex 1925, 58, Art. 470).

34. Should there be no group desiring to take over a religious building for the satisfaction of its religious needs and in accordance with Articles 2–7 of the present decree, the relevant MC or EC shall post a notice on the door of the religious building.

35. Should no one express the wish to take over the building on the specified conditions within one week of the posting of the notice, the MC or EC shall inform the EC above it, stating the date of the building, its conditions, the uses for which it is suitable and its own suggestions on this subject. In the case of an autonomous republic, where its CEC is not locally represented, the District or Regional EC shall determine the future use of the building and the objects contained in it, in accordance with Articles 40–42.

36. The use for other purposes of a religious building in use by believers (liquidation of a religious building) can be authorized only by a motivated decree of the Republican CEC or Regional or District EC, in a case where the building is indispensable for a government or social purpose. The decree must be communicated to the religious society.

37. Should the members of the religious society appeal to the Presidium of the CEC of the RSFSR within two weeks of having received notice of the decree, the case (of the liquidation of the religious building) shall be referred to the Presidium of the CEC of the RSFSR. The contract with the believers shall not cease to be valid or the use of the building removed from them until the decree has been confirmed by the Presidium of the CEC.

38. The lease of nationalized, municipalized or private premises for religious meetings (Art. 10, para. 2) can be broken by normal legal methods before the expiration of its term.

39. The liquidation of a religious building in a similar case must be carried out by the religious commission on the demand of the MC or District EC, in the presence of representatives of the local financial department and of other services if they are interested, as well as of a representative of the religious society.

40. When a religious building is liquidated, the ritual objects shall be apportioned as follows:

a. objects in platinum, silver or brocade, as also precious stones go to the treasury and are put in charge of the local financial authorities or of the organs of the People's Commissariat of Education should they be on its list;

b. objects of historical, artistic or collector's value shall be put in charge of the organs of the People's Commissariat of Education;

c. all other objects (icons, vestments, banners, etc.) shall revert to the believers for transfer to other religious buildings of the same rite; these objects shall be included in the general list of ritual objects;

d. objects of current use (bells, furniture, carpets, chandeliers) shall go to the treasury and be put in charge of the local financial authorities or the organs of the People's Commissariat of Education should they be on its list;

e. objects of transitory use, such as money, incense, candles, oil, wine, wax, wood and coal, destined for use strictly in accordance with the terms of the contract or in the celebration of the rites of the cult, shall not be confiscated where the existing religious society survives the liquidation of the religious building.

41. Religious buildings and the huts of the church watchmen, listed by local authorities responsible for the administration of State funds, may be handed over by the latter for the free use of the relevant ECs or MCs, on condition that they remain on the list of nationalized properties and that their allocation and use (unless the latter is subject to special conditions) are not decided without the knowledge and consent of the People's Commissariat of Finance of the RSFSR.

42. Local financial authorities shall retain closed religious buildings in their charge only if these are not within the competence of the People's Commissariat of Education as architectural monuments and cannot be used by the EC or MC for educational or cultural purposes (as schools, clubs, reading-rooms, etc.) or as dwellings.

43. Should the religious society fail to keep the terms of the contract or to carry out the orders of the religious commission (as to re-registration, repairs, etc.) the contract can be broken.

The right to break the contract lies with the CEC of an autonomous republic or the EC of the region or the district, which can do so on information received from a lower executive committee or council.

44. Should there be an appeal against the orders of the above-mentioned bodies (Art. 43) to the Presidium of the CEC of the RSFSR,

the building and the ritual objects shall not be confiscated before the Presidium of the CEC has made its decision known.

45. Permission to put up new religious buildings may be granted on application from religious societies, within the terms of the building regulations and of the special conditions imposed by the Permanent Religious Commission of the Presidium of the CEC of the RSFSR.

46. Should the religious building, owing to its age, be in danger of partial or total collapse, the local MC or EC has the right to request the executive body of the religious association to abstain from using it for religious services or meetings pending its inspection by a special technical commission.

47. At the same time as this request, the official who makes it, shall report to the building inspector on the urgent need for a technical inspection of the building. A copy of his report shall be sent for information to the body which has made the contract granting the use of the building and the ritual objects to believers.

48. The technical commission (Art. 46) chosen by the head of the building inspectorate or the chief engineer, shall consist of the following persons who have the right to a voice in the deliberations:

a. a representative of the local educational authority, if the People's Commissariat of Education is responsible for the building;

b. a representative of the corresponding branch of the local administration, of the Municipal Council or of the District police if the town is not the administrative centre of the district;

c. a representative of the religious society.

49. The decisions of the technical commission, as stated in its report, shall have force of law.

50. If the commission regards the building as in danger of collapse, it must state in its report whether the building must be demolished or merely repaired. If the latter, the report must state what repairs are necessary and how much time is needed for their completion. Until the repairs have been completed, the religious society is forbidden to hold meetings of any sort in the building.

51. In case of refusal by the believers to carry out the work required by the commission in its report, the contract granting them the use of the building and of the ritual objects shall be abrogated by order of the CEC of the autonomous republic or the EC of the district or region.

52. Should the technical commission decide that the building must be demolished, the contract with the believers shall be abrogated by

order of the Presidium of the CEC of the autonomous republic or the EC of the region or district.

53. Once the contract has been abrogated and the decision to demolish the building made with the consent of the local financial and educational authorities, the demolition shall be carried out by the religious commission of the relevant MC or district EC. The building materials obtained through demolition shall be sold, part of the proceeds being used to recover the cost of demolition and the remainder accruing to the State.

54. A religious association has the right to collect dues and accept voluntary donations, whether within or without the religious building, but only from its members and only for purposes related to the upkeep of the building and the ritual objects and the pay of the clergy and the executive body.

All forced levies for the benefit of religious societies are a crime punishable under the Penal Code of the RSFSR.

55. All ritual objects, whether donated or purchased out of donated sums must be included in the inventory of ritual objects.

All sums donated for the purpose of embellishing ritual objects or embellishing the religious building by the inclusion of donated objects must be listed in the inventory of ritual properties of which the religious society enjoys the use.

Donations in kind for purposes other than those mentioned above need not be listed in the inventory, any more than donations in money for purposes related to the use of the religious building or premises (repairs, heating, etc.) or for the upkeep of the clergy.

Voluntary donations in money from believers shall be listed in the parish ledgers kept by the treasurer.

56. Sums donated for purposes connected with the use of religious buildings and ritual objects can be spent by members of the executive bodies of religious societies or the representatives of groups of believers empowered to do so.

57. Provided the religious building or premises allocated to them for this purpose conform to structural and sanitary regulations, believers forming a religious society or group have the right to use them for religious gatherings without the knowledge and permission of the authorities.

Should the premises not be specially allocated for this purpose, believers wishing to hold a religious meeting must give notice to the

Rural Council in rural areas or the Municipal Council in urban communities.

58. Religious rites or ceremonies may not be held and ritual objects may not be introduced into any government, co-operative, social or private institution or concern.

This prohibition does not apply to religious rites performed at the request of the gravely sick or dying in prisons and hospitals, so long as they are performed in a special, isolated place.

59. For a religious procession or rite or ceremony to be held in the open, authorization must be obtained in each case from:

a. the religious commission of the MC in a town ranking as no less than a regional administrative centre;

b. from the Presidium of the MC or the Rural Council in towns which are not administrative centres, in workers' settlements and in holiday resorts;

c. from the District EC in rural areas.

Application for such an authorization must be made at least two weeks in advance. No such authorization is needed for religious ceremonies connected with burial.

60. If a procession forms part of a religious service and processes round the religious building, the authorities need not be notified, provided the procession does not impede the circulation in the street.

61. Religious processions, rites and ceremonies, held outside the area of the religious society's existence and normal activity, need a special authorization in each case from the body which has made the original contract. Such an authorization may be given with the preliminary consent of the EC of the district in which the procession, rite or ceremony is to be held.

62. A list of religious societies and groups of believers in their areas must be drawn up by the registering bodies (Art. 6).

63. Religious societies must submit full budgetary information, in the form and within the delays determined by the special religious commission of the Presidium of the CEC of the RSFSR, to the religious commissions of the relevant MCs and district ECs which shall communicate it to the regional ECs or the CECs of autonomous republics. These in turn shall forward it to the Permanent Religious Commission or the Presidium of the CEC of the RSFSR.

64. The registering bodies shall be responsible for supervising the activities of the religious societies, as well as for the safety of the

religious buildings and ritual objects of which they enjoy the use; in rural areas this responsibility lies with the local Rural Council.

II

65. All religious associations factually in existence at the date of promulgation of the present decree shall register within one year of its promulgation, in the form determined by the present decree.

66. In the event of any such society failing to comply with the above-mentioned condition, it shall be regarded as dissolved, and the consequences stated in the present decree shall follow.

67. As from the date of publication of the present decree, the following laws of the RSFSR cease to be valid:

1. Decree of the CEC of all Russia of 27th December 1921 concerning valuables found in churches and monasteries (Codex 1922, 19, Art. 215);

2. Decree of the Presidium of the CEC of all Russia of 30th July 1923 concerning the transfer from the old to the new calendar of the ten days rest granted to the Orthodox population by Article 112 of the Labour Code compiled in 1922 (Codex 1923, 70, Art. 678);

3. Decree of the CEC of all Russia of 14th August 1923 clarifying the decree on the transfer of the ten rest days from the old to the new calendar (Codex 1923, 72, Art. 707);

4. Decree of the Council of People's Commissars of 19th September 1923 on the sale of articles of religious use.

68. People's Commissars of the RSFSR are enjoined, within a month, to annul all circulars and orders abrogated by the present decree and to publish a list of those which remain valid.

Signed: President of the CEC of all Russia
M. Kalinin
Vice-President of the Council of
People's Commissars
A. Smirnov
Vice-Secretary of the CEC of all
Russia
A. Dossov[1]

[1] Codex of laws and decrees of the workers' and peasants' government, no. 23, 18th May 1929. Slight modifications were made on 1st January 1932 and published in Codex No. 8 on 28th January 1932; these have been included in the text printed above.

Appendix II

Document C: Articles of the Penal Code imposing penalties for religious crimes

Art. 142. *Breach of laws governing the separation of Church from State and of Education from the Church.*

Any breach of the laws governing the separation of the Church from the State and of Education from the Church is punishable by corrective labour for a maximum term of one year or a fine of 50 roubles.[1]

Art. 143. *Interference with the celebration of religious rites.*

Anyone hindering the celebration of religious rites which do not disturb the public order or interfere with the rights of citizens, is liable to corrective labour for a maximum period of six months or to public censure.[2]

Art. 227. *Interference with the rights of citizens under cover of religious rites.*

The organization or leadership of a group whose activity, carried on under cover of preaching religious doctrines or celebrating religious rites, is prejudicial to the health, persons or rights of citizens, or incites them to refuse to take part in all social activities or to perform their civic duties, as also the enrolment of children in such a group,

is punishable by deprivation of liberty for a maximum term of five years or by exile for the same term, with or without confiscation of property.

Active participation in the activities of such a group, as well as systematic incitement to the acts mentioned above,

are punishable by deprivation of liberty for a maximum term of three years or by corrective labour for a maximum term of one year.

If the activities mentioned in the second paragraph of the present article, or the persons who engage in them, do not represent a serious social danger, social pressure can be brought to bear on them.[3]

(The first part of the corresponding article in the Penal Code of the Ukraine is slightly different in its formulation and carries heavier penalties.[4])

[1] This Article adopted on 8th December 1960 replaces Articles 122–6 of the former Code.

[2] Article 127 of the former Code (lighter penalty).

[3] Article adopted on 25th July 1962 and published in *Vedomosti Verkhovnogo Sovieta RSFSR* (Official Journal) 29, 1962.

[4] Article adopted on 27th June 1961 and published in *Vedomosti Verkhovnogo Sovieta Ukrainskoy SSR* 28, 1961.

Art. 209. The organization or leadership of a group whose activity, carried on under cover of preaching religious doctrines or celebrating religious rites or *under any other pretext*, involves damage to the health of citizens, or *sexual corruption* or interference with the persons or rights of citizens, or incitement to refuse to take part in all social activities or to perform civic duties,

is punishable by deprivation of liberty for a maximum term of five years *and by exile of the same duration* with or without confiscation of property.[1]

Document D:[2] Statute concerning the administration of the Russian Orthodox Church passed by the Council on the Affairs of the Russian Orthodox Church on 31st January 1945

[1] Texts published in *Ugolovnoye zakonodatelstvo Soyuza SSR i soyuznikh respublik, Moscow*, 1963, vol. I, pp. 123, 142, 220.

[2] See note on page 418.

APPENDIX III

LIST – PROVISIONAL AND INCOMPLETE – OF BISHOPS OF THE RUSSIAN ORTHODOX CHURCH, MARTYRS FOR THEIR FAITH

This list includes the bishops of the Patriarchal Church and of the so-called Josephite schism, but not those of the Renewed (Living) Church. The names are given in probable chronological order.

1. Vladimir Bogoyavlensky, Metropolitan of Kiev, born in 1848, assassinated 25th January 1918, not far from the Monastery of the Caves. First martyr of the Russian Church.
2. Andronic Nikolsky, Archbishop of Perm, assassinated 4th June 1918.
3. Theophanus Ilchensky, Bishop of Solikamsk, Vicar to the Archbishop of Perm named above, drowned in the Kama 11th December 1918.
4. Basil, Archbishop of Chernigov, appointed by the All-Russian Council to investigate the assassination of the bishops of Perm, was himself assassinated, together with the other members of the Investigation Commission, in the train, on the return journey.
5. Hermogen, formerly Bishop of Saratov, tried to oppose Rasputin, and was removed from his see. After the Revolution, was appointed Bishop of Tobolsk. Was arrested in April 1918 and drowned in the river Tura 16th June 1918, together with the members of the delegation of the faithful who had come to negotiate for his release. Among those martyred was Bishop Hermogen's brother.
6. Isidor Kolokov, Bishop of Mikhailov, impaled at Samara.
7. Ambrosius Gudko, Bishop of Sarapul, killed at Sviasjk in January 1918.
8. Mitrophan Krasnopolsky, Archbishop of Astrakhan, thrown down from a high wall.

9. Leontii Vimpfen, Bishop of Enotai, Vicar of the diocese of Astra-khan, martyred with many priests of his diocese.
10. Platon Kulbush, Bishop of Revel, assassinated at Iuriev 14th January 1919.
11. Tikhon, Archbishop of Voronej, hanged in a church in December 1919.
12. Joachim Levitsky, Archbishop of Nijni Novgorod, hanged in a church at Sebastopol.
13. Nicodemus Kononov, Bishop of Belgorod.
14. Macarius Gnevushev, Bishop of Viazma.
15. Laurence Kniazev, Bishop of Balakhnin, Vicar of the diocese of Nijni Novgorod.
16. Pimen, Bishop of Vierny (Alma-Ata).
17. Herman, Bishop of Kamyshin, shot as hostage at Saratov.
18. Varsanuphii Vikhvelin, Bishop of Kirillov, Vicar of the diocese of Nijni Novgorod.
19. Sylvester, Archbishop of Omsk, died in the town prison.
20. Simon Shleev, Bishop of Ufa, killed at his home 6th July 1921.
21. Nazarius, Metropolitan of Kutaissi (Church of Georgia), shot in 1924.
22. Methodius Krasnoperov, Bishop of Petropavlovsk, killed in the spring of 1922.
23. Benjamin Kazansky, Metropolitan of Petrograd, executed 12(?) August 1922.
24. Philaret, Bishop of Kostroma, died in deportation at Archangel in 1923.
25. Seraphim, Bishop of Eloturovsk, died in prison in the Perm region in 1925.
26. Ieropheus Afonik, Bishop and Vicar of the diocese of Veliky Ustiug, killed in May 1928 (Josephite schism).
27. Peter Zverev, Archbishop of Voronej, died in the Solovki Islands, 25th January 1929.
28. Hilarion Troitsky, Bishop and Vicar of the diocese of Moscow, right hand of Patriarch Tikhon, outstanding theologian, deported in 1923 to Solovki, died in a Leningrad prison 15th December 1929.
29. Sergius, Bishop of Efremovo, shot at Buzuluk in 1929.
30. Maximus Zhizhilenko, Bishop of Serpukhov, doctor, shot in Moscow in 1930 (Josephite schism).

31. Basil, Bishop of Priluky, killed in Moscow in 1930–1 (Josephite schism).
32. Seraphim Meshcheriakov, Metropolitan of Stavropol. After having been deported to Solovki, he was shot at Rostov-on-Don in 1932 together with 120 members of the lower clergy.
33. Agapit Vishnevsky, Archbishop of Ekaterinoslav, died in prison.
34. Pimen, Metropolitan of Kharkov, died in prison in Kupiansk in 1933.
35. Theodosius Vashnetzov, Bishop of Moghilev, died in Siberia in 1933.
36. Nicodemus, Archbishop of Semyretchiey, died in deportation or shot in 1933.
37. Photius Purlevsky, Bishop of Semipalatinsk, shot in 1933.
38. Platon Rudnev, Bishop of Bogorodsk, deported to Solovki, shot in 1933.
39. Alexander Belozerov, Archbishop of Podolsk, died in 1934, in the Steppe, from hunger, in Kazakhstan.
40. Philip Gumilevsky, shot in the prison of Krasnoiarsk in 1934 (Josephite schism).
41. Arsen Zhadanovsky, Archbishop of Serpukhov, shot 30th June 1935.
42. Daniel Troitsky, died in Briansk prison in 1935 (brother of Bishop Hilarion, cf. No. 28).
43. Hermann Riashentzev 〔 martyred in
44. Serapion 〔 deportation at
45. Theodore Pozdeyev, formerly Rector of the 〔 Ust-Sysolsk
Moscow Theological Academy. 〕 in 1935.
46. Damascinus Tzedrik, Bishop of Glukhov, died in deportation in 1936 (Josephite schism).
47. Bartholomew Remov, Bishop and Vicar of the diocese of Moscow, shot 26th June 1936, for having directed a clandestine theological school in Moscow.
48. Peter Poliansky, Metropolitan of Krutitsy, *locum tenens* of the Patriarch, died in deportation in December 1936.
49. Constantine Diakov, member of the temporary Patriarchal Synod, Archbishop of Kharkov from 1923 to 1935, Metropolitan of Kiev and last Exarch of the Ukraine before the war, shot in October 1937.
50. Parthenus, Bishop of Ananiev, martyred in 1937.
51. Maximus, Bishop of Polon, shot in Jitomir in 1937.

52. Macarius, Bishop of Uman, shot in Jitomir in 1937.
53. George Deliev, Bishop of Ekaterinoslav, *idem.*
54. Philaret Lintchevsky, Bishop of Jitomir, *idem.*
55. Leo Cherepanov, shot in 1937.
56. Procopius Titov, Bishop of Kherson, shot in Jitomir in 1937.
57. Juvenal Maslovsky, Archbishop of Kursk, then of Riazan, *idem.*
58. Gleb Pokrovsky, Archbishop of Perm, *idem.*
59. Ignatius Sadkovsky, Bishop of Belev, *idem.*
60. Mitrophan Grinev, Bishop of Aksai, *idem.*
61. Paul Vvedensky, Bishop of Melekess, *idem.*
62. Seraphim Protopopov, Archbishop of Baku, *idem.*
63. Sophronius Arefeev, Bishop of Yakutia, *idem.*
64. Cyprian Soloviev, Bishop of Semipalatinsk, then of Viatka, *idem.*
    The last nine bishops in this list had been deported to the Solovki
    Islands as early as 1923.
65. Pachomius Kedrov, Bishop of Chernigov, shot in 1937.
66. Avercius Kedrov, brother of the above, Bishop of Zhitomir, shot
    in 1937.
67. Amphilocius, Vicar of the Yenissey region (Josephite schism), shot
    in 1937.
68. Stephen Zismerovsky, Archbishop of Vologda, *idem.*
69. Gurii Stepanov, Archbishop of Alatyr, imprisoned since 1918, shot
    in 1937.
70. Seraphim Alexandrov, Archbishop of Tver, member of the
    temporary Patriarchal Synod, shot in 1937.
71. Nicholas Dobronravov, Archbishop, *idem.*
72. Innocent Nikiforov, Archbishop of Klin, then of Orel, *idem.*
73. Theophanus Elansky, Vicar of the diocese of Nijni-Novgorod,
    shot in 1937.
74. Ambrosius Libinsky, Vicar of the diocese of Petrograd, *idem.*
75. Alexis Bui (Josephite schism), *idem.*
76. Raphael (Gumilev?), *idem.*
77. Tikhon Sharapov, *idem.*
78. Taras Khorov, *idem.*
79. Job (Rogozhin?), *idem.*
80. Anthony, *idem.*
81. Josaphat, *idem.*
82. Thaddeus, Archbishop of Kalinin, died in prison in 1937.
83. Anatole Grisiuk, Metropolitan of Odessa, member of the tem-

porary Patriarchal Synod, arrested for the second time 27th July 1936, died in deportation in the Far North 10th February 1938. In 1941, many thousands of believers gathered for a service celebrated in his memory in Odessa.

84. Boris Shipulin, Bishop of Kamenets-Podolsk, shot in 1938.
85. Benedict Plotnikov, Bishop of Kronstadt, condemned to death in 1922 and reprieved, appointed to the see of Novgorod in 1935 and to that of Kazan in 1936, shot in 1938.
86. Joseph Petrovykh, Metropolitan of Leningrad, head of the opposition group of the Right, shot in 1938.
87. Dimitry Liubimov, Archbishop of Gdovsk (Josephite schism).
88. Pitirim Krylov, Archbishop of Dimitrov, shot in 1938.
89. Nikon Purlevsky, Bishop of Belgorod, brother of Bishop Photius, (cf. No. 37), shot in 1938.
90. Nikon Lebedev, *idem*.
91. Hilarion Belsky, Vicar of the diocese of Smolensk (Josephite schism), shot in 1938.
92. Alexander Petrovsky, Archbishop of Kharkov, died in prison in 1939.
93. Methodius, Archbishop of the Far East, then of Piatigorsk, shot in 1939.
94. Eutychius, *idem*.
95. Eugene Zernov, Archbishop of the Amur region, deported to the Solovki Islands, then appointed to the see of Kotelnikovo and then that of Nijni-Novgorod, arrested in 1937 and disappeared.
96. Theophilus Bogoiavlensky, Archbishop of Kuban, disappeared in about 1932.
97. Nicholas, Bishop and Vicar of the diocese of Tsaritsyn, arrested in 1933. Disappeared.
98. Paul Kratirov, Bishop of Novo-Moskva, arrested *circa* 1935. Disappeared.
99. Paulinus Kroshechkin, Bishop of Rilsk, arrested in 1927. Disappeared.
100. Seraphim, Archbishop of Smolensk, arrested in 1936. Disappeared.
101. Peter Shibkov, Archbishop of Samara, arrested in 1937. Disappeared.
102. Arkadii Ostalsky, vicar of the diocese of Poltava, disappeared in 1937.

103. Cyril Smirnov, Metropolitan of Kazan, died in deportation *circa* 1938 (member of opposition group).
104. Josaphat Udalov, Bishop of Chistopol, arrested for the last time in 1937. Disappeared. (Josephite schism.)
105. Seraphim Samoilovitch, Archbishop of Uglitch, died in deportation *circa* 1935. (Josephite schism.)
106. Victor Ostrogradsky, Bishop of Glasov, disappeared *circa* 1933. (Josephite schism.)
107. Onuphrius Gagaliuk, Bishop of Kursk, disappeared in 1938.
108. Nicodemus Krotkov, Bishop of Simferopol, arrested for the last time in 1936 and deported to Kadalachka where he probably died.
109. Theodosius, Bishop of Poltava, arrested in 1938. Disappeared.
110. John Bulin, Bishop of Pechory, arrested in 1941. Disappeared.
111. Damascinus Maliuta, Bishop of Kamenets-Podolsk, arrested in 1944. Disappeared.
112. Seraphim Kushneruk, Bishop of Kherson, arrested in 1944, disappeared.
113. Pancratius, Bishop of Kursk, *idem.*
114. Anthony Martsenko, Archbishop of Tula, arrested in 1949, disappeared.
There is no information available, however, about the fate of the following bishops:
115. Chrysogonius Ivanovsky, consecrated Bishop of Iuriev in 1930.
116. Sergius Vasiliev, consecrated Bishop of Demian in 1932.
117. Joanicius Popov, consecrated Bishop of Kamyshin in 1932.
118. Alexander Toropov, consecrated Bishop of Kinechma in 1932.
119. Viacheslav, consecrated Bishop of Novgorod-Volynsk in 1932.
120. Benjamin Ivanov, consecrated Bishop of Stavropol in 1933.
121. Theodosius Kirik, consecrated Bishop of Nikolaev in 1933.
122. John Shirokov, Bishop of Volokolamsk.
123. Onisim, Bishop of Tula.
124. Vassian Piatnitsky, Bishop of Tambov.
125. Nicetas, Bishop of Borovichi.
126. Alexander Shchukin, Archbishop of Orel.
127. Nicholas Pokrovsky, Bishop of Polotsk-Vitebsk.
128. Dimitri Dobroserdov, Bishop of Kostroma.
129. Vassian Veretennikov, of Satkinsk.
130. Uarius, Bishop of Lipetsk. Etc.

PRESENT DAY SITUATION AND FORMATION
OF RUSSIAN ÉMIGRÉ CHURCHES

In May 1919, a central organization at Stavropol was established to administer the dioceses cut off from Moscow by the civil war. The status of this organization was later recognized by Patriarch Tikhon who, by a decree of 20th November 1920, conferred upon it supreme authority within the territories controlled by the Whites until such time as normal relations could be re-established with Moscow. The retreat of the White Armies and later their evacuation led this Administrative Centre of the Church to Novocherkask in the Crimea, then to Constantinople and finally to Yugoslavia where it was given asylum by the Patriarch of Serbia at Sermtsy-Karlovtsy.

More than two million Russians had left their country. The Supreme Administrative Authority of the Church which in 1921 counted thirty-four bishops presided over by the Metropolitan of Kiev (Mgr Antony Khrapovitsky), had to deal with the difficult problem of the religious organization of this shifting mass of émigrés, as well as of the émigrés who, for economic reasons, had settled in America before the revolution, and of the churches in mission countries.

To do so, the Russian Church abroad was divided into four regions: America, to which was delegated Metropolitan Platon Rozhyestvensky; the Far East (with its flourishing mission churches in Korea and in China, and to which the White Armies withdrew from Siberia) where the bishops appointed before the revolution kept their sees; Western Europe (in which the old consular chapels were able to supply the religious needs of the émigrés) where Archbishop Eulogius Georgievsky a former deputy of the Duma and member of the first Patriarchal Synod – an eminent, aesthetic and enlightened priest – was put in charge; and Eastern Europe (Balkan countries) administered directly by Mgr Antony Khrapovitsky.

Appendix IV

Two factors led to the break-up of this Supreme Authority: the renewal of semi-normal relations with Moscow, and the political passions which divided the émigrés. Mgr Eulogius was not content to accept the decision of the Supreme Authority and requested that his appointment to Western Europe be confirmed by Patriarch Tikhon (before the revolution the Church in Western Europe came under the Metropolitan of Petersburg). The Patriarch and the Holy Synod agreed to his request in a decree dated 8th April 1921. A few months later they provided him with a further proof of their confidence by raising him to the dignity of Metropolitan. (30th January 1922.)

In autumn 1921, the Supreme Administration of the Church called a general council which, by a two-thirds majority, adopted a resolution demanding the restoration of the monarchy and the re-establishment of the Romanov dynasty. The minority, which refused to support a political resolution of this nature, included thirty-four delegates, among them Mgr Eulogius, Mgr Anastasius Gribanovsky and Mgr Benjamin Fedchenkov.

The resolution, sent to the Geneva Conference, had unfortunate effects upon the Church in Russia. It may have influenced the fate of Mgr Benjamin and of Patriarch Tikhon . . . the latter was forced to dissolve the Supreme Administration in April 1922 and, in May of the same year, to put Mgr Eulogius in charge of all the parishes abroad.

The Supreme Administration was not prepared fully to accept the Patriarchal decrees: it dissolved itself but only to revive in the form of a Bishops' Synod, and refused to regard Mgr Eulogius as its canonical head (1st September 1922). Conflict inevitably followed. On the strength of the decree, Mgr Eulogius tried, somewhat tentatively, to extend his powers, while the Synod at Karlovtsy was doing its violent utmost to reduce them. The crisis came in 1926. On 21st January 1927, the Synod at Karlovtsy decided to depose Mgr Eulogius. This was the final breach: two parallel jurisdictions were established in Europe.

The Russian Church in America rejected the authority of the Synod at Karlovtsy and proclaimed its own complete autonomy.

Mgr Sergius, *locum tenens* of the Patriarchal throne, was secretly approached and asked to intervene. He would not do so and, in a confidential letter to the émigré bishops, advised them not to appeal to the Moscow Patriarchate to settle their differences. Since it had been clearly impossible to create a Central Administration recognized by all, he suggested that the émigrés place themselves under the jurisdiction of the local Orthodox Churches, or form their own independent communities in non-orthodox countries. The publication of this private letter is said to have been one of the reasons for the arrest of Mgr Sergius.

In 1927, when the Patriarchal Church was given legal status, it fell to Mgr Sergius to demand a written declaration of loyalty to the Soviet government from each émigré priest individually. To avoid an open breach with the Patriarchal Church, Mgr Eulogius submitted to this absurd demand but made it clear that by 'loyalty' he meant only strict political neutrality.

At the beginning of 1930, Mgr Eulogius agreed to participate in a great prayer meeting organized at Westminster by the Primate of the Anglican Church in order to protest against the persecution of the Church in the USSR. In the eyes of Moscow, this was a political crime. Mgr Sergius had, by order of the Soviet authorities, just issued a declaration denying that any persecution was taking place, and he ordered Mgr Eulogius to make his *mea culpa* and undertake never again to take part in any such meetings.

Mgr Eulogius felt he could not give way on this point. On 20th November 1930, he was stripped of his rank and placed under an interdict. He appealed for arbitration to the Ecumenical Patriarch. By a *tomos* of 17th February 1931, his H.B., Photius VII, took Mgr Eulogius and his diocese under his own jurisdiction, and conferred upon him the rank of Exarch for all Russian parishes in Western Europe, with the right to retain all the statutes and privileges of the Russian Church. Nevertheless, two bishops, Mgr Eleutherius, Metropolitan of Lithuania, and Mgr Benjamin Fedchenkov, and a few priests, refused to follow Mgr Eulogius and remained unconditionally faithful to Moscow. Thus three independent and sometimes mutually hostile jurisdictions were established in Europe:

1. The Jurisdiction of the Synod (or of Karlovtsy) definitely right wing, holding authoritarian views on matters of doctrine, and monarchist ones in policies. Since the death of Mgr Khrapovitsky in 1936, its head has been Mgr Anastasius Gribanovsky – hence the name 'Anastasian' sometimes applied to it.

2. Jurisdiction of the Ecumenical Patriarch (or Eulogian Jursidiction), apolitical and doctrinally broad-minded. It was within this Jurisdiction that the Theological Institute of St Sergius was able to develop, with its remarkable group of theologians, as well as the Christian Action of

Russian students – a useful movement of lay Christian action. Initiated and directed by Mgr Eulogius, these two organizations pioneered the participation of Orthodox Christians in the Ecumenical movement.

3. Moscow Jurisdiction, nationalist and *ipso facto* tending to be pro-Soviet, doctrinally rather conservative.

The following changes were brought about by the war of 1939:

1. The Bishops' Synod had to withdraw from Karlovtsy to Munich and thence to New York. It lost many of its earlier followers who, in 1945, transferred their allegiance with bewildering ease to the Patriarchate of Moscow (all Far-Eastern bishops, the Archbishop of Peking, Mgr Victor Svyatin, the Metropolitan of Paris, Mgr Serafim Lukyanov, Mgr Serafim Sobolev of Bulgaria, etc.) but in return attracted to itself much of the new emigration made up of several hundred thousand prisoners of war, deportees or merely fugitives who, despite the forced repatriation provided for under the Yalta agreement, had managed to remain outside the USSR. Most of these new émigrés left Europe and settled mainly in South America and Australia. Still headed by Mgr Anastasius, now almost ninety, the Synodal Church now has ramifications in four continents.

Invoking the authority of Patriarch Tikhon's decree of 1920, it maintains its autonomy. Passionately anti-communist, accusing other Orthodox churches of committing apostasy by maintaining relations with the Moscow Patriarchate, it tends more and more towards the tradition of the Russian Old-Believers. Its canonical legitimacy is doubted by several Orthodox churches.

2. In 1945, Mgr Eulogius, believing that relations with Moscow would now become normal, decided to lead his diocese back into the fold. But after his death in August 1946, the majority of clergy and laymen, led by Mgr Vladimir Tikhonitsky, reversed this decision and reaffirmed their connection with the Ecumenical Patriarchate.

The Moscow Patriarchate ceaselessly brought pressure on the Ecumenical Patriarchate to make it give up the Russian Exarchate. After many years of resistance, the Ecumenical Patriarch finally gave in and, in November 1965, unilaterally ended the existence of the Exarchate, which then became an independent entity – the Archbishopric of France and Western Europe and of Russian churches in exile.

3. In 1946, the refusal of some to accept the jurisdiction of the Ecumenical Patriarch naturally strengthened the Moscow Jurisdiction.

But it controls only some ten parishes in Western Europe. It receives substantial material aid from the Moscow Patriarchate.

4. During the war, the Russian Church in America recognized Patriarch Sergius, but at the Council of Cleveland in 1946, made its obedience to Moscow conditional upon the granting to it of a large measure of independence. Moscow having refused, it declared itself autonomous *de facto*, in the hope of creating a unified American Church which would include all the national Orthodox Churches represented in America. This Metropolitan American Church, as it calls itself, is much the largest and most active of those in America. The multi-national seminary of St Vladimir, and the Churches of Japan and of Alaska are under its jurisdiction. In most of its parishes, the services are in English.

The Synod is its rival but has little future, given its specifically Russian character, the Moscow Jurisdiction is much the smallest of the three.

APPENDIX V

TWO MOSCOW PRIESTS PROTEST AGAINST SOVIET HARASSMENT OF ORTHODOX CHURCH

To the Chairman of the Presidium of the Supreme Soviet of the Union of Soviet Socialist Republics, Comrade N. V. Podgorny

from: Citizens of the USSR:

> N. I. Eshliman *(priest)*
> *Ul. Pushkinskaya, 4/2 apt. 10*
> *Moscow, K–25.*

> G. P. Yakunin *(priest)*
> *Ul. Zhukovskovo, 7 apt. 13*
> *Moscow K–62.*

DECLARATION

We have forwarded identical declarations to the Chairman of the Soviet of Ministers of the USSR, Comrade A. P. Kosygin, and to the State Prosecutor of the USSR, Comrade R. A. Rudenko.

Comrade Chairman of the Presidium of the Supreme Soviet of the Union of Soviet Socialist Republics!

As citizens of the Soviet Union, we address you in protest against the illegal actions of the leaders and representatives of the Council on the Affairs of the Russian Orthodox Church of the Council of Ministers of the USSR. These actions flagrantly violate the principle of socialist law and the basic legislation of the Soviet Government regulating relations between the Soviet State and the Church.

It is well known that on 23rd January 1918, the Soviet government published the decree, 'On Separation of Church and State, and Schools from Church,' in which the fact of the independent existence of the Orthodox Church in our country is recognized. It is also well known that Article 124 of the Constitution of the USSR grants all citizens of the Soviet Union freedom of worship.

Besides these basic legislative documents defining the relations between the Soviet State and the Church, the decree from the All Russian Central Executive Committee and the Council of People's Commissars, 'On Religious Associations', dated 18th April 1929, is effective in our country to this day. This decree is a document that at the present time regulates relations between the Soviet State and religious organizations.[1]

In order to control the observances of laws determining relations between the State and the Church, and for mediation between Church and State in civil matters, the Soviet Government established a department: the Council on the Affairs of the Russian Orthodox Church.

Nevertheless, during the period 1957–64, under personal pressure from Kruschev, who permitted 'subjectivism and administrationism in the leadership', which was finally condemned by the Communist Party of the USSR, the Soviet Government and by all Soviet society, the council radically changed its function: from that of an official organ of arbitration to that of an unofficial and illegal organ of control over the Moscow Patriarchate.

Thus, the intrusion of the leaders and representatives of the council in the inner life of the Church took on forms which must be regarded as a flagrant violation of the very principles of socialist law and Soviet legislation relative to religion and the Church.

The *very method* of using unofficial verbal orders, which the leaders and representatives of the council chose as a means of systematic interference in the inner life of the Orthodox Church, is a violation of the principles of law.

The *actions* of the leaders and representatives of the council, which have been implemented by the above method, are violations of Soviet legislation on religion and the Church.

1. *Illegal registration of the clergy, as a means of interference in their posting* According to Soviet legislation a 'religious society may begin its activities only after registration' with the local authorities.

A registered religious society is obliged to inform the registering

[1] 'Kommunisticheskaya partiya i Sovetskoye pravitelstvo o religii i tserkvi,' Gospolitizdat, 1959, p. 116.

Appendix V

authority of the composition of its membership, of the staff of its executive and auditing bodies, and of its officiating clergy. The registering body have the right to remove individuals from the membership of the *executive body* of the religious society ('On Religious Associations', par. 2, 4, 8, 14).

By granting the right to remove individuals from the membership of the executive body of religious societies, Soviet law in no case grants civil authorities the right to remove clergymen when they are assigned or transferred.

It is clear that the law for registering clergy is in no way a sanctioning act, but only a *formalization (fiksiruiushchim)*.

Nevertheless, contrary to the law, representatives of the council have usurped the right to remove clergy, thus transforming the registration of clergy from a formal act to a sanctioning act.

By means of this juggling, the leaders and representatives of the council have established a practice in the Russian Church which has made it impossible to ordain, assign or transfer clergy without first obtaining *the verbal consent of the leaders or representatives* of the council on whom their registration depends.

Furthermore, the representatives of the council have widely employed the illegal practice of revoking, or threatening to revoke, the registration of the members of the clergy as a means of bringing administrative pressure on the Russian Orthodox Church.

The interference of officials of the council in the assignment and transfer of clergy, which involves a flagrant distortion of the principle of registration, has become a scandalous violation of the decree 'On Separation of Church and State', Article 124 of the Constitution of the USSR and of the decree, 'On Religious Associations'.

Moreover, the interference of the leaders and representatives of the council in the assigning and transferring of clergy is also a flagrant violation of the principle of socialist justice, for this interference is brought about by means of unofficial verbal orders.

2. *The illegal campaign of the mass closing of churches and monasteries, and the illegal liquidation of religious societies*

In accordance with the present Soviet law, every officially registered religious society has the right to obtain free of charge the use of a church building from the government, or to rent private or State-owned premises for its religious needs ('On Religious Associations', par. 10).

Appendix V

The rights of a religious community to the use of the church building, or leased premises, are protected by law: the transfer of a church building which is being used free of charge by a religious community to some other use (liquidation of the place of prayer) is permitted only by a reasoned decision initiated by the local government organizations at a level not lower than the Oblispolkom (Regional Executive Committee). If the members of the religious community, within a period of two weeks after being notified of this decision, appeal against it to the Presidium of the Supreme Soviet of the USSR, then the entire dossier concerning it is sent to the Presidium of the Supreme Soviet of the USSR. The contract with the believers only becomes void, and the building is only withdrawn from their use, after the Presidium of the Supreme Soviet of the USSR has ratified the decision of the local authority ('On Religious Associations', par. 36–7).

In contrast to the procedure for liquidating a place of prayer used free of charge, rented premises can only be legally taken away from the religious community before expiration of the contract by applying to a court of law ('On Religious Associations', par. 38).

The liquidation of a place of prayer *in no way signifies the dispersion of the religious community*, for according to the law, after the said liquidation has taken place, the religious community has the right to keep the objects of the cult ('icons, vestments, banners, covers, etc.') and transferable property ('money, as well as incense, candles, oil, wine, wax, firewood and coal') ('On Religious Associations', par. 40, items C and E).

The law also provides for the possibility of the building by the community of a new religious edifice ('On Religious Associations', par. 45), and in no way denies the religious community the right to acquire without charge or to lease another place of prayer in exchange for the one that has been liquidated. This right is envisaged in paragraph 10 of the decree, 'On Religious Associations'.

Such are the provisions of Soviet law in respect to the rights of a religious community to use a place of prayer.

Nevertheless, contrary to the law, these rights have been flagrantly violated.

It is well known that in our country, during the period 1961–4, and under the personal initiative of N. Kruschev, an active campaign was conducted for the massive closing of Orthodox churches.

No less than ten thousand churches and dozens of monasteries were closed during this campaign, among which was the most ancient sacred place of the Russian people – the Kiev Caves Monastery.

In practice the mass closing of churches was carried out by local government bodies by means of administrative measures, without observing the procedures envisaged in the law, and in an overwhelming majority of instances, even without any 'state or social necessity' which, according to the law, is the only reason for which a place of prayer may be closed ('On Religious Associations', par. 35).

The leaders and representatives of the Council on the Affairs of the Russian Orthodox Church, called upon to ensure the strict observance of the Soviet legislation 'On Religion and Church', not only failed to fulfil their obligations to assure the observance of the law, but they themselves actively participated in illegal acts violating the decree, 'On Separation of Church and State', Article 124 of the Constitution of the USSR and the decree, 'On Religious Associations'.

Thus, the representatives of the council, by means of 'administrative pressure', tried to get the agreement of the ruling bishops to abolish those parishes in which churches had been closed, and either to transfer the clergy to other parishes, or to retire them.

In this way the leaders and representatives of the council taking advantage of the canons of the Orthodox Church, according to which it is impossible for an Orthodox community to exist without an Orthodox priest at its head, in practice *transformed the closing of a church into the liquidation of a parish.*

In this way the authorities of the Council on the Affairs of the Russian Orthodox Church directly and actively participated in this anti-democratic campaign, depriving millions of believing citizens of the Union of Soviet Socialist Republics of their legal rights.

On the basis of the events described above it should be emphasized that the campaign for the mass closing of Orthodox churches was an open demonstration of contempt for the law based on a subjective and arbitrary interpretation of Soviet legislation, and a denial of the freedom of religious worship envisaged by the Constitution of the USSR.

Moreover, we consider it our civic duty to call your attention to the undeniable fact that the actively promoted campaign of mass closure of churches created an atmosphere of an anti-religious fanaticism which led to the barbarous destruction of a large number of irreplaceable works of art.

Appendix V

3. *The illegal registration of baptisms and of other religious rites, which in practice amounts to the registration of the religious affiliation of Soviet citizens, although this is forbidden by the Soviet Government*

Article 124 of the Constitution of the USSR guarantees citizens of the USSR freedom of conscience and recognizes the freedom of all citizens to participate in religious worship.

From this it follows that every citizen of the Soviet Union has the right to confess any religious conviction and to participate freely in the practice of the cult.

However, the leaders and representatives of the council called upon to ensure the strict observance of State laws concerning the Church and religion themselves have flagrantly violated the freedom of conscience guaranteed by the constitution.

During recent years the authorities of the council have imposed on the Russian Church a 'system' under which sacraments of baptism and matrimony can be performed only after prior and obligatory registration.

Every citizen of the USSR who wishes to be baptized, or to be married in the church, or to baptize his children, must first present his identification papers and (depending on the sacrament) his marriage certificate or birth certificate to the representative of the church council, who registers the documents on the form authorized by the representative of the council. The number of the person's identification card, surname, name and patronymic and home address are recorded, and attested to by the owner of the documents. Other religious rites are also subject to registration: anointing, communion of the sick at home, and religious funerals.

These registration forms are carefully scrutinized and noted by representatives of the local government authorities.

Ultimately, the information received in this way is used, under the guise of anti-religious propaganda, for discrimination against citizens who have exercised their right to religious freedom as envisaged by the Constitution of the USSR. Until recently, such citizens were 'worked over' at their place of work or at school, and subjected to 'administrative pressure'. They were the object of offensive caricatures, and their names appeared in the Press with unflattering comments, etc.

Still today anti-religious zealots continue to use the registration of religious rites for administrative intervention in the private religious lives of citizens.[1]

[1] 'Sovetskaya Rossiya,' August 12 1965, 'Vokrug kupeli.'

Appendix V

Thus, the practice of registering religious rites established by the leaders and representatives of the council serves as an instrument of discrimination in violation of the sacred principle of freedom of conscience, recognized and guaranteed by Article 124 of the Constitution of the USSR.

Moreover, the illegal practice of registering religious rites is a violation of the decree 'On Separation of Church and State', which, with the intention of guaranteeing freedom of conscience, emphasizes in particular the elimination 'from all official documents of any indication of religious affiliation', while the 'system' of registering religious rites, contrary to the decree, *in fact brings about the illegal documentation (fiksirovanie) of religious affiliation of USSR citizens.*

All this illegal practice of documenting citizens' religious affiliation, with discriminatory intentions, has been established by authorities of the Council on the Affairs of the Russian Orthodox Church by means of unofficial verbal orders to the executive organs of religious societies. Moreover, representatives of the council compel church councils to break the law, since, in accordance with Soviet law, the representative of the church council is a private individual and does not have the right to verify, and much less to register, such documents.

Clearly aware of the illegality of their actions and of the unpleasant consequences of possible lawful protests, the representatives of the council categorically refuse to confirm in writing their instructions concerning the method and form of registering religious rites. At the same time, the representatives of the council demand unconditional fulfilment of these instructions by removing from the ranks of the executive organs of church councils those persons who, not wishing to break the clearly defined Soviet law, refuse to obey verbal instructions.

Thus, in this case, the representatives of the council not only flout the principle of socialist justice and of Soviet legislation on religion and the Church, but also force Soviet citizens to do so by illegally making use of their official positions.

4. *The illegal restriction on the freedom of practising a religious cult*
Article 124 of the Constitution of the USSR grants all citizens the freedom of religious worship.

According to the decree presently effective, 'On Religious Associations', the celebration of church services is permitted both in and outside the church. The celebration of a service outside a church is permitted under the following conditions: for the celebration of a service in the open, if it is not an integral part of a service held in the church, a special permit from the local authority is needed; for the celebration of a service connected with a burial, no special permit is needed ('On Religious Associations', par. 58–61).

In respect to services performed in the homes of believers, Soviet law, naturally, has not established any restrictions. Up to recent times, in accordance with the law, the clergy of the Russian Church had the right to freely perform requiems (*panikhidas*) at cemeteries, as well as all other religious rites in the homes of believers.

In 1961 leaders and representatives of the council, in violation of the existing legislation, restricted the freedom of practising religious rites. Thus, for example, in the Moscow eparchy (diocese), during a specially organized re-registration of the clergy in 1961–2, verbal orders were given to all priests to the effect that rites performed at home, such as prayers, blessings of houses, parastases, burials and requiems (*panikhidas*), and also requiems (*panikhidas*) at cemeteries, be performed in each individual case only with the written permission of local authority (which in practice is almost never given). Moreover Trushin, a representative of the Council in Moscow and the Moscow region, gave priests their registration documents only after they had signed an undertaking to the effect that they would abide by this regulation.

The authorities of the council in the instance again flagrantly violated Article 124 of the Constitution of the USSR and the decree of the All Russian Central Executive Committee and the Council of People's Commissars, 'On Religious Associations', by illegally limiting the freedom of practising a religious rite.

5. Violation of the principle of freedom of conscience in respect to children
Without question, the principle of freedom of conscience proclaimed by the Constitution of the USSR applies also to children. There is not a single paragraph in Soviet legislation that forbids, or even restricts, the participation of children in the life of the Church. At the same time, the decree, 'On Separation of Church and State', which separates the schools from the Church, permits all citizens 'privately to teach and study religion' (Decree, par. 9).

Nevertheless, during recent times, the authorities of the council, violating the principle of separation of Church and State by means of interfering in the internal life of the Church, established a practice of forcibly keeping children out of Church life. Thus, during recent years, representatives of the council, by means of verbal instructions to bishops, pastors of churches and church wardens, forbade any participation of children and young people in religious worship. In some eparchies (dioceses), the violating of the principle of freedom of conscience in respect to children went so far that representatives of the council tried to prohibit children from taking communion, thus openly flouting the religious feelings of believing citizens.

Finally, and undoubtedly with the knowledge of the authorities of the council, in recent years a mass campaign was conducted in our country forcibly to keep Christian youth from entering churches at the time of the great church feasts.

6. *Violation of the principle of separation of Church and State by means o, administrative interference in the financial life of the church community*
According to the State's legislation, houses of prayer (churches) and objects used for worship are nationalized and are handed over to church communities on a contractual basis; but the financial assets of a community are not nationalized and are in no way within the competence of local authority (decree 'On Separation of Church and State' and the decree 'On Religious Associations', par. 55–6). Nevertheless, in violation of Soviet law, in 1961–2 representatives of the council obliged the executive bodies of church communities to give an account of their finances to the local authorities (Raiispokom: Regional Executive Committee) and to permit the representatives of the local authorities to investigate the financial state of the community without interference.

In practice, this has reached the point where representatives of the local authorities have assumed the role of managers of the church communities, flagrantly interfering in all aspects of the administrative-economic life of the Church. This is a scandalous violation of the decree, 'On Separation of Church and State', and Article 124 of the Constitution of the USSR and justly arouses the dissatisfaction of the believers.

7. *The illegal limitation of the number of members of a religious society to 'The Twenty (Dvadtsatka)' and the actual denial to the wide masses of believers of their legal right to participate in managing the administrative-economic life of the Russian Orthodox Church*
According to Soviet law, a religious society is recognized as a com-

munity of believers made up of *no less* than twenty adult citizens of the USSR. *The numerical growth of a religious society is not limited by law.* All local residents of the same faith *have the right* to become members of a religious society at any time after its founding, and to sign the contract which affords them the use of the building and of the objects used in the rites, 'obtaining, in this way, the equal right to manage the property with those persons who first signed the contract' ('On Religious Associations', par. 3, 31).

Such are the provisions of the law. The directors of the council, however, do not abide by these provisions. Representatives of the council, by means of administrative pressure on the executive organs of the communities, systematically limit the size of religious societies to from twenty to thirty members. In some instances they even pevent raising the number of members of a religious society to the minimum norm envisaged by the law.

Thus, the representatives of the council transformed the religious society previously quantitatively unlimited by law into a closed group (of twenty persons), depriving in this way masses of believing citizens of their legal right to participate in the management of the administrative-economic life of the parishes of the Orthodox Church. This has in fact led to a complete change in the structure of a religious society as established by law.

It should be emphasized that here again we are faced with a worthless substitution for the direct meaning of the legislation: according to the decree, 'On Religious Associations', a religious society is comprised of full and equal members who have signed the contract for acquiring the use of the building and the property of the cult, and of an executive organ elected by them at a general meeting. In contrast to this system, the representatives of the council burdened the parishes of the Russian Church with a structure in which is established an organ not envisaged by the law, the 'Twenty', as a substitute for the religious society and which deprives hundreds, and sometimes even thousands, of parishioners of their legal right to participate in the management of the administrative-economic life of the religious society, as well as to participate in the electing of its executive organ.

As a result, because of the illegal efforts of the representatives of the council, the overwhelming majority of believing citizens have been placed, in respect to religious societies, in the category of the 'deprived'.

Appendix V

A question naturally arises: why did the council find it necessary to deprive millions of believing citizens of the Orthodx faith of their legal rights to participate in the management of the administrative- economic life of the Russian Church?

8. *The illegal limiting of the staff of clergy, inhibiting the performing of religious rites*

In accordance with the principle of separation of Church and State, Soviet law in no way regulates the staffing of clergy, recognizing the church's right to solve this important question of internal ecclesiastical life by itself.

Nevertheless, in this case, the representatives of the council flagrantly violate Soviet law by taking advantage of the 'right' that it illegally acquired to remove clergy – transforming the registration of clergy from a formal act into a sanctioning act (see the first section) – and systematically diminishing the staff of clergy of the Russian Orthodox Church.

Consequently, a priest of the Russian Orthodox Church becomes physically unable properly to satisfy the religious needs of the multi-million mass of believing citizens. Here it is appropriate to note that at a time when the parishes of the Russian Orthodox Church severely need priests, many hundreds of priests have been retired as a result of the action of the representatives of the council. Thus, in such instances, the authorities from the council (1) violate the law on the separation of Church and State, and (2) illegally hamper the performing of religious rites.

SUMMARY

To summarize: the officials of the Council on the Affairs of the Russian Orthodox Church attached to the Council of Ministers of the USSR, rudely breaking Soviet legislation on religion and the Church, have:

1. Assumed for themselves the 'right' to remove priests, changing the registration of clergy from a formal act to a sanctioning act.

2. Assisted in the mass closing of Orthodox churches and monasteries by the illegal administrative anti-democratic methods initiated by Kruschev and, further, contrary to law, have in practice transformed the closing of places of worship into the liquidation of religious associations (parishes).

3. Have imposed on the Executive organs of religious associations an illegal system of registration of baptisms and other church rites, in violating Par. 3 of the decree, 'On Separation of Church and State', and in practice introducing the registration of the religious adherence of citizens of the USSR.

4. Illegally hindered the free exercise of religious worship, by forbidding priests to conduct church ceremonies in homes (except Holy Communion and Unction for the Sick) or requiems at cemeteries, without written permits from the local authorities in each specific instance.

5. Broken the principle of freedom of conscience in regard to children.

6. Illegally limited the number of members of religious associations to the 'Twenty', in practice deprived millions of believing citizens of the Orthodox faith from using their legal right to participate in the administrative and financial life of the Russian Church.

7. Illegally assumed the 'right' to restrict the size of the staff of priests of a religious association, thereby interfering in the internal life of the church.

All of these acts constitute an infraction of the decree 'On Separation of Church and State', Article 124 of the Constitution of the USSR and the Resolutions of the All Union Central Executive Committee and the Council of People's Commissars, 'On Religious Associations', and in most cases illegally hinder the celebration of religious rites.

Thus the leaders and representatives of the Council on the Affairs of the Russian Orthodox Church, by radically disturbing the lawful functions of the council, have transformed it into an overtly discriminating body, whose entire activity is directed towards the systematic abuse of the laws of separation of Church and State and of school from Church, and the systematic prevention of the conduct of religious rites, which is a criminally punishable act according to Articles 142 and 143 of the Civil Code of the RSFSR.

It is not surprising that in order to carry out their illegal activities the representatives of the council have chosen a method contrary to the principles of socialist legality by giving unofficial verbal orders and verbal instructions contrary to law, seeking thereby to hide their illegal activities and to keep clear of responsibility. This effort to keep out of the public view, so characteristic of all illegal activities, was carried so far by the leaders of the Council on the Affairs of the Russian

Orthodox Church that the building which houses its administration has no name plate on it, a small detail, but characteristic.

In this connection, this fact is to be noted, that in 1959 and 1965 there were published two collections of Party and State documents on religion and Church, and in neither the one nor the other is there even mention of the Council on the Affairs of the Russian Orthodox Church attached to the Council of Ministers of the USSR, in spite of its being the body authorized to deal with these questions.

Convincing evidence that the council hinders the carrying out of Soviet legislation on religion and Church, is the fact that, at the wish of the leaders of the council, there is no teaching on this legislation in the theological schools of the Moscow Patriarchate, in particular there is no mention of the law which is of such daily importance for priests as the Resolution of the All Union Central Executive Committee and the Council of People's Commissars, 'On Religious Associations', which gives the detailed juridical development of the Decree of 23rd January 1918.

The illegal practices of the leaders and representatives of the Council on the Affairs of the Russian Orthodox Church, which in violation of the laws on separation of Church and State have placed themselves in the position of unlimited dictators of the Russian Church, systematically abusing the principle of freedom of conscience and hindering the free conduct of religious worship, leads to warranted dissatisfaction of the believing citizens of the USSR, and discredits in the eyes of the broad public the rightful foundations of socialist society, thereby causing great harm to our Fatherland.

The principle of maintaining the solidity of socialist legality demands that the disgusting practice of the leaders and representatives of the Council on the Affairs of the Russian Orthodox Church, being a not yet outgrown inheritance of arbitrariness condemned by the Soviet public, must be definitely disclosed, carefully and comprehensively examined, and legally condemned, and the entire work of the council brought into strict correspondence with State legislation on religion and Church. In this connection it is necessary to restore to the Russian Orthodox Church, which for many years has suffered systematic discrimination on the part of the leaders and representatives of the Council on Affairs of the Russian Orthodox Church, the freedom for religious life which is guaranteed by the constitution. Furthermore, all the churches, monasteries and theological schools which have been illegally closed during the period 1961–4 should justly be returned to the Russian Orthodox Church.

Finally, in view of the fact that the relations between Church and State in principle are not secret, all the activities of the Council on the Affairs of the Russian Orthodox Church should be open to public scrutiny and subject to systematic public control, with the right of representation in that control of members of the Russian Orthodox Church.

On the basis of the above, we earnestly request you to take effective measures for the earliest possible uprooting of illegality and the re-establishment of the legal rights of the millions of believing citizens of the Soviet Union.

December 15th 1965   [*signatures*]

APPENDIX VI

DATA ON THE STATE OF THE CHURCH
IN THE USSR

DOCUMENT A: *Comparative tables showing the numbers of the Orthodox Church laity and clergy and listing the establishments in 1914, 1939, 1957 and 1962.*

DOCUMENT B: *Comparative statistics of believers and practice of religious rites in the rural province of Riazan in 1912, 1939, 1945–59, 1961.*

DOCUMENT C: *List of dioceses and their titular heads.*

DOCUMENT D: *List of churches open for worship in Moscow and Leningrad.*

DOCUMENT E: *List of works published by the press of the Moscow Patriarchate.*

DOCUMENT F: *Addresses of Ecclesiastical academies and seminaries.*

NOTE: The text of the documents listed at the end of Appendix I, Document D in Appendix II, and the contents of the tables listed above, can be found in the revised French edition and also in the German, Italian and Spanish translations; the document in Appendix V was written after these editions appeared and is only in the English edition.

NOTES
INDEX

NOTES

ABBREVIATIONS USED IN THE NOTES

JMP: Journal Moskovskoï Patriarkhii (Review of the Moscow Patriarchate)
NR: Nauka i Religia (Science and Religion)
Kom. Pr.: Komsomolskaïa Pravda
ICI: Informations catholiques internationales
SOEPI: Service œcuménique de presse et d'information

Chapter I

1. Cf. Pierre B. Struve, *Khristianstvo i Slavianstvo* (Christianity and the Slav world) in *Sotsialnaia i Ekonomicheskaia Istoria Rossii*, Paris, 1952, pp. 305–10.
2. G. P. Fedotov, *The Russian Religious Mind,* paperback edition, New York, 1960.
3. N. A. Klepinin, *Alexander Nevsky*, Ymca-Press, s. d. p. 205.
4. V. Kliuchevsky, *Znatchenie prep. Sergia dlia russkogo naroda i gosudarstya* (The significance of St Sergius for the Russian people and State) *Bogoslovsky Vestnik*, XI, 1892. This article was not included in the collected works of the famous historian, published in eight volumes in 1956. Cf. also, N. Zernov, *Saint Sergius, Builder of Russia,* London, 1939.
5. Prince E. Trubetzkoi, *Umozrenie v kraskakh* (A vision of the world expressed in colour), Moscow, 1914. This initial philosophical interpretation of the symbolism of icons might well be translated.
6. Useful details on the canonical position of the Russian Church in history are given in Jean Meyendorff's *L'Église orthodoxe hier et aujourd'hui*, Ed. du Seuil, 1960, pp. 93–101.

7. Cf. Jean Meyendorff, *Une controverse sur le rôle social de l'Église, La querelle des biens ecclésiastiques au XVIe siècle en Russie*, Chevetogne, 1956.

8. G. P. Fedotov, *Sviatye Drevnei Russi* (The saints of ancient Russia), Paris, 1931. A fundamental work and the source of all later studies of Russian sanctity. Cf. by the same author, *Sv. Filip, mitropolit moscovsky*, Paris 1928, p. 227; and *A Treasury of Russian Spirituality*, London, 1950.

9. On the 'Time of Troubles' and the *Raskol*, cf. the basic study by P. Pascal, *Avakum et les débuts du Raskol*, Paris, 1938.

10. On the Hesychast controversy and its ramifications cf. Jean Meyendorff, *Saint Grégoire Palamas et la Mystique orthodoxe*, Ed. du Seuil, 1959, pp. 150–73.

11. The best work on St Seraphim is *Sviatoi Serafim Sarovsky* by V. Iliine, Ymca-Press, Paris, 1930.

12. Cf. N. Struve, 'Église orthodoxe et mission', in *Messager Orthodoxe*, 10, 1960, pp. 2–12.

13. The best description of the religion of the Russian people is by Pierre Pascal in *La Revue de Psychologie des peuples*, 2, 1947, pp. 138–54; 3, 1947, pp. 262–84. An excellent outline of the main trends of Russian thought in the twentieth century, by the same author, is given in *Cahiers du monde russe et soviétique*, 5, 1962. For the development of ideas see also the admirable introduction to Russian culture, *La Russie absente et présente*, by V. Weidlé, Paris, 1949, pp. 237 and following, and the monumental *Histoire de la Philosophie russe* by Basil Zenkovsky 1–2, Paris, 1953–5. For the last period cf. N. Zernov, *The Russian Religious Renaissance*, Longman, 1963.

Chapter II

1. A. Kartashev, 'La Révolution et le Concile de 1917–18,' in *Russie et Chrétienté*, 1–2, 1950, pp. 7–42. The following pages are greatly indebted to this work.

2. A Wuyts s.j., *Le Patriarcat russe au Concile de Moscou de 1917–18*, OCA, No. 129, Rome, 1941, p. 244.

3. Cf. the complete text in Appendix I.

4. Cf. the account of this decree in *Voprosy istorii religii i ateizma*, V. Moscow, 1958 pp., 50–63.

5. Cf. the text of this message in Appendix I.

6. A. Kartashev, *art. cit.*, p. 41.
7. Cf. the text of the decree in Appendix I.
8. There is a French translation of these decrees in C. J. Dumont's 'L'Église orthodoxe russe en face du communisme,' *Économie et Humanisme*, 7–8, 1950, pp. 4–6.
9. Cf. *Novye moucheniki rossiiskii* (The New Russian Martyrs), Jordanville, 1949, pp. 10–24.
10. Circular of 21st February 1918.
11. Cf. the text of this message in Arch. Nikon Rklitsky, *Jizneopisanie blaj. Antonia, mitropolita Kievskago i Galitskago,* New York. 1960, vol. 6, pp. 51–3.
12. The legislative work of the council still awaits its historian.
13. S. Bulgakov has given an account of his ordination and of the prevailing atmosphere of the time in a posthumous work *Autobiograficheskie Zametki* (autobiographical notes), Paris, 1946, pp. 34–43. This thought-provoking book deserves to be translated into a Western language.
14. P. Pascal, *Les grands courants de la pensée mondiale contemporainne, Russie (U.S.S.R.),* II, Milan, 1960, p. 1158.
15. *Novye mucheniki*, etc., op. cit., p. 97.
16. Extracts from this message are given in the collection *Russkaia pravoslavnaia tserkov*, Munich, 1962, pp. 85–6.
17. Cf. the text of this circular in *Voprosy istorii religii i ateizma*, V. Moscow, 1958, pp. 16–20.
18. Cf. the distressing account of these profanations in the collection *O sviatykh moschakh* (On the sacred relics), Moscow 1961, 115 pages.
19. *Rul* (The Helm), 17th August 1923.

Chapter III

1. The English text of the Government's decree is given in W. G. Einhardt's *Religion in Soviet Russia*, London, 1929, p. 46.
2. Cf. the English text of this letter in *The Assault of Heaven*, London, 1924, Appendix I. The Russian text is given in *Russkaia pravoslavnaia tserkov'v SSSR* (The Russian Orthodox Church in USSR), Munich, 1962, pp. 96–7.
3. *Pravda*, No. 70, 1922.
4. ibid., No. 110, 1922.

5. ibid., No. 101, 1922.
6. For further details cf. A. Valentinov, *The Assault of Heaven*, Chapters III and IV.
7. *Izvestia*, 7th May 1922.
8. On the Living Church of S. Troitsky, *Tchto takoe Jivaïa Tserkov* (What is the Living Church?), Warsaw, 1928, p. 82. and R. Stupperich, *Die Lebende Kirche*, in the volume *Kirche im Osten*, Stuttgart, 1960, pp. 72–103.
9. Cf. *The Assault of Heaven*, Chapter XI.
10. The list of bishops deported at this time is given in *The Assault of Heaven*, Appendix 3. Cf. *Pravda*, 5th September 1922; 6th September 1922; 19th October 1922.
11. *Tserkovnye vedomosti*, Nos. 19–20, 1924, pp. 14–15. Information given by Bishop Nicholas Soloveï, a former member of the Living Church.
12. This Council was widely reported in the Soviet press. Cf. *Izvestia*, No. 99, 1923; *Pravda*, Nos. 98–101, 1923. The *Acts* of the Council were published by the State printing press: *Deiania 11 Vserossiiskogo pomestnogo sobora*, Mospolitgraf.
13. The Patriarch's arrest was universally reprobated. Telegrams of protest were sent to Moscow by the various French Churches and religious bodies, headed by Cardinal Louis Dubois, by three Protestant denominations of Great Britain, etc. Lord Curzon, the Foreign Minister of Great Britain, sent what amounted to an ultimatum to the Soviet Government, threatening to break off the semi-diplomatic relations which had just been established between the USSR and England.
14. This confession, signed on 16th June, was published in *Izvestia* on 27th June 1923.
15. Cf. the extracts from the first statement in Appendix. Extracts from the second have been published by J. Dumont in 'L'Église orthodoxe russe en face du communisme,' *Économie et Humanisme*, 7–8, 1950, p. 11.
16. *Novye mucheniki rossiiskie* (New Russian martyrs), Jordanville, 1949, pp. 105–24.
17. *Izvestia*, 15th April 1925, French translation in C. J. Dumont, *art. cit.*, pp. 12–14.
18. Cf. for the most serious criticism of the authenticity of this 'will', V. Vinogradov, *O nekotorykh vajneïchikh momentakh posledniego*

perioda jizni i deiatel'nosti sv. patriarkha Tikhona. (Some important points in the last period of the life and activity of the Patriarch Tikhon), Munich, 1959, pp. 40–57.

19. Cf. the text of the will and the act signed by the fifty-nine bishops who ratified it in *Jisneopisanie blazhenneĭchago Antonia, mitropolita Kievskago i Galitskago*, by Archbishop Nikon Rklitsky, Vol. VI, New York, 1960, pp. 207–8.

20. Cf. the text of this letter, ibid., pp. 209–12.

21. The Acts of this Council were published in *Vestnik Sv. Sinoda Prav. Rossiiskoĭ Tserkvi*, 6, 1925 (the official organ of the 'Renewed Church').

22. Paul B. Anderson, *L'Église et la Nation en Russie Soviétique*, Paris, 1946, p. 102.

23. ibid., p. 103.

24. Michel D'Herbigny, *L'Aspect religieux de Moscou*, Rome, 1926.

25. Cf. the text of this arrangement made by Mgr Peter, 6th October, a few days before his arrest, in Nikon Rklitsky, op. cit., p. 220.

26. Cf. the text of his proposal in Appendix I.

27. Cf. the text of this document in Appendix I.

28. Not unnaturally, this event was not mentioned in any of his official biographies.

29. Cf. the text of his pastoral letter in *Vestnik russkago studentcheskago khristianskago dvigenia*, I, 1927, pp. 28–9.

30. Cf. the description of religious life during this period in the review *Put'* (The Way) No. 2, 1926, pp. 3–12.

31. Cf. the text of this declaration in Appendix I.

32. M. Polsky *Kanonitcheskoe pologenie Vyscheĭ tserkovnoĭ vlasti v SSSR i zagranitseĭ* (The Canonical Position of the Supreme Authority of the Church in the USSR and Abroad), Jordanville, 1948, p. 66.

33. The principal texts giving the views of the various representatives of the opposition have been published in *Novye mucheniki rossiikie*, II, Jordanville, 1957, p. 318 and *passim*.

34. M. Polsky, op. cit., pp. 66–7.

35. For the sake of completeness there should also be mentioned the schism of the 'Gregorians', caused by a misunderstanding which was used to his own advantage by Gregory, Archbishop of Ekaterinenburg. This schism, which was confined to the basin of the Volga, was characteristic of the centrifugal tendencies in the Church.

36. *Rossia*, 9–11th October 1945.

37. Cf. the original text of the decree, which is still in force, in Appendix I.
38. *Bezbojnik* 6th February 1930.
39. *Vestnik Moskovskoï Patriarkhii*, 3, 1931 (decree of 20th February 1929).
40. A vivid account of the closing of the churches, as described in the Soviet press, is given by S. Troitsky, *Pochemu i kak zakryvaiutsia khramy v sovetskoi Rosii* (Why and how the churches in the USSR were closed), Belgrade, 1931, p. 54.
41. *Kom. Pr.*, 31st May 1930.
42. ibid., 8th March 1930.
43. My quotation of these statements is taken from P. Anderson, op. cit., pp. 129–34.
44. For Moscow cf. the inventory drawn up by P. Lev Liperovsky, *Sorok liet spustia* (Forty years after), Paris, 1960.
45. B. Mikorsky, *Razruchenie kulturno-istoricheskikh pamiatnikov v Kieve* (The Destruction of Cultural and Historical Monuments in Kiev from 1934–6), Munich, 1951, p. 22.
46. *Bezbojnik*, 22nd December 1929; 6th January 1930; 10th March 1930; *Vecherniaïa Moskva*, 27th December 1929, etc.
47. B. Pilniak, *Krasnoe Derevo* (Riga, 1929).
48. *Kommunisticheskaïa partia i sovetskoe pravitel'stvo o religii i tserkvi* (Decisions of the Communist Party and the Soviet Government on Religion and the Church), Moscow, 1959, p. 96.
49. *Izvestia*, 5th April 1923.
50. *Pravda*, 30th May 1923.
51. ibid., 4th May 1923.
52. ibid., 11th April 1923.
53. P. B. Anderson, op. cit., pp. 139–41.
54. A. Kishchkowsky, *Die sowjetische Religionspolitik und die Russische Orthodoxe Kirche,* Munich, 1957, p. 62.
55. An unpublished document.
56. N. Timasheff, *Religion in Soviet Russia*, London, 1943, p. 65.
57. *Materialy XXII s'ezda knss*, Moscow, 1961, p. 250.
58. Cf. the religious chronicle given in *Irenikon* for the years 1937–9; cf. also the list of the martyred bishops in Appendix III.
59. *Orlovskaïa Pravda*, 30th May 1937, quoted by P. B. Anderson, op. cit., pp. 180–5.
60. Private information from an unimpeachable source.

Notes

61. *Novye mucheniki rossiiskie, II,* pp. 120–22.
62. *Patriarkh Sergij i ego dukhovnoe nasledstvo* (The Patriarch Sergius and his spiritual inheritance), Moscow, 1947, p. 227.

Chapter IV

1. *Patriarkh Sergij i ego dukhovnoe nasledstvo,* Moscow, 1947, p. 234. The testimony] of the Archimandrite John Razumov who served the Patriarch as his *keleinik.*
2. Cf. Appendix 1 and note p. 418.
3. *Pravda o religii,* Moscow, 1942. pp. 83–94.
4. Cf. C. Simonov, *Jyvye i mertvye* (The living and the dead), Moscow, 1961, p. 67.
5. *Literaturnaia Moskva,* Moscow, 1955, p. 296.
6. *Pravda o religii,* pp. 86–92.
7. P. A. Smirnov, *Moskva v Ulianovske* (Moscow to Ulianovsk) in *Patriarkh Sergij,* pp. 237–45.
8. *Patriarkh Sergij,* pp. 287–94.
9. *Pravda o religii,* pp. 105–12.
10. ibid., p. 9. Cf. the French translation of this Introduction in *Russie et Chrétienté,* 1. 1946, pp. 73–7.
11. ibid., pp. 26–7.
12. ibid., pp. 121–2.
13. ibid., pp. 449–51.
14. *Pravda,* 9th November 1942. Cf. the French translation in *Le Clergé de l'U.R.S.S. et la Grande Guerre pour le salut de la patrie,* Moscow, 1944, p. 3.
15. ibid., pp. 27–8.
16. *Patriarkh Sergij,* p. 228.
17. ibid., pp. 144–51.
18. This is taken from a confidential dossier in the author's possession. Cf. V. Alekseev, *Le Drame de l'exarque Serge Voskresensky, Irenikon* 2, 1957, pp. 189–201.
19. A. Ionov, *Zapiski missionera* (Notes of a missionary), Sea-Cliff, New York, published by the author, 1952.
20. I have taken the content of the following paragraphs from the remarkable study by Friedrich Heyer *Die orthodoxe Kirche in der Ukraine von 1917 bis 1945,* Cologne, 1953, R. Muller Verlag.
21. These are still active today in the forests of the western Ukraine.

22. Bishop Manuel Tarnavsky was hanged in a wood on 22nd July 1942. At least thirty 'autonomous' priests were martyred.

23. During this same period the well-known uniate Metropolitan, Andrew Szepticky issued an appeal to the Orthodox for union. This appeal, considered by the Orthodox to be inopportune, remained unanswered.

Chapter V

1. *Patriarkh Sergij i ego dukhovnoe*, Moscow, 1947, p. 282.
2. Cf. *The Assault of Heaven*, London, 1924, appendix.
3. M. Polsky, *Kanonicheskoe pologenie vyshei tserkovnoi vlasti USSR i zagranitsei*, Jordanville, 1948, p. 99.
4. *Patriarkh Sergij . . .* , p. 172.
5. *Izvestia*, 21st May 1944.
6. *Patriarkh Sergij . . .* , pp. 308–9.
7. *JMP*, 2. 1945. Cf. the French translation of the most important passages in *Russie et Chrétienté*, 1, 1947, pp. 41–102.
8. Cf. the text in Appendix II.
9. *JMP*, 4, 1961, p. 6.
10. ibid., 3, 1947, p. 52.
11. ibid., 8, 1961, pp. 30–5.
12. ibid., 1954, p. 15.
13. N. Spassky, *Ne khochu obmanyvat'* (I am not going to deceive the people) Moscow, 1960, pp. 34–6.
14. *L'Église Orthodoxe Russe, Organisation, Situation, Activité*, Moscow, 1958, pp. 129–32.
15. See Appendix VI, Document E, and note, p. 418.
16. *L'Église Orthodoxe Russe . . .* pp. 80–104.
17. *JMP*, II, 1946, p. 40.
18. ibid., 2, 1946.
19. Cf. the French translation of this pastoral letter in C. J. Dumont 'L'Église orthodoxe russe face du communisme,' *Économie et Humanisme*, cahiers *Idées et Forces* 7–8, 1950, pp. 7–11.
20. *JMP*, 12, 1949, pp. 7–11.
21. *Conférence de toutes les églises et associations religieuses de l'U.S.S.R. pour la défense de la paix dans le monde* (Zagorsk, 9–12th May 1952). Moscow 1952, p. 320.
22. *Izvestia*, 21st March 1952.

23. ibid., 6th November 1956.
24. *JMP*, 12, 1956, p. 3.
25. ibid., 3, 1957, p. 42.
26. ibid., 1, 1957, pp. 36–8.
27. ibid., 5, 1962, p. 5.
28. ibid., 11, 1962, pp. 5–7.
29. ibid., 12, 1952, p. 11; 1962, p. 3.

Chapter VI

1. For further details cf. *Notes et Études Documentaires, No.* 1124, *Les relations extérieures du Patriarchat de Moscou.* This work, edited under the supervision of John Meyendorff, is practically exhaustive for the period between 1945 and 1951.
2. *JMP*, 12, 1945, pp. 14–17.
3. *Tserkonyi Vestnik* (The Church Messenger; the journal of the Russian Exarchate of Western Europe), 3, 1946, pp. 1–5.
4. ibid., 4, 1947, p. 5 and pp. 10–11.
5. *JMP*, 1, 1946, p. 16.
6. ibid., 5, 1946, p. 14.
7. ibid., 9, 1946, pp. 4–5.
8. ibid., 8, 1947, p. 8.
9. ibid.. 4, 1945, p. 8.
10. ibid., 8, 1950, pp. 4, 6.
11. ibid., 8, 1951, p. 43.
12. *Notes et Études Documentaires,* no. 1845, 6th March 1954, pp. 22–3.
13. *Orthodoxia*, 5–6, 1947, pp. 160–5.
14. *Ekklesia*, 15–111, 1948, pp. 94–5.
15. *JMP*, 8, 1948, pp. 23–7.
16. *Actes de la Conférence des chefs et représentants des Églises autocéphales orthodoxes réunie à l'occasion des solennités du 500ᵉ anniversaire de l'autocéphalie de l'Église Orthodoxe Russe, 8–18 juillet 1948*, Moscow (Publications of the Patriarchate) 1950, vol. 1, p. 447; 1952, vol. 2, p. 479.
17. The complete texts of the various resolutions is given in *Notes et Études Documentaires,* No. 1624.
18. *JMP*, 8, 1948–50.
19. *Izvestia*, 15th April 1950.

20. *L'Église orthodoxe russe dans la lutte pour la paix. Résolutions, messages, discours*, 1948–50. Moscow (Publications of the Patriarchate), 1950, pp. 41–4.

21. ibid., pp. 91–3.

22. *SOEPI*, 1st September 1950.

23. *JMP*, 1950, p. 17.

24. ibid., 8, 1952, pp. 3–7.

25. ibid., 5, 1953, pp. 4–8.

26. ibid., 8, 1953, pp. 47–53.

27. ibid., 9, 1953, pp. 7–11; 10, 1953, pp. 16–19.

28. ibid., 1, 1954, pp. 74–6; 3, pp. 66–7; 4, pp. 64–72; 5, pp. 75–80.

29. *SOEPI*, 24th February 1956.

30. ibid., 1st August 1958.

31. *JMP*, 2, 1956, pp. 20–41.

32. ibid., p. 6.

33. Cf. *JMP*, 9, 1953.

34. *JMP*, 6, 1957, p. 3.

35. ibid., 3, 1957, pp. 5–8.

36. ibid., 1, 1956, p. 10.

37. ibid., 6, 1957, p. 5.

38. ibid., 6, 1956 (the entire number is devoted to reunion).

39. ibid., 4, 1961, pp. 8–29.

40. ibid., 10, 1959, pp. 3–30.

41. ibid., 9, 1958, pp. 29–36.

42. ibid., 10, 1959, pp. 42–50.

43. ibid.

44. *Vestnik russkogo studentcheskogo khristianskogo dvigenia*, 64, 1962, pp. 11–14 (an article by P. B. Bobrinskoi).

45. *SOEPI*, 15th June 1962.

46. *JMP*, 10, 1958, p. 3.

47. ibid., 7, 1959, p. 10.

48. ibid., 5, 1961, pp. 55–7.

49. ibid., 11, 1960, pp. 40–7.

50. ibid., 6, 1961, pp. 55–7.

51. 21st September 1961.

52. *ICI*, no. 159, 1st January 1962, 9. 7.

53. ibid., no. 183, 1st January 1963.

54. *JMP*, 6, 1961, p. 4.

55. ibid., 7, 1961, pp. 55–7.
56. ibid., 5, 1962, pp. 25–6.
57. ibid., 4, 1959, p. 70.
58. ibid., 10, 1959, pp. 14–26.
59. ibid., 3, 1962, p. 16.
60. ibid., 2, 1962, pp. 23–31.

Chapter VII

1. *JMP*, 10, 1946. Speech by Professor N. Chepurin, Rector of the Moscow Academy, p. 5; 'Our former Academies, copying Western models in their theological studies, attributed too great a significance to human reason, whose usurpation in the realm of dogmatic truths must be rejected.'
2. Among other eminent Orthodox ecclesiastics, Nicodemus (d. 1948), Patriarch of the Rumanian Orthodox Church, Stephen, Exarch of Bulgaria (d. 1953), Alexander Tahan (d. 1958), Greek Patriarch of Antioch; and Michael, Greek Exarch of America (d. 1958), were former students of the Russian Academies.
3. Cf. the speech of the Metropolitan Gregory at the Inauguration of the Academy of Leningrad, *JMP*, 1946, 10, p. 9 onwards. Cf. also Mgr Cassian, *Rodoslovie dukha* (The genealogy of the spirit) in *Pravoslavnaia Mysl*, Paris, 8, 1949, pp. 12–13.
4. *JMP*, 1943, pp. 22–4.
5. The account of the restoration of the theological schools is taken from the study by A. V. Vedernikov: *Jysn dukhovnoi chkoly* (The Life of the Theological Schools), in *Patriarkh Sergij i evo dukhovnoe nasledstvo*, Moscow, pp. 383–401.
6. This condition is not always observed. Some students were admitted into the Seminaries after a secondary education of four classes only. Cf. Paul Darmansky: *Pobeg iz tmy* (I have fled from darkness), Moscow, 1961, p. 38.
7. This condition has recently been altered. The reference is now inspected by the rural dean and confirmed by the diocesan bishop. Instead of a baptismal certificate a simple notification of the date and, place of baptism suffices.
8. *JMP*, 5, 1962, pp. 20–1.
9. P. Darmansky, op. cit., p. 50.
10. A. Vedernikov, op. cit., pp. 395–6.

11. P. Darmansky, op. cit., p. 21.

12. *JMP*, 6, 1947, p. 6.

13. ibid., 7, 1955, p. 18; 11, 1956, p. 45.

14. ibid., 8, 1951, p. 58.

15. *L'Église Orthodoxe Russe, Organisation, Situation, Activité*, Moscow, 1958, p. 116.

16. *JMP*, 1, 1961, p. 19.

17. A. Verdernikov, op. cit., p. 398.

18. ibid.

19. P. Darmansky, op. cit., p. 44.

20. A. Vedernikov, op. cit., p. 397.

21. *JMP*, 6, 1053, p. 67.

22. *L'Église Orthodoxe Russe*, op. cit., p. 117.

23. *Golos Pravoslavia*, Berlin, 8–12, 1959 (Report of the vice-rector, L. Pariisky).

24. *JMP*, 11, 1955, p. 15.

25. ibid., 4, 1960, pp. 41–6.

26. *Messager de l'Exarchat pour l'Europe Occidentale du Patriarchat de Moscou*, Paris, 25, 1957, pp. 22–8.

27. *JMP*, 10, 1947, p. 29.

28. ibid., 7, 1960, p. 30.

29. ibid., 10, 1946, p. 5.

30. ibid., 10, 1947, pp. 30–1.

31. ibid., 9, 1955, p. 10.

32. ibid., 2, 1960, p. 42.

33. ibid., 11, 1960, pp. 22–9.

34. ibid., 10, 1946, p. 11–12.

35. *Golos Pravoslavia, art. cit.*

36. *JMP*, 12, 1955, pp. 28–9.

37. *ibid.*, pp. 29–30.

38. Cf. A. Schmemann, *The Revival of Theological Studies in the U.S.S.R.,* in *Religion in the U.S.S.R.*, Munich, 1960, pp. 29–43.

39. *Golos Pravoslavia, art. cit.*

40. *JMP*, 4, 1939, p. 20.

41. *Kom. Pr.*, 24th May 1957.

42. P. Darmansky, op. cit.

43. *Pravda*, 2nd December 1959.

44. *JMP*, 1, 1961, p. 19.

45. According to a report by V. Lossky.

46. *Anglo-Russian Theological Conference*, Moscow, July 1950: London 1956, p. 120.
47. Cf. *JMP*, 10, 1958, pp. 14–18.
48. *Vestnik russkogo studentcheskogo khristianskogo dvigenia*, pp. 62–3, and 67.
49. The cover has the date 1959 and the title page 1960.
50. *JMP*, 8, 1956, p. 11.
51. ibid., 10, 1958.
52. This second number which appeared in March 1963, bears on its cover the date 1961! It includes four liturgical and historical articles, two by N. Uspensky (Leningrad) and two by S. Troitsky, an émigré theologian, living in Belgrade, as well as a contribution by Bishop Michael Chub.
53. The closing of the seminaries of Kiev, Saratov and Stavropol was followed by an intense press campaign. Cf. for example S. Lvov, *Spasite nachi duchi* (S.O.S.) Moscow, 1961.

Chapter VIII

1. *Tserkovnye Vedomosti* (News of the Church), the journal of the émigré Synod, 1927, 3–4; 3–6; 11–12; 19–20; 21–2.
2. Apart from the *locum tenens*, these were the Metropolitan of Leningrad, Alexis Simansky; Archbishop Nicholas Yarushevich; the Metropolitan Sergius Voskresensky; Mgr Sergius Grishin; Alexis Sergeev; John Sokolov; Nicholas Mogilevsky.
3. Cf. the list of martyrs in Appendix III.
4. *Pravda o Religii v Rossii* (The truth about religion in the USSR), Moscow, 1942, pp. 141–2.
5. Only those who had fulfilled their term of punishment were released, and even these were required to give proofs of their loyalty. According to the evidence of a Soviet officer in the region of Perm, out of nine bishops in confinement there, only one was set free in 1945. (Cf. *Sotsialistichesky Vestnik*, 20th August 1946).
6. Cf. V. Alexeev, *Episkopat i Narod v S.S.S.R.*, 1941–53 (The Episcopate and the People in the U.S.S.R.). Roneotype edition, New York, 1954.
7. All the details given above are based on a very careful analysis of *The Review of the Moscow Patriarchate*.
8. Here are some examples: Mgr Benjamin Tikhonitsky, born in

Vyatka (Kirov) was appointed bishop of that town; Mgr Antony Krotevich, priest of Jitomir, was consecrated bishop of Jitomir. The first appointment of Mgr Boris Vik was for Saratov, the town where he was born. Mgr Cyril Pospelov, who had studied theology in Penza in 1900, was made bishop of this town in 1945. Mgr Onesimus Festinatov, born in Vladimir, where he completed his studies and served as a priest, has been its bishop since 1944.

9. Cf. chapter III.

10. *JMP*, 2, 1949, p. 22.

11. Information from a private source.

12. Cf. especially *Stalingradskaya Pravda*, 7th June 1959, and *JMP*, 8, 1959, p. 6.

13. Cf. *Kom. Pr.* 21st June 1961, and *JMP*, 6, 1961, p. 4.

14. These accusations, exaggerated and distorted by the anti-religious press, are not entirely baseless.

15. *JMP*, 8, 1960, pp. 55–7.

16. ibid., 10, 1955, pp. 11–12.

17. ibid., 7, 1961, p. 6.

18. Cf. the description given by A. Khomyakov of the farewell given by the people of Tula to Mgr Dimitri Muretov in *Messager Orthodoxe*, 9, 1960, pp. 31–2.

19. A private letter (1951).

20. *JMP*, 8, 1947, pp. 46–7.

21. *JMP*, 1, 1947, p. 44.

22. ibid., 1, 1956, p. 13.

23. ibid., 7, 1956, p. 18.

24. ibid., p. 21.

25. ibid., 12, 1955, p. 13.

26. This convent has since been closed.

27. *Istina*, 3, 1957, pp. 279–82. This description calls to mind the fervour of the people of Toulouse at the funeral of Cardinal Salièges.

28. *JMP*, 12, 1955, pp. 13–18.

29. The translation is taken from *Irenikon*, 2, 1962, pp. 283–6. Cf. the Russian text in *Vestnik russkogo khristianskogo studentcheskogo dvigenia*, 3–4, 1962, pp. 40–43.

30. *JMP*, 1, 1948, pp. 61–3.

31. ibid., 5, 1951, pp. 8–10.

32. *JMP*, 8, 1961, pp. 35–8. The prelate's medical career is described in *Bol'chaïa meditsinskaia entsiklopedia*, V, 1958.

33. *The Assault of Heaven*, London, 1924.
34. *JMP*, 4, 1952, p. 22. (Speech at a meeting of the workers of Moscow, 13th March 1952.)
35. Cf. chapter XIII. *Cf.* also the obituary in *JMP*, 1, 1962, pp. 14–22.
36. According to an unpublished manuscript in the author's possession.
37. *Cf.* the record of events in the Church's life in the *Review of the Moscow Patriarchate*, 1946–9.
38. *JMP*, 9, 1961, p. 45.
39. ibid., 5, 1960, pp. 31–3.
40. ibid., 1, 1954, p. 26.
41. ibid., 12, 1957, pp. 54–64; 8, 1958, pp. 65–72.
42. *JMP*, 1956, 1, p. 48; 2, p. 54; 3, p. 42.
43. ibid., 4, 1958, pp. 44–50.
44. ibid., 9, 1956, pp. 24–31.
45. ibid., 9, 1958, p. 35.
46. ibid., 6, 1958, pp. 73–5.
47. ibid., 4, 1959, p. 6.
48. ibid., 5, 1962, pp. 8–10.
49. ibid., 8, 1961, pp. 26–7.
50. ibid., 12, 1955, p. 25.
51. ibid., 8, 1959, pp. 25–8.
52. ibid., 5, 1961, p. 41.
53. ibid., 4, 1960, p. 11; 7, 1963, pp. 26–9.
54. ibid., 2, 1958, p. 10.
55. ibid., 4, 1957, pp. 57–60.
56. ibid., 9, 1963, p. 3.
57. ibid., 2, 1959, pp. 32–4.
58. ibid., 8, 1963, pp. 5–9.
59. ibid., 10, 1963, pp. 3–8.
60. ibid., 12, 1957, pp. 17–22.
61. ibid., 8, 1960, pp. 15–17.
62. ibid., 10, 1961, pp. 10–14.
63. ibid., 3, 1962, pp. 11–16.
64. ibid., 2, 1962, pp. 15–17.
65. A private letter from Mgr Sergius Korolev, Archbishop of Kazan, in the author's possession.
66. *Istina*, 3, 1957, p. 286.
67. *JMP*, 1, 1949, p. 13.
68. ibid., 1, 1950, p. 6.

69. This man has been described by P. Darmansky, *Pobeg iz tmy* (I have fled from darkness), Moscow, 1960, pp. 53–4. I have received a confirmation of the truth of this account from an ecclesiastic who met Tarassov in Leningrad.

70. *JMP*, 1, 1950, pp. 6–8. *Cf.* the French translation of this speech in *Russie et Chretienté*, 1–2, 1950, pp. 68–71.

71. ibid.

72. From a private letter.

73. This estimate is confirmed by a former seminarist who left the Church, Nicholas Trofimchuk. Cf. *Komsomolskaya Jizn*, 13th (June) 1963, article by N. Mirocshnichenko.

74. The second edition of this book was already at the press when I obtained information about the state of the clergy of the diocese of Riazan in *Voprosy istorii religii i ateizma*, vol. xi, Moscow, 1963, pp. 73–94. The clergy are there described as forward-looking, flexible, and zealous, and relatively well-educated.

75. Cf. the text of this protest in Appendix V.

Chapter IX

1. When the Patriarchate put its case for candidature to the World Council of Churches, it stated that it had between 20 and 30 million believers under its jurisdiction. Cf. *SOEPI*, 23rd November 1961. This number is vague enough, and it is probably below the truth.

2. In the USSR there are 30 million Mohammedans; 3 million Jews and Buddhists (?); 3–4 million Catholics; 2–3 million Protestants; 1 million Old Believers, etc. (These figures are approximate.)

3. A. Zalesky, *Ob otnocheniakh belorusskikh kolkhoznikov k religii i o roste ateisma* (On the Attitude of the Peasants of White Russia to Religion, and on the Development of Atheism) in *Sovetskaïa Etnografia*, 2, 1957, pp. 48–59.

4. ibid.

5. *Kommunist*, May 1960.

6. *Kom. Pr.*, 7th February 1962.

7. *Le Problème religieux en U.R.S.S.*, part 2. Data and documents on the organization of the different churches and religious bodies. *Notes et Études Documentaires*, No. 1931, p. 4.

8. *Literaturnaia Gazeta*, 30th January 1962.

9. *Kom. Pr.*, 25th August 1961.

10. Ibid., 26th December 1958.

11. ibid.

12. *Vestnik zapadno – evropeïskogo exarkhata*, Paris, May 1947, p. 3. An article by A. Sergeenko.

13. *Irenikon*, XXVII, 2, 1954.

14. *SOEPI*, 23rd November 1961. This is also the number given by G. Karpov in 1949: USSR *Information Bulletin*, Washington, January 1949, pp. 54–6. Karpov was well placed to know the facts.

15. *Stimme der Gemeinde*, 15, 1954, p. 343.

16. A. Zalesky, *art. cit.*

17. A private letter.

18. *JMP*, 8, 1959, p. 9.

19. This argument which I developed in a paper published in the *Vestnik russkogo studentcheskogo khristianskogo dvigenia*, 47, 1957, pp. 22–33, has been repeated by a number of later writers, including Jean Meyendorff, *L'Église Orthodoxe hier et aujourd'hui*, Paris, 1961, p. 134, and C. de Grünwald, who attributes it to Mgr Nicholas of Krutitsy, although this may only be a journalistic device: *La vie religieuse en U.R.S.S.*, Paris, 1961, p. 106.

20. Cf. N. Timasheff, *The Russian Orthodox Church Today*, St Vladimir Seminary's Quarterly, 3, 1958, p. 40. *SOEPI*, 27th February 1964.

21. A private letter.

22. *Vestnik russkogo studentcheskogo khristianskogo dvigenia*, 35, 1955, p. 40.

23. Confidential information.

24. *Notes et Études Documentaires*, No. 1931. op. cit., p. 3.

25. A. Sergeenko, *art. cit.*

26. Information sent by Mgr Boris, then Bishop of that See.

27. *JMP*, 3, 1947, p. 52.

28. Cf. *JMP*, 12, 1955, p. 7.

29. Radio Moscow in Italian, 11th December 1955, quoted by W. Kolarez, *Religion in the Soviet Union*, London, 1961, p. 80. This number corresponds with that which I have obtained by going through the complete files of the *JMP*.

30. *NR*, 2, 1962, p. 8.

31. *Le Monde*, 12th April 1960.

32. Data painstakingly gleaned from the *Review of the Moscow Patriarchate*.

33. *Bilan du Monde,* 1960, vol. 2, p. 758.

34. Cf. P. Mehnert, *L'Homme soviétique*, Paris, 1962, *passim*, or this poem by the well-known Soviet poet Boris Slutski:

May God grant happiness to women,
Grant them health, O God,
May we have a little less of it,
And they a little more,
They cannot bear burdens
That are too heavy for us to carry. . . .

in *Sovetskaia potaennaïa muza*, Munich, 1961, p. 134, or this: 'A peasant woman's work is harsh, harsher than her husband's. At forty she looks aged.' E. Doroche. *Derevensky Dnevnik*, in *Literaturnaia, Moskva*, 1956, p. 553.
35. *NR*, 9, 1961, p. 56.
36. Private letter (1961).
37. Cf. Chombart de Lauwe, *Les Paysans Soviétiques*, Paris, 1962, p. 73.
38. Cf. the periodical reports in the *Figaro* Lucien Laurat's numerical account is confirmed by many descriptions of peasant life in Soviet journals. Cf. the most recent: A. Soljenitsine, *Matrionin dvor*, *Novyi Mir*, 1, 1963, 1963, pp. 42–63 (French translation in *Temps Modernes*, 3, 1963).
39. Efim Doroche, *Derevensky Dnevnik*, in *Literaturnaia Moskva*, 1956, *passim*.
40. ibid., p. 553.
41. Chombart de Lauwe, op. cit., p. 297.
42. *Voprosy istorii religii i ateisma*, Moscow, 1963, p. 13.
43. *NR*, 8, 1962, pp. 74–5.
44. ibid., 2, 1960, pp. 81–2.
45. ibid., 2, 1959.
46. *JMP*, 10, 1954, p. 4.
47. Efim Doroche, op. cit., p. 594.
48. *Kom. Pr.*, 25th January 1962.
49. A private letter (1957).
50. *Istina*, 1, 1955, pp. 9–11.
51. *Dieu Vivant*, 21, 1952, p. 21.
52. Cf. S. Bulgakov, *Le Ciel sur la terre*, *Ostkirche*, Sonder-Heft der *Una Sancta*, Stuttgart, 1927, p. 21.
53. *Contacts*, 34, 195, pp. 134–7.
54. N. Gogol, *le Jour de la Résurrection*, *Extraits de ma correspondance avec mes amis*, 1846. Cf. French trans. in *Contacts*, 29, 1960, p. 38.

55. A private letter (1955).
56. *Istina*, I, 1955, pp. 14–15.
57. A private letter (1957).
58. *idem.* (1955).
59. *idem.* (1950).
60. *Istina*, I, 1955, p. 15.
61. ibid., p. 12.
62. E. de Linden, *Notes de voyage en U.R.S.S., Contacts,* 31, 1960, p. 213.
63. Private letter (1961).
64. *idem.* (1950).
65. *JMP*, 2, 1949, p. 22.
66. *Istina*, I, 1955, p. 11.
67. ibid., pp. 19–20.
68. P. Pascal, *Les Pèlerinages de l'Orthodoxie, Lumen Vitae.* vol. XIII, 2, 1958, pp. 258–66.
69. Private letter (1958).
70. *JMP*, 1956.
71. C. de Grünwald, op. cit., p. 209.
72. *JMP*, 8, 1957, pp. 20–21.
73. ibid., 7, 1949, p. 4.
74. *NR*, 4, 1962, pp. 28–9.
75. *JMP*, 10, 1958, pp. 10–11.
76. *NR*, 9, 1961, pp. 76–9.
77. *NR*, 4th December 1959.
78. *JMP*, 10, 1949, pp. 62–4.
79. P Pascal, *art. cit.*, p. 262 and 266.
80. A private letter (1957).
81. *NR*, 4, 1961, pp. 29–36.
82. *Pravda o peterburgskikh sviatyniakh* (The Truth about the Holy Places of Petersburg), Leningrad, 1962, pp. 112–15.
83. *NR*, 4, 1961, pp. 29–36.
84. *Pravda o peterburgskikh sviatyniakh*, op. cit., pp. 60–61.
85. *Kom. Pr.*, 28th March 1956; *Literaturnaia Gazeta*, 1st October 1959.
86. *Kom. Pr.*, 25th August 1961.
87. *NR*, 1st September 1959.
88. Elizabeth de Linden, *Notes de voyage en U.R.S.S. Contacts,* 31, 1960, pp. 41–5.

89. *NR*, 11, 1961, pp. 66–7.
90. ibid., 1st September 1959.
91. Manuscript notes of a journey made by E. de Linden (kindly lent to the author).
92. P. Darmansky, *Pobeg iz tmy* (I have fled from darkness), Moscow, 1960, p. 105.
93. Confidential information of unquestionable veracity.
94. *Uchitelskaia Gazeta*, 21st July 1959.
95. *Kom. Pr.*, 12th April 1960.
96. *Sovetsky Flot*, 29th March 1960.
97. V. Tendriakov, *Neobyknovennoe prikluchenie* (An extraordinary incident). NR, 7, 9, 10, 1961.

Chapter X

1. A. Erichev, *Sektanstvo i ego suchnost'* (The sects and their essence), Kiev, 1959.
2. Following the publications of extracts (cf. Voprosy filosofii, 1, 1960: *Voprosy istorii religii i ateizma*, VII, 1960), the more or less complete results of the expedition were published in volume IX of the *Voprosy religii i ateizma*, Moscow, 1961, p. 315, with the title *Sovremennoe sektanstvo*.
3. Cf. Introduction.
4. Described by P. Pascal, *Russie et Chrétienté*, 1949, 3–4, pp. 165–7.
5. *La Vie religieuse en U.R.S.S.*, Paris, 1960, p. 157.
6. *Kom. Pr.*, 18th November 1953.
7. *JMP*, 7, 1946, p. 31.
8. *Conférence de toutes les églises et associations religieuses de l'U.R.S.S. pour la défense de la paix dans le monde* (Zagorsk, 9–12th May 1952), Moscow, 1952.
9. *JMP*, 6, 1950, p. 40.
10. *NR*, 9, 1961, p. 47.
11. ibid., 8, 1962, pp. 76–9.
12. W. Kolarz, *Religion in the Soviet Union*, London, 1961, p. 141.
13. *Conférence* . . . , p. 257.
14. *JMP*, 12, 1958, p. 7.
15. W. Kolarz, op. cit., p. 141.
16. *Conférence* . . . , pp. 225–30.
17. W. Kolarz, op. cit., pp. 142–6.

18. *Russkaia Mysl'*, 2nd October 1962.

19. A. Erichev, op. cit., p. 18.

20. *JMP*, 1948, p. 76.

21. *Anti-religioznik*, 7, 1939.

22. *Sputnik Ateista*, pp. 147–9.

23. L. Mitrokhine, *Yzuchenie sektanstva v Tamboskoi oblasti* (A study of the sects in the Tambov province) *Voprosy filosofii*, 1. 1960.

24. Garkovenko, *Chto takoe religioznoe sektanstvo* (What are the religious sects?), Moscow, 1961, Voenizdat . . . , p. 104–5.

25. *My porvali s religiei* (We have broken with religion) Donbass,1959, pp. 30–4.

26. *NR*, 5, 1961, p. 91.

27. K. Grass, *Die russichen Sekten, Zweiter Band, Die weissen Tauben oder Skopzen*, Leipzig, 1914.

28. p. 152.

29. Col. 1785.

30. A. Erichev, op. cit., p. 58.

31. *NR*, 1962, pp. 19–25.

32. *Anti-religioznik*, 8, 1937.

33. *Sovremennoe sektantstvo*, p. 104.

34. W. Kolarz, op. cit., p. 356.

35. *Conférence*, p. 133.

36. *Sovremennoe sektantstvo*, p. 99.

37. Jidkov, Karev, etc., cf. *Bratsky Vestnik*, 1, 1953, pp. 50–1.

38. *Literaturnaia Gazeta*, 11th December 1959.

39. *Russkaia Mysl'*, 2nd October 1962.

40. *Bezbojnik*, 4, 1937.

41. *Literaturnaia Gazeta*, 11th December 1959.

42. B. Kandidov, *Tserkov' i chpionaj* (The Church and espionage), Moscow, 1938, p. 69.

43. *JMP*, 1, 1948, p. 76.

44. *Literatura i Jizn*, 14th December 1960.

45. *Anti-religioznik*, 10, 1931.

46. *NR*, 6, 1960, p. 85.

47. *Pravda Vostoka*, 13th November 1960.

48. *Sputnik Ateista*, p. 167. Cf. *Sovetskaia Moldavia*, 3rd July 1957.

49. W. Kolarz, op. cit., pp. 281–2.

50. *SOEPI*, 31st August 1962, Statement of pastor P. J. Dyck at the seventh Mennonite World Conference in Kitchener (Ontario).

51. W. Kolarz, op. cit., pp. 281–2.
52. *Sputnik Ateista*, p. 155.
53. *JMP*, 5, 1956, p. 61, W. Kolarz, op. cit., pp. 303–6.
54. *Bratsky Vestnik*, 3–4, 1954, p. 9.
55. *Pochemu my porvali s religiei*, Moscow, 1959, *passim*.
56. W. Kolarz, op. cit. pp. 306–12, gives a very detailed account of the geographical distribution of the Baptists.
57. *Kom. Pr.*, 17th June 1961.
58. *SOEPI*, 19th January 1962.
59. *Sovetskaia Rossia*, 9th August 1959.
60. *Iunost'*, 1, 1960, report by S. Krainov, Cf. French translation in *ICI*, 1st August 1960.
61. *Uchitelskaia Gazeta*, 7th June 1959.
62. *NR*, 9, 1961, p. 11.
63. ibid., p. 48.
64. ibid., pp. 47–54.
65. *Pochemu, my porvali s religiei*, p. 107.
66. *Iunost'*, *art. cit.*
67. *Sputnik Ateista*, p. 154.
68. *NR*, 12, 1961, p. 32. ibid., 1, 1963, p. 32.
69. *Literaturnaia Gazeta*, 12th April 1958.
70. *Pochemu*, etc., pp. 126–45.
71. *Literaturnaia Gazeta*, 14th March 1959.
72. F. Miatchine, *Moi razryv s sektantami triasunami* (I have broken with the trembling sectaries) Vladivostok, 1958, pp. 38–41.
73. *Izuvery* (The Fanatics), Moscow, 1961, pp. 27–44.
74. *Pochemu*, pp. 163–7.
75. *Izuvery*, p. 46.
76. *Conférence* . . . , p. 207.
77. W. Kolarz, op. cit., p. 325.
78. *My porvali* . . . Donbass, 1959, pp. 27–9; *Pochemu my porvali* . . . Moscow, 1959, pp. 146–59; *Sovetskaia Rossia*, 16th June 1958; *NR*, 11, 1961, p. 67.
79. *Kommunist Tadjikistana*, 15th March 1958.
80. *Kazakhstanskaia Pravda*, December 1957.
81. *Pravda Ukrainy*, 27th September 1959.
82. *Mohilevskaia Pravda*, 31st January 1958.
83. *Literaturnaia Gazeta*, 3rd September 1949. French translation in *Notes et Études Documentaires*, No. 1931, p. 27.

Notes

84. Bartochevich, *Svideteli' Yegovy*, Moscow, 1960, p. 114, p. 155.

85. *Year Book of Jehovah's Witness*, 1957, Brooklyn, 1958, p. 253.

86. Bartochevich, op. cit., pp. 140–8.

87. *Kazakhstanskaia Pravda*, 1st September 1957.

88. *Sovetskaia Moldavia*, 1st March 1957.

89. A. T. Moskalenko, *Kto takie Yegovisty* (Who are the Jehovists?), Moscow, 1959, p. 19.

90. *Kom. Pr.*, 15th June 1959.

91. *Anti-religioznik*, 5, 1939, p. 22.

92. *Krymskaia Pravda*, 7th September 1957.

93. I. Eliachevich, *Pravda o Churikove i Churikovtsach*, Leningrad, 1928. Cf. *Bezbojnik*, 3, 1938.

94. *Uchitelskaia Gazeta*, 13th January 1962.

95. A. L. Lounine, *Fiodorovtsy-krestonostsy*, Moscow, 1930.

96. *Sovremennoe sektanstvo*, pp. 164–5.

97. F. M. Poutintsev, *Vybory v sovety i razoblachennaia popovschina* (Elections to the soviets and the clerical clique unmasked), Moscow, 1938, p. 79.

98. *Osnovy nauchnogo ateisma* (Foundations of scientific atheism), Alma-Ata, 1961, p. 235.

99. *Sovremennoe sektanstvo*, p. 165.

100. *Anti-religioznik*, 5, 1939, p. 22.

101. F. M. Putintsev, op. cit., *passim*.

102. *JMP*, 2, 1948, pp. 65–6.

103. The main lines of what follows are taken from the study made by L. N. Mitrokhine, *Reaksionnaia deiatelnost 'istinno-pravoslavnoi tserkvi' na Tambovihine* (The reactionary activity of the 'True Orthodox Church' in the province of Tambov), *Sovremennoe Sektanstvo*, pp. 144–60.

104. *NR*, 5, 1961, p. 91.

105. Z. A. Nikolskaia, *Kharakteristike techenia tak nazyvaemych istinno-pravoslavnykh khristian*, *Sovremennoe sektanstvo*, pp. 161–88.

106. *Kom. Pr.*, March 15th 1959.

107. *Sovremennoe sektanstvo*, pp. 219–20.

108. *Sel'skoe khoziaistvo*, 22nd February 1959. *Kirovskaia Pravda*, 16th March 1959. *Stalinskoe plemia*, 13th September 1959. *Kommunist*, 24th March 1959. *Leninskoe znamia*, 5th July 1959. *Luganskaia Pravda*, 25th July 1959. *Pravda Yujnogo Kazakhstana*, 27th November 1959 *Izvestia*, 12th December 1959. *Sovetskaia Chuvachia*, 16th

Notes

July 1959. *Sovetskaia Sibir'*, 4th August 1959. *Zvezda*, 2nd August 1959. *Vecherniaia Moskva*, 29th July 1959. Evidently this was a synchronized campaign. Cf. *NR*, 3, 1960, pp. 53–6 (an account of the villages of the Altai).

109. *Sovremennoe sektanstvo*, pp. 172–4.
110. ibid., p. 175.
111. *Sovetskaia Kultura*, 13th January 1959.
112. *Trud*, 9th July 1960, quoted by W. Kolarz, op. cit., pp. 370–1.
113. *Osnovy nauchnogo ateisma*, Alma-Ata, 1961, pp. 242–3.

Chapter XI

1. *Anti-religioznik*, 10, 1932, pp. 39–40.
2. *SOEPI*, 15th June 1962.
3. *JMP*, 4, 1960, pp. 61–5.
4. The most complete study is that published by the *Documentation française* under the title *La Situation de l'Église Arménienne, Notes et Études Documentaires*, 8th December 1956, No. 2,239, p. 31. Cf. also W. Kolarz, op. cit., p. 150–75.
5. Aristide Brunello, *La chieza del silenzio*, Ostia, 1953, pp. 1–39.
6. W. Kolarz, *Religion in the Soviet Union*, London, 1961, pp. 207–213.
7. *Sovetskaia Kultura*, 5th September 1959.
8. *ICI*, 1st January 1962.
9. ibid.
10. W. Kolarz, op. cit., p. 212.
11. *JMP*, 2, 1945, p. 24.
12. *Die Zerstörung der Ukrainisch – Katolischen in der Sowjetunion Ostkirchliche Studien*, 1, pp. 3–38.
13. *JMP*, 4, 1946, p. 36.
14. The French text of this message in *La Documentation Catholique*, No. 54, 20th January 1946, col. 59–60.
15. *JMP*, 4, 1946, pp. 5–6.
16. The Acts of the Council have been published in the Ukrainian language: *Diiania Soboru greko-katolits'koi tserkvi u L'vovi 8–10 beresnia 1946*, Lvov, pp. 175.
17. *Die Zerstörung*, art. cit., p. 35.
18. *Acts of the Conference of the Leaders and Delegates of the Orthodox Churches*, Moscow 1949, vol. 2, pp. 226–32.
19. *JMP*, 1, 1956, pp. 16–20.

20. M. Polsky, *Novye mucheniki rossiiskii*, 11, Jordanville, 1957, pp. 94–6.
21. *JMP*, 10, 1949, p. 5.
22. *Bilan du Monde*, op. cit., p. 766.
23. *JMP*, 10, 1949, p. 5.
24. W. Kolarz, op. cit., p. 235.
25. *Pravoslanyi Visnik*, 7, 1957, p. 214.
26. *JMP*, 11, 1956, pp. 10–11.
27. R. Girault, *Carnet de voyage*, in *Lumière et Vie*, 55, 1961, p. 92.
28. *Pravoslanyi Visnik*, 7, 1957, p. 217.
29. *JMP*, 4, 1961, pp. 30–1.
30. *SOEPI*, 15th June 1962.
31. ibid.
32. ibid., 6th September 1957.
33. ibid., 15th June 1957.
34. ibid., 12th March 1964.

Chapter XII

1. *Choix*, No. 5, p. 109.
2. *NR*, 2, 1962, pp. 11–12.
3. June 1947.
4. 18th October 1947.
5. *Nauka i Jizn*, November 1949.
6. *Sovietskaia kniga*, 8, 1952.
7. *Istina*, 3, 1954, pp. 296–8.
8. C. Fotiev, *Za prava i svobodu v Rossii*, 6, 1958.
9. *NR*, 2, 1962, p. 12.
10. *Narodnoie obrazovanie* (National education), April 1949.
11. *Uchitelskaia Gazeta* (The Teachers' Journal), 25th November 1949. Cf., *Bolchevik*, 15th July 1948; *Leninskoe Znamia*, 8th October 1954.
12. *NR*, 1, 1962, p. 6.
13. ibid., 2, 1962, p. 14.
14. ibid.
15. ibid., 9, 1961, pp. 56–9.
16. ibid., 9, 1960, pp. 5–7.
17. Cf. for example, *Voprosy ateisticheskogo vospitania v chkole* (Problems of Atheist Education in the Schools), Moscow, 1960, p. 117. (40,000 copies).

18. *NR*, 1961, pp. 56–9. This example was followed by School n. 106 of the city of Gorky. Cf. *Uchitelskaia Gazeta*, 30th November 1963.

19, ibid., 1, 1962, p. 6.

20. ibid., 2, 1962, p. 13.

21. ibid., 12, 1961, p. 76.

22. ibid., 1962, p. 14.

23. ibid.

24. *Nachalnaia chkola*, February 1953 article entitled 'The 35th Anniversary of the Decree on the Separation between Church and State'.

25. *Kom. Pr.*, 20th March 1954.

26. *Molodoi kommunist*, January 1957. An article by J. Uskov.

27. Cf. the novel by V. Tendriakov, *Chudotovornaia* (The Miraculous Icon), Moscow, 1959.

28. *NR*, 3, 1961, p. 82.

29. *Oustav vsesoiuznogo leninskogo soiuza molodioji*, Moscow, 1961, p. 8.

30. *Kom. Pr.*, 20th March 1954.

31. *Notes et Études Documentaires*, No. 2,096, p. 22.

32. *Molodoi kolkhoznik*, March 1954; the article entitled 'The Sound of the Bells'.

33. *ICI*, 15th May 1962, p. 14.

34. *NR*, 8, 1962, p. 4.

35. ibid., 2, 1962, p. 12.

36. ibid., p. 13.

37. ibid., 8, 1963, p. 3.

38. ibid., p. 10.

39. ibid., p. 11.

40. *Sovetskaia Kultura*, 28th January 1964.

41. *ICI*, No. 115, 1960, p. 19.

42. Ibid. This number contains an excellent and very detailed account of these two centres of atheism.

43. *NR*, 2, 1962, p. 4.

44. ibid., 3, 1961; and also: 'Writers search for every excuse that will enable them to avoid discussions against religion. Apparently this is a sphere in which they do not excel. And, in general, our foremost writers stand aside from the fight against religion.' Cf. *NR*, 3, 1962, p. 10. It will be noticed that Iliichev in his report, refrains from calling on writers to take part in the war against religion.

45. *Znamia*, 5, 1958. The novel was later published as a book, and new editions are always being issued.

Notes

46. *NR*, 10, 1961, p. 76.

47. *Antidüring*, Moscow, 1953, p. 299.

48. I have summarized the main theses of Soviet atheism from the account given in *Sputnik Ateista*. Its standard is higher than that of most of the popular booklets published.

49. Only one brochure admits that several historical personalities may have contributed to the origin of the myth of Jesus. Its author also admits that the four Gospels date from the beginning of the second century, and even go farther back. But it is significant that this brochure was only published in a very limited edition of 8,000 copies: J. Krainev *L'Opposition entre l'Idéologie Chrétienne et le Communisme Scientifique*, Moscow, 1961.

50. *NR*, 1, 1962, pp. 8–10 (interview with Titov). This argument dates from before the space flights. Before the war the pilot Chkalov was quoted as an example: he had gone up to 10,000 metres and yet had not encountered God.

51. *Sputnik Ateista*, M. 1961, the penultimate illustration.

52. V. Zenkovsky, *O mnimom materializme russkoi nauki i filosofii* (On the Supposed Materialism of Russian Science and Philosophy) Munich, 1956, p. 72.

53. *NR*, 6, 1960, pp. 50–7.

54. *Sputnik Ateista*, pp. 113–15.

55. *NR*, 3, 1962, p. 12.

56. ibid., p. 18.

57. *Kommunist*, 15, 1961, pp. 45–6.

58. *Sputnik Ateista*, pp. 416–17.

59. ibid., p. 416.

60. ibid., p. 422.

61. ibid., p. 423.

62. ibid., pp. 419–20.

63. ibid., pp. 385–8.

64. *ICI*, No. 115, 1960, p. 19.

65. *NR*, 3, 1962, pp. 30–31. Cf. the French translation in *ICI*, No. 168, 1962, pp. 20–21.

66. H. Chambre, *Le Marxisme en Union Soviétique*, Paris, 1955, pp. 352–3.

67. *NR*, 8, 1962, p. 6.

68. ibid., 3, 1962, p. 15.

447

Notes

Chapter XIII

1. *JMP*, 2, 1957, p. 25.
2. Quoted by Jabinsky, *Prosviety* (Insights), Munich, 1957, p. 127.
3. *JMP*, 9, 1958, p. 12.
4. This is a poem written by Vostokov in 1951 in the concentration
   camp and dedicated to Mgr Athanasius:

   > For thirty years your austere ministry has continued:
   > Steadfast in all things, light shines in you,
   > Wisdom and truth send forth their rays,
   > That emanate from suffering and conflict.

   > The torrent of suffering has not extinguished gaiety:
   > You smile – and I am comforted,
   > You look at me, and bitterness is calmed . . .
   > O the divine depths of your humility

   > Which sparkles in your daily deeds,
   > Your behaviour, your eyes, your gentle speech . . .
   > Your simplicity is the sign which makes us see
   > Everything which is holy, heavenly and sublime.

   Stikhi (verses), Paris, 1960, p. 123. Cf. *JMP*, 1, 1957, p. 28. When this
   book was published, its author was again arrested and sentenced to
   three years imprisonment.

   Mgr Athanasius Sakharov died 28th October 1962. In the
   obituary notice published in *JMP*, 12, 1962, the anonymous author
   admits that Mgr Athanasius, who was consecrated bishop in 1921,
   spent the greater part of his life in exile.
5. *JMP*, 1955, p. 9.
6. Cf the table of contents in the last number of that year.
7. Quoted by the critic E. Gogochvili in *Sovietskaia Kultura*, No. 901,
   1959. Since this sentence no longer corresponds to the facts it has
   been omitted in the edition published in Moscow in 1962.
8. *JMP*, 11, 1956, p. 45.
9. *JMP*, 12, 1956, p. 7.
10. *JMP*, 10, 1957, p. 12–15.
11. *Istina*, 3, 1957, p. 288.
12. *Voprosy istorii religii i ateizma*, XI, Moscow, 1963, p. 80.
13. *Voprosy filosofii*, 8, 1959, p. 180.

14. ibid., 5, 1958.
15. *Rencontres des cultures – Rencontres des hommes*, fasc. II, *La Russie*.
16. *L'Église orthodoxe russe, organisation, situation, activité*, Moscow, 1961, p. 232.
17. *JMP*, 2, 1959, p. 6.
18. P. Darmansky, *Pobeg iz tmy* (I fled from darkness), Moscow, 1961, p. 111.
19. A. Yakuchevich, *Razdumie o vere* (Thoughts on belief), Moscow, p. 111.
20. Petition drawn up in September 1963, signed with the names of four women and passed to western tourists in Ukraine. The complete Russian text has been published by me in *Russkaia Mysl'*. A shortened French version appeared in *Jeunesse orthodoxe*, IV, 1963.
21. Cf. my commentary on the report in *ICI*, 1st March 1964.
22. The Soviet Press has not been very forthcoming on the adoption of this new anti-religious legislation.
23. *NR*, 4, 1961, p. 30.
24. Almost everywhere and even in the Iliichev report. But that is characteristic of the system. The first condemnation of the arbitrary closing of churches dates from December 1918. The term *administrirovanie* appears for the first time in paragraph 18 of the thirteenth congress of the Communist Party (May 1924). Since then administrative measures have continually been practised, encouraged at first, and then condemned in a purely formal manner.
25. Information given by a representative of the Moscow Patriarchate.
26. Cf. Chapter III, pp. 34–38.
27. *NR*, 12, 1963, p. 60. Financial arrangements are not made public, a fact which leads to all sorts of abuses.
28. Iou. Manine, in his anti-religious pamphlet, records the objections of the Metropolitan of Krasnodar, Victor Sviatine, *Reaksionnaia suchnost' sovremennoi khristianskoi morali*, Minsk, 1963, p. 38.
29. *Literaturnaia Gazeta*, 21st February 1964. The diocese contained upwards of forty parishes before 1959.
30. N. Spassky, *Ne khochu obmanyvat'* (I do not desire to deceive the people), Moscow, 1960, pp. 34–6.
31. 'The cost of icons, candles and other devotional articles which were sold in the churches, has been lowered to deprive the churches of their income and so prepare for their closing. At Pochaev it is forbidden for the monks to sell crosses, icons, incense and other

devotional objects or those needed for worship. The abbey is obliged to sell the candles at the same price that they have been bought from the Moscow Patriarchate without making any profit... The manufacture of candles by the monks themselves is forbidden.' (Petition addressed to the Eastern Patriarchs, September 1963.

32. *NR*, 8, 1963, p. 30.

33. Cf. the petition addressed to the Eastern Patriarchs: 'We entreat you to prevent the local authorities from seizing the money belonging to churches for the construction of cinemas, theatres and other needs, for the Church is separated from the State. The money given by the faithful must be used for the needs of the monasteries and churches.'

34. *JMP*, 4, 1961, p. 30. This is the only clear case of the shutting of a church described by the *JMP*.

35. *Literatura i Jizn*, 21st February 1960.

36. *NR*, 7, 1961, pp. 46-8.

37. The news appeared in the newspapers of the West in January 1964. There was a good deal of talk about it in Christian circles in Moscow.

38. The method used in the fight against the Church is described in detail in a petition addressed to the World Council of Churches (2nd February 1964) and published in *Situation des chrétiens en URSS*, II, Paris, 1965, 5-13, a publication of the *Comité d'Information sur le situation des chrétiens en URSS*.

39. ibid., p. 15.

40. *Kom. Pr.*, 14th June 1961; *Voiovnichy ateist*, 6, 1962, p. 23; 10, 1962, p. 2.

41. *Sovetskaia Moldavia*, 13th December 1960.

42. *Voprosy teorii i praktiki nauchnogo ateizma* (Theoretical and practical problems of scientific atheism), Novosibirsk, 1962, p. 199.

43. *Sovetskaia Rossia*, 1st June 1961.

44. *NR*, 9, 1961, p. 39. 'The relics of Tikhon of Zadonsk have ended their career and will never again be used to deceive the people.' Do the final words mean that the relics have been destroyed?

45. N. Yudine, *Pravda o peterburgskikh sviatyniakh*, Leningrad, 1962, p. 8.

46. *NR*, 10, 1961, p. 91.

47. Information given to a third party by representatives of the Moscow Patriarchate.

48. *NR*, 10, 1961, p. 91.

49. *Literaturnaia Gazeta*, 23rd August 1956.

50. *Novyi Mir*, 11, 1962, p. 123.
51. *NR*, 12, 1962, pp. 38–43.
52. *Literaturnaia Gazeta*, 8th February 1962.
53. Petition addressed to the Eastern Patriarchs (September 1963).
54. *Situation des chrétiens en URSS*, p. 15.
55. Account given by eye witnesses.
56. *ICI*, 15th May 1962, p. 14.
57. *NR*, 8, 1962, p. 82.
58. Zagorsk, where admission of novices has been forbidden, Pskovo-Pechery, under frequent attack in the press, Pukhtitsa (Esthonia), Riga, monastery of the Assumption at Odessa, Pochaev, Jirovitsy, Saint Flor (Kiev), Intercession of the Blessed Virgin (Kiev), etc.
59. Extracts from a twofold petition addressed to the World Council of Churches and to the government in the USSR, supported by three thousand signatures and handed to Western tourists in September 1962. The first of these petitions was published in full in *Esprit*, March 1963, pp. 431–3.
60. *Krokodil*, 29th February 1964, p. 7.
61. The full dossier of the measures taken against the Laura of Pochaev has been published in *Situation des chrétiens en URSS*, II, Paris, 1965, pp. 17–56.
62. Private letter. Cf. *NR*, 12, 1963, p. 66.
63. *JMP*, 5, 1961, p. 37.
64. According to the Soviet Press which continually mentions candidates for the seminary who are persuaded to give it up.
65. Compare *JMP*, 4, 1960, p. 41 and *JMP*, 5, 1961, p. 38.
66. Cf. Appendix.
67. *Izvestia*, 31st March 1964.
68. *Kom. Pr.*, 7th February 1962.
69. *NR*, 2, 1962, p. 37.
70. A. Ossipov, *Moi otvet veruiuchim* (My answer to believers), Leningrad, 1960, p. 16.
71. *JMP*, 4, 1963, p. 30.
72. ibid., p. 29.
73. Confidential information.
74. Cf. Appendix.
75. *JMP*, 10, 1960, p. 4. Restored to his office, Mgr Hermogenes was once more suspended in November 1965, *JMP*, 12, 1965.
76. ibid., 9, 1961, p. 4.

77. Confidential information.
78. *Izvestia*, 8th July 1960; *Sovetskaia Rossia*, 21st June and 20th July 1960; NR, 7, 1960, pp. 36–43.
79. NR, 5, 1961, pp. 62–3.
80. ibid, 8, 1962, p. 27.
81. Cf. Chapter VIII.
82. *JMP*, 2, 1960, p. 27 (decision of 30th December 1959).
83. Text in *JMP*, 3, 1960, pp. 33–5.
84. *Possev*, 23rd January 1962.
85. *Vestnik russkogo studentcheskogo khristianskogo dvigenia*, 64, 1962, pp. 29–31.
86. Private letter.
87. *JMP*, 8, 1961, pp. 5–15.
88. *JMP*, 8, 1961, pp. 15–17.
89. *Voprosy istorii religii i ateizma*, vol. XI, Moscow, 1963, p. 77.
90. NR, 7, 1962, p. 56.
91. ibid., I, 1964, p. 32: 'In their desire to reach more people some priests have gone so far as to break the law of the land. Thus Frs Zverev, Rojdestvensky, Yukov and Marussine of the diocese of Yaroslavl went to neighbouring villages for this purpose, even to those which were not dependent on their parishes. ... Fr Dositheus, of the province of Pskov, devoted himself to preaching religion outside the church which, as is known, is forbidden by law; he regularly visited his parishioners to administer the sacraments to them in their own homes.' *Ejegodnik muzeia istorii religii i ateizma*, VII, Moscow, 1964, p. 110.
92. NR, 6, 1963, p. 73.
93. A private letter.
94. Petition to the Eastern Patriarchs: 'In 1961 the local authorities (Minsk) forbade the admission of children of between three and eighteen in the churches and giving them communion of the sacred mysteries of Christ.'
95. NR, 2, 1962, p. 35.
96. ibid, 9, 1960, p. 50.
97. ibid., 4, 1962, p. 39; *Kom. Pr.*, 20th December 1961.
98. *Rabotchaia Gazeta*, 19th January 1962.
99. *Frunzevets*, 13th February 1960 quoted in *My porvali s religiei*, Moscow, 1901, pp. 230–4.
100. *Pravda*, 27th January 1962.

101. See Appendix II.
102. *Priokskaia Pravda*, quoted by *NR*, 3, 1964, p. 27.
103. *NR*, 12, 1961, p. 65; cf. *Sovetskaia Rossia*, 18th December 1959.
104. Cf. Appendix II.
105. *NR*, 1, 1963, p. 32.
106. N. Yudine, op. cit., p. 8.
107. Address given at the consecration of Mgr Nicodemus of Kostroma on 19th August 1961. Cf. French translation in *Messager de l'exarchat du patriarche russe en Europe Occidentale*, 38–9, 1961, pp. 68–9.
108. *JMP*, 10, 1962, p. 7.
109. A. Ossipov, op. cit. The Ossipov case caused much ink to flow: cf. Mgr John of San Francisco, 'L'Affaire Ossipov' in *Messager Orthodoxe*, 10, 1960, pp. 14–18.
110. A. Chertkov, *Ot boga k liudiam* (I have given up God for mankind), Moscow, 1962 (140,000 copies published).
111. C. de Grünwald, *La Vie religieuse en U.R.S.S.*, Paris, 1961, p. 132.
112. Cf. note 18.
113. N. Spassky, *Ne khochu obmanyvat'* (I will no longer deceive the people).
114. Oplesin (Nijnie Sergui); Victor Dechko; A. Klimenko; V. Rozin; A. Pivovarchuk; L. Nagorny (Lazo); V. Odaiskii (Kursk); A. Ovcharenko (Kursk); A. Krivocheev (Donets); B. Kosmin, I. Gussarov (Kuibyshev); A. Chertkov (Moscow); M. Trubachev; I. Gleba; G. Stiojko (Ukraine), etc.
115. *NR*, 3, 1964, p. 70.
116. *Novyi Mir*, 8, 1962, p. 271.
117. *NR*, 6, 1963, p. 73.
118. ibid., 1, 1959. Article entitled *Konets Nikolskoi Gory*.
119. *Tainy sviatykh mest* (The mysteries of the holy places), Moscow, 1961, pp. 76–8.
120. Petition addressed to the Eastern Patriarchs.
121. *NR*, 6, 1963, p. 73.
122. Petitions addressed to the World Council of Churches and the government of the URSS (September 1962).
123. Petition to the Eastern Patriarchs. Cf. *Situation des chrétiens en URSS*, II, pp. 27 following.
124. A. Kryvelev, *O formirovanii i raspzostranenii novykh obychaev i prazdnikov ou narodov SSRR* (The formation and diffusion of new

customs and festivals among the peoples of the URSS), *Sovetskaia Etnografia,* 6, 1963, pp. 15–24.

125. *Kom. Pr.* 29th November 1963.

126. ibid., 19th January 1964.

127. *NR,* 12, 1961, p. 76.

128. ibid., 3, 1962, p. 6.

129. ibid., 6, 1963, pp. 74–6; 8. 1963, pp. 75–77.

130. *Komsomolskaia Jizn',* 13, 1963.

131. ibid.

132. *Kom. Pr.,* 20th December 1963.

133. ibid., 15th August 1961.

134. The Russian text of the long speech by L. Iliichev on 25th November 1963 was reproduced in *Nauka i Religia.* I, 1964. A French translation may be found in *ICI,* 211, 1st March 1964.

135. The measures taken by the central committee of the Communist Party of the USSR to improve the atheistic education of the population (January 1964) were published in *Partinaia Jizn* (The life of the party) on 2nd January, 1964, pp. 22–5; they reproduced in part in *Pravda* of 2nd March 1964

136. *Izvestia,* n. 222, 1963.

137. *Kom. Pr.,* 25th August 1961.

138. *Krokodil.* 16, 1963, p. 2: in 1962, 59 marriages and 1,795 baptisms as against 10 marriages and 206 baptisms in 1961. These fluctuations are due to periodical tightening up of police control.

139. *Voprosy istorii religii i ateizma,* vol. XI, Moscow, 1963, p. 80. In a single country church (Prudskaia sloboda) in 1961 there took place 856 baptisms, 137 funerals and 27 marriages.

140. *NR,* 3, 1964, p. 27.

141. *Kom. Pr.,* 1st February 1964. Cf. Petition to the Eastern Patriarchs: 'At the beginning it was forbidden for children of school- or pre-school age to be servers at the liturgy; this applied throughout Russia and even in Moscow despite the parents' protests.'

142. Petition to the Eastern Patriarchs; in *NR,* 6, 1965, pp. 43–5 there is a whole article devoted to the children of Varava.

143. *Uchitel'skaia Gazeta,* 18th January 1964.

144. *Sel'skaia Jizn',* 14th June 1962.

145. *NR,* 1, 1964, p. 31.

146. *Kom. Pr.,* 29th November 1963.

147. *Esprit,* March 1963, p. 433.

148. *Frunzevets*, 13th February 1960.

149. *Kom. Pr.*, 29th November 1963.

150. *Komsomolskaia Jizn*, 1–2 1963.

151. *Kom. Pr.*, 29th November 1963.

152. See note 134.

153. *NR*, 2, 1964, pp. 7–11.

154. *Kom. Pr.*, 31st December 1963: 'I will follow your example' (three letters from the daughter of a member of the Jehovah's Witnesses sect).

155. *NR*, 2, 1962, pp. 34–6.

156. *Lumiere et Vie*, 55, 1961, p. 85.

157. *Kom. Pr.*, 21st June 1961.

158. *NR*, 2, 1962, pp. 34–6.

159. ibid., 12, 1961, pp. 70–1.

160. ibid., 2, 1962, p. 37.

161. This practice is in force throughout the USSR (information confirmed by Soviet citizens.)

162. *NR*, 10, 1961, pp. 34–60.

163. Manuscript prayer in circulation among believers in the USSR.

164. *Possev*, 21st January 1961 (letter from Russia).

165. *SOEPI*, 1st June 1962, quoting *Izvestia*.

166. *Gudok*, 23rd February 1964. It mentions a priest of the Kalinin province to whom even the members of the party go to have their children baptized.

167. Cf. especially *JMP*, 7, 1960, pp. 25–31.

168. V. Nekrasov, *Po obe storony okeana* (From both shores of the ocean), *Novyi Mir*, 11, 1962, p. 142. The author implicitly contrasts the unhampered and enlightened Christianity of Italy with the fanaticism of the persecuted laity of Russia.

INDEX

Abramovitch, Nicanor, Bishop of Kiev, 75
academies, organization of, 125–6
Adrian, Patriarch, 17
Afanassiev, E., 271
Albania, Orthodox church in, 101, 104
Aleshin, S., 173, 291
Alexander II, 20
Alexander III *see* Antioch, Patriarch of
Alexandria, Christopher, Patriarch of, 96, 97
Alexis, Metropolitan, 72, 78–79
  aims of external policy, 96
  allegiance to Stalin, 79–80
  calls Council of 1945, 80
  change of policy after Stalin's death, 106–8
  calls meeting of Orthodox Churches (1958), 108
  calls Conference of 1948, 101
  decorated by the State, 94
  delegated Patriarch by Sergius, 78
  development of external relations, 118
  elected Patriarch, 82
  imprisoned, 37
  in Leningrad, 62
  meets the Ecumenical Patriarch, 109–10
  on the priesthood, 171–2
  praises Stalin, 91
  protests American blockade of Cuba, 93
  receives Emperor Haile Selassie, 118
  restores theological studies (1944), 122
  visit to the Middle East and Bulgaria (1945–6), 97–98
Ambrose, Father, 19
Ammasisky, Mgr Nicholas, 57
Andrew, Archbishop of Saratov, 64
Anglicanism, Russian attitude towards, 103
Anissimov, Mgr Nestor, 144, 291
Anthony, Mgr, 143

anti-religious movement, 53–54
Anti-religioznik, 54
Antioch, Patriarch of, 96, 97
Armenian Church, 255–7
  relations with Russia, 104
Asseev, Nicholas, 281
Assumption, Feast of the, 198–9
Athanasius, Bishop of Korov, 291
atheism, 323–4
  among adults, 275–6
  houses of, 280
  in books and pamphlets, 276–8
  in films, 278–9
  in museums, 279–80
  in the press, 276
  in radio and television, 278–9
  in theatre, 279
  in youth organizations, 272–5
  lack of distinguished propaganda, 280–2
  nature of the arguments for, 282–9
  press campaign (1947–59), 267–9
  pressures on children, 327–31
  teaching in schools, 270–2
  the Iliichev report on religion, 295

Bachmann, Pastor Eugene, 265
Baltic countries, annexation of, 57–58
baptism
  prevalence of, 176–8
  restriction of (1962), 327–8
Baptist and Evangelical Union, 232–7
Barlaam, Bishop of Mukachevo, 93
Bartholomew, Metropolitan, 147
Baziak, Mgr Eugene, Bishop of Lvov, 259
Beirut, Metropolitan of, 107
Beky, Zoltan, statement on the Russian Church, 113–14
Bely, A., 20
benderovtsy, 75
Benjamin, Metropolitan, 36–37, 121
Berdyaev, 21

456

Index

Index

Index

Index

League of Militant Atheists, 54
  dissolved (1951), 61
Lemeshevsky, Mgr Manuel, 144, 158–9
Leningrad
  Academy, 123, 131–4
  Church of the Saviour, 205
  Monastery of St John, 206
  number of churches, 182–3
  seminary, 123
  Smolensky cemetery, 204–5
Leonidze, G., 254
Leontievtsy sect, 250
Leontyev, C., 19
Lipkovtsy, the, 74
liturgy, 192–4
'Living Church', origin of, 35–36
  council of 1923, 38–40
Luhacovici conference (1950), 104
Lutsk seminary, 123
Lvov, V., 23
Lutheran Church in Russia, 264–5

Macarius, Mgr, Archbishop of Lvov,
  263
Manchuria, Church in, 98
Marchenko, Mgr Antony, 144
marriage, 324
martyrs, repudiation of, 63–64
Matulionis, Bishop of Kaisedorys, 259
Melnik, Michael, 261, 262–3
'Men of God' sect, 225–6
Mennonites, 231–2
Messenger of the Patriarchate, 55
Michael, Mgr, 143
Mikhailovich, Tsar Alexis, 17
Mikhalkov, S., 287
Milov, Benjamin, 130
Minsk seminary, 123, 125
Mitin, M. B., 293
Mogilevsky, Metropolitan Nicholas,
  147, 183
Molokanes sect, 227–9
monasteries, present position, 90, 303–
  10
Mongol invasion, 11–12
Morosov, Pavlik, 331
Morzhakov, Joseph, Archbishop of
  Moscow and all Russia, 220–1
Moscow
  Academy, 120, 123, 127–31
  practising Christians in, 182
Mourashkovtsy sect, 238–9

Müller, W., 239
Muravyev-Uralsky, or -Apostol, Mgr
  Nicholas, 164, 291
museums of atheism, 279–80

Nekrassov, Victor, 301
Nestor, monk, 11
Netovtsy sect, 224
Neumann, Julia, 61
Nevsky, Alexander, 12
Nicholas, Metropolitan of Krutitsy,
  111, 155–7
  on the return of the exiles, 290
  persecution of, 312–16
  statement on the Ecumenical Move-
  ment, 112–13
Nicodemus, Archbishop, 109, 116, 117
  on Vatican Council, 11, 115
Nikitin, Seraphim (Vladimir), Bishop
  of Kursk, 165
Nikitin, Mgr Stephen, Bishop of
  Mozhaisk, 164
Nikon, Patriarch, 16
Nilus of Sora, 15
Novitsky, Mgr Benjamin, Bishop of
  Poltava, 291
Novitsky, G., 37

Odessa seminary, 123, 124, 170
Office for Publications, 89
Ogorodmikov, Professor, 272
Old Believers, 15, 16, 219–25
'Old Pomorians', 222–3
Oleschuk, F., 268
Olga, Princess, 10
Onesimus, Bishop of Vladimir, 143
  on religious festivals, 188
Optino, Monastery of, 19
Orthodox Churches, meeting of (1958),
  108–9
Orthodox Christian, The, 71
Ossipov, A., 133, 319–20
Ostapov, Father A., 131
Ossipova, Professor, 272

Paleologus, Princess Zoë (Sophia),
  14
Palladius, Archbishop of Lvov, 93
pan-Orthodox Conference *see* Conference of 1948
Pariisky, Professor L., 134
parishes, finance of, 86–8

460

Index

Index

Rotov, Archimandrite Nicodemus, 118, 166–8
Rublev, Andrew, 13
Rumanian Church, relations with Russia, 98, 104
Rujitsky, Archpriest Constantine, 130

St Alexis, 13
St Petersburg Academy, 120
St Seraphim of Sarov, 18
St Stephen, Bishop of Perm, 13
St Theodosius, 12
Sabbatarians *see Subbotniki* sect
Sagarda, A., 133
Samoilovich, Mgr Seraphim, 45
Saratov seminary, 123, 124
Sbovovsky, Professor K., 134–5
Schein, Archimandrite Sergius, 37
schisms, 245–50
schools, athesit teaching in, 270–2
Schuiia, massacre at, 35
sects
  'of the Red Dragon' *see Krasno-drakonovtsy* sects
  of Western origin, 231–43
  post-revolutionary, 243–52
  significance of, 251–2
Selassie, Emperor Haile, 118
seminaries, 123–5
  persecution (1959–65), 310–11
  suppression of (1960), 124
Sentsov, Nicholas, 273
Seraphim, Metropolitan of Bulgaria, 98
Serbian Church, relations with Russia, 95–104
Sergius, Bishop of Berlin, 143
Sergius, Bishop of Prague, 98
Sergius, Mgr, 143
Sergius of Radonej, 13
Sergius of Vladimir, Mgr and later Patriarch, 23, 42
  arrest and release (1926), 43
  attacked through relatives, 57
  congratulates Stalin on the 25th anniversary of the revolution, 65–66
  death, 67
  declaration of obedience to Soviet Government, 44
  elected Patriarch, 66–67
  memorandum of demands (1930), 48–52

  pastoral letter on outbreak of World War II, 59–61
  policy defined, 46–47
  work in Baltic States, 58
  work in Ulianovsk, 62
Sergueenko, Father A., 133
Settlement of 1945
  Church and State, 90–93
  Committee for pensions, 89
  departments of the Patriarchate, 88–89
  financial resources of the Church, 86–88
  monasteries, 90
  Office for publications, 89
  organization of the Church, 83–86
  State and Church, 93–94
Seventh Day Adventists, 239–40
Shchegolev, Mgr Donatus, 143
Shchegurov, Vladimir, 332
Sicobeev, Leonides, 36
Sidamanidze, Mgr Ephrem, 254
Sikorsky, Polycarp, Bishop of Loutsk, 74, 139
Silichev, Archbishop Seraphim, 57
Simansky, Alexis Vladimirov *see* Alexis, Metropolitan
Simonov, Constantine, 281
Skipetrov, Peter, 27
skoptsy sect, 226
Slipyii, Mgr Joseph, 260
Smirnov, Mgr Cyril, 45
Smolensky cemetery (Leningrad), 204–5
Smorodin, Nicholas, 238
Smorodinsty sect, 238
Soloviev, Sergius, 31
Solovyev, Vladimir, 19, 20
Soviet Government
  and financial resources of the Church, 87
  policy towards external relations of the Church, 101
Spasky, N., 87
Springovics, Archbishop Anthony, 260
Stadnitsky, Mgr Arsenius, 25, 44
Stalin, Joseph,
  consequences of death, 105–6, 114–15, 139–40
  praised by the Patriarch of Alexandria, 97
  reaction to World War II, 61